INVITATION TO THEOLOGICAL STUDIES SERIES

INVITATION TO BIBLICAL HEBREW

A Beginning Grammar

RUSSELL T. FULLER
KYOUNGWON CHOI

Invitation to Biblical Hebrew: A Beginning Grammar

Published by Kregel Publications, a division of Kregel, Inc., P.O. Box 2607, Grand Rapids, MI 49501.

ISBN 978-0-8254-2650-6

Printed in the United States of America

15 16 17 / 8 7 6 5

Table of Contents

Phonological Principles

MORPHOLOGICAL PRINCIPLES: PARTICLES

MORPHOLOGICAL PRINCIPLES: NOUNS AND ADJECTIVES

Morphological Principles: Strong Verb

PREFACE

Many friends and colleagues helped and encouraged this work along the way, most notably, Terry J. Betts of The Southern Baptist Theological Seminary, who first suggested the writing of this book and Eric A. Mitchell of Southwestern Baptist Theological Seminary, whose suggestions and corrections were most helpful and especially the students, who demonstrated that the book actually works. Additional thanks to Mark Mangano and Glenden Riddle for many helpful suggestions and corrections.

Of course, family support is a necessity for such projects. We thank our wives Donna and Jiyoun, and children, David, Christine, Katherine, and Hayyiym. Also we thank our parents, Thomas and Melba Fuller and Youngsam and Jung-Eun Choi, whose help over a lifetime can never be repaid.

We also thank the administration of The Southern Baptist Theological Seminary, R. Albert Molher, President, and Russell Moore, Dean of the School of Theology, whose support made the work possible.

We dedicate this work to our teacher, Isaac Jerusalmi, of Hebrew Union College-Jewish Institute of Religion in Cincinnati, Ohio, who taught us not only Hebrew, Aramaic, and Arabic, but also how to think about and teach a language. His wonderful influence as a teacher and scholar will always be with us; his friendship will always be dear.

Our hope and prayer in producing this work is that many will learn Biblical Hebrew to become better interpreters of the Word of God so as to glorify God, and His Son Jesus Christ, whom to know is eternal life.

Russell T. Fuller
Kyoungwon Choi

INTRODUCTION

In producing another elementary Hebrew grammar, we are aware that an ultimate Hebrew grammar will never be written. A grammar, no matter how well written, will never satisfy all. Each grammar represents the training, pedagogy, and personality of the author. This is particularly true for this grammar.

The deductive approach of this Grammar stresses the mastery of the fundamentals of Hebrew phonology (the sounds), those seemingly insignificant details, essential for understanding the language (Chapters 1-6), and of Hebrew morphology (the forms of the language), constructed from the phonology (Chapters 7-38). The Grammar explains and demonstrates the grammatical material. The exercises and drills at the end of each chapter (and the accompanying workbook) allows students to imitate the grammatical forms and to correct their errors with the provided keys in the workbook. Finally, they can repeat, repeat, and repeat the drills until the grammar becomes thoroughly mastered and ingrained. As a further aid to the student and teacher, lectures covering each chapter on video disks are included. In these lectures, the grammar is presented and examples of the drills are worked to clarify the material and to explain the process for learning and teaching the grammar.

This approach stresses phonology and morphology. This does not mean, however, that syntax is ignored. Basic syntax is discussed in the grammar. Yet, until phonology and morphology are mastered, syntax cannot be truly understood or appreciated. If a student cannot parse, he cannot understand or apply syntax effectively. Once the foundation of phonology and morphology is laid, syntax can be constructed for the student in manner both effective and practical. The truth is Hebrew cannot be learned in a year. But step-by-step – phonology then morphology then syntax – Hebrew can be learned in three or four semesters. This book is written for the first year of elementary Hebrew. We have almost completed a manual for intermediate syntax and composition that will supply a textbook for the second year of Hebrew.

Finally, this approach is directed towards the student, not towards the scholar. Hence, the language of the book is often popular rather than technical, colloquial rather than formal. Terms – sometimes unorthodox terms – are used that the students will understand and remember. This will hopefully take away some of the intimidation of learning the language. Some technical language is retained to give students a foundation to progress to advanced grammars. Making Hebrew more difficult through jargon is not so easy to overcome. Once the student learns the grammatical phenomenon, the terms and labels can be readily changed as the teacher desires.

The ultimate goal of this grammar, of course, is that students will master Hebrew so well that they will actually use it for ministry. This is the frustration of teaching and learning Hebrew. So often students leave college or seminary with a very weak understanding of Hebrew so that they simply throw their Hebrew away. Hebrew becomes simply a course to be endured to get the degree. Finally, the course is dropped from the theological curriculum because it is impractical. The solution for this problem is to teach the language in a thorough manner so that students will actually use it in ministry. This will only happen – not by computer programs – when students truly learn the language. This takes work, but so does an effective ministry that truly preaches the Word of God. May God raise up ministers who take the ministry seriously, versed in the original languages, orthodox in their doctrine, and love in their heart for God and His people.

Russell T. Fuller
Kyoungwon Choi

ABBREVIATIONS

!	Unexpected form
□	A Hebrew letter or root letter
*	Reconstructed or hypothetical form
=	Equals
«	Derives from
»	Changes to
1.2	Chapter.Section number
1-2	Chapter-Footnote number
G	Guttural letter
R_1	First root letter of a word
R_2	Second root letter of a word
R_3	Third root letter of a word

PHONOLOGICAL PRINCIPLES

CHAPTER 1
ALPHABET
VOWELS

1.1. The Consonants (The Alphabet)

Printed Letters	Letters with Final Forms	Names of the Letters	Phonetic Values	Transliteration	Cursive
א		Alef	silent letter	’	א
בּ ב		Bet	v, b	b̲, b	ב
גּ ג		Gimel	g	ḡ, g	ג
דּ ד		Dalet	d	d̲, d	ד
ה		He	h	h	ה
ו		Vav	v	v or w	ו
ז		Zayin	z	z	ז
ח		Ḥet	ch[2]	ḥ	ח
ט		Ṭet	t	ṭ	ט
י		Yod	y	y	י
כּ כ	ךְ[1]	Kaf	ch[2], k	k̲, k	ך כ
ל		Lamed	l	l	ל
מ	ם	Mem	m	m	ם מ
נ	ן	Nun	n	n	ן נ
ס		Samek	s	s	ס
ע		Ayin	silent letter	‘	ע
פּ פ	ף	Pe	f, p	p̄, p	ף פ
צ	ץ	Ṣade	s	ṣ	ץ צ
ק		Qof	k *or* q	q	ק
ר		Resh	r	r	ר
שׂ		Sin	s	ś	שׂ
שׁ		Shin	sh	š	שׁ
תּ ת		Tav	t	t̲, t	ת

[1] Final Kaf usually contains two vertical dots (1.7; 3.2.1 and footnote 3-4).

[2] To pronounce these letters, see 1.4.

1.2. Printed Letters: Hebrew, with its twenty-three letters or consonants, is read right to left. The letters בּ, גּ, דּ, כּ, פּ, תּ may occur with a dot, which originally changed pronunciation. In this grammar, only three of these letters – בּ, כּ, פּ – change pronunciation with a dot. (See 1.4).

1.3. Final Letters: Certain letters (כ, מ, נ, פ, צ) vary their form when ending a word. Except for מ, the final form straightens the bottom of the letter vertically.

Initial or Medial		Final	
כ	כַּדְכֹּד	שָׁלַךְ	ךְ
מ	מִן	שָׁם	ם
נ	נָבָא	תֵּן	ן
פ	פָּקַד	אַף	ף
צ	צָבָא	עֵץ	ץ

1.4. Phonetic Values (Sounds): Phonetic values, listed in 1.1, represent modern Israeli pronunciation.[3] The following consonants merit special attention.

א – Alef is a silent letter.

ב, בּ – Without the dot, the ב sounds like /v/; with the dot, the בּ sounds like /b/.

ח – This letter sounds like the clearing of the throat. (German *ch* as in machen, or the Scottish *ch* as in loch)

כ, כּ – Without the dot, the כ sounds like the ח above; with the dot, the כּ sounds like /k/.

ע – Ayin is a silent letter.

פ, פּ – Without the dot, the פ sounds like /f/; with the dot, the פּ sounds like /p/.

General Observations

1. Most letters may receive a dot, but the dot only in בּ כּ פּ changes pronunciation.
2. The silent letters (א, ע) originally had phonetic values (as in Arabic).
3. Some letters have the same sound. Both ט and ת, for example, represent the sound /t/. Originally, these letters represented different /t/ sounds (as in Arabic).

1.5. Guttural Letters

The four guttural letters – א ה ח ע (ר is a semi-guttural letter) – originally pronounced deep in the throat, display certain peculiarities (5.7).

---

[3] Phonetic values, listed here and in 1.1, represent modern Hebrew pronunciation. For a simplified phonological classification of modern Hebrew, see Appendix 1.

1.6. The Vowels (also called vowel points): Although Modern Hebrew does not distinguish short and long vowels in pronunciation,[4] carefully distinguish (not in sound, but in observation) short vowels from long vowels. The following chart lists the vowel signs (also called vowel points) with Modern Hebrew pronunciation.

	Short			**Long**		
Phonetic Value	Name of the Vowel	Vowel / with letter	Transliteration	Name of the Vowel	Vowel / with letter	Transliteration
A (as in father)	Pataḥ	□ַ / סַ	a	Qameṣ	□ָ / סָ	ā
E (they)	Segol	□ֶ / סֶ	e	Ṣere	□ֵ / סֵ	ē
The short Segol sounds like the /e/ in pet.				Ṣere-Yod	□ֵי / סֵי†	ê
				Segol-Yod	□ֶי / סֶי†	ey
I (be)	Ḥireq	□ִ / סִ	i	Ḥireq-Yod	□ִי / סִי†	î
O (note)	Qameṣ-Ḥatuf	□ָ / סָ	o	Ḥolem	□ֹ / סֹ	ō
				Ḥolem-Vav	□וֹ / סוֹ†	ô
U (flute)	Qibbuṣ	□ֻ / סֻ	u	Shureq	□וּ / סוּ†	û

Most vowels are written under its consonant (סָ); some are written to the left of its consonant (סוֹ); a few are written under and to the left of its consonant (סֵי). The sign † indicates an historic long vowel (1.8.2). An historic long vowel is a vowel that was long in Pre-Biblical Hebrew (Proto-Hebrew) and cannot be reduced (shortened) in Biblical Hebrew.

1.7. The Shewa: Hebrew also has a shewa, two vertical dots under a letter סְ (transliterated ᵊ), often indicating an indistinct vowel or slurred sound, like the "e" in the word "shewa" (chapter 3).

1.8. Observations on the Vowels

1. Short Vowels
    1. Short vowels may reduce to a shewa.
    2. Short vowels may lengthen to long vowels:
    Pataḥ □ַ may lengthen to Qameṣ □ָ
    Ḥireq □ִ may lengthen to Ṣere □ֵ
    Qameṣ-Ḥatuf □ָ may lengthen to Ḥolem □ֹ

[4] The distinction between Segol and Ṣere, Ṣere-Yod, Segol-Yod is sometimes an exception.

The lengthening or reducing of vowels will be considered later.

2. Long Vowels
   1. Long vowels written with Vav or Yod – סוֹ, סִי, for example – are historic long vowels. *These vowels never reduce to a short vowel or a shewa.*[5]
   2. Historic long vowels may be written defectively (partially) – that is, without the Yod or Vav.[6] The historic long Ḥireq-Yod, then, may be written סִי or defectively (partially) סִ. A dot under a letter, therefore, may be a short Ḥireq or an historic long Ḥireq-Yod written defectively. Distinguishing these options will be considered later.[7]
   3. Qameṣ, Ṣere, and Ḥolem, not historically long vowels, lengthen secondarily from short vowels.

1.9. Note on the Exercises

In studying the beginning chapters, students are tempted to try the exercises immediately without seriously studying the chapter or learning the vocabulary. While this method may work for a few chapters, eventually the student will spend an inordinate time on homework, with slight benefit and little profit. For the chapters and their exercises to have the intended effect, the student must study the chapter and work the exercises in the proper order. First, read and comprehend the chapter thoroughly, including the footnotes. Then master the vocabulary (chapter one is without vocabulary). Finally, work the drills. The chapter carefully studied and the order properly followed, the exercises will have the intended effect of correcting mistakes and of creating the proper habits to master the language.

EXERCISE ONE

I. Questions

1. How many consonants does Hebrew have? What direction is Hebrew read?
2. Which three letters with a dot change pronunciation in this grammar? Pronounce their sounds, with and without the dot.
3. Does Modern Hebrew distinguish short and long vowels in pronunciation? How should we distinguish them?
4. In relation to a consonant, where can a vowel be written?
5. What is a shewa?

---

[5] Very rarely, Qameṣ may be historic long, but usually, Qameṣ lengthens secondarily from Pataḥ.

[6] When written defectively, Shureq (וּ) is written as a Qibbuṣ (□ֻ).

[7] Some vowels lengthen by compensating the form for a peculiarity in the word. Vowels lengthened by compensation are like historic long vowels: *they never reduce to a short vowel or a shewa.*

6. What kind of vowels reduce to shewa?
7. List the vowels that can lengthen and indicate what they may lengthen to.
8. What is a historic long vowel? What long vowels are not historic long?
9. What is defective writing? List the vowels that may be written defectively and write them defectively.
10. Describe the proper order to learn the chapters and to work the exercises in this grammar.

II. Drills

1. Write the alphabet in order, giving the phonetic value for each letter: list the five final letters, the six letters that have a dot, and the gutturals.

2. Recite the alphabet orally.

3. Write the vowels and shewa with the letter ס – identify the phonetic value of each vowel; divide the vowels into short and long vowels and label all historic long vowels.

4. Identify and pronounce with /ā/ the following letters.

   שׁ פ ר ס צ ם ע כּ נ ט ל ז י ה

   ת ק גּ בּ ףּ שׂ ן ד א תּ ח ג ו א

   דּ פּ ך ב כ ץ

5. Identify and pronounce the following vowels.

   ◌ֵ ◌ֶי ◌ִי ◌וּ ◌ָ ◌ֶ ◌ֹ ◌ַ ◌ֵי ◌וֹ ◌ֻ ◌ִ

6. Identify and pronounce the following consonant-vowel combinations.

Chapter 2
Consonantal and Vocalic Yod/Vav
The Syllable

2.1. Introduction: Yod and Vav may be read as a consonant or as a vowel. To read a word properly, carefully distinguish between consonantal Yod/Vav and vocalic Yod/Vav. The syllable is the brick and mortar of Hebrew word structure, foundational for building and connecting mere letters and vowels into stately words.

2.2. Yod or Vav: Vowel or Consonant

1. Yod
   1. Vowel: If a Yod is without a vowel or a dot, and is preceded by a Ṣere, Ḥireq, or Segol; the Yod is a vowel – בֵּית, נָבִיא, תְּקוּמֶינָה.
   2. Consonant:
      1. If a Yod begins a word, it is a consonant – יוֹם, יָם.
      2. If a Yod has a dot, it is a consonant – דַּיָּן.
      3. If a Yod has a vowel, it is a consonant – שָׁמַיִם, הָיָה, יוֹם.
      4. If Yod is preceded by a vowel other than Ṣere, Ḥireq, or Segol; it is a consonant – בָּנוּי, בַּנַי.

2. Vav
   1. Vowel:
      1. A Vav, having a dot in its middle and beginning a word, is a vowel – וּמֹשֶׁה.
      2. A Vav, having a dot in its middle and preceded by a consonant, is a vowel – נוּן, סוּס.
      3. A Vav, having a dot at its top and preceded by a consonant, is a vowel – לוֹ, טוֹב.
   2. Consonant:
      1. A Vav, without a dot in its middle or at its top, is a consonant – מִצְוָה.
      2. A Vav, having a dot in its middle or at its top and preceded by a vowel or a shewa (two vertical dots under a letter סְ, see 1.7), is a consonant:
         מְצַוֶּה – the Vav is a consonant because preceded by a vowel (Pataḥ).
         מִצְוֹת – the Vav is a consonant because preceded by a shewa.

2.3. The Syllable – Definition: A Hebrew syllable must begin with a consonant (this includes the silent letters א, ע) and must have a single vowel. A Hebrew syllable may end with a vowel – בָּ, or with a consonant – בָּם.[1]

---

[1] בּ ָ is not a syllable because a vowel cannot begin a syllable (the Vav-conjunctive – וּמֹשֶׁה – being the only exception, 8.3.6); without a vowel, בם is not a syllable.

2.4. Open and Closed Syllables:

1. An open syllable ends with a vowel בָּ, or with a final א or ה – תָּה, נָא.
2. A closed syllable ends with a consonant (excluding final א or ה) – בָּם, נוּן.

2.5. Dividing Words into Syllables – Syllabifying

Syllabify from the end of the word (left to right), which may end with a consonant or with a vowel. First, locate the final vowel, then divide the syllable after the consonant with the final vowel. Then find the next vowel (moving to the right) and divide the syllable after its consonant.

1. מֵאָדָם – The final vowel (Qameṣ) is under the ד. Because a syllable must begin with a consonant, divide the syllable to the right of the ד – דָם | מֵאָ. Now repeat the process with the next syllable: find the vowel (Qameṣ) and divide the syllable to the right of its consonant (א) – דָם | אָ | מֵ. This word has three syllables. The last syllable is closed because the syllable ends with a consonant (ם). The other two syllables are open because they end in vowels: a Qameṣ (אָ) and a Ṣere (מֵ).
2. סֵ֫פֶר – The final vowel (Segol) is under the פ; therefore, divide the syllable to the right of the פ because a syllable must begin with a consonant – פֶר | סֵ֫. The last syllable ends in a consonant (ר) and is closed. The first syllable ends in a vowel (Ṣere) and is open.
3. שָׂפָה – The final vowel (Qameṣ) is under the פ; therefore, divide the syllable to the right of the פ because a syllable must begin with a consonant – פָה | שָׂ. Both syllables are open: the last syllable is open because it ends in a final ה (2.4.1); the first syllable is open because it ends in a vowel.

2.6. Accent

Most words in Hebrew have accent (also called stress or tone). Most Hebrew words accent the final syllable (also called ultima or milra[2]); some accent the next to last syllable (also called, penult or milel[3]). Hebrew never accents a syllable before the next to last (also called the antepenult syllable). Words accented on the next to last syllable will receive an accent mark – סֵ֫פֶר; words accented on the last syllable usually will not be given an accent mark – דָּבָר.

---

[2] Milra is an Aramaic word meaning "from below," that is, the last syllable.

[3] Milel is an Aramaic word meaning "from above," that is, the next to last syllable.

2.7. Syllable: Terminology

1. The syllable with the accent is called the tone syllable (or accented syllable or stress syllable) – דָבָר.
2. The syllable after the accent is called the post-tonic syllable – מֶ֫לֶךְ.
3. The syllable before the accent is called the pretonic syllable – דָבָר.
4. All syllables before the pretonic syllable are called pro-pretonic syllables:

דָ֫ם	אָ	הָ | מֵ
tonic	pretonic	two pro-pretonics

Exercise Two

I. Questions

1. When should Yod be read as a vowel? as a consonant?
2. When should Vav be read as a vowel? as a consonant?
3. Define a Hebrew syllable.
4. Define open and closed syllable.
5. Explain the process of dividing syllables.
6. Which syllables can receive the accent in Hebrew?
7. Define the following terms: tone, penult, antepenult, milel, milra, post-tonic, pretonic, pro-pretonic.

II. Vocabulary: For now, translate all verbs as a simple past or perfect tense.

אֶל־[4]	(prep.) unto, toward, to	אֵת	(prep.) with
מִן	(prep.) from, out of, because of, part of, than (in comparisons)	לֹא	no, not
		אָמַר	(verb) (he) said, has said
עַל	(prep.) on, upon, over, against	הָיָה	(verb) (it, he) came to be, became, happened, has happened, was, were
עָשָׂה	(verb) (he) did, made, has made		
הָלַךְ	(verb) (he) went, walked, has gone	נָתַן	(verb) (he) gave, has given
יוֹם	day	יָם	sea
עִיר	(fem.) city (irregular plural עָרִים)	מֶ֫לֶךְ	king
		הוּא	(pronoun) he

III. Drills

1. Write the alphabet in order: list the five letters that have final forms, the six letters that have a dot, and the gutturals; then give the phonetic value for each letter.

2. Recite the alphabet orally.

---

[4] The raised dash after the word is a Maqqef, see 5.5.

3. Write the vowels and shewa with the letter ס: identify the phonetic value of each vowel; divide the vowels into short and long vowels and label all historic long vowels.

4. Label consonantal Yod/Vav or vocalic Yod/Vav.

מִצְוָתִי   בַּ֫יִת   תְּשׁוּבֶ֫ינָה   מִצְוֹתַי   צַוֵּה

וָו   תּוֹרוֹתַי   יָמִים   יוֹמַ֫יִם

5. In the following words, divide the syllables, label them open or closed; tonic, post-tonic, pretonic, pro-pretonic; then pronounce the words.
Example: יֵאָמֵר[5]

יֵ | אָ | מֵר

closed tonic   open pretonic   open pro-pretonic

שָׁמַ֫יִם   חָמָס   וָעֹ֫שֶׁר   יִירַשׁ   אָלָה

יֵעָשׂוּ   וִיהִי   הוֹצִיאֵם   מָצָא   שָׂדֵ֫הוּ

עָשׂוּ   הוּא   טוֹבָה   לָעִיר   רָאִ֫יתָ

יַ֫יִן   מוֹעֵד   וָאָ֫רֶץ   עָלִ֫יתִי   רֹמֶ֫שֶׂת

---

[5] Until chapter 5, consider every ◌ָ as /ā/ (Qameṣ).

CHAPTER 3
THE SHEWA

3.1. Introduction: The shewa is an impoverished vowel, the low rent district of Hebrew – some are vocal about it; others are silent. The shewa is two vertical dots under a letter (◌ְ) to indicate the absence of a vowel:

1. Silent shewa, the absence of any sound, ends a syllable.
2. Vocal shewa,[1] an indistinct vocalic sound, begins a syllable. Vocal shewa comes in two flavors: simple vocal shewa, two vertical dots under a letter; composite shewa, a composite of a short vowel (Pataḥ, Segol, or Qameṣ-Ḥatuf) to the left of two vertical dots חֲ, חֱ, חֳ, usually under the guttural letters (א, ה, ח, ע, see 1.5).

3.2. Distinguishing between Silent Shewa and Simple Vocal Shewa

1. Single Shewa
   1. At the beginning of the word: The shewa is vocal because it begins a syllable – דְּבָרִים, שְׁמוּאֵל.
   2. In the middle of a word:
      1. If the vowel to the right of the shewa is long, the shewa is vocal[2] – קֹטְלִים (קֹ | טְלִים).
      2. If the vowel to the right of the shewa is short, the shewa is silent – יִקְטֹל.
      3. If a shewa is to the left of a vertical line called Metheg (or Gaya), the shewa is usually vocal, even if preceded by a short vowel – קָֽטְלָה qāṭᵊlāh, הַֽמְכַסֶּה ham(m)ᵊkasseh.[3]
   3. At the end of a word: The shewa is silent because it ends a syllable – מֶ֫לֶךְ, בָּרַךְ.[4]

2. Two Consecutive Shewas
   1. At the beginning of the word: Hebrew will not tolerate two consecutive shewas. If two vocal shewas begin a word, the first shewa becomes a short vowel,

---

[1] The vocal shewa usually reflects the remains of a reduced short vowel (1.8.1); the silent shewa usually reflects the absence of any vowel. In Modern Hebrew, simple vocal shewa is rarely pronounced.

[2] In an accented syllable, silent shewa may be to the left of a long vowel: לָ֫יְלָה (for the sign ◌֫, see 6.5.2). If the shewa under the Yod were vocal, then a vertical line called Metheg would appear to the left of the first Qameṣ. See 3.2.1.

[3] Although inconsistently found in the Hebrew Bible, the Metheg is used consistently in this grammar.

[4] Although examples of silent shewas in a final letter are usually restricted to ךְ, the final silent shewa is implicit in most words, for example, דָּבָר for the implied *דָּבָר(ְ). Notice again that in an accented syllable, a silent shewa may be to the left of a long vowel. Two silent shewas may be implied in some words – *יָמָיו(ְ). See footnote 3-2.

usually Ḥireq – *דְּבְרֵי » דִּבְרֵי – or Pataḥ under the guttural letters א, ה, ח, ע – *אֲדְמַת » אַדְמַת.[5]

2. In the middle of a word:
    1. The shewa on the right is silent because it is preceded by a short vowel and closes a syllable. The shewa on the left is vocal because it begins a new syllable – יִקְטְלוּ.
    2. The shewa is vocal if it occurs under a letter with a doubling dot (Dagesh Forte, 4.3.2) because קִטְּלוּ actually stands for *קִטְטְלוּ.
3. At the end of a word: both shewas are silent – קָטַלְתְּ.

3.3. Composite Shewa: Composite shewas occur under guttural letters (א, ה, ח, ע see 1.5) and are always vocal – אֲדָמָה, אֱלֹהִים, חֳלִי. These shewas are called Ḥatef ("hurried") vowels: Ḥatef-Pataḥ (□ֲ), Ḥatef-Segol (□ֱ), and Ḥatef-Qameṣ-Ḥatuf (□ֳ). The transliteration of composite shewas are: ª Ḥatef-Pataḥ; ᵉ Ḥatef-Segol; º Ḥatef-Qameṣ-Ḥatuf.

3.4. The Shewa and the Syllable

1. A syllable in Hebrew must begin with a consonant and have one vowel. *A consonant with a vocal shewa – including composite shewa – never constitutes a syllable in Hebrew.* A vocal shewa, which always begins a syllable, must attach to the following consonant and vowel combination.
   Example: קֹ | טְלִים – The shewa is vocal because it is to the left of a long vowel. The vocal shewa begins the following syllable and attaches to the consonant-vowel-consonant: לִים
2. Dividing syllables with silent and vocal shewas
    1. Silent shewa always ends a syllable; therefore, divide the syllable to the left of a silent shewa – מִקְ | נֶה
    2. Vocal shewa always begins a syllable; therefore, divide the syllable to the right of a vocal shewa – קֹ | טְלִים, כּוֹ | כְבֵי, קָ | טְלָה
3. Syllabifying with shewas
   As in 2.5, begin at the end of the word, locate the final vowel and the consonant above that final vowel. If a shewa is to the right of that final vowel and its consonant, then determine whether the shewa is silent or vocal (3.2). If the shewa is silent, divide the syllable to the left of the silent shewa – מִמְ | שָׁל. If the shewa is vocal, divide the syllable to the right of the vocal shewa – קֹ | טְלִים. Then repeat the process for every vowel in the word. Remember: *Every syllable has a vowel, and every vowel has a syllable.*

---

[5] This is the shewa fight: two vocal shewas at the beginning of the word will fight, leaving the first shewa a Ḥireq or Pataḥ. Moreover, within a word, when a vocal shewa (or political shewa, see footnote 12-1) follows a composite shewa (which is always vocal, 3.3), the composite shewa becomes the short vowel of the composite shewa: *נַעֲרְךָ » נַעַרְךָ.

Examples:

1. יִצְחָק – The final vowel (Qameṣ) and its consonant ח have a shewa to the right of them. The shewa is silent because it is to the left of a short vowel; therefore, divide the syllable to the left of the silent shewa – חָק | יִצְ. The last syllable is closed because it ends in a consonant[6] חָק, and the first syllable is closed because it ends in a consonant (with silent shewa) – יִצְ.
2. קֹטְלֵי – The final vowel (Ṣere-Yod) and its letter ל have a shewa to the right of them. The shewa is vocal because it is to the left of a long vowel (Ḥolem); therefore, divide the syllable to the right of the vocal shewa – טְלֵי | קֹ. The last syllable is open because it ends with a vowel – טְלֵי; the first syllable also ends with a vowel and is open – קֹ.
3. קָֽטְלָה – The final vowel (Qameṣ) and its letter ל have a shewa to the right of of them. The shewa is vocal because the shewa is to the left of a Metheg (3.2.1). Therefore, divide the syllable to the right of the vocal shewa: טְלָה | קָֽ. Both syllables are open: the last syllable ends in a ה (2.4.1) – טְלָה; the first syllable ends in a vowel – קָֽ.

Exercise Three

I. Questions

1. Define silent and vocal shewa. What do vocal and silent shewa usually reflect?
2. Describe a shewa at the beginning, middle, and end of a word. When is the shewa silent or vocal?
3. When can a silent shewa be preceded by a long vowel?
4. When is a silent shewa implied in many words?
5. Describe two consecutive shewas at the beginning, middle, and end of a word. When are they silent or vocal?
6. What kind of shewa occurs under a doubling dot (Dagesh Forte)?
7. Describe the Metheg. How does the Metheg affect the shewa?
8. Define the composite shewa. When do they occur?
9. Describe the process of syllabifying words with shewas.
10. Can a consonant with vocal shewa or composite shewa ever constitute a syllable?

---

[6] A silent shewa is implied under the ק – *יִצְחָקְ – but in an accented syllable, a silent shewa may be preceded by a long vowel (see footnotes 3-2 and 3-4).

II. Vocabulary

אֱלֹהִים	God	יָד	(f) hand
אֲשֶׁר	(relative pronoun) who, which, that, that which	אָב	father
		פָּנִים	face
יָשַׁב	(verb) (he) sat, dwelled	מֹשֶׁה	Moses
אִישׁ	man	שָׁמַע	(verb) (he) heard, obeyed
אֲנָשִׁים	men	רָאָה	(verb) (he) saw, looked
קָרָא	(verb) (he) called, read	יִשְׂרָאֵל	Israel
אֲדֹנָי	Lord, lord, master	שֵׁם	name

III. Drills

1. Identify each shewa as vocal or silent shewa.

יִשְׁמְרוּ יַבְנֶה הוֹשְׁבוּ יִקְרַב שְׁמוֹ

מָחֳרָת יֵשְׁבֵי יִתְרְעָם מֶֽשְׁלָה קַבְּרוּ[7]

2. First, identify each shewa as vocal or silent shewa. Second, divide each syllable, labeling them open or closed; tonic, post-tonic, pretonic, pro-pretonic; then pronounce the words. In checking your work, be sure every syllable has a vowel, and every vowel has a syllable.

אֲנַ֫חְנוּ לַ֫יְלָה יִמְשְׁלוּ אֲדָמָה אֱדֹם

הוּקְמוּ לְמַ֫עַן חַכְמֵי קֹטְלִים אֱמֶת

יִירְשׁוּ תּוֹרוֹתַ֫יִךְ נְבִיאַי יִתְרְעָם מֶֽשְׁלָה

וְשַׁוְעָתִי מִנְחָה בֶּֽרְכִי שֶֽׁמְרוּ שָׁמָ֫רְנוּ

---

[7] Doubling dot, Dagesh Forte.

Chapter 4
Dagesh

4.1. Introduction: A Dagesh is a dot in the middle of a letter.[1] There are two varieties of Dagesh: Dagesh Lene (or soft Dagesh) and Dagesh Forte (or strong Dagesh). The Dagesh is the nail of Hebrew that stabilizes a word and fixes the pronunciation of certain letters.

4.2. Dagesh Lene

1. Originally, Dagesh Lene differentiated the pronunciation of six letters (בּ, גּ, דּ, כּ, פּ, תּ). In Modern Hebrew pronunciation, only three of these letters (בּ, כּ, פּ) actually differ in pronunciation because of Dagesh Lene. These three letters have a plosive[2] pronunciation with the Dagesh Lene, and a spirantic[3] pronunciation without the Dagesh Lene.

   ב, בּ = ḇ, b
   כ, כּ = ḵ, k
   פ, פּ = p̄, p

   The other letters (ג, ד, ת), with or without Dagesh Lene, have a plosive pronunciation.

2. To remember the six letters that admit the Dagesh Lene, grammarians have made two (artificial) words בְּגַד כְּפַת (Bᵊgad Kᵊfat). These six letters are called "Bᵊgad Kᵊfat" letters.

3. Bᵊgad Kᵊfat letters admit the Dagesh Lene (usually) at the beginning of syllables:
   1. At the beginning of a word – בֵּן, פֶּה.
   2. In the middle or end of a word when the Bᵊgad Kᵊfat letter is to the left of a silent shewa – מִדְבָּר, יִקְבֹּר, שָׁמַ֫רְתְּ. At the end of a word (not at the beginning of the syllable), a Dagesh Lene is to the left of a silent shewa and can admit a silent shewa under the Dagesh Lene – שָׁמַרְתְּ (footnote 3-4).

4. Bᵊgad Kᵊfat letters will not admit the Dagesh Lene:
   1. When the Bᵊgad Kᵊfat letter is to the left of a vowel – יִבְחַר, עֶ֫בֶד.[4]
   2. When the Bᵊgad Kᵊfat letter is to the left of a vocal shewa – וְכֹל, אֲדָמָה.

---

[1] This excludes the vowel Shureq וּ, of course, and the Mappiq (4.6).

[2] A plosive sound is the complete stoppage and sudden release of the breath, like the /b/ in boy. (Compare the word "explosive.")

[3] Spirantic sound is the passage of breath through the partially closed oral cavity, like the /v/ in victory. (Compare the word "spirit.")

[4] This is also true at the beginning of a word when that word is preceded by a word ending in a vowel (and with a conjunctive accent that joins words together): וַיְהִי כֵן. Here the כ is without Dagesh Lene because the preceding word ends in a vowel (with an assumed conjunctive accent on וַיְהִי).

4.3. Dagesh Forte

1. Dagesh Forte indicates the doubling of a letter. Instead of writing the same letter consecutively – *קִטְטֵל, Hebrew frequently represents the first ט and silent shewa by a Dagesh Forte – קִטֵּל; therefore – קִטֵּל = *קִטְטֵל, שִׁלַּח = *שִׁלְלַח, יַלֵּד = *יַלְלֵד.

2. A shewa under a Dagesh Forte is a vocal shewa – קִטְּלוּ = *קִטְטְלוּ. The Dagesh Forte has an implied silent shewa; therefore, the shewa under the Dagesh Forte must be vocal according to 3.2.2.

3. Dagesh Forte may occur in any letter (including Bᵊgad Kᵊfat letters, which have a plosive pronunciation with Dagesh Lene or Dagesh Forte, 4.2.1) except the gutturals (א ה ח ע and ר, 1.5).[5]

4. *Dagesh Forte must be preceded by a vowel* (usually a short vowel, but a long vowel in an accented syllable – אֵלֶּה, הֵמָּה), קִבֵּר.

5. Dagesh Forte may not begin a word or end a word[6] – עַמִּי, but עַם.

4.4. Distinguishing between Dagesh Lene and Dagesh Forte

1. A Dagesh in a non-Bᵊgad Kᵊfat letter is a Dagesh Forte.

2. A Dagesh in a Bᵊgad Kᵊfat letter may be a Dagesh Lene or Dagesh Forte.
   1. Dagesh Lene occurs at the beginning of words – בֵּן, or to the left of a silent shewa – יִקְבֹּר.
   2. Dagesh Forte must be to the left of a vowel (usually, a short vowel) – שִׁלַּח; therefore, *Dagesh Forte never begins a word.*

4.5. The Dagesh and the Syllable

1. *The Dagesh Forte always indicates a closed syllable* because the Dagesh Forte represents a doubled letter with a silent shewa – קִטֵּל = *קִטְטֵל (two closed syllables).
2. Therefore, when dividing closed syllables with Dagesh Forte, the Dagesh Forte should be "wrapped," קִטֵּל (= *קִטְ | טֵל), to show doubling and the silent shewa.

---

[5] Certain letters with vocal shewa *may* omit the Dagesh Forte: וַיְהִי for *וַיְּהִי. These letters are the sibilants (/s/ letters), ס, צ, שׂ, שׁ; the liquid and nasal letters, ל, מ, נ; and the letters, ק, ו, י. These letters are known by the memory word (compare 4.2.2) SQeNeMLeVY, סְקֶנֶם לֵוִי (The ס stands for all sibilants).

[6] If a doubled consonant occurs at the end of a word, *עַמְםְ (two silent shewas), the word will be written עַם. The Dagesh hovers – *עַםּ. If something is added to the end of the word, the hovering Dagesh will land – עַמִּי.

When dividing a syllable with Dagesh Lene, do not wrap the Dagesh Lene because it does not represent doubling, but only the beginning of a syllable – יִקְ | בֹּר.

4.6. Mappiq

A ה in the final position of a word may receive a dot called a Mappiq – תָּמַהּ, גָּבַהּ. Although final ה is silent and does not close a syllable (2.4.1), a final הּ with Mappiq is pronounced and closes a syllable.[7] Transliterate Qameṣ He with Mappiq (הּ) as /āh/; Qameṣ with He without Mappiq /â/.

Exercise Four

I. Questions

1. Define Dagesh.
2. Define Dagesh Lene.
3. Which letters admit Dagesh Lene? What are these letters called (or remembered by)?
4. When do Bᵊgad Kᵊfat letters admit Dagesh Lene? When do they not admit Dagesh Lene?
5. Define Dagesh Forte.
6. What two things does the Dagesh Forte represent?
7. What kind of shewa is under a letter with a Dagesh Forte?
8. Which letters admit Dagesh Forte? Which letters do not admit Dagesh Forte?
9. What must precede the Dagesh Forte? Why?
10. Does a Dagesh Forte begin or end a word?
11. What is a hovering Dagesh? When does it occur?
12. What are SQeNeMLeVY letters? When do they affect the Dagesh Forte?
13. What are the three tests for distinguishing Dagesh Lene and Dagesh Forte?
14. How is a syllable divided with Dagesh Lene or Dagesh Forte? Which always indicates a closed syllable?
15. What is a Mappiq? How does a final הּ differ from a final ה?

[7] Very frequently, a final ה was added to aid the reading of an unpointed (i.e. vowelless) text. Thus, the word סוס could be read "horse" (masculine) or "mare" (feminine). To aid the reader, a ה was added to distinguish the reading – סוס = horse, סוסה = mare. Because the ה was added to aid reading, the ה did not close a syllable, but indicated a vowel, frequently Qameṣ – סוּסָה. Hence, the ה is "phony" for syllabification, but the הּ with Mappiq is a genuine ה that closes a syllable, not merely an aid to reading.

II. Vocabulary

בָּא	(he) came	דָּוִד	David
עָבַד	(he) served	בֵּן	son
עִם	(prep.) with	עֶבֶד	slave, servant
אָדָם	man, Adam	מִצְרַיִם	Egypt, Egyptian
יָדַע	(he) knew, knows	כִּי	(conj.) because, for, that, when, but, indeed
גַּם	(adv., conj.) also, indeed, moreover	דִּבֶּר	(he) spoke
אִשָּׁה	woman	דָּבָר	word, matter, thing
נָשִׁים	women		

III. Drills

1. Identify each Dagesh Forte, Dagesh Lene, Mappiq.

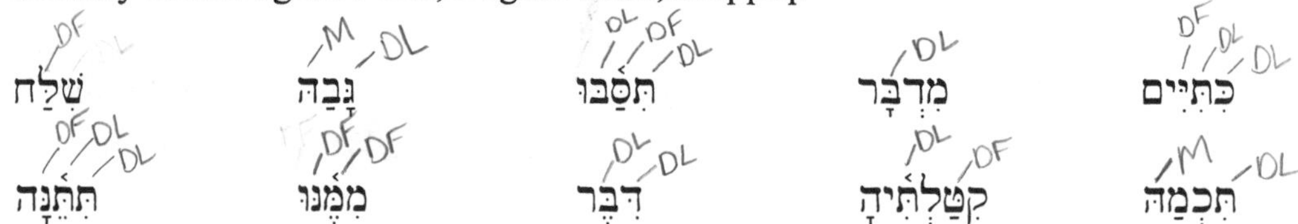

2. In the following order: label every Dagesh, Mappiq, shewa, then divide syllables, labeling them open or closed; tonic, post-tonic, pretonic, pro-pretonic. Then pronounce the words.

גֻּלְגֹּלֶת	תִּגְדַּל	נְקֻדִּים	תְּסַבֶּינָה	הִשְׁתַּמְּרִים
בִּקַּשְׁתּוּנִי	בְּלָגָה	יִקְבֹּר	תִּגְבַּהּ	פְּלִשְׁתִּים
תַּחְתֶּיךְ	תִּתִּי	שָׁמַרְתְּ	נֵרְדְּ	בִּתָּהּ

CHAPTER 5
QAMEṢ AND QAMEṢ-ḤATUF
CHARACTERISTICS OF GUTTURALS
QUIESCENT ALEF

5.1. Introduction: The Masoretes, the preservers of the traditional reading of the Hebrew text and the creators of the vowel signs or points, employed the same sign for /ā/ and /o/ (perhaps they had a similar sound), namely □ָ, which more frequently represents Qameṣ than Qameṣ-Ḥatuf.

5.2. Qameṣ-Ḥatuf: For the sign □ָ to be read as /o/, Qameṣ-Ḥatuf, two conditions must be true:

1. The sign □ָ must be in a closed syllable, *and*
2. The sign □ָ must be in an unaccented syllable.

If either statement is untrue for a syllable with the sign □ָ, read it as /ā/, Qameṣ.

5.3. The Metheg and the Qameṣ/Qameṣ-Ḥatuf

The word חָכְמָה may be read: (1) the shewa may be taken as a silent shewa, then the first syllable is closed, unaccented; therefore, read the vowel under the ח as a Qameṣ-Ḥatuf. (2) The shewa may be taken as a vocal shewa, then the vowel under the ח would be in an open syllable; therefore, the vowel is a Qameṣ. The difficulty is determining whether the shewa is vocal or silent. In this grammar, if the sign □ָ is unaccented and followed by a shewa, □ָ□ְ□֫, read the shewa as silent and the sign □ָ as a Qameṣ-Ḥatuf (/o/). If the shewa is vocal, a Metheg (3.2.1.2.3) will appear to the left of the Qameṣ, □ָֽ□ְ□֫.

Examples:

1. אָכְלָה – The unaccented vowel under the א is followed by a shewa. Because a Metheg does not occur to the left of that vowel, read the shewa as a silent shewa and the vowel as Qameṣ-Ḥatuf: ’okַlâ.
2. אָֽכְלָה – The unaccented vowel under the א is followed by a shewa, but a Metheg occurs to the left of the vowel under the א. Read the shewa as vocal and the vowel as Qameṣ: ’āk̲ᵊlâ.

5.4. The Dagesh Forte and the Qameṣ/Qameṣ-Ḥatuf

Because Dagesh Forte always represents a closed syllable (4.5.2), if a closed syllable is unaccented and has the sign □ָ, the sign □ָ is a Qameṣ-Ḥatuf – חָנֵּ֫נִי (ḥonnēnî for *חָנְנֵנִי).

5.5. Maqqef: A word may transfer its accent to the following word, marked by a raised dash called Maqqef. In the phrase, גַּ֫ם הֿ֫וּא, each word has its own accent, but the first word may transfer its accent to the following word, marked by a Maqqef – גַּם־ה֫וּא. Pronounce words linked by Maqqef as one word.

5.6. Maqqef and the Qameṣ-Ḥatuf: Words, having lost their accent and connected by Maqqef, often have Qameṣ-Ḥatuf: כָּל־רַע – the sign ◌ָ, in a closed unaccented syllable, is a Qameṣ-Ḥatuf.

5.7. The Characteristics of Gutturals[1]

1. Gutturals take composite shewas instead of simple vocal shewa.[2]
2. Gutturals (including ר) do not admit Dagesh Forte.
3. Gutturals prefer Pataḥ under them or before them. The word מֶ֫לֶךְ has two Segols; נַ֫עַר, the same noun pattern, would have two Segols, but the guttural ע transforms the Segols into Pataḥs.
4. Gutturals (הּ, ח, ע, but excluding א and ר) take Furtive Pataḥ
    1. A word ending in a guttural will receive a Furtive Pataḥ, a vocalic glide to help pronounce the guttural, when the vowel before the final guttural is not a Qameṣ or Pataḥ.
        - רֵעַ instead of *רֵע
        - רוּחַ instead of *רוּח
        - שָׁלוֹחַ instead of *שָׁלוֹח
    2. If a Pataḥ or Qameṣ occurs before a final guttural, a Furtive Pataḥ is not written – שָׁלַח. If the guttural does not end the word, a Furtive Pataḥ is not written – רֵעוֹ.
    3. Ignore Furtive Pataḥ in dividing syllables and in opening or closing of syllables – לֵחַ | שׁ. The last syllable is closed.

5.8. Quiescent Alef: Silent in modern pronunciation and even in the Biblical period, Alef could quiesce (become quiet or silent).[3] Having quiesced, the Alef was written without any vowel or shewa – מָלֵ֫אתִי. When syllabifying a word, ignore the quiescent Alef, so מָלֵ֫אתִי = תִי א לֵ | מָ. Usually, a word compensates for the quiesced Alef by lengthening the preceding short vowel (footnote 5-3).

---

[1] The semi-guttural ר acts like the gutturals in not admitting the Dagesh Forte and occasionally in preferring Pataḥ (5.7.3). Otherwise, ר behaves like a non-guttural letter.

[2] Gutturals may take silent shewa (שָׁלַ֫חְתִּי), but even in the silent shewa position, gutturals may take a composite (vocal) shewa: יַעֲשֶׂה for *יַעְשֶׂה.

[3] Alef frequently quiesces in the silent shewa position: *מָצַאְתִי » *מָצַאתִי » מָצָ֫אתִי. The form compensates for the quiesced Alef by lengthening the Pataḥ to Qameṣ under the second letter. Alef also quiesces at the end of the word – *מָצַא » מָצָא. The Alef quiesces and the Pataḥ under the second letter lengthens by compensation. Occasionally, the Alef may quiesce in the vocal shewa position (לֵאלֹהִים for *לֶאֱלֹהִים, see 8.2.5).

Exercise Five

I. Questions

1. What two conditions must exist for the sign ◻ָ to be read Qameṣ-Ḥatuf?
2. How does the Metheg affect the reading of Qameṣ/Qameṣ-Ḥatuf?
3. Explain how the Dagesh Forte affects the reading of Qameṣ/Qameṣ-Ḥatuf?
4. What is the importance of the Maqqef?
5. List the four characteristics of the gutturals.
6. When does ר act like a guttural letter? When does it usually not act as a guttural letter?
7. Discuss the gutturals with silent shewa.
8. Define Furtive Pataḥ. Which gutturals may take Furtive Pataḥ? Which gutturals do not take Furtive Pataḥ? When does Furtive Pataḥ occur? How does it affect the dividing of syllables and of the opening and closing of syllables?
9. What is a quiescent Alef? How does it affect syllabification? How does a word compensate for a quiescent letter?

II. Vocabulary

כֹּל, כָּל־	all, every, totality	לָקַח	(he) took, received
יהוה	LORD, Yahweh, the Divine Name	שָׁם	(adv.) there
בַּ֫יִת	house	עָלָה	(he) went up
הִנֵּה	(particle) look, see, behold	יָצָא	(he) went out
אָכַל	(he) ate	שָׁלַח	(he) sent
כֹּהֵן	priest	כַּאֲשֶׁר	(conjunction) as
יְרוּשָׁלַ֫יִם	Jerusalem	יְהוּדָה	Judah

III. Drills

1. Identify each Qameṣ or Qameṣ-Ḥatuf.

2. Word Breakdown: In the following order: label every Dagesh Forte and Lene, Mappiq; vocal and silent shewa; Qameṣ, Qameṣ-Ḥatuf. Next divide syllables, labeling them open or closed. Then pronounce the words.

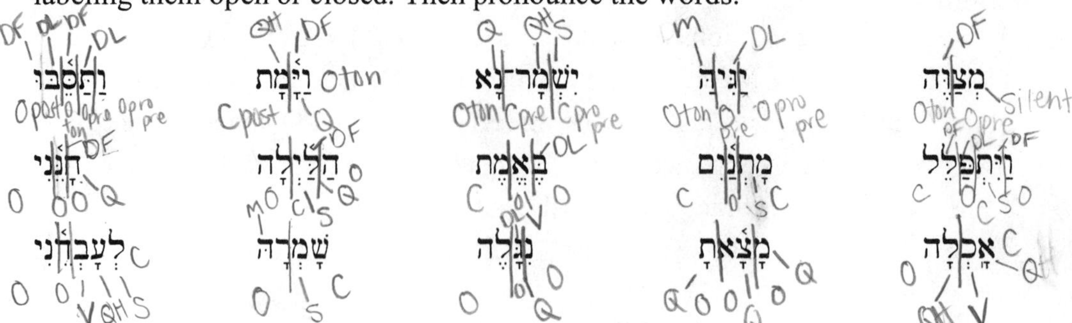

CHAPTER 6
RULES OF PROTO-HEBREW
RULES OF SYLLABLES
NOTES ON HEBREW SYNTAX

6.1. Introduction: Chapter six is the heart of the grammar – with every chapter flowing into or out of chapter six. We have now come to the Hebrew Sinai – master these laws and you can master Hebrew.

6.2. Rules of Proto-Hebrew (Pre-Biblical Hebrew)

1. Qameṣ in Biblical Hebrew was a Pataḥ in Proto-Hebrew[1] – דָּבָר « *דַּבַר.
2. Vocal shewa (□ְ, □ֱ, □ֶ֑, □ֲ) in Biblical Hebrew was a short vowel (frequently Pataḥ) in Proto-Hebrew – דְּבַר « *דַּבַר.[2]
3. Historic long vowels (1.8.2) are the same in Proto-Hebrew and Biblical Hebrew: סוּסִים is both Proto-Hebrew and Biblical Hebrew.
4. The short vowels (Pataḥ, Ḥireq, Qibbuṣ, and Qameṣ-Ḥatuf) in Biblical Hebrew are the same in Proto-Hebrew: גַּם is both Proto-Hebrew and Biblical Hebrew.

6.3. The Five Rules of Syllables in Biblical Hebrew[3] (review 2.6 and 2.7)

דָּ | בָ֫ר (1 2)   מֶ֫ | לֶךְ (3 4)   דְּ ¦ בָ | רִ֫ים[4] (5)

1. In a closed accented syllable, Hebrew *prefers* a long vowel.
2. In an open pretonic syllable, Hebrew *requires* a long vowel.[5]
3. In a closed unaccented syllable, Hebrew *requires* a short vowel.
4. In an open accented syllable, Hebrew *prefers* a short vowel.
5. In an originally open pro-pretonic syllable, Hebrew reduces the original short vowel to a vocal shewa. (The vocal shewa, unable to constitute an independent syllable, attaches to the pretonic syllable – דְּבָ 3.4.1.)

---

[1] Rarely, Qameṣ is an historic long vowel. Also in Proto-Hebrew, Ṣere was a Ḥireq, and Ḥolem was a Qameṣ-Ḥatuf or a Qibbuṣ. The Ṣere and Ḥolem lengthen secondarily from short vowels (1.8.2). Segol is a secondary vowel usually from Ḥireq.

[2] Silent shewa is the absence of a vowel – even in Proto-Hebrew.

[3] Of course, there are exceptions to these "rules," but these rules apply for almost all syllables in Hebrew.

[4] The dotted line indicates an original syllable division.

[5] Moreover, in an open post-tonic syllable, Hebrew *requires* a long vowel – קָטָ֑לְתָּ (for the sign □֑, see 6.5.2).

6.4. Proto-Hebrew and the Five Rules of Syllables

1. דָּבָר was originally *דַּבַר in Proto-Hebrew (6.2.1).
    1. In Biblical Hebrew, the Pataḥ under the ב lengthens to Qameṣ in a closed accented syllable (6.3.1 rule one).
    2. The Pataḥ under the ד lengthens to Qameṣ in a pretonic open syllable (6.3.2 rule two).
2. מֶ֫לֶךְ: The Proto-Hebrew of this word will be explained in chapter 15.
    1. Any closed unaccented syllable – whether post-tonic, pretonic, or pro-pretonic – requires a short vowel (לֶךְ) (6.3.3 rule three).
    2. Frequently, an open accented syllable receives a short vowel (מֶ֫) (6.3.4 rule four).
3. דְּבָרִים was originally *דַּבַרִים in Proto-Hebrew.
    1. The last syllable (רִים), closed and accented with a historic long vowel, never lengthens or reduces (1.8.2).
    2. The next syllable בַ, in the pretonic open position, lengthens the original Pataḥ to Qameṣ.
    3. The next syllable דַ, in the originally open pro-pretonic position, reduces the original Pataḥ to a vocal shewa and attaches to the בָ to form a syllable (6.3.5 rule five; 3.4.1).

6.5. Notes on Hebrew Syntax

1. Basic Sentence Structure
    1. The usual word order of a Hebrew sentence is Verb-Subject-Object – שָׁמַע מֹשֶׁה קוֹל "Moses (he) heard a voice." The order may vary for emphasis: מֹשֶׁה שָׁמַע קוֹל "(As for) Moses (he) heard a voice," or קוֹל מֹשֶׁה שָׁמַע "A voice – Moses heard."
    2. Third person verbs (he, she, it, they) have an inherent or implied pronoun. If the sentence, however, has an explicit subject, the inherent or implied pronoun is omitted in translation – שָׁמַע מֹשֶׁה "Moses (he) heard" becomes "Moses heard." Without the explicit subject, translate the inherent or implied pronoun – שָׁמַע "he heard."[6]

2. Disjunctive Accents – Sof Pasuq/Silluq and Athnaḥ
   Often overlooked, the Masoretic accents furnish important information for syntax.[7] The accents group words of a sentence into smaller units, thereby clarifying the syntax of the sentence.

[6] Hebrew is like Greek here.

[7] The accents also supply the traditional Jewish interpretation of the text.

1. Sof Pasuq and Silluq: Biblical Hebrew sentences end in Sof Pasuq: **:** (two stacked diamonds) and a Silluq: □ֽ (a vertical line, like the Metheg) under the accented syllable of the last word in a sentence. (The boxes represent words, not root letters.)
   :□□□□□□□□□□□□□
2. Athnaḥ: The Athnaḥ □֑ divides the sentence in half according to syntactical and exegetical considerations.[8] Like the Silluq, the Athnaḥ marks the accented syllable. (The boxes represent words, not root letters.)
   :□□□□□□ □□□□□□

3. Pausal Forms
   The Silluq and the Athnaḥ often lengthen a short vowel in the accented syllable to a long vowel (מַ֫יִם » מָ֑יִם). This lengthening of the short vowel indicates a pause in pronunciation, as the pause in English after periods, semi-colons, and commas. Words that lengthen short vowels (usually with Silluq and Athnaḥ) in accented syllables are said to be in pause or a pausal form.

Exercise Six

I. Questions

1. Write the four rules of Proto-Hebrew and the five rules of syllables (with their examples) for Biblical Hebrew.
2. What is the normal word order in Hebrew? Discuss the problem of translating third person verbs.
3. What is the importance of the accents? Describe the Sof Pasuq, Silluq, and Athnaḥ. How do Silluq and Athnaḥ frequently affect short vowels?
4. Discuss the syntactical and exegetical significance of the Athnaḥ.
5. When is a word in pause? How is a pausal form indicated?

II. Vocabulary

אַחַר, אַחֲרֵי	(prep.) after, behind	קוֹל	voice, sound
גּוֹי	people, nation	עַתָּה	(adverb) now
כֹּה	(adverb) thus, so	שָׁמַר	(he) kept, watched, guarded
עָבַר	(he) passed over, transgressed	מַ֫יִם	water
נָבִיא	prophet	שָׁמַ֫יִם	heaven, heavens, sky
אַבְרָהָם	Abraham	עָמַד	(he) stood, has stood

[8] Often the half of the verse before the Athnaḥ gives the main idea of the verse. (This is especially true in poetry.) The second half explains, specifies, enumerates, or qualifies the first half of the verse. Moreover, the Athnaḥ may be exegetically important marking the emphasis of the verse. See 2 Sam 12:7; Jer 1:10.

אַהֲרֹן	Aaron	רֹאשׁ	head

III. Drills

1. Word Breakdown: In the following order: label every Dagesh Forte and Lene, Mappiq; vocal and silent shewa; Qameṣ and Qameṣ-Ḥatuf. Next, divide syllables labeling them open or closed. Then pronounce the words.

    יְגַדְּלוּ   אָכְלָה   כְּכָל־עַמִּים   לָהּ   הִשְׁתַּלְּחוּ

    יַשְׁמִיעַ   עָרְמָה   הִמָּצֵא   הִסַּבִּי   מִמִּצְרַיִם

2. Put the following Biblical Hebrew words into Proto-Hebrew[9] according to the rules of Proto-Hebrew.

    מַמְתָּק   כּוֹכָבִים   בָּשָׂר   נָבִיא   עָמָל

    עֲמָלִים   יָד   נְבִיאוֹת   סוּס   הַיָּדַיִם

3. Put the following Proto-Hebrew words into Biblical Hebrew words according to the five rules of syllables of Biblical Hebrew.

    שַׁמַיִם   נַחַשׁ   יַשַׁרוֹת   נַבִיאִים   כּוֹכַב

    דַּבַרִים   תּוֹרוֹת   מַהְלַךְ   עַמַלִי   מַשְׁקוֹף

4. Translation: Because of the brevity of the following sentences, only Sof Pasuq and Silluq will be used.

    1. דָּבָר אַבְרָהָם דִּבֵּר׃
    2. כֹּה אָמַר מֹשֶׁה אֶל־אַהֲרֹן׃
    3. בָּא נָבִיא אֶל־יְרוּשָׁלִָם׃
    4. רָאָה אָדָם שָׁמָיִם׃
    5. לָקַח כֹּהֵן עֶבֶד מִן־מִצְרָיִם׃
    6. הָלַךְ מֹשֶׁה עִם אַהֲרֹן׃
    7. יָצָא מִן־עִיר׃
    8. בָּא אֶל־יִשְׂרָאֵל׃

[9] Restore vocal shewas to Pataḥ.

MORPHOLOGICAL PRINCIPLES: PARTICLES

Chapter 7
The Article ה and the Interrogative מה־
The Marker of the Definite Direct Object: אֵת (אֶת־)

7.1. Introduction: Down from Sinai, we now examine the idolatries of particles,[1] those demons only exorcised through memory – mostly. First comes the article and the interrogative מה. Hebrew has a definite article (the), but not an indefinite article (a, an). The article and the interrogative מה connect to their words similarly.

7.2. The Form of the Article: The attaching (or pointing) of the article to a noun or adjective. The article attaches to the beginning of a word.

1. הַ▣: The article before non-guttural letters is pointed הַ▣ (with a Dagesh Forte in the following letter: הַ▣□□) – הַדָּבָר, הַמֶּ֫לֶךְ.
2. Guttural letters (including ר) will not admit Dagesh Forte (4.3.3):
   1. הָ: The article before the gutturals א, ע, and ר is pointed הָ – *הַאָדָם » הָאָדָם, הָעִיר, הָרֹאשׁ.
      Initial א, ע, and ר reject the Dagesh, and the Pataḥ lengthens to Qameṣ by compensation.[2]
   2. הַ: The article before the gutturals ה and ח is pointed הַ, without following Dagesh Forte – הַהֵיכָל, הַחוֹמָה.
      Consider the Dagesh Forte "implicit" or "implied" in the ה or ח.
   3. Certain gutturals with Qameṣ:
      1. הֶ: The article before חָ or unaccented הָ and עָ is pointed הֶ, without following Dagesh Forte – הֶהָרִים, הֶעָפָר, הֶחָכָם, הֶחָ֫יִל.
      2. הָ: The article before accented הָ֫ is pointed הָ – הָהָ֫ר.

7.3. The Translation of the Article

Translate a noun or an adjective without the article with or without the English indefinite article according to context. Translate the noun or the adjective with the article with the English definite article "the."

1. Without article: דָּבָר, "word" or "a word," מֶ֫לֶךְ, "king" or "a king."
2. With article: הַדָּבָר, "the word," הַמֶּ֫לֶךְ, "the king."

---

[1] Particles are small, uninflected elements of a language, such as articles, prepositions, conjunctions, interjections, and adverbs.

[2] See footnote 1-7.

7.4. The Interrogative מה – what?, how?

The interrogative מה is pointed like the article.

1. ▣־מַה: The interrogative מה before non-guttural letters is pointed ▣־מַה, with a Dagesh Forte in the following letter and a Maqqef connecting the words ☐☐▣־מַה – מַה־דָּבָר. Sometimes the interrogative מה occurs without the Maqqef before guttural letters.

2. The Guttural Letters
   1. ־מָה: Interrogative מה before the guttural letters, א, ע, ר, or before the article[3] is pointed ־מָה – *מַה־אֵיבָה » מָה־אֵיבָה.
      The initial א rejects the Dagesh Forte, and the Pataḥ lengthens to Qameṣ by compensation.[4]
   2. ־מַה: The interrogative מה before the guttural letters ה (excluding the article) and ח is pointed ־מַה, without Dagesh Forte – מַה־הֵיכָל.
      Consider the Dagesh Forte "implicit" or "implied" in the ה or ח.
   3. ־מֶה: Gutturals (excluding ר) with Qameṣ are pointed ־מֶה, without following Dagesh Forte – מֶה־אָמַרְתָּ.

7.5. Translation of the Interrogative מה

מֶה־אָדָם "What (is) man," "How (is) man." Supply some form of "to be" (is, was, will be, and so forth) in translating clauses without verbs in Hebrew.

7.6. Review of the Article and the Interrogative מה:

Article ה	Interrogative מה
1. ▣הַ: before non-gutturals – הַדָּבָר	1. ▣־מַה: before non-gutturals – מַה־דָּבָר
2. הָ: before א, ע, ר – הָרֹאשׁ	2. ־מָה: before א, ע, ר (or the article) – מָה־רֹאשׁ
3. הַ: before ה, ח – הַהֵיכָל	3. ־מַה: before ה (excluding the article), ח – מַה־הֵיכָל
4. הֶ: before חָ and unaccented הָ, עָ – הֶעָמָל	4. ־מֶה: before G[5] (excluding ר) – מֶה־עָמָל
5. הֶ: before accented הָ – הֶהָר	

[3] Generally, before the article and certain pronouns (הֵמָּה, הֵם), the Pataḥ lengthens to a Qameṣ: מָה־הַדָּבָר.

[4] See footnote 1-7.

[5] "G" stands for guttural letters.

7.7. The Marker of the Definite[6] Direct Object: אֵת (אֶת־)

1. If the direct object of a verb is definite, the direct object is usually, but not always, preceded by אֵת (or אֶת־) – רָדַף דָּוִד אֶת־הַמֶּלֶךְ "David pursued the king." The particle אֵת precedes the definite direct object (the king), which has the article. רָדַף הַמֶּלֶךְ אֶת־דָּוִד "The king pursued David." The particle אֵת precedes the definite direct object (David), being a proper noun.
2. If the direct object of a verb is not definite, the direct object is not preceded by אֵת (אֶת־) – שָׁמַר הָאִישׁ סוּס "The man kept a horse."

Exercise Seven

I. Questions

1. What are the five ways that an article can be attached to a noun/adjective?
2. Discuss the translation of a word with and without the article.
3. What are the four ways that the interrogative מה can be attached to a word? How is it attached before an article?
4. How is the interrogative מה translated?
5. When is a word considered definite in Hebrew?
6. When is the definite direct object marker אֵת used? When is it not used?

II. Vocabulary

מַה־, מָה־, מֶה־	what, how?	לֶחֶם	bread
עַם	(with article הָעָם[7]) people	פְּרִי	fruit
הַר	(with article הָהָר[7]) mountain	הֵיכָל	temple, palace
גַּן	(with article הַגָּן[7]) garden	רָדַף	(he) pursued, persecuted
אֶרֶץ	(with article הָאָרֶץ[7]) (f) earth, land	עָפָר	dirt, ground
צִוָּה	(he) commanded	שָׁאוּל	Saul
בָּשָׂר	flesh	פַּרְעֹה	Pharaoh

III. Drills

1. Word Breakdown: In the following order: label every Dagesh Forte and Lene, Mappiq; vocal and silent shewa; Qameṣ and Qameṣ-Ḥatuf. Next, divide syllables labeling them open or closed. Then pronounce the words.

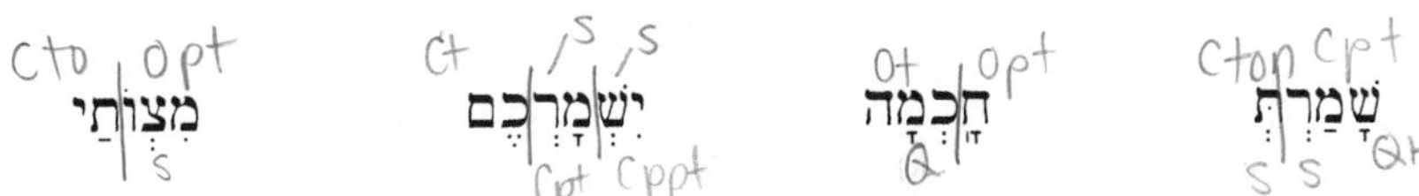

[6] Consider a word definite if: (1) it has the definite article – הַמֶּלֶךְ, (2) it is a proper name – שְׁמוּאֵל (Samuel), (3) it has a pronominal suffix – דְּבָרוֹ (his word). More accurately, אֵת marks an accusative.

[7] Rarely, because of the article, the Pataḥ under the first root letter becomes Qameṣ.

2. Put the following Biblical Hebrew words into Proto-Hebrew according to the rules of Proto-Hebrew.

3. Put the following Proto-Hebrew words into Biblical Hebrew according to the five rules of syllables.

4. Attach the article to the following words and translate all vocabulary words.

אוֹר	עָמָל	חַ֫יִל	יְפָעָה
הֵיכָל	אִשָּׁה	רֹאשׁ	חָכָם

5. Attach the interrogative מה to the following words and translate all vocabulary words.

זֶה	שֶׁהָיָה	הָיָה	הֵיכָל
אַתָּה	עָשִׂית	רָאִיתָ	עִיר

6. Translation

1. יוֹם הַיּוֹם; מֶ֫לֶךְ הַמֶּ֫לֶךְ; עִיר הָעִיר; הֵיכָל הַהֵיכָל; אָדָם הָאָדָם; הַר הָהָר
2. עָפָר הֶעָפָר; עֶ֫בֶד הָעֶ֫בֶד; אֶ֫רֶץ הָאָ֫רֶץ
3. גַּן הַגָּן; עַם הָעָם; לֶ֫חֶם הַלֶּ֫חֶם; אֲנָשִׁים הָאֲנָשִׁים
4. מֶה־אָדָם מַה־יִּשְׂרָאֵל מָה־אֱלֹהִים מָה־הַהֵיכָל מָה־הַדָּבָר
5. רָדַף שָׁאוּל אַחֲרֵי־דָוִד אֶל־יְהוּדָֽה׃
6. יָשַׁב מֹשֶׁה עַל־הָהָֽר׃
7. עָשָׂה אֱלֹהִים אֶת־אָדָם מִן־הֶעָפָֽר׃
8. עָבַר שָׁאוּל אֶת־הַדָּבָר אֲשֶׁר אָמַר יהוִה׃
9. רָאָה מֹשֶׁה אֶת־אֱלֹהִים פָּנִים אֶל־פָּנִֽים׃
10. שָׁלַח פַּרְעֹה אֶת־אַבְרָהָם אֶל־יְרוּשָׁלִָֽם׃

CHAPTER 8
INSEPARABLE PREPOSITIONS
THE CONJUNCTIVE VAV

8.1. Introduction: The inseparable prepositions (ב in, with; כ like, as, according to; ל to, for) connect inseparably to the beginning of a word. The conjunctive Vav (and, but, even), pointed like the inseparable prepositions, also inseparably connects to the beginning of a word. In Proto-Hebrew, the inseparable prepositions and the conjunctive Vav had a Pataḥ: בַ, כַ, לַ, וַ.

8.2. Attaching or Pointing Inseparable Prepositions ב, כ, ל

Point the inseparable prepositions with:

1. לְ (Vocal shewa): לְדָבָר (to a word), בְּמָקוֹם (in a place), כְּנָבִיא (like a prophet)
   The original Pataḥ under the inseparable preposition reduces to a vocal shewa in an originally open pro-pretonic syllable (6.3.5) – *לַדָבָר » לְדָבָר.

2. לִ:
   1. Before a vocal shewa – לִשְׁמוּאֵל (for Samuel), בִּצְדָקָה (in righteousness), כִּנְבִיאִים (like prophets)
      The original Pataḥ under the inseparable preposition reduces to a vocal shewa in an originally open pro-pretonic syllable (6.3.5) – *לְשְׁמוּאֵל. Hebrew will not permit two consecutive vocal shewas; therefore, a "shewa fight" occurs with the first vocal shewa becoming a Ḥireq[1] – *לְשְׁמוּאֵל » לִשְׁמוּאֵל.
   2. Before יְ – לִילָדִים (for children), בִּיהוּדָה (in Judah), כִּירֻשָּׁה (like a possession):
      *לַיְלָדִים » *לְיְלָדִים » *לִיְלָדִים » לִילָדִים
      1 2 3 4
      The original Pataḥ under the inseparable preposition reduces to a vocal shewa in an originally open pro-pretonic syllable (1). The two vocal shewas (2) fight, leaving a Ḥireq under the inseparable preposition (3). Then the consonantal Yod quiesces (the Yod becomes "quiet" and loses its shewa) becoming a vowel: Ḥireq-Yod (4).[2]

---

[1] See 3.2.2.

[2] This is the "Hebrew love story." The Yod drops the shewa to resume its love with the Ḥireq, its old flame.

3. לַ, לֶ, לָ (Qameṣ-Ḥatuf):

   לַאֲדָמָה (to land), בַּאֲדָמָה (in land), כַּאֲדָמָה (like land)
   לֶאֱדֹם (to Edom), בֶּאֱדֹם (in Edom), כֶּאֱדֹם (like Edom)
   לָחֳדָשִׁים (to months), בָּחֳדָשִׁים (in months), כָּחֳדָשִׁים (like months)

   *לַאֲדָמָה » *לְאֲדָמָה » לַאֲדָמָה
   1 2 3

   The original Pataḥ (1) under the inseparable preposition reduces to a vocal shewa in an originally open pro-pretonic syllable (6.3.5). The two vocal shewas (2) fight, and the first vocal shewa becomes a short vowel corresponding to the vowel of the following composite shewa (3).

4. לָ (Qameṣ) – כָּזֶה, בָּזֹאת, לָ֫מַּיִם

   The inseparable preposition, in the pretonic open position, may lengthen the original Pataḥ to Qameṣ (6.3.2) – *בַּזֹאת » בָּזֹאת. Frequently, however, a shewa occurs in the pretonic open position – לְמֶ֫לֶךְ. The shewa occurs so frequently with the inseparable prepositions that the shewa appears in syllables that "break" the rules (6.3.2).

5. לֵ or לַ – these are limited to two words:

   כֵּאלֹהִים, בֵּאלֹהִים, לֵאלֹהִים – אֱלֹהִים
   כַּיהוה, בַּיהוה, לַיהוה – יהוה

   1. אֱלֹהִים is like 8.2.3, so one expects *לֶאֱלֹהִים. Here, however, the א quiesces (thereby losing its shewa, compare 5.8 and 8.2.2), and the Segol lengthens to Ṣere by compensation for the quiescing of the Alef.[3]
      *לֶאֱלֹהִים » *לֶאלֹהִים » לֵאלֹהִים
   2. יהוה is also like 8.2.3, but the Hebrews read אֲדֹנָי (Lord) for יהוה (Divine Name) to keep from profaning the Lord's name. The Hebrews, then, attached the inseparable preposition belonging to אֲדֹנָי to יהוה – לַאֲדֹנָי = לַיהוה (for the corresponding short vowel, review 8.2.3).

[3] See footnotes 1-7 and 5-3.

6. ◘לַ: The inseparable preposition supplants the ה of the article, but retains the pointing of the article.[4]

Article	Article with Inseparable Preposition	
הַמֶּ֫לֶךְ	לַמֶּ֫לֶךְ	to the king
הָאָדָם	לָאָדָם	to the man
הַהֵיכָל	לַהֵיכָל	to the palace
הֶעָפָר	לֶעָפָר	to the dirt
הָהָר	לָהָר	to the mountain

8.3. Conjunctive Vav ו

Point the conjunctive Vav (and) virtually like the inseparable prepositions ל, ב, כ (except for 8.3.6):

1. וְ (Vocal shewa): וְדָבָר (like 8.2.1)
2. וִ before יְ: וִיהוּדָה (like 8.2.2)
3. וַ, וֶ, וָ (Qameṣ-Ḥatuf): וַאֲדָמָה (like 8.2.3)
4. וָ (Qameṣ): וָלַ֫יְלָה (like 8.2.4). A vocal shewa is possible (like 8.2.4).
5. וֵ or וַ in two words: וֵאלֹהִים and וַיהוה (like 8.2.5)
6. וּ:[5]
    1. before (simple) vocal shewas:[6] וּדְבַר, וּדְבָרִים
    2. before the labial (lip) letters במף (called בּוּמָף letters): וּבֵית, וּמִדְבָּר, וּפָרָה

[4] In Hebrew, ה between vowels may drop out – *לְהַמֶּ֫לֶךְ » לַמֶּ֫לֶךְ. Compare the Hiph'îl imperfect – *יְהַקְטִיל » יַקְטִיל (footnote 22-3).

[5] This differs from the pointing of inseparable prepositions.

[6] This is the only exception to the rule that a vowel cannot begin a syllable (2.3; footnotes 12-1 and 15-7).

8.4. Review of the Inseparable Prepositions and the Conjunctive Vav:

Inseparable Prepositions: בַ, כַ, לַ	Conjunctive Vav ו
1. לְ: originally open, pro-pretonic syllable – לְדָבָר	1. וְ: originally open, pro-pretonic syllable – וְדָבָר
2. לִ: 1) before vocal shewa – לִשְׁמוּאֵל 2) before יְ – לִיהוּדָה	2. וִ: before יְ – וִיהוּדָה
3. Gלֶ: corresponding short vowel before a composite shewa – לֶאֱדֹם	3. Gוַ: corresponding short vowel before a composite shewa – וֶאֱדֹם
4. ☐לְ/לָ: pretonic open may receive Qameṣ or shewa – לְלַיְלָה/לָלַיְלָה	4. ☐וְ/וָ: pretonic open may receive Qameṣ or shewa – וְלַיְלָה/וָלַיְלָה
5. לַ/לֵ: לַיהוה/לֵאלֹהִים	5. וַ/וֵ: וַיהוה/וֵאלֹהִים
6. ☐לַ: the preposition supplants the ה of the article – לַדָּבָר	6. וּ: 1) before (simple) vocal shewa – וּשְׁמוֹ 2) before בּוּמָף (labial letters) – וּבֵן

EXERCISE EIGHT

I. Questions

1. What was the original proto-vowel under the inseparable prepositions and the conjunctive Vav?
2. List how the inseparable prepositions attach to words.
3. List how the conjunctive Vav attaches to words.
4. Although the inseparable prepositions and the conjunctive Vav connect similarly to words, how do they differ?
5. What is the only exception to the rule that a vowel cannot begin a syllable?

II. Vocabulary

זָבַח	(he) slaughtered, sacrificed	בֵּין	(prep.) between
זֶבַח	sacrifice	תּוֹרָה	law, instruction
מִזְבֵּחַ	place of sacrifice,[7] altar	זָהָב	gold
אֲדָמָה	land, ground	יָרַד	(he) went down
מָלַךְ	(he) ruled, was king	...וְ	and, but, even, now
עֵץ	tree	כֶּסֶף	silver
יוֹסֵף	Joseph	בָּנָה	(he) built
יַרְדֵּן	Jordan (with the article הַיַּרְדֵּן)	לָמָּה, לָמָה	מה + ל prep. for what, why?

[7] מ at the beginning of a word sometimes expresses "place of."

III. Drills

1. Word Breakdown: In the following order: label every Dagesh Forte and Lene, Mappiq; vocal and silent shewa; Qameṣ and Qameṣ-Ḥatuf. Next, divide syllables labeling them open or closed. Then pronounce the words.

   יִשְׁבְּרוּ　　שֹׁלֵחַ　　חָכְמָה　　תִּתֵּנָּה

2. Put the following Proto-Hebrew words into Biblical Hebrew according to the five rules of syllables.

   כַּנַפַּיִם　　וַכוֹכַב

3. Put the following Biblical Hebrew words into Proto-Hebrew according to the rules of Proto-Hebrew.

   וְדָבָר　　נָעִים

4. Attach the following particles and translate all vocabulary words.

   Article

   ה אָדָם　　ה עָפָר　　ה חֹשֶׁךְ　　ה עִיר

   Interrogative מה

   ה עַיִן　　ה עָפָר　　ה חֲלוֹם　　ה פַּחַד

   Inseparable Preposition ב

   יִשְׂרָאֵל　　מַיִם　　אֲרִי　　שְׁמוּאֵל

   אֱדוֹם　　הַמְּלָכִים　　יהוה　　יְהוּדָה

   Conjunctive ו

   יְרוּשָׁלַיִם　　חֳלִי　　אֲרִי　　מֹשֶׁה

   יֶלֶד　　מַיִם　　יהוה　　יְהוּדָה

5. Translation

1. הַלֶּ֫חֶם בַּלֶּ֫חֶם כַּלֶּ֫חֶם וָלֶ֫חֶם וּבַלֶּ֫חֶם
2. כַּאֲדָמָה וְלַאֲדָמָה בָּאֲדָמָה וַאֲדָמָה וּמָה־אֲדָמָה
3. כִּיהוּדָה וְלִיהוּדָה וִיהוּדָה מַה־יְּהוּדָה
4. וּבַ֫יִת לְבַ֫יִת לָבַ֫יִת וְהַבַּ֫יִת וּבַבַּ֫יִת
5. כַּיהוה וְלַיהוה לֵאלֹהִים כֵּאלֹהִים
6. אָכַל דָּוִד לֶ֫חֶם בַּהֵיכָֽל׃
7. לֹא עָבַר מֹשֶׁה הַיַּרְדֵּֽן׃
8. עָשָׂה אֱלֹהִים אֶת־הַשָּׁמַ֫יִם וְאֶת־הָאָֽרֶץ׃
9. נָתַן מֹשֶׁה לְיִשְׂרָאֵל אֶת־הַתּוֹרָֽה׃
10. יָרַד יוֹסֵף אֶל־מִצְרַ֫יִם עִם הָאֲנָשִֽׁים׃

Chapter 9
The Preposition מִן
The Interrogative ה
Notes on Hebrew Syntax

9.1. Introduction: The מִן preposition (from, out of) may be a separable preposition – מִן־דָּבָר or an inseparable preposition – מִדָּבָר. The מִן preposition as a separable preposition is only a vocabulary item, but as an inseparable preposition, מִן deserves attention. The interrogative ה occurs at the beginning of a sentence or clause to introduce a question.

9.2. Attaching or Pointing the Inseparable Preposition מִן

Point the inseparable מִן:

1. מִ▣: With non-guttural letters

   *מִנְשָׁמַיִם » *מִשְׁשָׁמַיִם » מִשָּׁמַיִם from heaven(s)

   1 2 3

   The nun (1) of the מִן assimilates[1] with the first letter of the word (2) and appears as a Dagesh Forte (3).

2. מִ: Before יְ[2]

   *מִיְּהוּדָה » *מִיְהוּדָה « מִיהוּדָה

   1 2 3

   The Dagesh Forte (1) disappears (2) according to footnote 4-5, and the Yod quiesces, becoming a Ḥireq-Yod (3).[3]

3. מֵ: With guttural letters (including ר)

   *מִהַמֶּלֶךְ » מֵהַמֶּלֶךְ

   1 2

   The Dagesh Forte is rejected (1) and the Ḥireq lengthens to Ṣere by compensation (2).

---

[1] The letter /n/ also assimilates in English, as for instance, with the Latin prefix "in" (incompetent, incomparable, incurable), which negate words – illegal for inlegal, irresponsible for inresponsible. Assimilation may be partial: impossible for inpossible (not, ippossible, which would be full assimilation).

[2] Compare 8.2.2 and 8.3.2.

[3] See footnote 8-2.

9.3. The Interrogative ה: The inseparable particle ה, which introduces a question, has a Proto-Hebrew form הַ.

Point the interrogative ה:

1. הֲ: Before non-guttural letters (including ר) with a vowel – הֲשָׁלוֹם. The ה, commonly standing in the open pro-pretonic position, reduces the original Pataḥ to a composite shewa (Ḥatef-Pataḥ because of the guttural, compare 6.3.5; 8.2.1). Like the inseparable prepositions (8.2.4), the interrogative ה has a vocal shewa in the original open pretonic position: הֲלֹא « *הְלֹא, thus breaking the rules (6.3.2; 8.2.4).

2. הַ:
   1. Before vocal shewa – הַשְׁמוּאֵל. The interrogative ה cannot maintain the composite shewa because a word cannot begin with two vocal shewas (8.2.2; 3.2.2). The interrogative ה maintains its original Pataḥ.
   2. Before gutturals (excluding ר) – הַאֵלֵךְ. This may be implicit doubling (compare 7.2.2).[4]

3. הֶ: Before a guttural (excluding ר) with a Qameṣ – הֶאָמַרְתִּי (compare 7.2.2).

9.4. Review of the Pointing of the Preposition מן and the Interrogative ה

Preposition מן	Interrogative ה
1. מִ◻: before non-gutturals – מִשָּׁאוּל	1. הֲ: normal before a vowel – הֲשָׁלוֹם
2. מִ: before יְ – מִיהוּדָה	2. הַ: 1) before vocal shewa – הַשְׁמוּאֵל
3. מֵ: before gutturals – מֵהַמֶּלֶךְ	2) before a guttural (excluding ר) – הַאֵלֵךְ
	3. הֶ: before Gָ (excluding ר) – הֶאָב

9.5. Hebrew Syntax: Sentences and Clauses without Verbs

As mentioned earlier (7.5), sentences and clauses (especially clauses introduced by אֲשֶׁר, כִּי, and מַה־) sometimes occur without an explicit verb. Furnish a form of the English verb "to be" (is, are, was, were, will be, and so forth) in translating clauses without verbs into English. Context determines the appropriate tense to be supplied. Usually, the preceding verb determines the tense of a following clause without a verb.

דָּוִד אָדָם "David (is, was, will be) a man."

הָאִישׁ אֲשֶׁר בַּהֵיכָל "The man who (is, was, will be) in the palace."

[4] In examples like הַהֵיכָל, only context determines whether the word has the article or the interrogative ה.

9.6. Hebrew Syntax: Disjunctive Accents – Zaqef Qaton, Zaqef Gadol, Segolta

1. Zaqef Qaton
   The Masoretes further divided longer sentences by a Zaqef Qaton (small Zaqef), two vertically stacked dots (like the simple shewa sign) placed over the accented syllable of a word – אֶ֔רֶץ. Short verses may not have Zaqef Qaton. (The boxes represent words, not root letters.)

   :□□□ □̈□□ □□□ □̈□□

2. Zaqef Gadol
   The Zaqef Gadol (great Zaqef), two vertically stacked dots with a vertical line to the left of the dots (□), also indicates a break (disjunctive accent) and marks the accented syllable. It occurs on the first word of a sentence or the first word after a Zaqef Qaton or Athnaḥ. The Zaqef Qaton is generally stronger than the Zaqef Gadol. (The boxes represent words, not root letters.)

   :□□□ □ □□ □□ □□ □
   :□□□ □ □□□ □ □□ □

3. Segolta
   The Segolta (an inverted segol □), a disjunctive accent that does not mark the accent syllable, substitutes for the first Zaqef Qaton in the Athnaḥ segment of a verse. Segolta is generally found in longer verses. (The boxes represent words, not root letters.)

   :□□□ □□□ □□□ □□□

9.7. Verb Forms: Third Person Plural (Masculine and Feminine)

1. These forms end in Shureq (וּ) with a vocal shewa under the second root letter:[5]
   Third masculine singular
   אָמַר "He said" שָׁלַח "He sent" דִּבֶּר "He spoke"

   Third common[6] plural
   אָמְרוּ "They said" שָׁלְחוּ "They sent"
   דִּבְּרוּ "They spoke" אָמְרוּ הָאֲנָשִׁים "The men said"

---

[5] The reduction patterns of the verb will be explained later.

[6] Common means masculine and feminine.

2. Verbs that end in ◌ָה replace the ◌ָה with Shureq (וּ) without a vocal shewa under the second root letter.

   Third masculine singular

   בָּנָה "He built" הָיָה "He was" בָּנָה דָוִד "David built"

   Third common plural

   בָּנוּ "They built" הָיוּ "They were" בָּנוּ הָאֲנָשִׁים "The men built"

EXERCISE NINE

I. Questions

1. List how the inseparable מִן preposition attaches to words.
2. Describe assimilation for Hebrew and for English.
3. List how the interrogative ה attaches to words.
4. When Hebrew clauses are without a verb, what English verb is added for translation?
5. Discuss the accents: Zaqef Qaton, Zaqef Gadol, and Segolta. Which of these accents marks the accented syllable?
6. How do third person plural verbs end? How does this affect the second root letter?

II. Vocabulary

עוֹד	(adverb) again, still, yet	מִן	from, out of (the preposition can be compounded on another preposition – מֵעִם from with; מֵעַל from upon. This is common after verbs expressing motion.)
יְהוֹשֻׁעַ	Joshua		
כָּתַב	(he) wrote		
תְּהִלָּה	glory, praise		
לַיְלָה	night (This word is not feminine because the final ◌ָה is unaccented. The ending is an accusative ending. See 10.11.)	מְאֹד	(adverb) very, exceedingly
		אוֹר	light
סוּס	horse	חֹשֶׁךְ	darkness
שְׁמוּאֵל	Samuel	עוֹלָם	eternity
מִי	who? (אֶת־מִי whom?)	עַד	(prep. and conj.) unto, to, as far as, when, until, עַד עוֹלָם: forever
שָׁלוֹם	peace, health		

III. Drills

1. Word Breakdown: In the following order: label every Dagesh Forte and Lene, Mappiq; vocal and silent shewa; Qameṣ and Qameṣ-Ḥatuf. Next, divide syllables labeling them open or closed. Then pronounce the words.

   בַּבַּ֫יִת קְטַלְתִּ֫יהָ תְּקוּמֶ֫ינָה יִשְׁמְרֶ֫ךָ

2. Put the following Proto-Hebrew words into Biblical Hebrew according to the five rules of syllables.

   עֲמַלוֹ   מִדְבַּר

3. Put the following Biblical Hebrew words into Proto-Hebrew according to the rules of Proto-Hebrew.

   כּוֹכָב   חֲכַם

4. Attach the following particles and translate all vocabulary words.

   Article

   חֳלִי   הָר   אֱלֹהִים

   Interrogative מה

   אוֹר   חָ֫יִל   מֶ֫לֶךְ

   Inseparable Preposition כ

   יְרוּשָׁלַ֫יִם   שֶׁ֫בֶת   יִלוֹד

   Conjunctive ו

   יִשְׂרָאֵל   בֵּין   אִשָּׁה

   Interrogative ה

   חָכָם   עַם   יְהוּדָה   אֲרִי

   Preposition מן

   זֶה   הָיָה   אַתָּה   יְרוּשָׁלַ֫יִם

5. Translation

1. הַעִיר, הָעִיר, וּמֵהָעִיר, בְּעִיר, מַה־בָּעִיר
2. בַּלַיְלָה, מִלַּיְלָה, וּמָה־הַלַּיְלָה
3. לַתְּהִלָּה, וּתְהִלָּה, בִּתְהִלָּה
4. הַדָּבָר, כַּדָּבָר, וּמֵהַדָּבָר, מָה־הַדָּבָר
5. וְכֶסֶף, כַּכֶּסֶף, הָאֲדָמָה, מֵאֲדָמָה
6. שָׁמַע שָׁאוּל אֶל־אָדָם וְלֹא שָׁמַע אֶל־אֱלֹהִים׃
7. הַשְׁמוּאֵל נָבִיא׃
8. בָּא שָׁאוּל אֶל־הַהֵיכָל וְהוּא לֹא דִבֶּר אֶל־הַכֹּהֵן׃
9. אָכַל אָדָם פְּרִי מֵהָעֵץ אֲשֶׁר בַּגָּן׃
10. נָתַן פַּרְעֹה לְיוֹסֵף כֶּסֶף וְזָהָב וְגַם אִשָּׁה׃
11. בָּא הָאָדָם אֶל־הַגָּן אֲשֶׁר עָשָׂה אֱלֹהִים וְשָׁם דִּבֶּר אֶל־אֱלֹהִים׃
12. לָקַח דָּוִד אֶת־הַלֶּחֶם מֵהַהֵיכָל וְעַל־הָהָר עָלָה כַּאֲשֶׁר אָמַר הַכֹּהֵן׃
13. הָלְכוּ מֹשֶׁה וְאַהֲרֹן אֶל־פַּרְעֹה בַּלַּיְלָה וְלֹא שָׁמַע פַּרְעֹה אֶל־יְהוָה׃

6. Saul was obedient to man, not to God.
Saul listened to Adam and he did not to God

7. Is Samuel a prophet?

8. Saul came into the temple, but as for him he did he said no to the priest

9. Adam ate the fruit which is from the garden

10. The Pharoh gave to Joseph, silver and gold also a woman

11. The man came to the garden that God made and there he spoke to God

12. David took the bread from the temple and he went up the mountain as the priest said.

13. Moses and Aaron, they heard Pharoah in the night because he did not obey the Lord

Summary of Rules: Chapters 7-9

Article ה

1. ⊡הַ: before non-gutturals – הַדָּבָר
2. הָ: before א, ע, ר – הָרֹאשׁ
3. הַ: before ה, ח – הַהֵיכָל
4. הֶ: before חָ and unaccented הָ, עָ – הֶעָמָל
5. הָ: before accented הָ֫ – הָהָר

Interrogative מה

1. ⊡מַה־: before non-gutturals – מַה־דָּבָר
2. מָה־: before א, ע, ר (or the article) – מָה־רֹאשׁ
3. מַה־: before ה (excluding the article), ח – מַה־הֵיכָל
4. מֶה־: before G (excluding ר) – מֶה־עָמָל

Inseparable Prepositions: ב, כ, ל

1. לְ: originally open, pro-pretonic syllables – לְדָבָר
2. לִ: 1) before vocal shewa – לִשְׁמוּאֵל
   2) before יְ – לִיהוּדָה
3. Gלֲ: corresponding short vowel before a composite shewa – לֶאֱדֹם
4. □֫לְ/לָ: pretonic open may receive Qameṣ or shewa – לְלַ֫יְלָה/לָלָ֫יְלָה
5. לַ/לֵ: לַיהוה/לֵאלֹהִים
6. ⊡לַ: the preposition supplants the ה of the article – לַדָּבָר

Conjunctive Vav ו

1. וְ: originally open, pro-pretonic syllables – וְדָבָר
2. וִ: before יְ – וִיהוּדָה
3. Gוַ: corresponding short vowel before a composite shewa – וֶאֱדֹם
4. □֫וְ/וָ: pretonic open may receive Qameṣ or shewa – וְלַ֫יְלָה/וָלַ֫יְלָה
5. וַ/וֵ: וַיהוה/וֵאלֹהִים
6. וּ: 1) before (simple) vocal shewa – וּשְׁמוֹ
   2) before בּוּמָף (labial letters) – וּבֵן

Preposition מן

1. ⊡מִ: before non-gutturals – מִשָּׁאוּל
2. מִ: before יְ – מִיהוּדָה
3. מֵ: before gutturals – מֵהַמֶּלֶךְ

Interrogative ה

1. הֲ: normal before a vowel – הֲשָׁלוֹם
2. הַ: 1) before vocal shewa – הַשְׁמוּאֵל
   2) before a guttural (excluding ר) – הַאֵלֵךְ
3. הֶ: before G (excluding ר) – הֶאָב

*G stands for guttural letters.

MORPHOLOGICAL PRINCIPLES: NOUNS AND ADJECTIVES

Chapter 10
Nouns and Adjectives: The Absolute State
Syntax of Adjectives with Nouns

10.1. Introduction: Review the laws of the Hebrew Sinai (chapter 6), and they will take you to the Hebrew promised land. Hebrew nouns and adjectives have gender (masculine, feminine, but not neuter), number (singular, plural and dual), and state (absolute – for a word standing independently or absolutely; and construct – for a word constructed onto or connected with another word).

10.2. Hebrew Nouns

In general, Hebrew has two noun patterns:

1. Segolate nouns: Nouns with originally one short vowel (at least in the singular)[1] – מֶ֫לֶךְ « *מַלְךְ.
2. Non-Segolate nouns: Nouns with more than one originally short vowel (or with a long vowel), some examples.

   דָּבָר « *דַּבַר two originally short vowels
   נָבִיא « *נַבִיא an historic long vowel and an original short vowel
   סוּס « סוּס an historic long vowel

   Segolate nouns will be covered in chapters 15-16; chapters 10-13 will cover non-Segolate nouns.

10.3. Nouns and Adjectives: Masculine and Feminine Singular Absolute

Masculine singular absolute nouns and adjectives do not have a characteristic ending, but feminine singular absolute nouns and adjectives have a characteristic ending, ◌ָ֫ה – an accented Qameṣ with a ה. The adding of the Qameṣ and ה shifts the accent to the end of the word. A box, in which the last letter of the word is placed, emphasizes the shifting of the accent – ◌ָ֫ה.

Nouns	Boxes	Examples		
		1	2	3
Masculine Singular Absolute:	None	סוּס horse	נָבִיא prophet	עוֹלָם eternity
Feminine Singular Absolute:	◌ָ֫ה	סוּסָ֫ה mare	נְבִיאָ֫ה prophetess	

[1] This excludes mono-syllabic words like יָד, which follows the non-Segolate pattern.

Adjectives	Boxes	Examples	
		4	5
Masculine Singular Absolute:	None	יָשָׁר straight	חָכָם wise
Feminine Singular Absolute:	□ָה	יְשָׁרָה straight	חֲכָמָה wise

1. Explanation of the Forms

Nouns

1. Masculine:

סוּס is a mono-syllabic (one-syllable) noun with an historic long vowel (1.8.2 and 6.2.3).

Feminine:

The feminine ending shifts the accent to the end of the word – סוּסָה.

2. Masculine:

נָבִיא is a noun with two syllables: the first syllable has a Qameṣ, which was a Pataḥ in Proto-Hebrew (6.2.1) – *נַבִיא. Because the first syllable is in the pretonic open position, the original Pataḥ lengthens to Qameṣ (6.3.2) – *נַבִיא » נָבִיא.

Feminine:

נְבִיאָה: The accent shifts from the ב to the א. The original Pataḥ in the first syllable, now in the pro-pretonic open position, reduces to vocal shewa (6.2.2; 6.3.5)[2] – *נַבִיאָה » נְבִיאָה.

3. עוֹלָם is a masculine noun with two syllables: the first syllable with a historic long Ḥolem-Vav, the final syllable with a Qameṣ, which was a Pataḥ in Proto-Hebrew. The original Pataḥ lengthens to Qameṣ in a closed accented syllable (6.3.1) – *עוֹלַם » עוֹלָם.

Adjectives

4. Masculine:

יָשָׁר is an adjective with two syllables: both syllables have Qameṣ, which were Pataḥs in Proto-Hebrew – *יַשַׁר (6.2.1). Biblical Hebrew lengthens Pataḥ to

---

[2] The vocal shewa usually indicates an original short vowel (normally Pataḥ), (6.2.2 and footnote 2-6).

Qameṣ in closed accented syllables (6.3.1) and in pretonic open syllables (6.3.2) – *יַשַׁר » *יַשָׁר » יָשָׁר.

Feminine:
יְשָׁרָה: The accent shifts from the שׁ to the ר. The original Pataḥ under the שׁ, in the pretonic open position, lengthens to Qameṣ (6.3.2). The original Pataḥ under the י, in the open pro-pretonic position, reduces to vocal shewa (6.3.5) – *יַשַׁרָה » *יַשָׁרָה » יְשָׁרָה.

5. חָכָם is like יָשָׁר, except the guttural, in the originally open pro-pretonic syllable, takes a composite shewa instead of a simple vocal shewa (5.7.1).

2. Attaching the Feminine Singular Absolute Boxes.
Follow a three step process:
The feminine singular absolute of יָשָׁר
1. Restore Proto-Hebrew vowels – יַשַׁר (6.2.1)
2. Attach the box – יַשַׁ□ָה
3. Work the rules of syllables – יַשָׁ□ָה (6.3.2) » יְשָׁ□ָה (6.3.5)

10.4. Nouns and Adjectives: Masculine and Feminine Plural Absolute

The endings are □ִים for the masculine plural absolute and □וֹת for the feminine plural absolute.

Nouns	Boxes	Examples		
		1	2	3
Masculine Plural Absolute:	□ִים	סוּסִים	נְבִיאִים	עוֹלָמִים
		horses	prophets	eternities
Feminine Plural Absolute:	□וֹת	סוּסוֹת	נְבִיאוֹת	
		mares	prophetesses	

Adjectives	Boxes	Examples	
		4	5
Masculine Plural Absolute:	□ִים	יְשָׁרִים	חֲכָמִים
Feminine Plural Absolute:	□וֹת	יְשָׁרוֹת	חֲכָמוֹת

Like 10.3.1, original Pataḥs in an open pretonic syllable lengthen to Qameṣ (6.3.2), and reduce to vocal shewa in originally open pro-pretonic syllables (6.3.5). Attach these boxes like 10.3.2:

The feminine plural absolute of חָכָם

1. Restore Proto-Hebrew vowels – חַכַם (6.2.1)
2. Attach the box – חַכַ֫מוֹת
3. Work the rules of syllables – *חַכָ֫מוֹת (6.3.2) » חֲכָ֫מוֹת (6.3.5). Note the composite shewa under the guttural (5.7.1).

10.5. Attaching the Feminine Plural Absolute Ending to a Feminine Singular Absolute Noun Ending in □ָ֫ה

Most feminine nouns end in □ָ֫ה – שָׂפָ֫ה. Before attaching the feminine plural absolute ending to these words, remove the feminine singular box (□ָ֫ה). A feminine plural absolute box should never have a ה of the feminine singular absolute in it – *banish the* ה *and its Qameṣ first.*

Example: The feminine plural absolute of שָׂפָה

1. Remove the box of the feminine singular absolute – שָׂפ
2. Restore the proto-vowel Pataḥ (6.2.1) – שַׂפ
3. Attach the feminine plural absolute box – שַׂ֫פוֹת
4. Work the rules of syllables – שָׂ֫פוֹת (6.2.2)

10.6. Nouns and Adjectives: Masculine and Feminine Dual Absolute[3]

The box for the dual absolute is □ַ֫יִם. Attach this box like 10.3.2.

יָדַ֫יִם "two hands," יוֹמַ֫יִם "two days"

1. יָדַ֫יִם is the dual of יָד (hand). The original Pataḥ (6.2.1) under the Yod lengthens to Qameṣ in an open pretonic syllable (6.3.2) – *יַדַ֫יִם » יָדַ֫יִם.
2. יוֹמַ֫יִם is the dual of יוֹם (day).
   The historic long Ḥolem-Vav never changes.

10.7. Hebrew Boxes for the Absolute State:

	Singular	Plural	Dual
Masculine	None	□ִ֫ים	□ַ֫יִם
Feminine	□ָ֫ה	□֫וֹת	□ַ֫יִם

10.8. Syntax of Adjectives with Nouns

Adjectives modify nouns:

1. Attributively: The adjective gives an attribute to the noun: a good horse, a good mare. In English, the attributive adjective precedes its noun; in Hebrew, the attributive adjective follows its noun.

---

[3] Somewhat rare, the Hebrew dual is confined normally to body parts occurring in pairs: eyes, ears, hands, and to a few common words: two days, two years.

סוּס טוֹב	a good horse	Literally: a horse, a good (one)
סוּסָה טוֹבָה	a good mare	Literally: a mare, a good (one)
הַסּוּס הַטּוֹב	the good horse	Literally: the horse, the good (one)
הַסּוּסָה הַטּוֹבָה	the good mare	Literally: the mare, the good (one)
סוּסִים טוֹבִים	good horses	Literally: horses, good (ones)
סוּסוֹת טוֹבוֹת	good mares	Literally: mares, good (ones)
הַסּוּסִים הַטּוֹבִים	the good horses	Literally: the horses, the good (ones)
הַסּוּסוֹת הַטּוֹבוֹת	the good mares	Literally: the mares, the good (ones)

The attributive adjective follows its noun and agrees with it in gender, number, and definiteness:[4] if the noun has the article, the attributive adjective has the article; if the noun is without the article, the attributive adjective is without the article.

2. Predicatively: The predicate adjective asserts or declares something about a noun: the horse is good; the man is good. In English, the predicate adjective follows a linking verb (is, are, was, were, feel, for instance); in Hebrew, the noun usually precedes the adjective.[5] Moreover, the noun has the article, but its adjective is without the article. English translation must supply a form of "to be" (am, is, are, was, and so forth).

הַסּוּס טוֹב	The horse (is) good.
הַסּוּסָה טוֹבָה	The mare (is) good.
הַסּוּסִים טוֹבִים	The horses (are) good.
הַסּוּסוֹת טוֹבוֹת	The mares (are) good.

The predicate adjective usually follows its noun – though it may precede its noun for emphasis – and it agrees with its noun in gender and number, *but not in definiteness.*

10.9. Demonstrative Adjectives: Attributive and Predicative Use

Near Demonstrative

Singular	Plural
זֶה This (m) זאת This (f)	אֵלֶּה These (c)

[4] See footnote 7-6.

[5] The adjective placed before the noun frequently emphasizes the adjective – טוֹב הַסּוּס *good* the horse (is) = the horse (is) good.

Far Demonstratives (occur with article)

Singular	Plural
הַהוּא That (m)	הָהֵ֫מָּה, הָהֵם Those (m)
הַהִיא That (f)	הָהֵ֫נָּה, הָהֵן Those (f)

1. Attributive Use: Like other adjectives (10.8.1-2), the attributive demonstrative adjective follows its noun and agrees with it in gender, number, and definiteness:

הַסּוּס הַזֶּה	This horse
הַסּוּס הַהוּא	That horse
הַסּוּסָה הַזֹּאת	This mare
הַסּוּסָה הַהִיא	That mare
הַסּוּסִים הָאֵ֫לֶּה	These horses
הַסּוּסוֹת הָהֵן	Those mares

2. Predicate Use: Only the near demonstrative adjectives are used predicatively. The near demonstrative adjective occurs before its noun and agrees with it in gender and number, *but not in definiteness* – the near demonstrative adjective is without the article; its noun has the article:

זֶה הַסּוּס	This (is) the horse
זֹאת הַסּוּסָה	This (is) the mare
אֵ֫לֶּה הַסּוּסִים	These (are) the horses
אֵ֫לֶּה הַסּוּסוֹת	These (are) the mares

10.10. Substantives: Adjectives used for Nouns

In English, plural adjectives can function as nouns – the dead tell no tales. The adjective "dead" functions as a noun meaning "dead men." In Hebrew, plural and singular adjectives can function as a noun – הַטּוֹב the good man; הַטּוֹבִים the good men.

10.11. The Accusative □ָה

The accusative □ָה (unaccented)[6] attaches to nouns (frequently definite nouns) and to the adverb שָׁם. The meaning of this accusative □ָה is direction towards a place or destination to a place.

Noun		With Accusative □ָה	
מִצְרַ֫יִם	Egypt	מִצְרַ֫יְמָה	to, towards Egypt
בַּ֫יִת	house	בַּ֫יְתָה (or בֵּ֫יתָה)	to, towards a house

[6] Most feminine nouns end in accented Qameṣ ה – □ָ֫ה; the accusative □ָה ends in an unaccented □ָה – □֫□ָה.

הַיָּם	the sea	הַיָּ֫מָּה	to, towards the sea
הָעִיר	the city	הָעִ֫ירָה	to, towards the city

Adverb

שָׁם	there	שָׁ֫מָּה	to, towards there

EXERCISE TEN

I. **Questions**

1. What are the basic noun patterns in Hebrew?
2. Write the boxes for the feminine singular absolute, feminine plural absolute, masculine plural absolute, and dual absolute.
3. Explain the vowel changes for the word דָּבָר when the masculine plural absolute box is added.
4. List the three steps for the attaching of the masculine plural absolute box to דָּבָר.
5. List the four steps for the attaching of the feminine plural absolute box to אֲדָמָה.
6. What letter cannot go in the box of the feminine plural absolute? Why?
7. Define attributive and predicate adjective. What is the word order for the attributive and predicate adjective? How does the attributive adjective agree with its noun? How does the predicate adjective agree with its noun?
8. How does the accusative ה differ from the feminine singular absolute ending?

II. **Vocabulary**

אָז	(adv.) then, at that time	מִדְבָּר	wilderness
טוֹב	(adj.) good	זֶה	this (m)
יָשָׁר	(adj.) straight, right	זֹאת	this (f)
גָּדוֹל	(adj.) great	אֵ֫לֶּה	these (c = common, masculine and feminine)
רָשָׁע	(adj.) evil, wicked		
קָדוֹשׁ	(adj.) holy	הַהוּא	that (m)
רַע	(adj.) (f. רָעָה) evil	הַהִיא	that (f)
חָכָם	(adj.) wise	הָהֵ֫מָּה, הָהֵם	those (m)
פְּלִשְׁתִּים	Philistines	הָהֵ֫נָּה, הָהֵן	those (f)

III. **Drills**

1. Word Breakdown: In the following order: label every Dagesh Forte and Lene, Mappiq; vocal and silent shewa; Qameṣ and Qameṣ-Ḥatuf. Next, divide syllables labeling them open or closed. Then pronounce the words.

לִשְׁפֹּל   עַמֵּי־הָאֱלֹהִים   תִּתּוֹ   הֻגַּ֫שְׁתִּי

2. Attach the following particles and translate all vocabulary words.

Article

חֲלוֹם רֶ֫גֶל

Preposition ל

מִדְבָּר חֲלוֹם

Interrogative ה

אָדָם מֶ֫לֶךְ

Preposition מִן

שֶׁהָיָה הֵיכָל

Conjunctive ו

פַּ֫חַד אֱלֹהִים

Interrogative מָה

זֹאת אֲדָמָה

3. Attach the boxes and translate all vocabulary words – Follow 10.3.2. or 10.5. and list all steps.

1. Feminine singular absolute בָּר
2. Masculine plural absolute עָמָל
3. Feminine plural absolute אֲדָמָה
4. Feminine singular absolute נָבִיא
5. Feminine plural absolute בְּרָכָה
6. Dual absolute יוֹם
7. Masculine singular absolute דָּבָר
8. Feminine singular absolute צַדִּיק
9. Masculine plural absolute כּוֹכָב
10. Feminine singular absolute חָכָם
11. Feminine plural absolute תְּפִלָּה
12. Feminine singular absolute גָּדוֹל

4. Translation

1. עָבַר יְהוֹשֻׁעַ אֶת־הַיַּרְדֵּן עִם־הָעָם וְיִשְׂרָאֵל בָּאָרֶץ עַד־הַיּוֹם הַזֶּה׃
2. נָתַן פַּרְעֹה לְאַבְרָהָם כֶּסֶף וְזָהָב כִּי יָרַד אַבְרָהָם מִצְרַיְמָה מִן־יְרוּשָׁלָיִם׃
3. עָשָׂה יְהוָה אֶת־הַטּוֹב לַיּוֹם הַטּוֹב וְאֶת־הָרָשָׁע לַיּוֹם הָרָע׃
4. בָּנָה אַהֲרֹן מִזְבֵּחַ וְעַל־הַמִּזְבֵּחַ הַקָּדוֹשׁ הַהוּא זָבַח זֶבַח כַּאֲשֶׁר צִוָּה יהוה
אֶת־מֹשֶׁה׃
5. מֹשֶׁה הָיָה גָּדוֹל בָּאָרֶץ מְאֹד כִּי כָתַב אֶת־הַתּוֹרָה אֲשֶׁר נָתַן יְהוָה׃
6. הָלַךְ שָׁאוּל הָעִירָה וְלֹא רָדַף אַחֲרֵי־דָוִד כִּי שָׁלַח שְׁמוּאֵל הַנָּבִיא אֶת־דָּוִד
אֶל־הַפְּלִשְׁתִּים׃
7. אָכַל יִשְׂרָאֵל לֶחֶם וּבָשָׂר בַּמִּדְבָּר וְלֹא שָׁמַר הַגּוֹי אֶת־הַדָּבָר אֲשֶׁר דִּבֶּר יְהוָה׃
8. אָמַר דָּוִד טוֹב הַדָּבָר אֲשֶׁר דִּבְּרוּ הַנְּבִיאִים הַקְּדוֹשִׁים׃

1. Joshua crossed over the Jordan with the people, and Israel has been in the land to this day
2. Pharaoh gave to Abraham silver and gold because Abraham went down to Egypt from Jerusalem
3. The Lord made the good man for the good day and the wicked man for the evil day
4. Aaron built an altar and upon that holy altar he offered a sacrifice as the Lord commanded Moses
5. Moses was very great in the land because he wrote the law which the Lord gave
6. Saul went to the city, but he did not pursue after David because Samuel the prophet sent David to the Philistines
7. Israel ate bread and meat in the wilderness, but the nation did not keep the word which the Lord spoke
8. David said, "The word is good which the holy prophets spoke"

CHAPTER 11
NOUNS AND ADJECTIVES: THE CONSTRUCT STATE
ABSOLUTE AND CONSTRUCT STATE: SPECIAL CASES

11.1. Introduction: Nouns and adjectives not standing absolutely or alone (for the absolute state, see chapter 10) are constructed onto (or connected with) another noun. These nouns are in the construct state. A word (or words) in the construct state connects to a word in the absolute state and forms a grammatical unit called a construct package. In Hebrew, the word in the construct state always occurs before the word in the absolute state. Only the last word in the construct package is in the absolute state; all preceding words are in the construct state. For instance, in דְּבַר אֱלֹהִים (the word of God), the first word דְּבַר is constructed onto אֱלֹהִים; therefore, דְּבַר is in the construct state, and אֱלֹהִים is in the absolute state.[1] Most construct packages consist of two words, a few have more than two words: דִּבְרֵי־בְנֵי־יִשְׂרָאֵל (the words of the sons of Israel). The last word (יִשְׂרָאֵל) is in the absolute state; the prior two words are in the construct state.

11.2. The Construct Package and the Accent: Practically, the construct package has only one accent.[2] The word in the absolute state has accent; the word (or words) in the construct state is virtually without accent. Although the Maqqef connects the words within a construct package occasionally, the Maqqef will be used for all boxes (10.3) of the construct forms to emphasize the (practical) loss of the accent.

11.3. Nouns and Adjectives: Masculine Singular Construct
For all these forms, the accent (virtually) shifts to the following word.

Nouns	Box	Examples		
		1	2	3
Masculine Singular Construct:	־☐	סוּס־	נְבִיא־	דְּבַר־

Adjectives	Box	Examples		
		4	5	
Masculine Singular Construct:	־☐	יְשַׁר־	חֲכַם־	

[1] In a construct package, the word in the absolute state is a genitive (as in Arabic).

[2] When a Maqqef (see 5.5) connects words within a construct package, the word (or words) in the construct state completely surrenders its accent. Without a Maqqef, words in the construct state usually receive a conjunctive or a weak disjunctive accent. The words in the construct state are *practically* without accent.

1. Explanation of the Forms
   Nouns:
   1. סוּס־ – Because סוּס is a mono-syllabic noun with an historic long vowel (1.8.2.1), סוּס is unchanged in the construct state.
   2. נְבִיא־ – The final syllable, with the historic long vowel (1.8.2.1), is unchanged. In the first syllable, the original Pataḥ *נַבִיא (6.2.1), in an originally open pro-pretonic syllable, reduces to vocal shewa (6.3.5 and compare 10.3.1).
   3. דְּבַר־ – Both syllables originally had Pataḥ *דַבַר (6.2.1). The final syllable, closed and unaccented, preserves the original Pataḥ (6.3.3); the first syllable, an originally open pro-pretonic syllable, reduces the original Pataḥ to vocal shewa (6.3.5).

   Adjectives:
   4. יְשַׁר־ – This adjective is like the noun in 11.3.1.
   5. חֲכַם־ – This adjective is like 11.3.1, except the guttural, in the originally open pro-pretonic syllable, takes a composite shewa instead of a simple vocal shewa.

2. Attaching the Masculine Singular Construct Box
   Masculine singular construct of יָשָׁר:
   1. Restore the Proto-Hebrew vowels – יַשַׁר (6.2.1)
   2. Add the box – יַשַׁ□־
   3. Work the rules of syllables – יַשַׁ□־ (6.3.3), יְשַׁ□־ (6.3.5)

11.4. Nouns and Adjectives: Masculine Plural Construct

Nouns	Box	Examples		
		1	2	3
Masculine Plural Construct:	□ֵי־	סוּסֵי־	נְבִיאֵי־	דִּבְרֵי־

Adjectives	Box	Examples	
		4	5
Masculine Plural Construct:	□ֵי־	יִשְׁרֵי־	חַכְמֵי־

1. Explanation of the Forms
   Nouns:
   1. סוּסֵי־ – The historic long Shureq (1.8.2) never changes, even in the construct state.
   2. נְבִיאֵי־ – The final syllable with the historic long Ḥireq-Yod (1.8.2) is unchanged. In the first syllable, the original Pataḥ *נַבִיאֵי (6.2.1), in an

originally open pro-pretonic syllable, reduces to vocal shewa (6.3.5 and compare 10.3.1).

3. דִּבְרֵי־ – This word was originally *דַּבַרַי־. Both the first and second syllables, in originally open pro-pretonic position, reduce to vocal shewas – *דְּבְרֵי־ (6.3.5). Since a word cannot begin with two vocal shewas, the first vocal shewa becomes a Ḥireq – דִּבְרֵי־ (3.2.2).

Adjectives:

4. יִשְׁרֵי־ – This adjective is like the noun in 11.4.1.
5. חַכְמֵי־ – This adjective is like 11.4.1, except the guttural receives a Pataḥ (5.7.3) instead of a Ḥireq (3.2.2).

2. Attaching the Masculine Plural Construct Box
   Masculine plural construct of חָכָם:
   1. Restore the Proto-Hebrew vowels – חַכַם (6.2.1)
   2. Add the box – חַכַמֵי־
   3. Work the rules of syllables – חְכְמֵי־ (6.3.5), חַכְמֵי־ (3.2.2)

11.5. Nouns and Adjectives: Feminine Singular Construct

Nouns	Box	Examples	
		1	2
Feminine Singular Construct:	־ת□[3]	סוּסַת־	נְבִיאַת־

Adjectives	Box	Examples	
		3	4
Feminine Singular Construct:	־ת□	יְשַׁרַת־	חַכְמַת־

1. Explanation of the Forms
   Nouns:
   1. סוּסַת־ – The historic long Shureq (1.8.2) is unchanged.
   2. נְבִיאַת־ – The middle syllable, with the historic long Ḥireq-Yod (1.8.2), is unchanged; under the first letter, the original Pataḥ *נַבִיאַת־ (6.2.1), in an originally open pro-pretonic syllable, reduces to vocal shewa (6.3.5 and compare 10.3.1).

[3] The ending ת□ was the original feminine ending – *תּוֹרַת. When this form received accent *תּוֹרַ́ת, the ת disappeared, and the original Pataḥ lengthened to Qameṣ by compensation for the loss of the ת – *תּוֹרָ. The (phoney) ה was added to aid in reading an unpointed text: the ה indicates a preceding Qameṣ תורה = תּוֹרָה (footnote 4-7).

Adjectives:

3. יִשְׁרַת־ – This adjective was originally *יַשַׁרַת־. The Pataḥs of the first two syllables, in the originally open pro-pretonic position, reduce to vocal shewas – *יְשְׁרַת־ (6.3.5). The first vocal shewa becomes a Ḥireq (3.2.2).
4. חַכְמַת־ – This adjective is like 11.5.1; 11.4.1, except the guttural receives a Pataḥ (5.7.3) instead of a Ḥireq (3.2.2).

2. Attaching the Feminine Singular Construct Box

Feminine singular construct of נְבִיאָה

Words ending in ָה follow a four step process:

1. Remove the feminine singular absolute box ָה – נְבִיא

   Never place the ה *of the feminine singular absolute in a box.*
2. Restore the Proto-Hebrew vowels – נַבִיא (6.2.3; 6.2.2)
3. Add the box – נַבִיאַת־
4. Work the rules of syllables – נְבִיאַת־ (6.3.5)

11.6. Nouns and Adjectives: Feminine Plural Construct

Nouns	Box	Examples	
		1	2
Feminine Plural Construct:	☐וֹת־	סוּסוֹת־	נְבִיאוֹת־

Adjectives	Box	Examples	
		3	4
Feminine Plural Construct:	☐וֹת־	יִשְׁרוֹת־	חַכְמוֹת־

1. Explanation of the Forms

Nouns:

1. סוּסוֹת־ – The historic long Shureq (1.8.2.1) is unchanged.
2. נְבִיאוֹת־ – The historic long Ḥireq-Yod (1.8.2) is unchanged. Under the first letter, the original Pataḥ *נַבִיאוֹת (6.2.1), in an originally open pro-pretonic syllable, reduces to a vocal shewa (6.3.5 and compare 10.3.1).

Adjectives:

3. יִשְׁרוֹת־ – This adjective was originally *יַשַׁרוֹת. The Pataḥs, in the originally open pro-pretonic position, reduce to vocal shewas *יְשְׁרוֹת (6.3.5). Because a word cannot begin with two vocal shewas, the first vocal shewa becomes a Ḥireq (3.2.2).

4. חַכְמוֹת־ – This adjective is like 11.5.1.3; 11.4.1, except the guttural receives a Pataḥ (5.7.3) instead of a Ḥireq (3.2.2.1).

2. Attaching the Feminine Plural Construct Box
Feminine plural construct of חֲכָמָה:
1. Remove the feminine singular absolute box – ◌ָה חֲכָמ
Never place a ה of the feminine singular absolute in a box.
2. Restore the Proto-Hebrew vowels – חֲכַמ (6.2.1; 6.2.2)
3. Add the box – חֲכַמוֹת־
4. Work the rules of syllables – חֲכְמוֹת־ (6.3.5), חַכְמוֹת־ (3.2.2)

11.7. Nouns: Masculine and Feminine Dual Construct

The form is like the masculine plural construct: ◌ֵי־ – יְדֵי. The original Pataḥ under the Yod reduces to vocal shewa in an open pro-pretonic syllable (6.3.5). Attaching this box is like 11.4.1.

11.8. Hebrew Boxes: Absolute and Construct

	Absolute Singular	Construct Singular	Absolute Plural	Construct Plural	Absolute Dual	Construct Dual
Masculine	None	◌־	◌ִים	◌ֵי־	◌ַיִם	◌ֵי־
Feminine	◌ָה	◌ַת־	◌וֹת	◌וֹת־	◌ַיִם	◌ֵי־

11.9. Syntax of a Construct Package

1. In a construct package, only the last word in the package (the word in the absolute state) may have the article: a word in the construct state *never* has an article. If the last word in a construct package has the article (or is definite, see footnote 7-6), the entire package is definite.[4]
דְּבַר הָאָדָם "the word of the man," not *הַדְּבַר אָדָם or *הַדְּבַר הָאָדָם
The last two constructions are impossible because a word in the construct state *never* has the article.

2. In a construct package, the word in the absolute state often functions like an adjective to modify the word in the construct state.

מְקוֹם הַקֹּדֶשׁ the place of holiness = the holy place
מֹאזְנֵי צֶדֶק scales of righteousness = righteous scales
אִישׁ אֱלֹהִים man of God = godly man

[4] Therefore, if a direct object is a definite construct package, אֵת (אֶת־), the marker of the definite direct object (7.7), often preceeds the construct package – שָׁמַר יוֹסֵף אֶת־דְּבַר־הַחֲלוֹם "Joseph kept the matter (word) of the dream."

11.10. Absolute and Construct State: Special Cases

1. Contraction: Words with accented יִ֫◌ often contract to י◌ֵ when unaccented.[5]

	Absolute Singular		Construct Singular	Absolute Dual	Construct Dual
1.	[6]עַ֫יִן	eye, well	עֵין־	עֵינַ֫יִם	עֵינֵי־
2.	[6]בַּ֫יִת	house	בֵּית־	מַ֫יִם	מֵי־

2. Irregular and Special Nouns
Language tends to conform rare, irregular forms to more common, regular forms. Common irregular forms, however, often survive the pressure of a language to conform. These forms require special attention.

	Absolute Singular		Construct Singular	Absolute Plural	Construct Plural
1.	בֵּן	son	בֶּן־	בָּנִים	בְּנֵי־
2.	אִישׁ	man	אִישׁ־	אֲנָשִׁים	אַנְשֵׁי־
3.	אִשָּׁה	woman	אֵשֶׁת־	נָשִׁים	נְשֵׁי־
4.	יוֹם	day	יוֹם־	יָמִים	יְמֵי־
5.	עַם	people	עַם־	עַמִּים	עַמֵּי־
6.	הַר	mountain	הַר־	הָרִים	הָרֵי־
7.	עִיר	city (f)	עִיר־	עָרִים	עָרֵי־
8.	רֹאשׁ	head	רֹאשׁ־	רָאשִׁים	רָאשֵׁי־

1. בֵּן: The original Proto-Hebrew was בִּן. In a closed accented syllable, the Ḥireq lengthens to Ṣere, בֵּן (6.3.1). When the word loses its accent in the construct, the Ṣere shortens to Segol in a closed unaccented syllable, בֶּן־ (6.3.3). The expected form in the absolute plural is *בֵּנִים, but בָּנִים is the actual form. Perhaps פָּנִים assimilated to the דְּבָרִים pattern. The construct plural form is regular.
2. אִישׁ: The singular and the plural indicate different roots – אישׁ in the singular, אנשׁ in the plural.
3. אִשָּׁה: This word indicates perhaps three different roots: (ת)אנשׁ(?) in the absolute singular, אשׁת in the construct singular, נשׁ in the plural. Notice the absolute plural form נָשִׁים is a feminine word with an apparent masculine plural ending.
4. יוֹם: The singular root is יום, the plural root – ים.

[5] Another common contraction is aw » ô, for example, *הַוְשִׁיב » הוֹשִׁיב.

[6] When contraction occurs, the Ḥireq is lost. Actually, the contraction occurred before the Ḥireq was added.

5. עַם: The original root was עמם, but Hebrew rarely wrote the same letter consecutively; therefore, Hebrew wrote עַם with a hovering Dagesh – *עַםּ. When something is written at the end of the word, as in the plural, the hovering Dagesh Forte lands – עַמִּים (footnote 4-6).
6. הַר: This is like עַם (הרר root) except the hovering Dagesh Forte cannot land in a ר (5.7.2), so the preceding Pataḥ lengthens to Qameṣ by compensation – *הַרִּים » הָרִים.
7. עִיר: In the plural, the root is ערר. When the hovering Dagesh lands, the preceding Pataḥ lengthens by compensation.
8. רֹאשׁ: The plurals have the irreducible Qameṣ by compensation for the quiesced Alef (footnote 1-7).

EXERCISE ELEVEN

I. Questions

1. Describe the absolute and construct state: especially discuss the role of accent.
2. Write the boxes for the construct state: feminine singular and plural, masculine singular and plural, and dual.
3. Explain the vowel changes for the word דָּבָר, when adding the masculine plural construct box.
4. Discuss the attaching of the masculine plural construct box to דָּבָר and the feminine singular construct box to שָׂפָה.
5. In the feminine construct box, which letter is never placed in a box? Why?
6. In a construct package, which word has the article?
7. How does the word in the absolute state sometimes function in a construct package?
8. List the two common contractions in Hebrew.

II. Vocabulary: Add all words and forms (absolute/construct) of 11.10 to this vocabulary

שָׁפַט	(he) judged	צַדִּיק	(adj.) righteous
מִשְׁפָּט	judgment, justice, custom	עַיִן	(f) eye, well
מִצְוָה	commandment	לְעֵינֵי	to the eyes of, before
צְדָקָה	righteousness	לִפְנֵי־	to the face of, before[7]
שָׂרַי/שָׂרָה	Sarah	אַחֵר	(adj.) another, other
שָׁכַח	(he) forgot		(plural, אֲחֵרִים)
בָּחַר בְּ	(he) chose	אַף	also, even
זָקֵן	(adj.) old, elder	שְׁלֹמֹה	Solomon

[7] See 14.4.4.

III. Drills

1. Word Breakdown: In the following order: label every Dagesh Forte and Lene, Mappiq; vocal and silent shewa; Qameṣ and Qameṣ-Ḥatuf. Next, divide syllables labeling them open or closed. Then pronounce the words.

   כָּל־הָאָ֫רֶץ   גֻּלְגֹּ֫לֶת   יַ֫יִן   הַמְּלָכִים

2. Attach the following particles and translate all vocabulary words.
   Interrogative מה

   זֶ֫בַח   תְּהִלָּה   הָרִים

   Conjunctive ו

   שֶׁ֫בֶת   יהוה   חֲלוֹם

   Interrogative ה

   עַ֫יִן   יְלִיד   אֱדוֹם

3. Attach the boxes and translate all vocabulary words – For each answer give the following steps:
   1) Remove the feminine singular absolute box, ◌ָה (if necessary).
   2) Restore the Proto-Hebrew vowels.
   3) Attach the appropriate box.
   4) Work the five rules of Hebrew syllables.

   1. Masculine plural construct דָּבָר
   2. Masculine singular construct חָכָם
   3. Masculine plural construct כּוֹכָב
   4. Feminine singular construct סוּסָה
   5. Feminine plural absolute אֲדָמָה
   6. Feminine plural construct צְדָקָה
   7. Masculine singular construct עָמָל
   8. Masculine plural absolute נָבִיא
   9. Feminine singular construct אֲדָמָה
   10. Masculine singular construct צַדִּיק
   11. Feminine singular construct תְּפִלָּה
   12. Feminine plural construct חָכָם

4. Translation

1. בַּיָּמִים הָהֵמָּה שָׁפַט שְׁמוּאֵל אִישׁ אֱלֹהִים אֶת־יִשְׂרָאֵל בִּצְדָקָה וּבְנֵי־שְׁמוּאֵל הָיוּ רָעִים בְּעֵינֵי־יְהוָה׃
2. אָכְלוּ מֹשֶׁה וְהָעָם עִם־יהוה עַל־הָהָר לָחֶם׃
3. רְשָׁעִים אַנְשֵׁי הָעִיר לַיהוה מְאֹד׃
4. לָקַח פַּרְעֹה אֶת־שָׂרָה אֵשֶׁת אַבְרָהָם וְלֹא יָדַע כִּי אַבְרָהָם נָבִיא׃
5. רָאָה שָׁאוּל וְהִנֵּה עָמַד שְׁמוּאֵל לִפְנֵי־בֵית־יְהוָה וְלֹא דִבֶּר לְשָׁאוּל דָּבָר׃
6. שָׁכְחוּ בְנֵי־יִשְׂרָאֵל אֶת־מִצְוֹת־יְהוָה וּמֹשֶׁה שָׁמַר אֶת־דְּבַר־יהוה כָּל־הַיָּמִים׃
7. אֵלֶּה הַדְּבָרִים אֲשֶׁר דִּבֶּר מֹשֶׁה אֶל־כָּל־בְּנֵי־יִשְׂרָאֵל בַּמִּדְבָּר׃
8. בָּחַר יהוה בְּדָוִד לִמְלֹךְ עַל־כָּל־יִשְׂרָאֵל וְהַדָּבָר הָיָה רַע בְּעֵינֵי־שָׁאוּל׃

1. in the days those days Samuel a man of God judged Israel with righteousness the sons of Samuel were evil the eyes of the Lord.

2.

3. men of the city were wicked to YHWH

4. Prophet Abraham

5. Saul looked and behold Samuel stood before the house of the Lord, he did not speak a word to Saul

6. The sons of Israel forgot the commandments of the Lord but Moses kept the word of the Lord all the days.

7. These are the words which Moses speaks to all of the sons of Israel in the wilderness

8. King became

CHAPTER 12
PRONOMINAL SUFFIXES WITH MASCULINE NOUNS

12.1. Introduction: When receiving pronominal suffixes, nouns and adjectives undergo the same vowel changes discussed in the last two chapters (6.3).

12.2. Boxes for Pronominal Suffixes for Masculine Nouns and Adjectives

	Singular Noun	Plural Noun	
1cs	□ִי	□ַי	my
2ms	□ְךָ (vocal shewa)[1]	□ֶיךָ	your
2fs	□ֵךְ	□ַיִךְ	your
3ms	□וֹ	□ָיו	his
3fs	□ָהּ	□ֶיהָ	her
1cp	□נוּ	□ֵינוּ	our
2mp	□ְכֶם (silent shewa)[1]	□ֵיכֶם	your
2fp	□ְכֶן (silent shewa)[1]	□ֵיכֶן	your
3mp	□ָם	□ֵיהֶם	their
3fp	□ָן	□ֵיהֶן	their

1. Attach the boxes in the left column with singular nouns; the boxes in the right column with plural nouns.
2. The forms 1cs and 1cp are first common singular and first common plural.
3. Many boxes of the plural nouns have Ṣere or Segol (except 1cs, 2fs, 3ms): Segol when the final syllable has a Qameṣ (2ms, 3fs: Compare the Segol with the article הֶעָמָל.); otherwise, a Ṣere.

12.3. סוּס : Singular and Plural with Pronominal Suffixes

	Singular Noun		Plural Noun	
1cs	סוּסִי	my horse	סוּסַי	my horses
2ms	סוּסְךָ	your horse	סוּסֶיךָ	your horses
2fs	סוּסֵךְ	your horse	סוּסַיִךְ	your horses
3ms	סוּסוֹ	his horse	סוּסָיו	his horses
3fs	סוּסָהּ	her horse	סוּסֶיהָ	her horses

[1] These shewas are technically medial (or political shewas, since, like politicians, they are on both sides of issues) shewas: silent enough to close a syllable, vocal enough to keep the Dagesh Lene out of the following כ. This "middle" shewa falls between silent and vocal shewa. *For now, consider the shewa of the 2ms vocal and the shewa of the 2mp, 2fp silent.*

1cp	סוּסֵ֫נוּ	our horse	סוּסֵ֫ינוּ	our horses
2mp	סוּסְכֶם	your horse	סוּסֵיכֶם	your horses
2fp	סוּסְכֶן	your horse	סוּסֵיכֶן	your horses
3mp	סוּסָם	their horse	סוּסֵיהֶם	their horses
3fp	סוּסָן	their horse	סוּסֵיהֶן	their horses

When the pronominal suffix is attached to the word סוּס, the accent shifts down the word: סוּס – סוּ֫סִי. סוּס never changes because of the historic long Shureq (1.8.2; 10.3.1; 11.3.1).

12.4. דָּבָר: Singular and Plural with Pronominal Suffixes

	Singular Noun		Plural Noun	
1cs	דְּבָרִי	my word	דְּבָרַי	my words
2ms	דְּבָרְךָ	your word	דְּבָרֶ֫יךָ	your words
2fs	דְּבָרֵךְ	your word	דְּבָרַ֫יִךְ	your words
3ms	דְּבָרוֹ	his word	דְּבָרָיו	his words
3fs	דְּבָרָהּ	her word	דְּבָרֶ֫יהָ	her words
1cp	דְּבָרֵ֫נוּ	our word	דְּבָרֵ֫ינוּ	our words
2mp	דְּבַרְכֶם	your word	דִּבְרֵיכֶם	your words
2fp	דְּבַרְכֶן	your word	דִּבְרֵיכֶן	your words
3mp	דְּבָרָם	their word	דִּבְרֵיהֶם	their words
3fp	דְּבָרָן	their word	דִּבְרֵיהֶן	their words

1. Explanation of the Forms
   Form דָּבָר with suffixes from the original form *דַּבַר (6.2.1).
   1. The Singular Noun
      1. For all forms except 2mp, 2fp, the accent shifts down the word, leaving the original Pataḥ under the ב in the open pretonic position; therefore, the original Pataḥ lengthens to Qameṣ (*דַּבָרִי, 6.3.2). The original Pataḥ under the ד, in the open pro-pretonic position, reduces to vocal shewa – דְּבָרִי (6.3.5).
      2. For the forms 2mp, 2fp, the accent shifts over the כֶם, כֶן suffixes. This leaves the preceding syllable closed and unaccented; therefore, the original Pataḥ remains under the ב – *דַּבַרְכֶם (6.3.3). The Pataḥ under the ד, in the open pro-pretonic syllable, reduces to vocal shewa – דְּבַרְכֶם (6.3.5).

3. The 2ms form – דְּבָרְךָ – frequently has a Metheg because the last letter of the root has a vocal shewa.[2]

2. The Plural Noun
   1. The forms with suffixes 1cs-1cp shift the accent over the last letter of the root. The original Pataḥ of the second root letter, in the open pretonic position, lengthens to Qameṣ – *דַּבָרַי (6.3.2). The original Pataḥ under the first letter of the root, now in the open pro-pretonic position, reduces to vocal shewa – דְּבָרַי (6.3.5).

   2. The forms with suffixes 2mp-3fp shift the accent over the suffixes. The Pataḥs under the first and second root letters, in the open pro-pretonic position *דַּבַרֵיכֶם, reduce to vocal shewas (6.3.5) – *דְּבְרֵיכֶם. The first shewa becomes Ḥireq דִּבְרֵיכֶם (3.2.2).

   3. If a word begins with a guttural, for example חָכָם, the guttural will receive a composite shewa (usually Ḥatef-Pataḥ) – עֲמָלַי (compare 11.3.1) and a Pataḥ when two vocal shewas begin a word – חַכְמֵיהֶם (11.5.1; 3.2.2).

2. Attaching Pronominal Suffixes on Masculine Nouns.
   Attach a 1cs suffix on the singular noun דָּבָר
   1. Restore the Proto-Hebrew vowels – דַּבַר (6.2.1)
   2. Add the pronominal suffix box – דַּבַ֫רִי
   3. Work the rules of syllables – *דַּבָרִי (6.3.2), דְּבָרִי (6.3.5)

12.5. Syntax: The Pronominal Suffix

Because a noun with a pronominal suffix is definite, אֵת (or אֶת־) frequently precedes a direct object with a pronominal suffix[3] – שָׁמַר הָאִישׁ אֶת־סוּסוֹ The man kept his horse.

EXERCISE TWELVE

I. Questions
1. List the boxes of the pronominal suffixes for singular and plural nouns.
2. Explain the vowel pattern changes when a 1cs and 3mp pronominal suffixes attach to the singular noun דָּבָר, and when a 3mp pronominal suffix attaches to the plural of the noun דָּבָר.

---

[2] Footnote 3-3 (3.2.2).

[3] Footnote 7-4.

3. What is a political (medial) shewa?
4. Discuss the attaching of pronominal suffixes to masculine nouns.

II. Vocabulary

חָרָה	to be hot, angry	לֵאמֹר	saying
אַף	nose	הֵ֫מָּה	they
חָרָה אַפִּי[4] בְּ	my nose became hot, i.e., I became angry with	חָכְמָה	wisdom
		אֵלִיָּ֫הוּ	Elijah
זָכַר	(he) remembered	עָזַב	(he) abandoned, left, forsook
כָּבוֹד	(noun) glory, riches	כֵּן	so, thus, rightly
בָּטַח	(he) trusts, trusted	שָׁאַל	(he) asked
כְּנַ֫עַן	Canaan	צָבָא	army, host
כָּבֵד	(adj.) heavy, severe	שֵׁם	name (with suffix 3ms שְׁמוֹ)

III. Drills

1. Word Breakdown: In the following order: label every Dagesh Forte and Lene, Mappiq; vocal and silent shewa; Qameṣ and Qameṣ-Ḥatuf. Next, divide syllables labeling them open or closed. Then pronounce the words.

פְּלִשְׁתִּים צוֹת כְּתָנְתִּי וַיִּרֶב

2. Attach the following particles and translate all vocabulary words.
Article

עַ֫יִן הָרִים הוֹד

Preposition ל

אִשָּׁה יְדֵי הַמֶּ֫לֶךְ

Preposition מן

עָפָר פַּ֫חַד חָצִיר

---

[4] אַף, אַפִּי: Note the hovering Dagesh, footnote 4-6.

3. Attach the boxes with suffixes and translate all vocabulary words – for each answer give the following steps.
   1) Restore the Proto-Hebrew vowels
   2) Attach the appropriate pronominal suffix box
   3) Work the five rules of Hebrew syllables

Singular Nouns

1. 2ms דָּבָר
2. 2mp עָמָל
3. 3ms נָבִיא
4. 3fs נָחָשׁ
5. 1cp כּוֹכָב

Plural Nouns

6. 1cp דָּבָר
7. 3mp נָבִיא
8. 2ms נָחָשׁ
9. 1cs שַׁבָּת
10. 3fp כּוֹכָב

4. Translation

1. חָרָה אַף־יהוה בִּבְנֵי־יִשְׂרָאֵל כִּי הָלְכוּ אַחֲרֵי־אֱלֹהִים אֲחֵרִים אֲשֶׁר בְּאֶרֶץ־כְּנָעַן׃
2. יהוה אֱלֹהַי וְאוֹרִי בִּשְׁמוֹ בָּטַח הַצַּדִּיק׃
3. בַּיּוֹם הַהוּא בָּאוּ אַנְשֵׁי־הָעִיר אֶל־הֵיכַל־יהוה בִּירוּשָׁלַיִם וְלֹא רָאוּ אֶת־הַכֹּהֵן וְלֹא שָׁמְעוּ אֶת־קוֹל־הַמֶּלֶךְ׃
4. חָרָה אַף־שָׁאוּל בְּדָוִד מְאֹד כִּי רָאָה כִּי הָלַךְ הָעָם אַחֲרֵי־דָוִד וְאַחֲרֵי־אֲנָשָׁיו׃
5. נָתַן אֱלֹהִים לִשְׁלֹמֹה חָכְמָה וְכָבוֹד כִּי לֹא שָׁאַל לְזָהָב וְלְכֶסֶף׃
6. הָאֵלֶּה הָאֲנָשִׁים אֶת־שָׁאוּל אֲשֶׁר עָזְבוּ אֶת־אֱלֹהִים וַאֲשֶׁר שָׁכְחוּ אֶת־עַמּוֹ׃
7. אָמְרוּ הָרְשָׁעִים מִי יהוה וּמִי נְבִיאוֹ וּמַה־דְּבָרוֹ׃
8. הָיָה דְּבַר־יהוה אֶל־אֵלִיָּהוּ לֵאמֹר חָרָה אַפִּי בִּבְנֵי־יִשְׂרָאֵל כִּי זָבְחוּ לֵאלֹהִים אֲחֵרִים׃

CHAPTER 13
PRONOMINAL SUFFIXES WITH FEMININE NOUNS
MORE IRREGULAR NOUNS

13.1. Introduction: Boxes with pronominal suffixes for feminine nouns and adjectives are like the pronominal suffixes for masculine nouns and adjectives (12.2).

13.2. תּוֹרָה: Singular and Plural with Pronominal Suffixes

	Singular Noun		Plural Noun	
1cs	תּוֹרָתִי	my law	תּוֹרוֹתַי	my laws
2ms	תּוֹרָתְךָ	your law	תּוֹרוֹתֶ֫יךָ	your laws
2fs	תּוֹרָתֵךְ	your law	תּוֹרוֹתַ֫יִךְ	your laws
3ms	תּוֹרָתוֹ	his law	תּוֹרוֹתָיו	his laws
3fs	תּוֹרָתָהּ	her law	תּוֹרוֹתֶ֫יהָ	her laws
1cp	תּוֹרָתֵ֫נוּ	our law	תּוֹרוֹתֵ֫ינוּ	our laws
2mp	תּוֹרַתְכֶם	your law	תּוֹרוֹתֵיכֶם	your laws
2fp	תּוֹרַתְכֶן	your law	תּוֹרוֹתֵיכֶן	your laws
3mp	תּוֹרָתָם	their law	תּוֹרוֹתֵיהֶם	their laws
3fp	תּוֹרָתָן	their law	תּוֹרוֹתֵיהֶן	their laws

1. Explanation of the Forms
   When adding pronominal suffixes to most feminine words, connect the pronominal suffix to the original feminine form (footnote 11-3). Restore the original feminine form for singular nouns by removing the feminine singular absolute box תּוֹ֫רָה » תּוֹר and by adding the feminine singular construct box ◻ַת » תּוֹרַת (without Maqqef) and then by restoring the Proto-Hebrew vowels. For the original feminine form for plural nouns, remove the feminine singular absolute box and connect the feminine plural construct box ◻וֹת (without Maqqef). The following discussion assumes these observations.
   1. The Singular Noun
      1. For all forms except 2mp and 2fp, the accent shifts to the restored ת of the feminine (or to the ךָ of the 2ms form) – *תּוֹרַתִי. The original Pataḥ, in the open pretonic position, lengthens to Qameṣ – תּוֹרָתִי (6.3.2). The historic long Ḥolem-Vav never changes.
      2. For the forms 2mp and 2fp, the accent shifts over the כֶם, כֶן suffixes, leaving the preceding syllable closed and unaccented; therefore, the original Pataḥ remains under the last root letter – תּוֹרַתְכֶם (compare 12.4.1).

3. The 2ms form – תּוֹרָֽתְךָ – frequently has a Metheg because the feminine marker ת has a vocal shewa.

2. The Plural Noun
Although the accent shifts, the preceding vowels are unchanged because they are historic long Ḥolem-Vavs.

2. Attaching Pronominal Suffixes to Feminine Words.
Attach a 1cs suffix to the singular noun תּוֹרָה:
   1. Remove the feminine singular absolute box ◌ָ֫ה – תּוֹר
   2. Add the feminine singular construct box (without Maqqef) and restore proto-vowels – תּוֹרַת
   3. Add the box of the pronominal suffix – תּוֹרַתִ֫י. *Always place the restored feminine* ת *in the box. Never place a* ה *of the feminine singular absolute in the box.*
   4. Work the rules of syllables – תּוֹרָתִי (6.3.2)

13.3. צְדָקָה: Singular and Plural with Pronominal Suffixes

	Singular Noun		Plural Noun	
1cs	צִדְקָתִי	my righteousness	צִדְקוֹתַי	my righteous acts
2ms	צִדְקָֽתְךָ	your righteousness	צִדְקוֹתֶ֫יךָ	your righteous acts
2fs	צִדְקָתֵךְ	your righteousness	צִדְקוֹתַ֫יִךְ	your righteous acts
3ms	צִדְקָתוֹ	his righteousness	צִדְקוֹתָיו	his righteous acts
3fs	צִדְקָתָהּ	her righteousness	צִדְקוֹתֶ֫יהָ	her righteous acts
1cp	צִדְקָתֵ֫נוּ	our righteousness	צִדְקוֹתֵ֫ינוּ	our righteous acts
2mp	צִדְקַתְכֶם	your righteousness	צִדְקוֹתֵיכֶם	your righteous acts
2fp	צִדְקַתְכֶן	your righteousness	צִדְקוֹתֵיכֶן	your righteous acts
3mp	צִדְקָתָם	their righteousness	צִדְקוֹתֵיהֶם	their righteous acts
3fp	צִדְקָתָן	their righteousness	צִדְקוֹתֵיהֶן	their righteous acts

1. Explanation of the Forms
   1. Singular Noun
      1. For all forms except 2mp and 2fp, the accent shifts to the restored ת of the feminine (or to the ךָ of the 2ms form) – *צַדַקַתִ֫י. The Pataḥ under the last root letter, in the open pretonic position, lengthens to Qameṣ (6.3.2) – *צַדַקָתִי. The remaining Pataḥs, in the open pro-pretonic position, reduce to vocal shewas (6.3.5) – *צְדְקָתִי. The first shewa becomes Ḥireq (3.2.2) – צִדְקָתִי.

2. For the forms 2mp and 2fp, the accent shifts over the כֶם, כֶן suffixes, leaving the preceding syllable closed and unaccented; therefore, the original Pataḥ remains under the last root letter – *צַדַקַתְכֶם (compare 12.4.1 and 13.2.1). The other Pataḥs, in the open pro-pretonic position, reduce to vocal shewas (6.2.5) – *צְדְקַתְכֶם. The first shewa becomes Ḥireq (3.2.2) – צִדְקַתְכֶם.
3. If a word begins with a guttural, such as אֲדָמָה, the guttural takes a Pataḥ under the first letter when two vocal shewas begin a word – אַדְמַתְכֶם (3.2.2).

2. Plural Noun
The original form is *צַדַקוֹת: when suffixes are attached, the accent shifts, and the original Pataḥs, in the open pro-pretonic position, reduce to vocal shewas (6.3.5) – *צְדְקוֹתַי. The first shewa becomes Ḥireq – צִדְקוֹתַי (3.2.2).

2. Attaching Pronominal Suffixes to Feminine Words
Attach a 1cs suffix to the plural noun צְדָקָה
1. Remove the feminine singular absolute box ◌ָה – צְדָק
2. Add the feminine plural construct box (without Maqqef) and restore proto-vowels – צַדַקוֹת (6.3.2; 6.3.5)
3. Add the box of the pronominal suffix – צַדַקוֹתַ◌ָי. *Always place the restored feminine* ת *in the box, never a* ה *of the feminine singular absolute.*
4. Work the rules of syllables – *צְדְקוֹתַי (6.3.5), צִדְקוֹתַי (3.2.2)

13.4. More Irregular Nouns (11.10.2.)

	Absolute Singular		Construct Singular	Absolute Plural	Construct Plural
1.	אָב	father	אֲבִי־	אָבוֹת	אֲבוֹת־
2.	אָח	brother	אֲחִי־	אַחִים	אֲחֵי־
3.	אָחוֹת	sister	אֲחוֹת־		
4.	בַּת	daughter	בַּת־	בָּנוֹת	בְּנוֹת־
5.	אֵם	mother	אֵם־	אִמּוֹת	אִמּוֹת־
6.	שֵׁם	name	שֵׁם־/שֶׁם־	שֵׁמוֹת	שְׁמוֹת־
7.	בַּ֫יִת	house	בֵּית־	בָּתִּים	בָּתֵּי־

1. אָב: The singular construct preserves the genitive ending – Ḥireq-Yod. The plural forms unexpectantly end in וֹת (Compare 11.10.2).
2. אָח: The singular construct is like אָב. The masculine plural absolute form reveals a root אחח (the Dagesh Forte is implicit); The masculine plural construct has the singular root אח (indicated by the reduction of the vowel under the Alef).

3. אָחוֹת: This word shows irregularities with suffixes. See appendix two.
4. בַּת: The plural root is בן – בָּנוֹת, בְּנוֹת־.
5. אֵם: The root is אמם: for the plurals (and suffix forms) the hovering Dagesh Forte lands, and the Ṣere reduces to Ḥireq in closed unaccented syllables.
6. שֵׁם: The expected singular construct form (שֵׁם־) occurs rarely; the irregular form (שֶׁם־) is common (breaking the rules of syllables, 6.3.3). The plural forms end unexpectantly in וֹת.
7. בַּיִת: The singular construct contracts ay » ê (11.10.1); the plural form is unbelievable – בָּתִּים (bāttîm).

For irregular nouns (11.10 and 13.4) with pronominal suffixes, see appendix three.

Exercise Thirteen

I. Questions

1. Write the boxes of the pronominal suffixes for singular and plural nouns.
2. How do you restore feminine nouns ending in ◌ָה to their Proto-Hebrew forms in the singular and in the plural?
3. Discuss the attaching of the boxes of pronominal suffixes to feminine nouns in the singular and plural.
4. With feminine nouns, which letter is always placed in the box of pronominal suffixes? Which letter is never placed in the box?

II. Vocabulary: Add the irregular nouns (13.4) in all forms (absolute and construct) to the vocabulary

אָחוֹת	sister	אֵם	mother
בַּת	daughter	אֱמֶת	truth
עֵדָה	congregation	קָבַץ	(he) assembled, gathered together
יַיִן	wine	שָׂמַח	(he) rejoices, rejoiced
בְּרִית	covenant	בָּכָה	(he) wept
כָּרַת	(he) cut	שָׁתָה	(he) drank
כָּרַת בְּרִית	he cut a covenant = he made a covenant	הָרַג	(he) killed
חוֹמָה	city wall	יִצְחָק	Isaac
רָעָב	famine, hunger	מָשַׁל	(he) ruled
אָח	brother	מָשַׁל בְּ	(he) ruled over

III. Drills

1. Word Breakdown: In the following order: label every Dagesh Forte and Lene, Mappiq; vocal and silent shewa; Qameṣ and Qameṣ-Ḥatuf. Next, divide syllables labeling them open or closed. Then pronounce the words.

   וַתְּסֻבּוּ   בָּשְׁתָּם   תְּוָשַׁבְנָה   יְבָרְכוּ

2. Attach the following particles and translate all vocabulary words.

   Interrogative מה

   חָיִל   מֶלֶךְ   חֹשֶׁךְ

   Conjunctive ו

   יִלּוֹד   חֲלוֹם   בַּיִת

   Interrogative ה

   עַיִן   בֵּין   אִשָּׁה

3. Attach the boxes and translate all vocabulary words. List all steps.
   1. fs construct תּוֹרָה
   2. fp absolute אֲדָמָה
   3. mp construct כּוֹכָב
   4. fs construct צְדָקָה

4. Attach the boxes with suffixes and translate all vocabulary words. List all steps.

Singular Nouns			Plural Nouns		
1.	3ms	אַמָּה	6.	1cs	מִלְחָמָה
2.	3fs	חוֹמָה	7.	3fs	תְּפִלָּה
3.	3fp	יְשׁוּעָה	8.	2ms	שָׁנָה
4.	2mp	מִצְוָה	9.	1cp	אֲדָמָה
5.	2ms	עָפָר	10.	2mp	דָּם

5. Translation

1. כָּרַת אַבְרָהָם בְּרִית עִם פַּרְעֹה וְלֹא אָכְלוּ לֶחֶם וְלֹא שָׁתוּ יָיִן׃
2. דִּבַּר־יהוה צַדִּיק תּוֹרָתוֹ אֱמֶת׃
3. אֵלֶּה הַמִּצְוֹת וְהַמִּשְׁפָּטִים אֲשֶׁר נָתַן יהוה לְמֹשֶׁה עַל־הָהָר׃
4. קָבַץ מֹשֶׁה אֶת־כָּל־עֲדַת־יִשְׂרָאֵל לִפְנֵי־יהוה כַּאֲשֶׁר צִוָּה יהוה בָּהָר הַקָּדוֹשׁ׃
5. בָּכוּ כָּל־בְּנֵי־יִשְׂרָאֵל כִּי חָרָה אַף־יהוה בְּדָוִד וּפְלִשְׁתִּים שָׂמְחוּ בַּיּוֹם הַהוּא׃
6. בְּחָכְמָתוֹ מָשַׁל שְׁלֹמֹה בְּיִשְׂרָאֵל׃
7. כִּי הָיָה הָרָעָב כָּבֵד בָּאָרֶץ עָלָה אַבְרָהָם מִמִּצְרַיִם הוּא וְשָׂרָה וְיִצְחָק׃
8. שָׁכְחוּ בְּנֵי־יִשְׂרָאֵל אֶת־מִצְוֹתָיו וְגַם תּוֹרוֹתָיו וְלֹא עָזַב אֱלֹהִים אֶת־הַבְּרִית אֲשֶׁר
כָּרַת עִם־אַבְרָהָם׃

1. Abraham made a covenant with Pharaoh, but they did not eat food and they did not drink wine

3. These are the commandments and judgements that the Lord gave to Moses on the mountain

5. All the sons of Israel wept because the Lord was angry with David, but the Philistines rejoiced in that day.

7. Because the famine was severe in the land, Abraham went up from Egypt, he and Sarah and Isaac

Chapter 14
Prepositions with Pronominal Suffixes

14.1. Introduction: Prepositions take pronominal suffixes like nouns and adjectives, but many forms must be memorized. Because they are exceedingly common in the Hebrew Old Testament, these prepositions must be thoroughly learned.

14.2. Inseparable Prepositions ל and ב with Pronominal Suffixes

1cs	לִי	to me	בִּי	in me
2ms	לְךָ	to you	בְּךָ	in you
2fs	לָךְ	to you	בָּךְ	in you
3ms	לוֹ	to him	בּוֹ	in him
3fs	לָהּ	to her	בָּהּ	in her
1cp	לָ֫נוּ	to us	בָּ֫נוּ	in us
2mp	לָכֶם	to you	בָּכֶם	in you
2fp	לָכֶן	to you	בָּכֶן	in you
3mp	לָהֶם	to them	בָּם/בָּהֶם	in them
3fp	לָהֶן	to them	בָּהֶן	in them

The pronominal suffixes with the inseparable prepositions ל and ב generally follow the boxes of the pronominal suffixes of the singular noun (12.2) with the following differences:

1. In the 2fs and 1cp, the connecting vowel is Qameṣ instead of Ṣere: ◌ָ֫ךְ, ◌ָ֫נוּ.

2. In the 2mp-3fp, the prepositions, in the open pretonic position, lengthen the original Pataḥ to Qameṣ (6.3.2) – *לַכֶם » לָכֶם.

3. In the 3mp-3fp forms, the endings are הֶם, הֶן instead of ◌ָם, ◌ָן.[1]

14.3. Prepositions עִם and אֵת with Pronominal Suffixes and the Marker of the Definite Direct Object with Pronominal Suffixes

Absolute	עִם	root עמם	אֵת	root אתת	אֵת	root את (marker of direct object)
Construct	עִם־		אֶת־		אֶת־	
1cs	עִמִּי	with me	אִתִּי	with me	אֹתִי	me
2ms	עִמְּךָ	with you	אִתְּךָ	with you	אֹתְךָ	you

[1] This variation drops the ה between vowels (footnote 8-4), as in בָּהֶם, or with the ה dropped – בָּם.

2fs	עִמָּךְ	with you	אִתָּךְ	with you	אֹתָךְ	you
3ms	עִמּוֹ	with him	אִתּוֹ	with him	אֹתוֹ	him
3fs	עִמָּהּ	with her	אִתָּהּ	with her	אֹתָהּ	her
1cp	עִמָּ֫נוּ	with us	אִתָּ֫נוּ	with us	אֹתָ֫נוּ	us
2mp	עִמָּכֶם	with you	אִתְּכֶם	with you	אֶתְכֶם	you
2fp	עִמָּכֶן	with you	אִתְּכֶן	with you	אֶתְכֶן	you
3mp	עִמָּם/עִמָּהֶם	with them	אִתְּהֶם	with them	אֶתְהֶם/אֹתָם	them
3fp	עִמָּהֶן	with them	אִתְּהֶן	with them	אֶתְהֶן/אֹתָן	them

1. These prepositions (and the marker of the direct object) take the suffixes of the singular noun.

2. The first two prepositions end in a doubled consonant, עממ and אתת. Hebrew frequently avoids writing consecutive consonants by the Dagesh Forte (4.3.1). Furthermore, Hebrew does not allow a Dagesh Forte in the final letter of a word if that final letter closes the syllable; therefore, the final letter, if doubled, will not admit a Dagesh Forte and the Dagesh hovers, *עִם, *אֵת (footnote 4-6). When these forms receive a pronominal suffix, the hovering Dagesh Forte lands – עִמִּי, אִתִּי.

3. עִם has a Qameṣ under the מ in 2mp-3fp forms; the 3mp form of עִם has a variant form עִמָּם (footnotes 14-1 and 8-4).

4. אֵת (with) has a vocal shewa under the ת in 2mp-3fp forms. It has a Ṣere in a closed accented syllable (6.3.1), but with a pronominal suffix, the Ṣere becomes a Ḥireq in a closed unaccented syllable – אִתּוֹ (6.3.3).

5. The pronominal suffixes generally follow the pattern of the pronominal suffixes with the inseparable ל and ב (14.2).

6. The marker for the definite object אֵת has an original root את (not אתת as the preposition אֵת [with]). The forms 1cs-1cp have a Ḥolem after the first letter and attach suffixes like the prepositions עִם and אֵת. The forms 2mp-3fp have a Segol with the first letter (perhaps assimilating to the final Segol). The forms 3mp and 3fp may also have a variant form with Ḥolem like the 1cs-1cp forms: אֹתָם, אֹתָן.

14.4. Prepositions אֶל, עַל, and לְפָנִים with Pronominal Suffixes

Absolute	אֶל	to, unto	עַל	upon, over	לְפָנִים	to the face, before
Construct	אֶל-		עַל-		לִפְנֵי-	to the face of
1cs	אֵלַי	unto me	עָלַי	upon me	לְפָנַי	to my face, before me
2ms	אֵלֶ֫יךָ	unto you	עָלֶ֫יךָ	upon you	לְפָנֶ֫יךָ	before you
2fs	אֵלַ֫יִךְ	unto you	עָלַ֫יִךְ	upon you	לְפָנַ֫יִךְ	before you
3ms	אֵלָיו	unto him	עָלָיו	upon him	לְפָנָיו	before him
3fs	אֵלֶ֫יהָ	unto her	עָלֶ֫יהָ	upon her	לְפָנֶ֫יהָ	before her
1cp	אֵלֵ֫ינוּ	unto us	עָלֵ֫ינוּ	upon us	לְפָנֵ֫ינוּ	before us
2mp	אֲלֵיכֶם	unto you	עֲלֵיכֶם	upon you	לִפְנֵיכֶם	before you
2fp	אֲלֵיכֶן	unto you	עֲלֵיכֶן	upon you	לִפְנֵיכֶן	before you
3mp	אֲלֵיהֶם	unto them	עֲלֵיהֶם	upon them	לִפְנֵיהֶם	before them
3fp	אֲלֵיהֶן	unto them	עֲלֵיהֶן	upon them	לִפְנֵיהֶן	before them

1. These prepositions take the pronominal suffixes of plural nouns.[2]

2. When the first syllable is open and pretonic, the original short vowels lengthen – אֵלֶ֫יךָ, עָלַ֫יִךְ. When the first syllable is in an originally open pro-pretonic position, the original short vowels reduce to Ḥatef-Pataḥ – אֲלֵיכֶם, עֲלֵיכֶן.

3. In the 2ms and 3fs forms, the vowel under the second letter (לֶ) is Segol (instead of Ṣere) when followed by a syllable with a Qameṣ (12.2.3).

4. The Hebrew word for face, פָּנִים, is always plural. To attach the pronominal suffixes, remove the masculine plural absolute box ◌ִ֫ים (compare the removing of feminine singular and plural absolute before adding suffixes, 13.2.2 and 13.3.2), then add the boxes of the plural nouns. פָּנִים with the inseparable preposition לְ means "to the face" (before). With the pronominal suffixes 1cs-1cp, the original Pataḥ, in the open pretonic syllable, lengthens to Qameṣ – לְפָנַי (6.3.2). With the pronominal suffixes 2mp-3fp (and in the construct state), the original Pataḥs, in open pro-pretonic syllables, reduce to vocal shewas *לְפְנֵיכֶם (6.3.5). Then the first shewa becomes Ḥireq לִפְנֵיכֶם (3.2.2.1).

[2] These suffixes, in fact, may not be plural suffixes because their original forms have a Yod – אלי and עלי, as in Arabic.

14.5. The Inseparable Preposition כ with Pronominal Suffixes

1cs	כָּמ֫וֹנִי	like (as) me	1cp	כָּמ֫וֹנוּ	like (as) us
2ms	כָּמ֫וֹךָ	like (as) you	2mp	כָּכֶם	like (as) you
2fs	כָּמוֹךְ	like (as) you	2fp	כָּכֶן	like (as) you
3ms	כָּמ֫וֹהוּ	like (as) him	3mp	כְּמוֹהֶם[3]	like (as) them
3fs	כָּמ֫וֹהָ	like (as) her	3fp	כְּמוֹהֶן[3]	like (as) them

1. In the forms 1cs-1cp and 3mp-3fp, the pronominal suffixes are attached directly[4] to *כַּמוֹ, an extended form of כ. Note the 3mp-3fp endings pull the tone to the end of the word, leaving the כ in an open pro-pretonic syllable, thus reducing the original Pataḥ to shewa.

2. The forms 2mp-2fp attach directly to the inseparable preposition כ. The first letter, always in the pretonic position, receives a Qameṣ.

3. Note the following variations in the pronominal suffixes: 1cs נִי for י□ִ, 3ms הוּ for וֹ, and 3fs הָ for ה□ָ. These suffix variations have consonantal buffers to attach suffixes to a word ending in a vowel to avoid consecutive vowels.

14.6. The Preposition מִן with Pronominal Suffixes

1cs	מִמֶּ֫נִּי	from me	1cp	מִמֶּ֫נּוּ	from us
2ms	מִמְּךָ	from you	2mp	מִכֶּם	from you
2fs	מִמֵּךְ	from you	2fp	מִכֶּן	from you
3ms	מִמֶּ֫נּוּ	from him	3mp	מֵהֶם	from them
3fs	מִמֶּ֫נָּה	from her	3fp	מֵהֶן	from them

1. The forms 1cs, 3ms, 3fs, and 1cp reduplicate the preposition מִן – מנמן before attaching the pronominal suffixes. These suffixes connect to the preposition with a Segol.

2. The 3ms form, מִמֶּ֫נּוּ, is contracted from *מִמֶּנְהוּ (note the variant suffix הוּ for וֹ); the 3fs form, מִמֶּ֫נָּה, is contracted from *מִמֶּנְהָ (note the variant suffix הָ for ה□ָ).

3. The forms 2ms and 2fs only partially reduplicate, מנם instead of מנמן.

---

[3] Variant forms – כָּהֵם, כָּהֵן.

[4] That is, the suffixes are without connecting vowels: so נוּ instead of נוּ□ֵ֫ in the 1cp.

4. The forms 2mp-3fp attach to the preposition מִן without reduplication.

EXERCISE FOURTEEN

I. Questions

1. List the differences between the pronominal suffix boxes of the nouns and the pronominal suffixes on the prepositions לְ and בְּ.
2. Explain why the suffixed forms of עִם receive a Dagesh Forte.
3. Which prepositions take the suffixes of the singular noun? Which take the suffixes of the plural noun?
4. Explain the variation עִמָּם and עִמָּהֶם.
5. Discuss the formation of לְפָנִים, with and without pronominal suffixes.
6. Discuss the attaching of pronominal suffixes to the כְּ preposition. Also list the suffix variations and explain the purpose of the suffix variations.
7. Discuss the attaching of pronominal suffixes to the מִן preposition.

II. Vocabulary

יוֹאָב	Joab	אֲבִימֶלֶךְ	Abimelek
מַלְאָךְ	messenger, angel	בָּקָר	cattle
קָרַב	(he) came near, approached	צֹאן	sheep
פָּשַׁע	(he) revolted, transgressed	עֵת	time, season
פָּשַׁע בְּ	(he) revolted against	שָׁכַב	(he) lay down, slept
פֶּשַׁע (*i*)	rebellion, revolt, transgression	שָׂנֵא	(he) hates, hated
יָרֵא	(he) feared	אַבְשָׁלוֹם	Absalom

III. Drills

1. Word Breakdown: In the following order: label every Dagesh Forte and Lene, Mappiq; vocal and silent shewa; Qameṣ and Qameṣ-Ḥatuf. Next, divide syllables labeling them open or closed. Then pronounce the words.

   קָטְלָה   חֵרוּ   פְּלִשְׁתִּים   חָכְמָתוֹ

2. Attach the following particles and translate all vocabulary words.
   Article

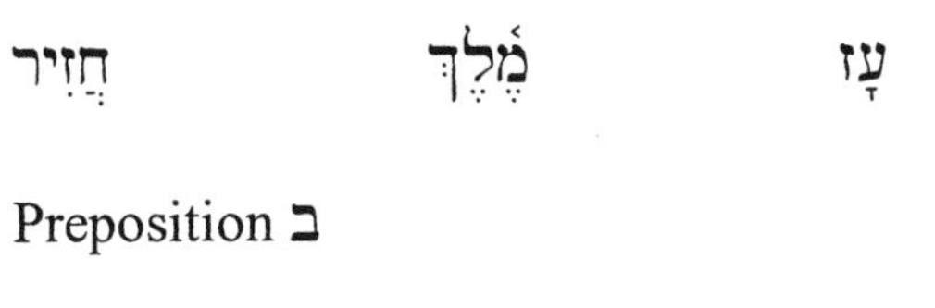

   עָז   מֶלֶךְ   חֲזִיר

   Preposition בְּ

   אֲדָמָה   יְלִיד   אֱלֹהִים

Preposition מִן

חֲלוֹם　　　　שְׁמוּאֵל　　　　עִיר

3. Attach the boxes and translate all vocabulary words. List all steps.
   1. fp construct גְּדוֹלָה
   2. fp absolute בְּרָכָה
   3. ms construct חָכָם
   4. mp construct צַדִּיק

4. Attach the boxes with suffixes and translate all vocabulary words. List all steps.

Singular Nouns			Plural Nouns		
1.	2fs	שָׁנָה	4.	2fs	תְּפִלָּה
2.	2ms	אַמְלָכָה	5.	3mp	עָפָר
3.	1cs	אָדָם	6.	3ms	מִצְוָה

5. Attach the suffixes to the prepositions and translate.

1.	1cs	לְ	6.	2fp	לְפָנִים
2.	2ms	עִם	7.	3fs	אֶל
3.	3ms	אֵת (with)	8.	2mp	מִן
4.	1cp	לְפָנִים	9.	2ms	כְּ
5.	3mp	כְּ	10.	2fs	מִן

6. Translation

1. הָרַג יוֹאָב אֶת־אַבְשָׁלוֹם כִּי פָּשַׁע בְּדָוִד וּבַאֲנָשָׁיו׃

2. לָקְחוּ מַלְאֲכֵי אֲבִימֶלֶךְ אֶת־שָׂרָה אֵשֶׁת־אַבְרָהָם וַאֲבִימֶלֶךְ לֹא קָרַב אֵלֶיהָ
כִּי שָׁמַר אֱלֹהִים אֹתוֹ מִכָּל־רָע׃

3. אַחַר הַדְּבָרִים הָאֵלֶּה נָתַן אֲבִימֶלֶךְ לְאַבְרָהָם זָהָב וָכֶסֶף צֹאן וּבָקָר וְגַם שָׂדֶה׃

4. בָּעֵת הַהוּא דִּבֶּר אֲבִימֶלֶךְ לְאַבְרָהָם לֵאמֹר יהוה עִמְּךָ וְהוּא בָּחַר בְּךָ לְמֶלֶךְ
עַל־כָּל־הַגּוֹיִם עַד־עוֹלָם׃

5. בָּא שְׁמוּאֵל הַנָּבִיא אֶל־הָעִיר הַזֹּאת כִּי בָהּ הָיוּ הָרְשָׁעִים אֲשֶׁר לֹא
יָרְאוּ אֶת־יְהוָה׃

6. יהוה אֲדֹנֵינוּ מַה־גָּדוֹל שִׁמְךָ בְּכָל־הָאָרֶץ׃

7. שָׁכַב מֹשֶׁה עַל־הָאֲדָמָה וְלֹא יָדַע כִּי קְדוֹשָׁה הָאֲדָמָה הָהִיא לַיהוָה׃

8. אָמַר אֵלִיָּהוּ יהוה הוּא הָאֱלֹהִים מִי כָמוֹהוּ בַּשָּׁמַיִם וּמִי כְעַמּוֹ יִשְׂרָאֵל
עַל־הָאָרֶץ׃

CHAPTER 15
SEGOLATE NOUNS

15.1. Introduction: Segolate nouns (10.2.1) derive their name from their characteristic Segols – מֶלֶךְ, קֶבֶר.[1] The absolute and construct state of these nouns are identical in the singular.[2] With pronominal suffixes, however, the Segols disappear and the forms radically change to מַלְכִּי and קִבְרִי (1cs suffix).

15.2. The Development of the Segolate Noun

*מַלְכַּם » *מַלְךַ » *מַלְךְ » *מַלֶךְ » מֶלֶךְ

1 2 3 4 5

The Segolate noun מֶלֶךְ was originally *מַלְכַּם[3](1). First, Segolate nouns dropped final Mems (2). Then, the final short case vowel dropped (3). This left the form with a cluster of two consonants – לְךְ. Generally, Hebrew will not tolerate the clustering of consonants, so a Segol was inserted between the second and third root letter (4). Finally, the Segol assimilated the sound of the original Pataḥ under the first root letter to the Segol under the second root letter (5). Forms with pronominal suffixes (מַלְכִּי), however, retained the original vowel under the first root letter because suffixed forms never clustered consonants (3). Only with the clustering of consonants are Segols secondarily inserted. Forms with pronominal suffixes have three varieties based on the original short vowel under the first root letter:

מֶלֶךְ « *מַלְךְ (*a*) סֵפֶר « *סִפְר (*i*) קֹדֶשׁ « *קָדְשׁ (*o*)

15.3. Singular Segolate Nouns: Absolute, Construct, and with Pronominal Suffixes

Absolute	מֶלֶךְ	(*a*) king	סֵפֶר	(*i*) book	קֹדֶשׁ	(*o*) holiness
Construct	מֶלֶךְ	king of	סֵפֶר	book of	קֹדֶשׁ	holiness of
Base forms	*מַלְךְ		*סִפְר		*קָדְשׁ	
1cs	מַלְכִּי	my king	סִפְרִי	my book	קָדְשִׁי	my holiness
2ms	מַלְכְּךָ	your king	סִפְרְךָ	your book	קָדְשְׁךָ	your holiness
2fs	מַלְכֵּךְ	your king	סִפְרֵךְ	your book	קָדְשֵׁךְ	your holiness
3ms	מַלְכּוֹ	his king	סִפְרוֹ	his book	קָדְשׁוֹ	his holiness
3fs	מַלְכָּהּ	her king	סִפְרָהּ	her book	קָדְשָׁהּ	her holiness

---

[1] Segolate nouns are also accented characteristically on the first syllable in the singular absolute.

[2] Only context can determine whether מֶלֶךְ is in absolute state (king) or in construct state (king of).

[3] Originally, Hebrew nouns ended with a ם (Mem). The second Pataḥ (under the כ) was a case vowel (accusative, as still seen in Arabic) – *מַלְכֻּם nominative, *מַלְכִּם genitive, *מַלְכַּם accusative.

1cp	מַלְכֵּ֫נוּ	our king	סִפְרֵ֫נוּ	our book	קָדְשֵׁ֫נוּ	our holiness
2mp	מַלְכְּכֶם	your king	סִפְרְכֶם	your book	קָדְשְׁכֶם	your holiness
2fp	מַלְכְּכֶן	your king	סִפְרְכֶן	your book	קָדְשְׁכֶן	your holiness
3mp	מַלְכָּם	their king	סִפְרָם	their book	קָדְשָׁם	their holiness
3fp	מַלְכָּן	their king	סִפְרָן	their book	קָדְשָׁן	their holiness

Pronominal suffixes attach to the proto-forms – *מַלְךְ, *סִפְרְ, and *קָדְשְׁ – not to the forms with Segols (15.2). The short vowel under the first root letter will be supplied to construct the forms מֶ֫לֶךְ (*a*), סֵ֫פֶר (*i*), and קֹ֫דֶשׁ (*o*).

15.4. Plural Segolate Nouns: Absolute and Construct[4]

In the plural, Segolate nouns follow two patterns: a pattern resembling the דָּבָר pattern and a plural Segolate pattern without a Dagesh Lene in the third root letter (R_3), מַלְכֵי. The Segolate singular pattern , by contrast, requires a Dagesh Lene in the third root letter if it is a Bᵊgad Kᵊfat letter – מַלְכִּי.

1. Absolute: From the singular, the expected plural absolute form would be *מַלְכִּים; however, the actual form is מְלָכִים (סְפָרִים, קֳדָשִׁים[5]). This follows the דָּבָר pattern – דְּבָרִים.[6]

2. Construct: The construct form, מַלְכֵי, is closer to the expected form – *מַלְכֵּי[7] (סִפְרֵי, קָדְשֵׁי). This is the plural Segolate pattern, which is without Dagesh Lene in the third root letter (R_3).

[4] Segolate nouns in the dual follow the singular Segolate pattern – *אָזְנְ, *חָפְנְ, but attach the pronominal suffixes of plural nouns – אָזְנָיו, חָפְנֶ֫יךָ.

[5] The Qameṣ-Ḥatuf under the first root letter is probably a substitute for Ḥatef-Qameṣ-Ḥatuf.

[6] Another common view postulates an original plural form – *מַלַךְ.

[7] The shewa is medial, therefore, without Dagesh Lene in the כ – מַלְכֵי. Segolate nouns in the plural never allow Dagesh Lene in the third root letter (R_3) (footnote 12-1).

15.5. Plural Segolate Nouns with Suffixes

Like the plural absolute and construct forms, plural Segolate nouns with suffixes follow two patterns: the דָּבָר pattern or the plural Segolate pattern, which is without Dagesh Lene in the third root letter (R_3).

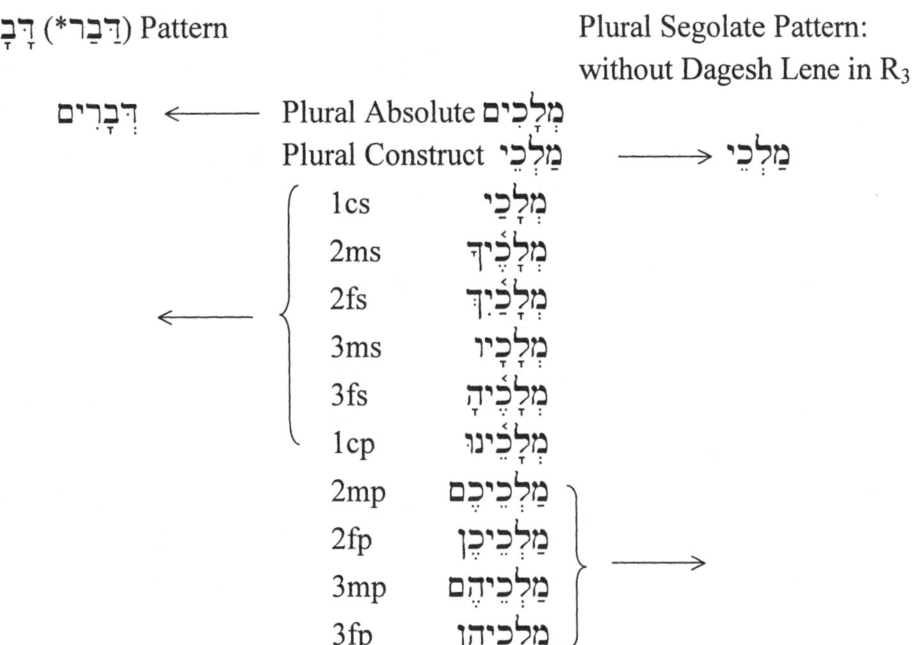

15.6. Plural Segolate Nouns: Absolute, Construct, and with Pronominal Suffixes

Absolute	מְלָכִים	kings	סְפָרִים	קֳדָשִׁים	– דָּבָר Pattern: דְּבָרִים
Construct	מַלְכֵי	kings of	סִפְרֵי	קָדְשֵׁי	– Plural Segolate Pattern: without Dagesh Lene in R_3
1cs	מְלָכַי	my kings	סְפָרַי	קֳדָשַׁי	1cs-1cp follows דָּבָר Pattern – דְּבָרַי
2ms	מְלָכֶיךָ	your kings	סְפָרֶיךָ	קֳדָשֶׁיךָ	
2fs	מְלָכַיִךְ	your kings	סְפָרַיִךְ	קֳדָשַׁיִךְ	
3ms	מְלָכָיו	his kings	סְפָרָיו	קֳדָשָׁיו	
3fs	מְלָכֶיהָ	her kings	סְפָרֶיהָ	קֳדָשֶׁיהָ	
1cp	מְלָכֵינוּ	our kings	סְפָרֵינוּ	קֳדָשֵׁינוּ	
2mp	מַלְכֵיכֶם	your kings	סִפְרֵיכֶם	קָדְשֵׁיכֶם	2mp-3fp follow Plural Segolate Pattern: without Dagesh Lene in R_3
2fp	מַלְכֵיכֶן	your kings	סִפְרֵיכֶן	קָדְשֵׁיכֶן	
3mp	מַלְכֵיהֶם	their kings	סִפְרֵיהֶם	קָדְשֵׁיהֶם	
3fp	מַלְכֵיהֶן	their kings	סִפְרֵיהֶן	קָדְשֵׁיהֶן	

1. The forms 1cs-1cp follow the דָּבָר pattern as if the original form was *מַלַךְ (compare the absolute plural form – מְלָכִים, 15.4.1).

2. The forms 2mp-3fp follow the plural Segolate pattern (without the Dagesh Lene in the third root letter) – מַלְכֵיכֶם, and the first root letter has the original short vowel of the proto-form of the singular – *מַלְךְ (compare the construct plural form – מַלְכֵי, 15.4.2).

3. The two most common Segolate nouns of the Ḥolem class – קֹדֶשׁ and שֹׁרֶשׁ – have Qameṣ-Ḥatuf (sometimes Ḥatef-Qameṣ-Ḥatuf in קֳדָשׁ) under the first root letter in the plural instead of the expected vocal shewa (6.3.5). Perhaps the Qameṣ-Ḥatuf substitutes for the Ḥatef-Qameṣ-Ḥatuf. Sometimes, the expected vocal shewa occurs in Biblical Hebrew – רְחָמִים (רֹחֶם) (see 16.5).

15.7. Attaching Pronominal Suffixes to Segolate Nouns

Follow a three step process

1. Determine the appropriate pattern
   1. Singular Segolate pattern with Dagesh Lene in R_3, if a Bᵊgad Kᵊfat letter, for singular nouns.
   2. דָּבָר pattern (plural absolute and 1cs-1cp suffixed forms for plural nouns)
   3. Plural Segolate pattern without Dagesh Lene in R_3, if a Bᵊgad Kᵊfat letter (plural construct and 2mp-3fp suffixed forms for plural nouns).

2. Attach the appropriate box

3. Work the rules of syllables

Example: 3ms suffix on the singular of מֶלֶךְ (*a*)[8]

1. Singular Segolate pattern with Dagesh Lene in R_3 (if Bᵊgad Kᵊfat letter) – מַלְכְּ
2. Attach the box – מַלְכּוֹ
3. Work the rules of syllables – מַלְכּוֹ (6.3.3)

Example: 3ms suffix on the plural of מֶלֶךְ (*a*)

1. The דָּבָר pattern (*דַּבָר) – מַלַךְ
2. Attach the box – מַלָכָיו
3. Work the rules of syllables – מְלָכָיו (6.3.2; 6.3.5)

[8] The letter in the parentheses (15.3) indicates the vowel under R_1 for the Segolate singular or plural patterns (not the דָּבָר pattern).

Exercise Fifteen

I. Questions

1. Where does the term "Segolate noun" come from?
2. What two forms in the singular are always identical in Segolate nouns?
3. Describe the historical development of Segolate nouns.
4. What three varieties do the singular Segolate nouns follow?
5. What pattern does the dual follow and which pronominal suffixes do they take?
6. What three patterns do the Segolate nouns follow with pronominal suffixes?
7. Describe the irregularity in the Segolate plural of קֹ֫דֶשׁ.
8. Describe the attaching of pronominal suffixes to Segolate nouns.

II. Vocabulary

שָׁנָה	year	מִלְחָמָה	war, battle
דֶּ֫רֶךְ (*a*)	way, road	כִּכָּר	(f) valley, plain, round, loaf of bread
בֹּ֫קֶר (*a*)	morning	אַחְאָב	Ahab
נָהָר	river	לוֹט	Lot
חֹק (pl. חֻקִּים)	statute, law, rule	צֶ֫דֶק (*i*)	righteousness
עֶ֫רֶב (*a*)	evening	חַיִּים	life (always in the plural)
נָשָׂא	(he) lifted up	סֵ֫פֶר (*i*)	scroll, book
חָטָא	(he) sinned (missed the mark)		

III. Drills

1. Word Breakdown: In the following order: label every Dagesh Forte and Lene, Mappiq; vocal and silent shewa; Qameṣ and Qameṣ-Ḥatuf. Next, divide syllables labeling them open or closed. Then pronounce the words.

   כָּתְבָהּ   לֵאלֹהִים   וַתַּסֵּ֫בוּ   יְשָׁ֫לוּךְ

2. Attach the following particles and translate all vocabulary words.
   Interrogative מה

   יֶ֫רַח   רֹאשׁ   חָלַ֫מְתָּ

   Conjunctive ו

   יְפִי   פַּר   עָמָל

Interrogative ה

עָמָל　　　　עָשִׂיתִי　　　　אֵימָה

3. Attach the boxes and translate all vocabulary words. List all steps.
    1. dual construct עַפְעַפַּיִם
    2. mp construct בֶּגֶד (*i*)
    3. mp absolute קֹדֶשׁ (*o*)
    4. mp construct דֶּלֶת (*a*)
    5. mp absolute סֵפֶר (*i*)

4. Attach the boxes with suffixes and translate all vocabulary words. List all steps. (see 15.7)

	Singular Nouns			Plural Nouns
1.	1cs עָקָר		6.	2ms תּוּשִׁיָּה
2.	3fp רִקְמָה		7.	3fp בֶּגֶד (*i*)
3.	3ms אֶרֶץ (*a*)		8.	1cs צְדָקָה
4.	3mp סֵפֶר (*i*)		9.	2ms שֹׁרֶשׁ (*o*)
5.	1cp קֹדֶשׁ (*o*)		10.	3ms אֹזֶן (*o*) dual

5. Attach the suffixes to the prepositions and translate.

1.	2ms אֶל		4.	1cp כ
2.	3mp מִן		5.	3ms עִם
3.	1cs לְפָנִים		6.	2fs אֵת (direct object)

6. Translation

1. הָלַךְ דָּוִד בְּדֶרֶךְ יהוה כָּל־יְמֵי חַיָּיו וְאַחְאָב עָבַד אֱלֹהִים אֲחֵרִים כָּל־יָמָיו׃
2. בַּשָּׁנָה הַהִיא עָבְרוּ יְהוֹשֻׁעַ וְיִשְׂרָאֵל אֶת־הַיַּרְדֵּן וּמֹשֶׁה לֹא עָבַר אֶת־הַנָּהָר
כִּי לֹא שָׁמַע בְּקוֹל־יהוה בַּמִּדְבָּר׃
3. זָכַר בֶּן־הַמֶּלֶךְ אֶת־תּוֹרַת מֹשֶׁה אֲשֶׁר צִוָּה יהוה אֹתוֹ בַּמִּדְבָּר עַל־כָּל־יִשְׂרָאֵל
מִצְוֹת מִשְׁפָּטִים וְחֻקִּים׃
4. אָמְרוּ לוֹ עַבְדֵי־פַרְעֹה זֹאת יַד אֱלֹהִים וְרַע הָיָה הַדָּבָר הַזֶּה בְּעֵינֵי־פַרְעֹה׃
5. נָשָׂא שְׁמוּאֵל אֶת־עֵינָיו וְלֹא רָאָה אֶת־הָאֲנָשִׁים אֲשֶׁר עָמְדוּ לִפְנֵי־הַכֹּהֵן בַּהֵיכָל׃
6. יָשַׁב אַבְרָהָם בְּאֶרֶץ כְּנַעַן וְלוֹט יָשַׁב בְּעָרֵי כִּכַּר הַיַּרְדֵּן׃
7. עָשׂוּ פְלִשְׁתִּים מִלְחָמָה אֶת־בְּנֵי־יִשְׂרָאֵל וַיהוה לֹא נָתַן אֹתָם בְּיָדָם׃
8. עָשָׂה לוֹ אַהֲרֹן מִזְבֵּחַ כִּדְבַר־יהוה אֲשֶׁר דִּבֶּר אֱלֹהִים לְמֹשֶׁה עַבְדּוֹ׃

CHAPTER 16
SEGOLATE NOUNS WITH GUTTURALS
SEGOLATE PREPOSITIONS

16.1. Introduction: In a Segolate noun, the presence of a guttural often changes Segols into Pataḥs (5.7.3). Like the Segolate nouns without gutturals (chapter 15), these Segolates follow three patterns (15.7). Moreover, some prepositions follow the Segolate pattern.

16.2. Segolate Nouns with Gutturals

1. If the final root letter (R_3) of a Segolate noun is a guttural, the preceding Segol becomes a Pataḥ (5.7.3) – *נֵצֶח » נֵ֫צַח.
2. If the second root letter (R_2) of a Segolate noun is a guttural, both Segols become Pataḥ (5.7.3) – *נֶעֶר » נַ֫עַר.
3. If the first root letter (R_1) of a Segolate noun is a guttural, the Segols frequently remains – הֶ֫בֶל.

16.3. Segolate Proto-forms

As with Segolate nouns without gutturals, Segolate nouns with gutturals have three varieties (compare 15.2).

נַ֫עַר « *נַעְרְ (*a*) נֵ֫צַח « *נִצְחְ (*i*) פֹּ֫עַל « *פָּעְלְ (*o*)

16.4. Singular Segolate Nouns (having a Guttural): Absolute, Construct, and with Pronominal Suffixes

Absolute	נַ֫עַר	(*a*) lad	נֵ֫צַח	(*i*) perpetuity	פֹּ֫עַל	(*o*) work
Construct	נַ֫עַר	lad of	נֵ֫צַח	perpetuity of	פֹּ֫עַל	work of
Base forms	*נַעְרְ		*נִצְחְ		*פָּעְלְ	
1cs	נַעֲרִי	my lad	נִצְחִי	my perpetuity	פָּעֳלִי	my work
2ms	נַעַרְךָ	your lad	נִצְחֲךָ	your perpetuity	פָּעָלְךָ	your work
2fs	נַעֲרֵךְ	your lad	נִצְחֵךְ	your perpetuity	פָּעֳלֵךְ	your work
3ms	נַעֲרוֹ	his lad	נִצְחוֹ	his perpetuity	פָּעֳלוֹ	his work
3fs	נַעֲרָהּ	her lad	נִצְחָהּ	her perpetuity	פָּעֳלָהּ	her work
1cp	נַעֲרֵ֫נוּ	our lad	נִצְחֵ֫נוּ	our perpetuity	פָּעֳלֵ֫נוּ	our work
2mp	נַעַרְכֶם	your lad	נִצְחֲכֶם	your perpetuity	פָּעָלְכֶם	your work
2fp	נַעַרְכֶן	your lad	נִצְחֲכֶן	your perpetuity	פָּעָלְכֶן	your work
3mp	נַעֲרָם	their lad	נִצְחָם	their perpetuity	פָּעֳלָם	their work
3fp	נַעֲרָן	their lad	נִצְחָן	their perpetuity	פָּעֳלָן	their work

1. In the suffixed forms (except 2ms, 2mp, and 2fp) with a middle guttural (נער, פעל), the form takes a composite shewa under the guttural instead of a silent shewa (5.7.1; footnote 5-2) – *נַעְרֵי » נַעֲרֵי.[1]

2. In the 2ms, 2mp, and 2fp forms, the composite shewa becomes a Pataḥ to avoid a medial shewa and a vocal shewa consecutively (3.2.2) – *נַעֲרְךָ » נַעַרְךָ; *נַעֲרְכֶם » נַעַרְכֶם.[2]

16.5. Plural Segolate Nouns (having a Guttural): Absolute, Construct, and with Pronominal Suffixes

Absolute	נְעָרִים	lads	נְצָחִים	פְּעָלִים	– דָּבָר Pattern: דְּבָרִים
Construct	נַעֲרֵי	lads of	נִצְחֵי	פָּעֳלֵי	– Plural Segolate Pattern: without Dagesh Lene in R_3
1cs	נְעָרַי	my lads	נְצָחַי	פְּעָלַי	
2ms	נְעָרֶיךָ	your lads	נְצָחֶיךָ	פְּעָלֶיךָ	
2fs	נְעָרַיִךְ	your lads	נְצָחַיִךְ	פְּעָלַיִךְ	1cs-1cp follows
3ms	נְעָרָיו	his lads	נְצָחָיו	פְּעָלָיו	דָּבָר Pattern – דְּבָרַי
3fs	נְעָרֶיהָ	her lads	נְצָחֶיהָ	פְּעָלֶיהָ	
1cp	נְעָרֵינוּ	our lads	נְצָחֵינוּ	פְּעָלֵינוּ	
2mp	נַעֲרֵיכֶם	your lads	נִצְחֵיכֶם	פָּעֳלֵיכֶם	2mp-3fp follow
2fp	נַעֲרֵיכֶן	your lads	נִצְחֵיכֶן	פָּעֳלֵיכֶן	Plural Segolate
3mp	נַעֲרֵיהֶם	their lads	נִצְחֵיהֶם	פָּעֳלֵיהֶם	Pattern: without
3fp	נַעֲרֵיהֶן	their lads	נִצְחֵיהֶן	פָּעֳלֵיהֶן	Dagesh Lene in R_3

1. As in the Segolate nouns without gutturals, the plural absolute and the suffixed forms 1cs-1cp follow the דָּבָר pattern (15.6; 15.7).

2. The plural construct and the suffixed forms 2mp-3fp follow the plural Segolate pattern without a Dagesh Lene in the third root letter. The middle guttural letter takes a composite shewa, which echoes the vowel under R_1, instead of a silent shewa (5.7.1 footnote 5-2; 16.4.1) – *נַעְרֵי » נַעֲרֵי.

3. פֹּעַל is regular in the plural with the vocal shewa under the first root letter (contrast קָדָשַׁי, 15.6.3).

---

[1] They may take silent shewa also – תַּחְתַּי.

[2] The shewa under the third root letter is medial – silent enough to close the syllable; vocal enough to keep the Dagesh Lene out of the כ (footnotes 12-1 and 15-7).

16.6. Attaching Pronominal Suffixes to Segolate Nouns with Gutturals

The first three steps are like 15.7, but add a fourth step for the shewa problem.

Example: 1cs suffix on the singular of נַעַר (*a*)

1. Determine the appropriate pattern: the singular Segolate pattern with Dagesh Lene in R_3 if it is a Bᵊgad Kᵊfat letter – נַעְר
2. Attach appropriate box – נַעְ□י
3. Work the rules of syllables – נַעְרִי (6.3.3)
4. Account for the guttural with silent shewa: they often become composite shewa under gutturals in the silent shewa position – נַעֲרִי (5.7.1 footnote 5-2).

16.7. Prepositions of the Segolate Pattern or Resembling the Segolate Pattern

	לְמַעַן	תַּחַת	אַחַר (אַחֲרֵי)
	"for the sake of"	"under, below, instead of"	"after, behind"
1cs	לְמַעֲנִי	תַּחְתַּי	אַחֲרַי
2ms	לְמַעַנְךָ	תַּחְתֶּיךָ	אַחֲרֶיךָ
2fs	לְמַעֲנֵךְ	תַּחְתַּיִךְ	אַחֲרַיִךְ
3ms	לְמַעֲנוֹ	תַּחְתָּיו	אַחֲרָיו
3fs	לְמַעֲנָהּ	תַּחְתֶּיהָ	אַחֲרֶיהָ
1cp	לְמַעֲנֵנוּ	תַּחְתֵּינוּ	אַחֲרֵינוּ
2mp	לְמַעַנְכֶם	תַּחְתֵּיכֶם	אַחֲרֵיכֶם
2fp	לְמַעַנְכֶן	תַּחְתֵּיכֶן	אַחֲרֵיכֶן
3mp	לְמַעֲנָם	(תַּחְתֵּיהֶם) תַּחְתָּם	אַחֲרֵיהֶם
3fp	לְמַעֲנָן	(תַּחְתֵּיהֶן) תַּחְתָּן	אַחֲרֵיהֶן

1. לְמַעַן – This Segolate preposition takes singular pronominal suffixes (compare נַעַר 16.4). This preposition, also a conjunction, combines the inseparable preposition לְ with the word מען – "intent, purpose": for (my) intent or purpose, for (my) sake.

2. תַּחַת – This Segolate preposition takes a singular root *תַּחְתְּ with plural endings (compare the dual, footnote 15-4). Note that the second root letter (a guttural) takes a silent shewa (instead of a composite shewa as נַעֲרִי).

3. אַחַר – This preposition is not a Segolate word (as the accent indicates, see footnote 15-1), but it resembles the Segolate noun נַעַר with suffixes – נַעֲרִי, אַחֲרַי. The preposition אַחַר, however, takes plural suffixes.

Exercise Sixteen

I. Questions

1. How does a guttural in the second root position (R_2) change the pointing of Segolate nouns (chapter 15) with and without pronominal suffixes? How does a guttural in the third root position (R_3) change the pointing of Segolate nouns with and without pronominal suffixes?
2. Describe the attaching of pronominal suffixes to Segolate nouns with gutturals. How does it differ from Segolate nouns without a guttural?
3. Describe the pattern and the suffixes (singular or plural) of the prepositions לְמַ֫עַן, תַּ֫חַת, אַחַר.

II. Vocabulary

נַ֫עַר (*a*)	lad, boy
דַּ֫עַת (*a*)	knowledge
לְמַ֫עַן	so that, in order that, for the sake of
בֵּית־אֵל	Bethel
יֵשׁ	there is, there are
חֶ֫סֶד (*a*)	loyalty, lovingkindness, steadfast love
חַטָּאת	(f) sin, sin-offering
חֶ֫רֶב (*a*)	(f) sword
לֵב, לֵבָב	heart (with suffix לִבִּי)
נָפַל	(he) fell
שַׂר	official, leader, prince
רַב	(adj.) much, many
תַּ֫חַת	under, instead of
אַשְׁרֵי	happy, blessed

III. Drills

1. Word Breakdown: In the following order: label every Dagesh Forte and Lene, Mappiq; vocal and silent shewa; Qameṣ and Qameṣ-Ḥatuf. Next, divide syllables labeling them open or closed. Then pronounce the words.

   צְפַרְדֵּעַ   פִּתְאֹם   אֳנִיָּה   קָדְשֵׁיכֶם

2. Attach the following particles and translate all vocabulary words.

   Article

   אָפִיק   דִּין   חָצִיר

   Preposition לְ

   גַּאֲוָה   יָם   מְזִמָּה

Preposition מִן

רַעֲנָן שְׁגָגָה חֵךְ

3. Attach the boxes and translate all vocabulary words. List all steps.

1.	dual construct	אֹ֫זֶן (*o*)	4.	fp construct	צַדִּיק
2.	mp construct	נַ֫עַר (*a*)	5.	mp absolute	מֶ֫לֶךְ (*a*)
3.	fp absolute	חָכָם	6.	mp construct	פֹּ֫עַל (*o*)

4. Attach the boxes with suffixes and translate all vocabulary words. List all steps.

	Singular Nouns			Plural Nouns	
1.	2ms	קֹ֫דֶשׁ (*o*)	5.	2fp	תַּנּוּר
2.	1cp	פְּעֻלָּה	6.	3ms	קֹ֫דֶשׁ (*o*)
3.	2ms	נַ֫עַר (*a*)	7.	2ms	פֹּ֫עַל (*o*)
4.	3fs	בָּקָר	8.	1cp	אֲדָמָה

5. Attach the suffixes to the prepositions and translate.

1.	3fp	אֶל	4.	3ms	כְּ
2.	1cs	מִן	5.	3ms	אֵת (with)
3.	2fs	לְמַ֫עַן	6.	3ms	תַּ֫חַת

6. Translation

1. שָׁאַל שְׁלֹמֹה מֵעִם־יהוה חָכְמָה וּבְחָכְמָתוֹ שָׁפַט אֶת־יִשְׂרָאֵל בְּצֶ֫דֶק וּבֶאֱמֶת׃
2. בָּנָה אַבְרָהָם מִזְבֵּחַ בְּבֵית־אֵל וְשָׁם זָבַח זֶ֫בַח כִּי יהוה כָּרַת עִמּוֹ בְּרִית
לְמַ֫עַן שְׁמוֹ׃
3. הֲיֵשׁ לְךָ אָב הֲיֵשׁ לְךָ אִשָּׁה הֲיֵשׁ לְךָ בֵּן׃
4. אָמַר שְׁמוּאֵל אֶל־דָּוִד הָרַג שָׁאוּל אֶת־עַבְדְּךָ וּבַלַּ֫יְלָה הַהוּא בָּא הָעִ֫ירָה
אֶל־בֵּית־אָבִיךָ׃
5. טוֹב עָשָׂה יהוה עִם־עַבְדּוֹ כִּי לְעוֹלָם חַסְדּוֹ׃
6. הָלְכוּ צַדִּיקִים בִּדְרָכָיו אַף שָׂמְחוּ בְּתוֹרוֹתָיו וּבְחֻקָּיו׃
7. דִּבֶּר מֹשֶׁה לָעָם בְּכִכַּר הַיַּרְדֵּן לֵאמֹר אֵ֫לֶּה הַתּוֹרוֹת הַמִּצְוֹת וְהַחֻקִּים
אֲשֶׁר צִוָּה אֹתְךָ יהוה אֱלֹהֶ֫יךָ׃
8. אַשְׁרֵי הָאִישׁ אֲשֶׁר עָזַב חַטָּאתוֹ וַאֲשֶׁר שָׁמַר אֶת־דְּבַר־יהוה בְּלֵב יָשָׁר׃

MORPHOLOGICAL PRINCIPLES: STRONG VERB

CHAPTER 17
INDEPENDENT PRONOUNS
THE VERB: QAL PERFECT

17.1. Introduction: This chapter begins the systematic study of the verb. Thoroughly memorize the verbal forms in chapters 17-19. These verbal forms are essential to mastering chapters 21-25. The independent pronouns are closely associated with the perfect and imperfect of the verb.

17.2. The Independent Pronouns

1cs	[1]אָנֹכִי/אֲנִי	I	1cp	אֲנַחְנוּ	we
2ms	אַתָּה	you	2mp	אַתֶּם	you
2fs	אַתְּ	you	2fp	אַתֶּן	you
3ms	הוּא	he	3mp	הֵם/הֵמָּה	they
3fs	הִיא	she	3fp	הֵן/הֵנָּה	they

1. These pronouns are essentially subject pronouns; contrast the object pronouns in 14.3 (marker of direct object).

2. These pronouns with a finite verb (perfect, imperfect, imperative) are frequently emphatic – אָמַרְתָּ "you said," אַתָּה אָמַרְתָּ "*you* said."

17.3. The Verb: Qal Perfect (Qātal[2])

1cs	קָטַלְתִּי	I killed, have killed
2ms	קָטַלְתָּ	you killed, have killed
2fs	קָטַלְתְּ	you killed, have killed
3ms	קָטַל	he killed, has killed
3fs	קָטְלָה	she killed, has killed
1cp	קָטַלְנוּ	we killed, have killed
2mp	קְטַלְתֶּם	you killed, have killed
2fp	קְטַלְתֶּן	you killed, have killed
3cp	קָטְלוּ	they killed, have killed

[1] The pausal form retracts the accented syllable for the following pronouns – אָנִי, אָנֹכִי, אָתָּה.

[2] The perfect is also called Qātal based on the perfect 3ms – קָטַל.

1. The vowel under the second root letter (R_2, Pataḥ in שָׁמַר), the thematic vowel, lengthens or reduces under certain conditions. Moreover, the thematic vowel may indicate certain verbal notions, such as active/passive.

2. The perfect, also called the suffixed conjugation, attaches the pronominal element to the end of the verb:

   2ms קָטַ֫לְ(אַ)תָּ(ה)
   2fs קָטַלְ(אַ)תְּ
   1cp קָטַ֫לְ(אֲנַחְ)נוּ
   2mp קְטַלְ(אַ)תֶּם
   2fp קְטַלְ(אַ)תֶּן

   The other persons (1cs, 3ms, 3fs, 3cp) do not attach the independent pronouns.

3. Endings of the Perfect
   1. Syllabic endings (1cs, 2ms, 1cp, 2mp, 2fp) are syllables, at least one consonant and only one vowel[3] (Consider the 2fs ending, although without a vowel, a syllabic ending.).

      1. Syllabic Endings (except 2mp and 2fp): The accent remains over the second root letter (R_2) and the thematic vowel Pataḥ;[4] therefore, the original Pataḥ under the first root letter lengthens in the open pretonic position – *קַטַלְתִּי » קָטַ֫לְתִּי (6.3.2).

      2. Syllabic Endings 2mp and 2fp: The accent shifts over the suffixes, leaving the thematic vowel (Pataḥ) in a closed unaccented syllable (6.3.3). The original Pataḥ under the first root letter in the originally open pro-pretonic position, reduces to vocal shewa – *קַטַלְתֶּם » קְטַלְתֶּם (6.3.5).

   2. Vocalic endings (3fs, 3cp) end in a vowel.[5]
      Vocalic Endings: Verbs follow a slightly different vowel reduction pattern from nouns (6.3). *With a vocalic ending, the thematic vowel reduces in the open pretonic position* (the noun, by contrast, lengthens vowels in the open

---

[3] The 2mp, 2fp forms have two consonants and a vowel.

[4] The Pataḥ in a closed accented syllable breaks rule 6.3.1, thus allowing a lengthened form in pause קָטָ֫לְתִּי (6.3.1).

[5] The 3fs ends in a phony ה to read a Qameṣ before the ה; therefore, the ending is vocalic (footnote 11-3).

pretonic position [6.3.2]). Then the original Pataḥ under the first root letter lengthens in the open pretonic position.

*קַטַלוּ » *קַטְלוּ » קָֽטְלוּ 3cp

1 2 3

The original form (1) reduces the thematic vowel in the open pretonic position (2). Then the original Pataḥ under the first root letter lengthens in the open pretonic position (3).

3. Non-Ending (3ms): The 3ms is without ending and implies the third person.

17.4. Qal Perfect: Meaning

1. Hebrew varies the meaning of the verbal action with seven basic stems (Qal, Niph‘al, Pi“ēl, Pu“al, Hithpa“ēl, Hiph‘îl, Hoph‘al). The Qal stem is the light (not heavy) stem because the stem is not made “heavy” by adding stem prefixes to the verb or by modifying the verb internally. The Qal expresses the simple action of the verb. Other types of action will be considered later.

2. For now, translate the perfect as a simple past tense or a perfect tense according to the context.

Exercise Seventeen

I. Questions

1. In a sentence, how do the independent pronouns usually function?
2. What is a thematic vowel? How does it function in the perfect?
3. How do the independent pronouns connect to the perfect?
4. What is a syllabic ending? Which perfect forms have a syllabic ending?
5. What is a vocalic ending? Which perfect forms have a vocalic ending?
6. Which form is without an ending?
7. How does the reduction pattern of the nouns differ from the perfect verb with vocalic endings?
8. How should the perfect be translated?

II. Vocabulary

אָנֹכִי/אֲנִי	I	הֵם/הֵמָּה	they (m)
אַתָּה	you (m)	הֵן/הֵנָּה	they (f)
אַתְּ	you (f)	קֹדֶשׁ (*o*)	holiness, holy
הוּא	he	צִיּוֹן	Zion
הִיא	she	מָקוֹם	place
אֲנַחְנוּ	we	לָכֵן	therefore

אַתֶּם	you (m)	תָּמִיד	continually, regularly
אַתֶּן	you (f)	צֵל	shade

III. Drills

1. Word Breakdown: In the following order: label every Dagesh Forte and Lene, Mappiq; vocal and silent shewa; Qameṣ and Qameṣ-Ḥatuf. Next, divide syllables labeling them open or closed. Then pronounce the words.

   חַטָּאתוֹ　　אֱמִתּוֹ　　חָגִּי　　תִּשְׁבְּרוּ

2. Attach the following particles and translate all vocabulary words.

   Interrogative מָה

   חֳלִי　　אָדָם　　שָׁמַר

   Conjunctive וּ

   אֱדוֹם　　יְלוֹד　　מֶלֶךְ

   Interrogative הֲ

   שַׁבָּת　　שְׁמַרְתֶּם　　אַתָּה

3. Attach the boxes and translate all vocabulary words. List all steps.

   1. ms construct נַ֫עַר (*a*)
   2. mp construct צֶ֫דֶק (*i*)
   3. fs construct אֲדָמָה
   4. mp absolute חֶ֫רֶב (*a*)
   5. ms construct עָמָל
   6. fp absolute מִלְחָמָה

4. Attach the boxes with suffixes. List all steps.

   Singular Nouns
   1. 3fp פֹּ֫עַל (*o*)
   2. 1cs צְדָקָה
   3. 3fs עָפָר

   Plural Nouns
   4. 3fs בֶּ֫גֶד (*i*)
   5. 1cp חֹ֫פֶן (*o*) dual
   6. 2ms אֲדָמָה

5. Attach the suffixes to the prepositions.
   1. 2fp לִפְנֵים
   2. 1cs מִן
   3. 3fp תַּ֫חַת
   4. 2ms בְּ

6. Write and recite orally the perfect for the roots כתב and מלך.

7. Translation

1. אָמַר פַּרְעֹה לַיהוָה הִיא גַּם הִיא אָמְרָה אֵלַי אָחִי הוּא׃
2. גַּם יָדַעְתִּי כִּי לָקַחְתָּ לְךָ אֶת־שָׂרָה אֵשֶׁת־אַבְרָהָם לְאִשָּׁה לָכֵן חָרָה אַפִּי בְּךָ וּבְבֵיתֶךָ׃
3. אָמְרָה הָאִשָּׁה טוֹבִים הָעֵצִים לְצֵל וְלָעֵצִים הַטּוֹבִים פֶּרִי׃
4. שְׁמַעְתֶּם אֶת־קוֹל־אֱלֹהִים בַּמִּדְבָּר הַגָּדוֹל הַהוּא וְהֵמָּה רָאוּ אֶת־יהוֹה בְּהֵיכָלוֹ פָּנִים אֶל־פָּנִים׃
5. מִי עָלָה בְּהַר־יהוָה וּמִי עָמַד בִּמְקוֹם קָדְשׁוֹ׃
6. הֲלֹא שָׁלַחְנוּ לָכֶם מַלְאָכִים יִשְׂרָאֵל הֲלֹא דִּבֶּר יהוה אֲלֵיכֶם בְּיַד נְבִיאָיו בְּצִיּוֹן׃
7. לָכֵן כֹּה אָמַר יהוה אֱלֹהֵי־יִשְׂרָאֵל כִּי לֹא שְׁמַעְתֶּם דְּבָרַי עָזַבְתִּי אֶתְכֶם וְאֶת־בְּנֵיכֶם כַּאֲשֶׁר עֲזַבְתֶּם אֹתִי וְאֶת־מִשְׁפָּטָי׃
8. עֵינַי תָּמִיד אֶל־יהוָה כִּי נָשָׂא חַטָּאת עֲבָדָיו׃

CHAPTER 18
THE VERB: THE IMPERFECT AND VOLITIVES
PROHIBITIONS WITH אַל AND לֹא

18.1. Introduction: The imperfects and volitives reduce their thematic vowels, with vocalic endings, like the perfect.

18.2. The Verb: Imperfect (Yiqtōl[1])

1cs	אֶקְטֹל	I will kill	אֶשְׁלַח	I will send
2ms	תִּקְטֹל	You will kill	תִּשְׁלַח	You will send
2fs	תִּקְטְלִי	You will kill	תִּשְׁלְחִי	You will send
3ms	יִקְטֹל	He will kill	יִשְׁלַח	He will send
3fs	תִּקְטֹל	She will kill	תִּשְׁלַח	She will send
1cp	נִקְטֹל	We will kill	נִשְׁלַח	We will send
2mp	תִּקְטְלוּ	You will kill	תִּשְׁלְחוּ	You will send
2fp	תִּקְטֹלְנָה	You will kill	תִּשְׁלַחְנָה	You will send
3mp	יִקְטְלוּ	They will kill	יִשְׁלְחוּ	They will send
3fp	תִּקְטֹלְנָה	They will kill	תִּשְׁלַחְנָה	They will send

1. Thematic Vowels (17.3.1):
    1. The thematic vowel, the vowel under the second root letter (R_2), varies according to the verb. Many verbs have Ḥolem for a thematic vowel (יִקְטֹל); some verbs have Pataḥ (יִשְׁלַח), especially with a guttural for the second or third root letter.[2] For now, always use Ḥolem for the thematic vowel.

    2. With vocalic endings, thematic vowels, in the open pretonic position, reduce to vocal shewa – *יִקְטָלוּ[3] » יִקְטְלוּ (17.3.3.2).

2. The Prefixed Elements: The imperfect, the prefixed conjugation,[4] attaches the pronominal element to the beginning of the word (The vowels differ between the imperfect preformatives and the independent pronouns.).

---

[1] The imperfect is also called Yiqtōl based on the imperfect 3ms – יִקְטֹל.

[2] Pataḥ is also the imperfect thematic vowel for stative verbs (21.2).

[3] The Qameṣ-Ḥatuf lengthens in accented closed syllables (6.3.1) to Ḥolem – יִשְׁמָר־ » יִשְׁמֹר (compare יִשְׁמָר־נָא).

[4] Of course, this designation of prefixed conjugation, though not strictly accurate because some forms (2fs, 2mp, 3mp, and 2, 3fp) have suffixed elements, is commonly accepted.

1cs	אֶ(נִי)קְטֹל	(אֲנִי)
2ms	(א)תִּ(ה)קְטֹל	(אַתָּה)
2fs	(א)תִּקְטְלִי	(אַתְּ)
1cp	(אנח)נִ(ו)קְטֹל	(אֲנַחְנוּ)
2mp	(א)תִּ(ם)קְטְלוּ	(אַתֶּם)
2fp	(א)תִּ(ן)קְטֹלְנָה	(אַתֶּן)

3. Endings of the imperfect
   1. Syllabic endings (17.3.3): Syllabic endings occur in the 2fp, 3fp forms – תִּקְטֹלְנָה.
   2. Vocalic endings (17.3.3): Vocalic endings occur in the 2fs, 2mp, 3mp forms – יִקְטְלוּ, תִּקְטְלוּ, תִּקְטְלִי.[5]
   3. Non-Endings (17.3.3) occur in 1cs, 2ms 3ms, 3fs, and 1cp.
   4. The short vowel of the first syllable, always closed and unaccented, never reduces (6.3.3). All preformatives have Ḥireq except the 1cs which has Segol (under the influence of the guttural א). Memorize these imperfect preformatives by the memory word (4.2.2) – אֵיתָן: א = 1cs, י = 3ms, 3mp, etc., ת = 2ms, etc., נ = 1cp.

18.3. Qal Imperfect: Meaning

For now, translate the imperfect as a future tense.

18.4. Volitives: the Cohortative, Imperative, and Jussive

Volitives express the will or desire of the speaker. For the first person (I or we), the volitive is called cohortative; for the second person (you: singular or plural), the volitive is called imperative; for the third person (he, she, it, they), the volitive is called jussive (though the jussive can occur in first and second persons). All volitives forms are related to the imperfect.

1. Cohortatives: Form the cohortative by adding the vocalic ending Qameṣ and (phony) ה to the first person forms (singular and plural) of the imperfect. The vocalic ending reduces the (originally short) thematic vowel to vocal shewa (18.2.1).

---

[5] The 2mp and 3mp forms occasionally end with a Nun – יִקְטְלוּן, תִּקְטְלוּן, but still consider them vocalic endings.

	Imperfect	Cohortative	
Singular	אֶקְטֹל	אֶקְטְלָה	Let me kill or I *will* kill
Plural	נִקְטֹל	נִקְטְלָה	Let us kill or We *will* kill

Translate the cohortative like a proposition, "let us kill," or as a future when the cohortative emphasizes the desire or wish of the speaker: "we *will* kill."

2. Imperatives: Derive the imperatives from the imperfect second person forms by dropping the prefixed pronominal element of the imperfect. If two vocal shewas begin the word (2fs, 2mp), the first vocal shewa becomes a Ḥireq (3.2.2; footnote 3-5).

	Imperfect	Imperative		Imperative	
2ms	תִּקְטֹל	קְטֹל	Kill	שְׁלַח	Send
2fs	תִּקְטְלִי	קִטְלִי (« קְטְלִי*)	Kill	שִׁלְחִי	Send
2mp	תִּקְטְלוּ	קִטְלוּ (« קְטְלוּ*)	Kill	שִׁלְחוּ	Send
2fp	תִּקְטֹלְנָה	קְטֹלְנָה	Kill	שְׁלַחְנָה	Send

The 2ms imperative also has an emphatic form – קָטְלָה[6] kill (emphatic imperative).

3. Jussives: For now, the jussive form is identical to the third person forms of the imperfect (3ms, 3fs, 3mp, 3fp). Context determines whether a third person imperfect translates as a future or as a jussive.

3ms	יִקְטֹל	He will kill (imperfect) or Let him kill (jussive)
3fs	תִּקְטֹל	She will kill (imperfect) or Let her kill (jussive)
3mp	יִקְטְלוּ	They will kill (imperfect) or Let them kill (jussive)
3fp	תִּקְטֹלְנָה	They will kill (imperfect) or Let them kill (jussive)

18.5. Prohibitions with לֹא and אַל

With prohibitions (negative commands such as, "do not kill"), Hebrew has two constructions.

1. The imperfect with לֹא – לֹא תִקְטֹל "you will not kill" or "you must not kill"

2. The jussive with אַל[7] – אַל תִּקְטֹל "do not kill"

[6] Distinguish קָטְלָה (Qameṣ-Ḥatuf), the emphatic imperative, from קָטְלָה (Qameṣ), the perfect 3fs.

[7] אַל takes the second person jussive (18.4).

Normally the jussive with אַל is the simple warning or prohibition – “do not keep”; the imperfect with לֹא is the stronger, more emphatic prohibition – “you will not keep” (i.e., thou shalt not keep), “you must not keep.” The imperfect with לֹא is commonly found in divine prohibitions (ten commandments, for instance).[8] Hebrew never negates an imperative.

Exercise Eighteen

I. Questions

1. In the Imperfect, which forms have syllabic endings, vocalic endings, or no endings?
2. Vocalic endings in the Imperfect also may end with what letter?
3. How does the thematic vowel vary in the imperfect? When does the thematic vowel reduce?
4. What are אֵיתָן letters?
5. Define volitive. What are the various volitives called?
6. How are the various volitives formed?
7. How is the imperfect translated? How are the volitives translated?
8. How does Hebrew express prohibition? Can Hebrew ever express prohibition with an imperative?

II. Vocabulary: The verbs will now be listed without vowels.

שֶׁ֫קֶר (*i*)	falsehood, deception, lie	שַׁבָּת	sabbath, rest
נְעוּרִים	youth	יְהוֹנָתָן	Jonathan
לכד	capture	אֵשׁ	(f) fire
טוּב	good thing(s), goodness	חִזְקִיָּ֫הוּ	Hezekiah
שׂרף	burn	דָּם	blood
מָחָר	tomorrow	אַשּׁוּר	Assyria
אַל	no, not	דָּמִים	bloodshed, murder (plural of דָּם)

III. Drills

1. Word Breakdown: In the following order: label every Dagesh Forte and Lene, Mappiq; vocal and silent shewa; Qameṣ and Qameṣ-Ḥatuf. Next, divide syllables labeling them open or closed. Then pronounce the words.

יִתְּעַנּוּ   תִּתֵּ֫נָּה   קְטָלְכֶם   צִיּוֹן

[8] The jussive with אַל is commonly found when an inferior is speaking with a superior; the imperfect with לֹא is common when a superior speaks with an inferior.

2. Attach the following particles and translate all vocabulary words.
   Article

   חָג   עֶרֶשׂ   נְבִיאִים

   Preposition כ

   הֶעָמָל   רַע   יהוה

   Interrogative ה

   שָׁמַר   שְׁמַרְתֶּם   אֲדָמָה

3. Attach the boxes and translate all vocabulary words. List all steps.
   1. fp absolute תְּפִלָּה
   2. mp absolute סֵפֶר (*i*)
   3. fp construct אֲדָמָה

4. Attach the boxes with suffixes and translate all vocabulary words. List all steps.

   Singular Nouns
   1. 1cp נַעַר (*a*)
   2. 2fs דָבָר

   Plural Nouns
   3. 2mp נֵצַח (*i*)
   4. 1cs צְדָקָה

5. Attach the suffixes to the prepositions and translate.
   1. 1cs כְּ
   2. 2fp לְמַעַן
   3. 3ms אֶל
   4. 3mp לְ

6. Write and recite orally the perfect, imperfect, imperative (including the emphatic imperative), cohortatives, and jussive 3ms, 3fs of the roots כתב and משל.

7. Translation
   1. הָיָה דְבַר־יהוֹה אֶל־הַנָּבִיא לֵאמֹר יִשְׁפֹּט אֱלֹהִים אֶת־אַשּׁוּר כִּי עָשָׂה חִזְקִיָּהוּ
      אֶת־הַיָּשָׁר בְּעֵינֵי־יהוָה׃
   2. בַּיּוֹם הַהוּא תִּזְכְּרוּ אֶת־הַבְּרִית אֲשֶׁר כָּרַת עִמָּכֶם יהוָה וְגַם אַתֶּם תִּכְתְּבוּן
      בְּסֵפֶר אֶת־הַבְּרִית הַזֹּאת׃
   3. שָׁפְטָה אֹתִי יהוה כְּצִדְקִי וּשְׁמֹר אֹתִי מֵאַנְשֵׁי דָמִים לְמַעַן טוּבֶךָ׃

4. אָמַר שְׁמוּאֵל בָּעֵת הַהִיא לָֽכְדוּ פְּלִשְׁתִּים אֶת־הָעִיר וְאֶת־שָׁאוּל וְאֶת־יְהוֹנָתָן
בְּנוֹ הָֽרְגוּ בֶּחָרֶב׃

5. פִּשְׁעֵי נְעוּרַי אַל־תִּזְכֹּר כְּחַסְדְּךָ זְכָר־לִי־אַתָּה׃

6. צִוָּה יהוה אֶת־יְהוֹשֻׁעַ לִכֹּד אֶת־הָעִיר וּשְׂרֹף אֹתָהּ בָּאֵשׁ׃

CHAPTER 19
PARTICIPLES: ACTIVE AND PASSIVE
INFINITIVES: ABSOLUTE AND CONSTRUCT

19.1. Introduction

Participles and infinitives are hybrid forms: the participle is the offspring of a verb and of an adjective (a verbal adjective); the infinitive is the offspring of a verb and of a noun (a verbal noun). In form and in function (syntax), the participle acts like a verb at times; at other times, like an adjective. Similarly, the infinitive at times acts like a verb, at other times, like a noun.

19.2. Active Participle (Qōtēl[1])

1. Form

Masculine Singular Absolute	קֹטֵל		Construct	קֹטֵל
Masculine Plural Absolute	קֹטְלִים		Construct	קֹטְלֵי
Feminine Singular Absolute	קֹטְלָה		Construct	קֹטְלַת
or Absolute	קֹטֶלֶת	(T-form)	Construct	קֹטֶלֶת
Feminine Plural Absolute	קֹטְלוֹת		Construct	קֹטְלוֹת

1. The characteristic of the active participle is the historic long Ḥolem (usually written defectively 1.8.2) between the first and second root letters. The T-form participle has the original feminine ת with Segolate formation (footnote 11-3, 15.1).

2. Adjectival characteristics: The endings of the participle are adjectival endings.

3. Verbal characteristics: *Participles with adjectival endings (except T-form) reduce the thematic vowel like the verb with vocalic endings* (17.3.3). Thus, the original Ḥireq under the second root letter (R_2) reduces to vocal shewa (verb reduction pattern, 17.3.3).

2. Function (syntax)

 1. Adjectival Use:

  1. When modifying a noun, the participle follows its noun and functions as an adjective:

  הָאִישׁ הַקֹּטֵל the man, the one killing (the man who kills)

  הָאִשָּׁה הַקֹּטְלָה the woman, the one killing (the woman who kills)

[1] The active participle is also called the Qōtēl form – קֹטֵל.

2. When not modifying a noun, the participle, like an adjective, may function as a noun (substantive use)[2]:

הַקֹּטֵל the one killing (the killer)
הַיֹּשֵׁב the one dwelling (the dweller)
יֹשֵׁב a dweller

2. Verbal Use: The verbal participle occurs without the article. The subject of the participle usually precedes the participle though it may follow the participle.

הָאִישׁ קֹטֵל the man is killing (the man kills)[3]
קֹטְלִים הֵמָּה they are killing (they kill)

3. Aspect and Tense of the Active Participle
The verbal participle expresses durative or continual action (aspect). The context determines the tense, but usually it is a present tense. With the adjectival participle, context determines tense and aspect, though again, it is usually durative action (aspect) and present tense.

19.3. Passive Participle (Qāṭûl)

1. Form

Masculine Singular Absolute	קָטוּל	Construct	קְטוּל
Masculine Plural Absolute	קְטוּלִים	Construct	קְטוּלֵי
Feminine Singular Absolute	קְטוּלָה	Construct	קְטוּלַת
Feminine Plural Absolute	קְטוּלוֹת	Construct	קְטוּלוֹת

The masculine singular absolute has a Qameṣ under the first root letter. The original Pataḥ lengthens in the open pretonic position to Qameṣ. In the other forms, the original Pataḥ in an open pro-pretonic position reduces to vocal shewa.

2. Function (syntax)
The function of the passive participle resembles the active participle:
   1. Adjectival Use:
      1. Modifying a noun הָאִישׁ הַקָּטוּל
the man, the one killed – the man who is killed (19.2.2)

---

[2] 10.10.

[3] If both the noun and the participle are without the article (אִישׁ קֹטֵל), the construction is ambiguous: adjectival participle, "a man who kills"; or verbal participle, "a man is killing." Context determines the appropriate translation.

2. Substantive use הַקָּטוּל the killed one (ms) (19.2.2)

2. Verbal Use: הֵמָּה קְטוּלִים they are killed (19.2.2)

3. The aspect and tense of the passive participle are the same as the active participle (19.2.2).

19.4. Infinitive Absolute and Construct[4]

1. Infinitive Absolute (Qātôl)
   1. Form
      קָטוֹל killing

   2. Function (syntax):
      1. The infinitive absolute frequently occurs before or after a verb and emphasizes some aspect of the verb, often making a strong assertion. Translate the infinitive absolute, before or after a verb, "really, surely, indeed."
         קָטוֹל קָטַל (literally, killing, he has killed) he has indeed killed (he has surely killed, or he has really killed)
         קָטַל קָטוֹל (literally, he has killed a killing) he has indeed killed (he has surely killed, or he has really killed)

      2. Sometimes, the infinitive absolute intensifies the action of the verb:
         שָׁמוֹר שָׁמַר he has completely kept, or he has carefully kept

2. Infinitive Construct (Qᵊtōl)
   1. Form
      קְטֹל killing

   2. Function (syntax)
      1. Translate an infinitive construct as an English infinitive or gerund:
         קְטֹל to kill, killing

      2. The infinitive construct with the ל preposition often expresses purpose:
         לִקְטֹל in order to kill, or for the purpose of killing

---

[4] The terms "absolute" and "construct" as describing infinitives and nouns are analogous: the absolute noun stands absolutely or by itself; the infinitive absolute stands by itself, without suffixes or prepositions. The noun in the construct state connects to the following noun; the infinitive construct frequently connects to the following noun and takes suffixes and prepositions.

EXERCISE NINETEEN

I. Questions

1. Define participle and infinitive.
2. In form and function, how does the active participle act like a verb and like an adjective?
3. What is the usual aspect and tense of the participle?
4. Describe the function (syntax) of the infinitive absolute and construct.
5. How do the terms "absolute" and "construct" describe the infinitive absolute and infinitive construct?

II. Vocabulary

בְּתוֹךְ	(preposition) in the midst of	אֵין	there is no/not (literally: "non-existence of," construct of אַ֫יִן)
נָא	now, please		
ברח	flee	כִּסֵּא	chair, throne
אוֹ	or	כְּסִיל	fool (noun), insolent, stupid (adj.)
שַׁ֫עַר (*a*)	gate		
אֹ֫הֶל (*o*)	tent	אִם	if
עֵלִי	Eli	בְּהֵמָה	large animal, cattle, crocodile (?)
מצא	find, discover, present	שִׁלוֹ, שִׁלֹה	Shiloh

III. Drills

1. Word Breakdown: In the following order: label every Dagesh Forte and Lene, Mappiq; vocal and silent shewa; Qameṣ and Qameṣ-Ḥatuf. Next, divide syllables labeling them open or closed. Then pronounce the words.

   תּוּשִׁיָּה   מָשִׁיחַ   בְּקַשְׁתַּ֫נִי   חָכְמָתָהּ

2. Attach the following particles and translate all vocabulary words.

   Interrogative מה

   הַוָּה   יָגוֹן   הַמֶּ֫לֶךְ

   Conjunctive ו

   צְדָקָה   יהוה   אוֹר

   Interrogative ה

   הַוָּה   עָרִיץ   פְּלֵיטָה

3. Attach the boxes and translate all vocabulary words. List all steps.
    1. ms construct מֶ֫לֶךְ (*a*)
    2. mp construct נַ֫עַר (*a*)
    3. fp absolute שָׂפָה

4. Attach the boxes with suffixes and translate all vocabulary words. List all steps.

    Singular Nouns
    1. 2fp מַמְלָכָה
    2. 1cp קֹ֫דֶשׁ (*o*)

    Plural Nouns

    3. 3fs בֶּ֫גֶד (*i*)
    4. 2fs שָׂפָה

5. Attach the suffixes to the prepositions and translate.
    1. 2fs לְ
    2. 3mp אֶל
    3. 3fs אֵת (with)
    4. 2fp אֵת (direct object)

6. Write and recite orally the Qal perfect, imperfect, imperative (five forms), cohortatives, and jussive 3mp, 3fp, participles: active and passive, infinitive absolute and construct of the root זכר.

7. Translation
    1. אָמַר אֱלֹהִים אֶל־הָאִישׁ הֶאָכוֹל אָכַ֫לְתָּ מִפְּרִי הָעֵץ אֲשֶׁר בְּתוֹךְ הַגָּן׃
    2. אָמַר יהוה אֶל־מֹשֶׁה הִנֵּה אֲנִי נֹתֵן לָכֶם אֶת־הָאָ֫רֶץ וְהִנֵּה אָנֹכִי שֹׁלֵחַ
       אֶת־מַלְאָכִי לִפְנֵיכֶם׃
    3. שִׂמְחוּ עַמִּים כִּי יהוה מֹשֵׁל בָּאָ֫רֶץ יִרְאוּ גּוֹיִם כִּי יהוה שֹׁפֵט אֶת־בְּנֵי־אָדָם׃
    4. אָמַר הַכְּסִיל בְּלִבּוֹ אֵין־אֱלֹהִים אֵין־צְדָקָה וְאֵין־אֱמֶת׃
    5. קָֽרְאוּ הַנָּשִׁים הָעֹמְדוֹת לִפְנֵי הֵיכַל הַמֶּ֫לֶךְ אֵין־לָ֫נוּ לֶ֫חֶם וְאֵין־לָ֫נוּ מָ֫יִם׃
    6. צִוָּה אֶת־עַמּוֹ יהוה לִשְׁמֹר אֶת־תּוֹרָתוֹ מְאֹד׃
    7. אָמַר יהוה אֶל־מֹשֶׁה זָכוֹר אֶזְכֹּר הַנֹּשֵׂא אֶת־שְׁמִי לַשָּׁ֫קֶר׃
    8. שִׁמְרוּ אֶת־תּוֹרוֹתַי וְאֶת־חֻקַּי כִּתְבוּ אֹתָם עַל־לִבְּךָ רִדְפוּ אֹתָם כָּל־יְמֵי חַיַּ֫יִךְ׃

CHAPTER 20
VAV-CONSECUTIVE
HEBREW SYNTAX: ACCENTS – REVIA, TIFḤA

20.1. Introduction

The Vav can attach to a perfect or an imperfect to form the Vav-consecutive, a prominent characteristic of Hebrew narrative.

20.2. The Form of the Vav-Consecutive

1. Past time: Vav-consecutive with the imperfect (Vayyiqtōl): וַיִּקְטֹל, וָאֶקְטֹל. A Vav, pointed like an article (7.2), attaches to an imperfect form.[1] The Vav, like the article, takes a Pataḥ with a Dagesh Forte in the following letter (וַתִּקְטֹל). The Alef of the 1cs form rejects the Dagesh and lengthens the preceding Pataḥ to Qameṣ – וָאֶקְטֹל.

2. Future time: Vav-Consecutive with the Perfect (Vᵊqātaltî):
(1) וְקָטַלְתִּי, (2) וּמָשַׁלְתִּי, (3) וּקְטַלְתֶּם, (4) וַאֲמַרְתֶּם, (5) וִידַעְתֶּם
A Vav-conjunctive (8.3) attaches to the perfect.[2] The first form has the usual vocal shewa (in an originally open pro-pretonic syllable). The second and third forms have a Shureq before a labial letter (בּוּמָף letters) or before a vocal shewa. The fourth form has the Pataḥ, the corresponding vowel before a Ḥatef-Pataḥ. The last form has a Ḥireq (see 8.3.3).

20.3. The Meaning of the Vav-Consecutive

1. Past time: The perfect indicates past action in Hebrew; however, if an author relates a narrative in the past with succession (this happened ... and (then) this happened ... and (then) this happened ...), then the author often begins the narrative with a verb in

---

[1] Although the form resembles an imperfect and is usually identical to the jussive form, in reality, the form is a preterite (simple past tense). The Vav-consecutive, pointed וַ◙, tends to retract the accent to the penult syllable when the final syllable is closed with a shortened (or a short) final vowel, *and* the penult syllable is open with a long vowel.

[2] The conjunctive Vav tends to shift the accent to the end of the word in 1cs and 2ms forms – וְקָטַלְתִּ֫י, וְקָטַלְתָּ֫. (The Qameṣ remains under the first root letter.) The Vavs on the Vav-consecutives appear to convert the וַיִּקְטֹל form to a perfect in meaning and the וְקָטַל form to an imperfect in meaning. Hence these forms are sometimes referred to as "inverted forms" – inverted imperfect (וַיִּקְטֹל) and inverted perfect (וְקָטַל). While these terms are misleading, for the beginner, the idea of the Vav-consecutive converting the tense may help in learning the construction for the beginning student.

the perfect or with וַיְהִי[3] and continues the narrative with Vav-consecutives of the imperfect.[4]

זָכַר הַמֶּלֶךְ אֶת־סֵפֶר־יהוה וַיִּכְתֹּב לָעָם מִצְוָה וַיִּשְׁפֹּט אֶת־הָעָם וַיִּשְׁמֹר אֶת־דְּבַר־יהוה׃

"The king remembered the book of the Lord, and (then) he wrote to the people a commandment, and (then) he judged the people, and (then) he kept the word of the Lord."

2. Future time: The imperfect indicates future action, but if an author relates a narrative in the future with succession, then the author often begins the narrative with an imperfect verb or with וְהָיָה and continues the narrative with Vav-consecutives of the perfect.[5]

יִזְכֹּר הַמֶּלֶךְ אֶת־סֵפֶר־יהוה וְכָתַב לָעָם מִצְוָה וְשָׁפַט אֶת־הָעָם וְשָׁמַר אֶת־דְּבַר־יהוה׃

"The king will remember the book of the Lord, and (then) he will write to the people a commandment, and (then) he will judge the people, and (then) he will keep the word of the Lord."

20.4. The Vav-Consecutive with an Infinitive Construct

Hebrew often begins a sentence with וַיְהִי or וְהָיָה, thus establishing the tense as past (וַיְהִי) or future (וְהָיָה) for a following infinitive construct[6] (with prefixed preposition ב or כ, but not ל). This construction is a temporal clause followed by Vav-consecutives.

1. Past

וַיְהִי בִּזְכֹר (or כִּזְכֹר) הַמֶּלֶךְ אֶת־סֵפֶר־יהוה וַיִּכְתֹּב לָעָם מִצְוָה וַיִּשְׁפֹּט אֶת־הָעָם וַיִּשְׁמֹר אֶת־דְּבַר־יהוה׃

Literally: And it was in (or as) the remembering of the king the book of the Lord and (then) he wrote to the people a commandment, and (then) he judged the people, and (then) he kept the word of the Lord.

Translation: (And it was) When the king remembered the book of the Lord then[7] he wrote to the people a commandment, and (then) he judged the people, and (then) he kept the word of the Lord.

---

[3] וַיְהִי is the Vav-consecutive with imperfect of the verb הָיָה. וַיְהִי was so common that narratives and even books can begin with this word. (Also notice that וַיְהִי does not have the Dagesh Forte in the Yod of the preformative according to the rule of SQeNeMLeVY, footnote 4-5.) Indeed, narratives can even begin with any Vav-consecutive.

[4] For now, translate all Vav-consecutives with the imperfect as a past tense.

[5] For now, translate all Vav-consecutives with the perfect as a future tense.

[6] Infinitives are without tense in Hebrew. וַיְהִי sets the tense as past for the following infinitive construct and narrative; וְהָיָה sets the tense as future for the following infinitive construct and narrative.

[7] The first Vav-consecutive form in this construction is neatly translated "then" or "that."

2. Future

וְהָיָה בִּזְכֹּר (or כִּזְכֹּר) הַמֶּ֫לֶךְ אֶת־סֵפֶר־יהוה וְכָתַב לָעָם מִצְוָה וְשָׁפַט אֶת־הָעָם
וְשָׁמַר אֶת־דְּבַר־יהוה׃

Literally: And it will be in (or as) the remembering of the king the book of the Lord and (then) he will write to the people a commandment, and (then) he will judge the people, and (then) he will keep the word of the Lord.

Translation: (And it will be) When the king will remember the book of the Lord then he will write to the people a commandment, and (then) he will judge the people, and (then) he will keep the word of the Lord.

20.5. The Vav-Consecutive with כִּי

For the past tense, Hebrew also frequently begins a sentence with וַיְהִי, followed by כִּי and a perfect verb, continued by a Vav with the imperfect (Vayyiqtōl). For the future tense, Hebrew begins the sentence with וְהָיָה, followed by כִּי and an imperfect verb, continued by Vav with the perfect (Vᵊqātaltî). These are also temporal clauses.

1. Past

וַיְהִי כִּי זָכַר הַמֶּ֫לֶךְ אֶת־סֵפֶר־יהוה וַיִּכְתֹּב לָעָם מִצְוָה וַיִּשְׁפֹּט אֶת־הָעָם וַיִּשְׁמֹר
אֶת־דְּבַר־יהוה׃

Literally: And it was when the king remembered the book of the Lord and (then) he wrote... etc.

Translation: (And it was) When the king remembered the book of the Lord that he wrote... etc.

2. Future

וְהָיָה כִּי יִזְכֹּר הַמֶּ֫לֶךְ אֶת־סֵפֶר־יהוה וְכָתַב לָעָם מִצְוָה וְשָׁפַט אֶת־הָעָם וְשָׁמַר
אֶת־דְּבַר־יהוה׃

Literally: And it will be when the king will remember the book of the Lord and (then) he will write... etc.

Translation: (And it will be) When the king will remember the book of the Lord that he will write... etc.

20.6. Hebrew Syntax: Accents – Revia, Tifḥa

Revia and Tifḥa group and separate words in a sentence. In general, they do not divide or separate words as strongly as the Segolta or Zaqef (Qaton or Gadol).

1. Revia: The Revia, a diamond-shaped accent mark that separates or disjoins words, marks the accented syllable. (The following boxes represents words, not root letters.)

   :□□□ □̇□ □□ □□□ □̇□

2. Tifḥa: Also marking the accented syllable of a word, the Tifḥa (□) occurs one or (at the most) two words before both Silluq and Athnaḥ. (The following boxes represents words, not root letters.)

   :□ □□ □□ □□ □□□

EXERCISE TWENTY

I. Questions

1. Discuss the forms of the Vav-consecutives for past and future time.
2. Discuss the meaning of the Vav-consecutives for past and future time.
3. Discuss the Vav-consecutive with the infinitive construct. How does הָיָה influence the infinitive construct?
4. How should a Vav-consecutive attached to a perfect be translated?
5. How should a Vav-consecutive attached to an imperfect be translated?
6. Discuss the Vav-consecutive with כִּי.
7. Can the Vav-consecutive begin narratives and books?
8. Describe the Revia and Tifḥa. Where does the Tifḥa occur?

II. Vocabulary

מִשְׁפָּחָה	family, clan	וַיְהִי	and he (it) was (sg.)
פַּחַד (*a*)	trembling, terror	וַיִּהְיוּ	and they were (pl.)
אוֹיֵב	(participle) enemy	וְהָיָה	and he (it) will be
יִרְאָה	fear	וְהָיוּ	and they will be
רוּחַ	spirit, wind	מָשִׁיחַ	anointed one, Messiah
בְּרָכָה	blessing	זעק	cry out
יֶתֶר (*i*)	remainder, the rest	קרע	tear up, tear away
שֹׁפֵט	(participle) a judge	בֶּגֶד (*i*)	garment

III. Drills

1. Word Breakdown: In the following order: label every Dagesh Forte and Lene, Mappiq; vocal and silent shewa; Qameṣ and Qameṣ-Ḥatuf. Next, divide syllables labeling them open or closed. Then pronounce the words.

   תְּקַדְּשִׁי   תְּצַוּוּ   וַתִּשֶּׂאנָה   כְּדָרְלָעֹמֶר

2. Attach the following particles and translate all vocabulary words.
   Article

   קָצִיר   הָגִיג   עֶבֶד

   Preposition ב

   חֲמוֹר   כֶּסֶף   הַמִּדְבָּר

   Preposition מִן

   הָעָם   כֶּסֶף   חֲמוֹר

3. Attach the boxes and translate all vocabulary words. List all steps.
   1. mp construct עָמָל
   2. mp absolute קֹדֶשׁ (*o*)
   3. fp construct תְּהִלָּה

4. Attach the boxes with suffixes and translate all vocabulary words. List all steps.

Singular Nouns			Plural Nouns		
1.	1cs	עַתּוּד	4.	1cp	שֹׁרֶשׁ (*o*)
2.	2fs	שִׂמְלָה	5.	3ms	שְׂבָכָה
3.	2fp	נַעַר (*a*)	6.	3mp	יֶלֶד (*a*)

5. Attach the suffixes to the prepositions and translate.

1.	3fs	תַּחַת	3.	1cp	מִן
2.	2fs	לְפָנִים	4.	1cs	כ

6. Write and recite orally the Qal perfect, imperfect, imperative (5), cohortatives, and jussive 3ms, 3fs, participles: active (5) and passive (4), infinitive absolute and construct, Vav-consecutive with imperfect and with perfect 3ms of the root כתב.

7. Translation

1. וְיֶתֶר דִּבְרֵי שְׁלֹמֹה וְכָל־אֲשֶׁר עָשָׂה וְהֵיכָלוֹ אֲשֶׁר בָּנָה וְהַכִּסֵּא אֲשֶׁר־עָשָׂה
הֲלֹא הֵם כְּתוּבִים עַל־סֵפֶר לְמַלְכֵי יִשְׂרָאֵל׃

2. וַיְהִי כִּשְׁמֹעַ דָּוִד אֶת־דִּבְרֵי־הַמַּלְאָכִים וַיִּרְדֹּף אֶת־הָאֲנָשִׁים הַפֹּשְׁעִים בּוֹ
אֶל־הָעִיר׃

3. וַיְהִי אַחֲרֵי־כְתֹב מֹשֶׁה אֶת־הַתּוֹרָה וַיִּקְרַב הָעָם אֶל־הַיַּרְדֵּן וּמֹשֶׁה לֹא עָבַר
אֶת־הַיַּרְדֵּן וַיִּשְׁפְּטוּ הַשֹּׁפְטִים אֶת־יִשְׂרָאֵל יָמִים רַבִּים׃

4. אָמַר יְהוָה אִם שָׁמֹעַ תִּשְׁמְעוּ בְּקֹל־עֲבָדַי הַנְּבִיאִים וְקָבַצְתִּי אֶתְכֶם מֵהַגּוֹיִם
וְשָׁלַחְתִּי עֲלֵיכֶם בִּרְכָתִי וְשָׁמַרְתִּי אֶתְכֶם מִכָּל־רָע׃

5. וַיְהִי כִּי קָרְאוּ בְנֵי־יִשְׂרָאֵל אֶל־יְהוָה וַיִּשְׁמְעוּ פְלִשְׁתִּים אֶת־הַדָּבָר
וַיִּבְרְחוּ אֶל־אַרְצָם וְלֹא עָשׂוּ מִלְחָמָה בְּיִשְׂרָאֵל עוֹד׃

6. דִּבֶּר הַנָּבִיא כֹּה אָמַר יְהוָה אֱלֹהֵי יִשְׂרָאֵל קִרְעוּ לְבַבְכֶם וְאַל בִּגְדֵיכֶם
זִכְרוּ אֶת־יְהוָה וְאַל־אֱלֹהִים אֲחֵרִים׃

7. וְהָיָה כִּי־תִקְרְאוּ אֵלַי וְשָׁמַעְתִּי מִשָּׁמַיִם וְשָׁכַחְתִּי אֶת־חַטַּאתְכֶם וְרָדַפְתִּי
אֶת־שְׁלוֹמְכֶם׃

CHAPTER 21
THE STATIVE VERB
THE PERFECT: ADDITIONAL TENSE OPTIONS

21.1. Introduction

The stative verb[1] is a conjugated adjective, an adjective converted into a verb: כבד "to be heavy," גדל "to be great," קטן "to be small."

21.2. Thematic Vowels

The thematic vowel (18.2.1), the vowel appearing under the second root letter (R_2) of a verb (or verbal), varies. The following observations are general; exceptions occur because of the "weakness" (29.1) of the verb. The thematic vowels are more easily learned and discussed if viewed as colors.

Colors: A (Pataḥ) = red; E (Ṣere, Ḥireq in a closed unaccented syllables) or Î (Ḥireq-Yod) = green; O (Ḥolem, Qameṣ-Ḥatuf in a closed unaccented syllable) = orange

QAL	
Standard	**Stative**
A/Ō כתב	Ē/A מלא
A/Ē נתן	A-ē/A כבד
A/A שלח	A/A גדל
	Ō/A קטן

1. The letter before the slash (/) is the thematic vowel for the perfect; the letter after the slash is the thematic vowel for the imperfect-imperative: perfect/imperfect-imperative.

2. In the perfect, the smaller case letter refers to the 3ms form (and the pausal 3ms, 3cp and 3fs forms).

3. The standard verbs must have a red vowel (A) in the perfect; the stative verbs must have a red vowel (A) in the imperfect-imperative.

4. Notice the stative perfect evolves from all green (Ē), to slightly green/mostly red (A-ē), to all red (A) (analogy to the standard Qal).

5. In the Qal, the thematic vowels for particular verbs must be learned by observation.

[1] The non-stative verbs, chapters 17-20, are designated standard verbs. Biblical Hebrew does not strictly separate stative and standard verbs: some stative verbs have become standard verbs in form and meaning; some standard verbs have become stative verbs in meaning.

21.3. Stative Verbs: Perfect

	כבד A-ē/	קטן Ō/
1cs	כָּבַ֫דְתִּי	קָטֹ֫נְתִּי
2ms	כָּבַ֫דְתָּ	קָטֹ֫נְתָּ
2fs	כָּבַדְתְּ	קָטֹנְתְּ
3ms	כָּבֵד	קָטֹן
3fs	כָּבְדָה	קָטְנָה
1cp	כָּבַ֫דְנוּ	קָטֹ֫נּוּ
2mp	כְּבַדְתֶּם	קְטָנְתֶּם
2fp	כְּבַדְתֶּן	קְטָנְתֶּן
3cp	כָּבְדוּ	קָטְנוּ

1. כבד: The stative perfect of כבד is identical to the standard verb (for example, קטל), except the 3ms has a Ṣere thematic vowel (21.2.2).

2. קטן: This verb has a Ḥolem for the thematic vowel (or Qameṣ-Ḥatuf in the closed unaccented syllables in the 2mp, 2fp). In the 1cp form, קָטֹ֫נּוּ contracts from קָטֹ֫נְנוּ.

21.4. Stative Verb: Imperfect

	כבד /A	קטן /A
1cs	אֶכְבַּד	אֶקְטַן
2ms	תִּכְבַּד	תִּקְטַן
2fs	תִּכְבְּדִי	תִּקְטְנִי
3ms	יִכְבַּד	יִקְטַן
3fs	תִּכְבַּד	תִּקְטַן
1cp	נִכְבַּד	נִקְטַן
2mp	תִּכְבְּדוּ	תִּקְטְנוּ
2fp	תִּכְבַּ֫דְנָה	תִּקְטַ֫נָּה
3mp	יִכְבְּדוּ	יִקְטְנוּ
3fp	תִּכְבַּ֫דְנָה	תִּקְטַ֫נָּה

Cohortative 1cs	אֶכְבְּדָה	אֶקְטְנָה
Jussive 3ms	יִכְבַּד	יִקְטַן
Imperfect with Vav-consecutive	וַיִּכְבַּד	וַיִּקְטַן

Stative verbs have a Pataḥ for the thematic vowel in the imperfect. For the imperfect 2fp, 3fp of קטן, the Nun of the suffix assimilates to the Nun of the root – *תִּקְטַנְנָה » תִּקְטַנָּה.

21.5. Stative Verb: Imperative

	כבד /A	קטן /A
2ms	כְּבַד	קְטַן
2fs	כִּבְדִי	קִטְנִי
2mp	כִּבְדוּ	קִטְנוּ
2fp	כְּבַדְנָה	קְטַנָּה
Emphatic	כָּבְדָה	

Stative verbs have a Pataḥ for the thematic vowel in the imperative. קְטַנָּה (2fp) contracts from *קְטַנְנָה.

21.6. Stative Verb: Active Participle

	Absolute	Construct	Absolute	Construct
ms	כָּבֵד	כְּבֵד	קָטֹן	קְטֹן
fs	כְּבֵדָה	כְּבֵדַת	קְטַנָּה	קְטַנַּת
mp	כְּבֵדִים	כְּבֵדֵי	קְטַנִּים	קְטַנֵּי
fp	כְּבֵדוֹת	כְּבֵדוֹת	קְטַנּוֹת	קְטַנּוֹת

Participles of the stative verbs are verbal adjectives. These follow noun reduction patterns (6.3), not verbal reduction patterns of the participles of standard verbs (19.2.1). *The active participle masculine singular is always identical to the stative perfect 3ms.* Notice in the construct forms, the Ṣere or Ḥolem thematic vowels – even in construct – do not reduce.

21.7. Stative Verb: Infinitives

Absolute	Construct
כָּבוֹד	כְּבַד
קָטוֹן	קְטַן

21.8. The Perfect: Additional Tense Options

The perfect, a past tense, can also be translated as a present tense. This is especially common with:

1. Stative verbs – כָּבֵד he is heavy, אָהֵב he loves, שָׂנֵא he hates
2. Standard verbs that express a state of mind – זָכַר he remembers, בָּטַח he trusts, יָדַע he knows

Translate these verbs, both stative and standard, with the past tense if the context requires it.

Exercise Twenty-One

I. Questions

1. Define a stative verb. Compare and contrast stative verbs to standard verbs in form and in meaning.
2. Give the colors for the following thematic vowels: A, Ē, Î, Ō.
3. In the perfect of the standard verb, what is the thematic vowel? In the imperfect of the stative verbs, what is the thematic vowel?
4. What does the slash (/) indicate?
5. List all possible thematic vowels for the perfect/imperfect-imperative.
6. What does a smaller case letter in A-ē/A indicate?
7. How does the stative perfect differ from the standard perfect in כבד and in קטן?
8. How does the stative participle differ from the standard active participle? Which form of the participle and of the perfect are always identical in the stative verb?
9. Discuss when the perfect may be translated as a present tense.

II. Vocabulary

גדל	(A/A) be (become) great, mature, strong	צָרָה	distress
		אָהֵב, אָהַב	(A/A or A-ē/A) to love
עֹז	(with suffix עֻזִּי) strength, might, power	שׁכן	dwell, settle
		כְּלִי	vessel, weapon
מָוֶת	(construct מוֹת, see footnote 11-5) death	בַּעַל	owner, lord, Baal
		כָּבֵד	(A-ē/A) to be heavy
מוֹאָב	Moab	זָקֵן	(A-ē/A) to be old
מָגֵן	shield	קבר	bury

III. Drills

1. Word Breakdown: In the following order: label every Dagesh Forte and Lene, Mappiq; vocal and silent shewa; Qameṣ and Qameṣ-Ḥatuf. Next, divide syllables labeling them open or closed. Then pronounce the words.

   מִגְדָּלֶיהָ　　　עֲנִיֵּי　　　וַיִּטְּשֵׁהוּ　　　וְרָדְפֵהוּ

2. Attach the following particles and translate all vocabulary words.
   Interrogative מה

   רָשָׁע　　　יְגוֹן　　　עִוֵּר

Conjunctive ו

בַּבַּ֫יִת   עֳנִי   עָרִיץ

Interrogative ה

רָשָׁף   עֲלִיל   סֶ֫מֶל

3. Attach the boxes and translate all vocabulary words. List all steps.
   1. mp construct צַדִּיק
   2. mp absolute נַ֫עַר (*a*)
   3. fp construct אֲדָמָה

4. Attach the boxes with suffixes and translate all vocabulary words. List all steps.

   Singular Nouns
   1. 3ms הַוָּה
   2. 2fp מֶ֫לֶךְ (*a*)

   Plural Nouns
   3. 1cs אֲנָפָה
   4. 3mp קֹ֫דֶשׁ (*o*)

5. Attach the suffixes to the prepositions and translate.
   1. 1cs אֵל
   2. 2ms תַּ֫חַת
   3. 1cp כְּ
   4. 2fs עִם

6. Write and recite orally the Qal perfect, imperfect, imperative, cohortatives, and jussive 3mp, 3fp, participles and the infinitives of the root זָקֵן (A-ē/A).

7. Translation

1. וּשְׁמוּאֵל הָיָה נַעַר וַיִּגְדַּל וַיִּקְרַב אֶל־הַהֵיכָל לִזְבֹּחַ זָבַח׃

2. אַחַר הַדְּבָרִים הָאֵלֶּה הָיָה דְבַר־יהוה אֶל־אַבְרָהָם לֵאמֹר מָגֵן לְךָ אָנֹכִי
וְהַר עֹז לָךְ[2]׃

3. אָמַר אֵלִיָּהוּ הַנָּבִיא קִבְצוּ אֶת־כָּל־יִשְׂרָאֵל הָהָרָה וְקָרְאוּ נְבִיאֵי הַבַּעַל
בְּשֵׁם־אֱלֹהֵיהֶם וַאֲנִי אֶקְרָא בְּשֵׁם יְהוָה אֱלֹהֵי־יִשְׂרָאֵל׃

4. וַיְהִי אַחֲרֵי מוֹת־מֹשֶׁה עֶבֶד־יְהוָה וַיִּקְבְּרוּ בְנֵי־יִשְׂרָאֵל אֹתוֹ בְּהָרֵי מוֹאָב
וְלֹא יָדַע אִישׁ אֶת־הַמָּקוֹם הַהוּא עַד־הַיּוֹם הַזֶּה׃

5. בָּא יוֹם יהוה יוֹם חֹשֶׁךְ וְצָרָה וַיהוה שֹׁפֵט אֶת־הָרְשָׁעִים וְהוּא הֹרֵג
אֶת־הַפֹּשְׁעִים׃

---

[2] Pausal form of לְךָ.

6. עָשָׂה מוֹאָב מִלְחָמָה אֶת־יִשְׂרָאֵל וַיִּבְרַח יִשְׂרָאֵל מִפְּנֵי־מוֹאָב וַיִּשְׁלַח יִשְׂרָאֵל
מַלְאָכִים אֶל־מֶלֶךְ־מוֹאָב לִכְרֹת עִמּוֹ בְּרִית־שָׁלוֹם׃

7. וַיְהִי כִּמְלֹךְ דָּוִד עַל־כָּל־יִשְׂרָאֵל וַיִּפְשַׁע אַבְשָׁלוֹם בְּאָבִיו וְרַע בְּעֵינֵי־כָל־הָעָם
הוּא׃

8. מָשְׁלוּ פְּלִשְׁתִּים בְּיִשְׂרָאֵל וַיִּשְׁכֹּן הָעָם בָּאֳהָלִים וּבֶהָרִים וְאֵין חֶרֶב וּכְלִי לָהֶם׃

CHAPTER 22
OVERVIEW OF THE STRONG VERB

22.1. Introduction

A "weak verb" is a verb with a weak letter: Vav, Yod, Nun or a guttural letter. A strong verb is a verb (with three letters) without a weak letter. So far, only the Qal of the strong verb has been presented. Now, the rest of the strong verb, the so-called derived stems[1] (Pi"ēl, Pu"al, Hithpa"ēl, Hiph'îl, Hoph'al, and Niph'al), will be surveyed.

22.2. Derived Stems: The Names of the Stems

The names of the derived stems are formed from the root פעל. Memorize the spelling of the following words, especially the English transliterations: these derived stems are essential for mastering the strong verb.

פִּעֵּל[2]	Pi"ēl	הִפְעִיל	Hiph'îl
פֻּעַל	Pu"al	הָפְעַל	Hoph'al
הִתְפַּעֵּל	Hithpa"ēl	נִפְעַל	Niph'al

In the word Pi"ēl, the "P" represents the first root letter of the word (R_1); the "i," the vowel under the first letter; the """," the doubled second root letter (R_2); the "e," the thematic vowel under the second root letter; the "l," the third root letter (R_3).

22.3. Derived Stems: Characteristics – Boxes

	Pi"ēl (Pa"ēl)	Pu"al	Hithpa"ēl
Perfect	□⊡□	□⊡□	הִתְ□⊡□
Imperfect	יְ□⊡□	יְ□⊡□	יִתְ□⊡□
Imperative	□⊡□		הִתְ□⊡□
Infinitive	□⊡□		הִתְ□⊡□
Participle	מְ□⊡□	מְ□⊡□	מִתְ□⊡□

	Hiph'îl (Haph'îl)	Hoph'al	Niph'al
Perfect	הִ□□□	הָ□□□	נִ□□□
Imperfect	יַ□□□	יָ□□□	יִ□⊡□
Imperative	הַ□□□		הִ□⊡□
Infinitive	הַ□□□		הִ□⊡□/נִ□□□
Participle	מַ□□□	מָ□□□	נִ□□□

---

[1] So-called because they seem to be derived from the Qal.

[2] The Dagesh Forte in the Ayin is hypothetical.

Memorize these boxes by properly spelling the name of the stem. The names of the stems virtually supply the boxes.

1. The Pi"ēl, Pu"al, and Hithpa"ēl: The Dagesh Forte in the second root letter and the preceding short vowel under the first root letter (a closed unaccented syllable) characterizes these stems.
    1. The stem name Pi"ēl aids only in the perfect: outside the perfect, the Pi"ēl is actually a Pa"ēl – a Pataḥ (not a Ḥireq) precedes the Dagesh Forte of the second root letter. The 1cs preformative (Alef) of the imperfect takes a Ḥatef-Pataḥ.

    2. Pu"al: A Qibbuṣ under the first root letter precedes the Dagesh Forte of the second root letter. The 1cs preformative (Alef) of the imperfect takes a Ḥatef-Pataḥ.

    3. Hithpa"ēl: A Pataḥ under the first root letter precedes the Dagesh Forte of the second root letter. The preformative syllable הִתְ (יִתְ in the imperfect, מִתְ in the participle) precedes the verbal root.

2. The Hiph'îl and Hoph'al: The preformative ה attached to the verbal root[3] characterizes these stems.
    1. Hiph'îl: The stem name aids only in the perfect. The preformative ה has a Ḥireq under it, and the first root letter has a silent shewa. Except for the perfect, the Hiph'îl is actually a Haph'îl. The preformative letter ה has a Pataḥ under it, and the first root letter has a silent shewa. In the imperfect and participle, the preformative (אֵיתָן for the imperfect, מ for the participle) supplants the ה of the Haph'îl (Hiph'îl).

    2. Hoph'al: In the perfect, the preformative ה has a Qameṣ-Ḥatuf followed by a silent shewa under the first root letter. In the imperfect and participle, the preformative (אֵיתָן for the imperfect; מ for the participle) supplants the ה of the Hoph'al.

3. Niph'al: The preformative נ attached to the verbal root characterizes the Niph'al. In the perfect, the participle, and one option of the infinitive absolute, the preformative נ has a Ḥireq under it, with a following silent shewa under the first root letter. In the imperfect, the preformative (אֵיתָן) has a Ḥireq under it; in the imperative and the infinitive construct and one option of the infinitive absolute, the

[3] In the imperfect and participle, the ה between vowels drops: *יְהַקְטִיל » יַקְטִיל, *מְהַקְטִיל » מַקְטִיל (see footnote 8-4).

preformative ה has a Ḥireq under it. The imperfect, imperative, infinitive construct and one option of the infinitive absolute have a Dagesh Forte in the first root letter (R_1, the assimilated נ of the Niph'al) and a Qameṣ under it.

22.4. Thematic Vowels (Perfect/Imperfect-Imperative) of the Derived Stems

Derived Conjugations			
Active	(Qal)	Pi"ēl A-ē/Ē	Hiph'îl A-î/Î-ē
Passive		Pu"al A/A	Hoph'al A/A
Reflexive	Niph'al A/Ē-a	Hithpa"ēl A-ē/Ē-a	

1. The letter before the slash (/) is the thematic vowel for the perfect; the letter after the slash is the thematic vowel for the imperfect-imperative: perfect/imperfect-imperative.

2. In the perfect, the smaller case letter refers to the 3ms form (also 3fs and 3cp in the Hiph'îl); in the imperfect-imperative, the smaller case letter refers to the 2fp and 3fp forms.

3. "A" stands for Pataḥ (red, rarely Qameṣ); "Ē" for Ṣere (green); "Î" for Ḥireq-Yod (green).

4. The Active and Reflexive
   1. The perfect is predominately red.
      Exceptions: 3ms is green in Pi"ēl and Hithpa"ēl; 3ms, 3fs, 3cp (the threes) are green in Hiph'îl.
   2. The imperfects-imperatives are green in the active (the imperfects-imperatives of the Hiph'îl are /Î-ē) and predominately green in the reflexive.
      There are exceptions in the reflexive: 2fp, 3fp are red.

5. The passive is all red A/A (Communist).

6. *If the details are forgotten, remember A/Ē for all stems except the Pu"al, Hoph'al A/A. Memorize A/Ē for the chart: Pi"ēl has a little green (3ms) in the perfect; Niph'al has a little red (2, 3fp) in the imperfect-imperative; Hithpa"ēl is the most colorful A-ē/Ē-a; Hiph'îl has the Ḥireq-Yod A-î/Î-ē; the Pu"al and Hoph'al are Communists (all red) A/A.*

22.5. Thematic Vowels of Infinitives and Participles

1. Infinitives (Exclude the Pu“al and Hoph‘al because they are rare.)
    1. Infinitive Absolute
        1. Orange: Niph‘al, Pi“ēl (!)
        2. Green: Pi“ēl, Hiph‘îl (□ֵ), Hithpa“ēl

        The orange forms probably reflect ā » ō. These vowels generally follow the final vowel of the derived stem names: Hithpa“ēl, the final vowel “e” is green; Niph‘al, the final vowel “a” (ā » ō), reflects orange. The Pi“ēl form is exceptional.

        Exceptions: The Pi“ēl can be either orange or green; the Hiph‘îl has a Ṣere.
    2. Infinitive Construct

        Green: Pi“ēl, Hiph‘îl (□ִי), Hithpa“ēl, Niph‘al

2. Participles
    1. Green: Pi“ēl, Hiph‘îl (□ִי), Hithpa“ēl (pretonic reduction except for the historic long Ḥireq-Yod of the Hiph‘îl)
    2. Red: Pu“al, Hoph‘al, Niph‘al (irreducible Qameṣ)

    These vowels follow the final vowel of the derived stem names: for example, Pi“ēl, the final vowel “e,” is green; Hoph‘al, the final vowel “ā,” is *irreducible* Qameṣ.

22.6. Synopsis of the Strong Verbs: Derived Stems

	Pi“ēl (Pa“ēl) A-ē^3ms^/Ē	**Pu“al** A/A	**Hithpa“ēl** A-ē^3ms^/Ē-a^2fp, 3fp^
Perfect	□▣□	□▣□	הִתְ□▣□
Imperfect	יְ□▣□	יְ□▣□	יִתְ□▣□
Imperative	□▣□		הִתְ□▣□
Infinitive	□▣□		הִתְ□▣□
Participle	מְ□▣□	מְ□▣□	מִתְ□▣□

	Hiph‘îl (Haph‘îl) A-î^3ms, 3fs, 3cp^/Î-ē^2fp, 3fp^ No Vowel Reduction	**Hoph‘al** A/A	**Niph‘al** A/Ē-a^2fp, 3fp^
Perfect	הִ□□□	הָ□□□	נִ□□□
Imperfect	יַ□□□	יָ□□□	יִ▣□□
Imperative	הַ□□□		הִ▣□□
Infinitive	הַ□□□		נִ□□□/הִ▣□□
Participle	מַ□□□	מָ□□□	נִ□□□

In the imperfect, the Yod (י) stands for all imperfect preformatives (אֵיתָן)

1. Infinitives:
   1. Infinitive Absolute
      1. Orange: Niph‘al, Pi“ēl (!)
      2. Green: Pi“ēl, Hiph‘îl (□ֵ), Hithpa“ēl

   2. Infinitive Construct
      Green: Pi“ēl, Hiph‘îl (□ִי), Hithpa“ēl, Niph‘al (!)

2. Participles
   1. Green (pretonic reduction): Pi“ēl, Hithpa“ēl, Hiph‘îl (□ִי)

   2. Red (irreducible Qameṣ): Pu“al, Hoph‘al, Niph‘al

Exercise Twenty-Two

I. Questions

1. Define strong verb and weak verb. What are the “weak” letters?
2. List the derived stems (spell them properly).
3. What two derived stems have a variant name? What are the variant names?
4. How should the boxes of the derived stems be memorized?
5. What is the characteristic of Pi“ēl, Pu“al, Hithpa“ēl? Hiph‘îl, Hoph‘al? Niph‘al?
6. When does the He drop in the Hiph‘îl and Hoph‘al?
7. When does the Nun assimilate in the Niph‘al?
8. If the details of the thematic vowels are forgotten, what thematic vowel pattern should be remembered?
9. How are the thematic vowels of the infinitive and participles memorized?

II. Vocabulary

יְשׁוּעָה	salvation	סָבִיב	all around, all about, surrounding
מכר	sell	שָׂפָה	lip, shore
ילד	bear a child	עֹלָה	burnt offering
שִׂמְחָה	rejoicing, joy	אֶבֶן (*a*)	(f) stone
יִרְמְיָה, יִרְמְיָהוּ	Jeremiah	נֶפֶשׁ (*a*)	soul, life
לָשׁוֹן	tongue, language	בֵּית לֶחֶם	Bethlehem
אֲרוֹן	(with article הָאָרוֹן) ark, chest	אֱדוֹם	Edom

III. Drills

1. Word Breakdown: In the following order: label every Dagesh Forte and Lene, Mappiq; vocal and silent shewa; Qames and Qames-Hatuf. Next, divide syllables labeling them open or closed. Then pronounce the words.

   עָיְפָה　　הַשְׁבִּית　　מְלוֹאָהּ　　יְשָׁדְדֵם

2. Attach the following particles and translate all vocabulary words
   Article

   הָרָה　　יְלָלָה　　עָב

   Preposition לְ

   אֱלֹהִים　　מְבוּכָה　　שֶׁבֶת

3. Attach the boxes and translate all vocabulary words. List all steps
   1. fp construct　מִלְחָמָה
   2. dual construct　אֹזֶן (*o*)
   3. fs construct　תְּפִלָּה

4. Attach the boxes with suffixes and translate all vocabulary words. List all steps

   Singular Nouns
   1. 2ms　קֹדֶשׁ (*o*)
   2. 1cs　צְדָקָה

   Plural Nouns
   3. 2fs　חֶרֶב (*a*)
   4. 1cs　חָכָם

5. Attach the suffixes to the prepositions and translate
   1. 1cp　עַל
   2. 1cs　לְמַעַן
   3. 3ms　אֵת (direct object)
   4. 2ms　לְפָנִים

6. Write and recite orally the Qal perfect, imperfect, imperative (5), cohortatives, and jussive 3ms, 3fs, participles, infinitives, Vav-consecutive with imperfect 3ms and with perfect 3ms of the root קטן (Ō/A).

7. Write out the boxes for the derived stems and the thematic vowels for the derived stems, including the thematic vowels for the infinitives and the participles.

8. Translation

1. עָשָׂה יִשְׂרָאֵל אֶת־הָרַע בְּעֵינֵי־יְהוָה וַיִּמְכֹּר יהוה אֹתָם בְּיַד־אֹיְבֵיהֶם מִסָּבִיב
וַתִּכְבַּד מְאֹד יַד־יְהוָה עֲלֵיהֶם׃

2. הַדָּבָר אֲשֶׁר הָיָה אֶל־הַנָּבִיא מֵאֵת יְהוָה לֵאמֹר בְּשַׁעַר בֵּית יהוה תִּקְרָא
אֶת־הַדָּבָר הַזֶּה וְאָמַרְתָּ שִׁמְעוּ דְבַר־יהוה כָּל־הַהֹלְכִים אֶל־הַשְּׁעָרִים הָאֵלֶּה׃

3. וַיְהִי אֲרוֹן יְהוָה בְּאֶרֶץ־פְּלִשְׁתִּים וַיִּקְרְאוּ פְלִשְׁתִּים לַכֹּהֲנִים עָזְבוּ אֶת־הָאָרוֹן
אֲשֶׁר לָקַחְנוּ׃

4. זֶה סֵפֶר הַתּוֹרָה אֲשֶׁר נָתַן מֹשֶׁה לִבְנֵי־יִשְׂרָאֵל נִשְׁמְרָה אֶת־הַתּוֹרוֹת הָאֵלֶּה
וּמִצְוֹתָיו נִשְׁמָעָה׃

5. הֶאָמוֹר אָמַר הַנָּבִיא לָכֶם כִּי בָא יוֹם מִשְׁפָּט הֲלֹא אָמַרְתִּי לָכֶם כִּי דִבְרֵי
שֶׁקֶר הֵמָּה׃

6. וַיְהִי בַּיָּמִים הָהֵם וַיִּגְדַּל מֹשֶׁה וַיִּשְׁכֹּן בְּמִצְרַיִם וַיִּקְרָא לְעַבְדֵי פַרְעֹה לֵאמֹר
בֶּן־מִי אֲנִי וְהֵמָּה לֹא אָמְרוּ לוֹ דָבָר׃

7. כָּתַב הַנָּבִיא אֶת־הַדְּבָרִים הָאֵלֶּה עַל־הָאֲבָנִים הַגְּדוֹלוֹת אֶשְׂמַח בַּיהוָה כִּי נָתַן
לְעַמּוֹ יְשׁוּעָה׃

CHAPTER 23
THE INTENSIVES: PI"ĒL, PU"AL, HITHPA"ĒL

23.1. This chapter (and the next two chapters), building upon chapter 22, focuses on the forming, parsing, and meaning of the intensive stems – Pi"ēl, Pu"al, Hithpa"ēl.

23.2. Forming the Intensive Stems – Pi"ēl, Pu"al, Hithpa"ēl

To form the intensive stems properly, follow a three step process:

1. Memorize the boxes by spelling the stems properly (22.2 and 22.3).[1]

	Pi"ēl (Pa"ēl)	Pu"al	Hithpa"ēl
Perfect	□▣□	□▣□	□▣□הִתְ
Imperfect	□▣□יְ	□▣□יְ	□▣□יִתְ
Imperative	□▣□		□▣□הִתְ
Infinitive	□▣□		□▣□הִתְ
Participle	□▣□מְ	□▣□מְ	□▣□מִתְ

Remember: the 1cs preformative (Alef) of the imperfect takes a Ḥatef-Pataḥ in the Pi"ēl and Pu"al.

2. Memorize the thematic vowels.

	Pi"ēl	Pu"al	Hithpa"ēl
Perfect/Imperfect-Imperative	A-ē/Ē	A/A	A-ē/Ē-a
Infinitive Absolute	Ē or Ō	–	Ē
Infinitive Construct	Ē	–	Ē
Participle	Ē	A	Ē

3. Know the Qal stem thoroughly: especially, the preformative and sufformative elements on the root.[2]

23.3. Examples of Forming Intensive Stems

1. Pi"ēl perfect 1cs שׁבר
   1. Boxes: □▣□ (Pi"ēl) שִׁבר
   2. Colors: A-ē/Ē שִׁבֵּר
   3. Qal stem: שָׁבַרְתִּי שִׁבַּרְתִּי

      Answer: שִׁבַּרְתִּי

[1] The Dagesh Forte may be omitted in the letters ס, צ, שׂ, שׁ, ל, מ, נ, ק, ו, י with a vocal shewa (footnote 4-5).

[2] Elements within the Qal verbal root are unnecessary for forming the intensive stems.

1. Step one derives the boxes from the stem name Pi"ēl: Dagesh Forte in the second root letter, Ḥireq under the first root letter.
2. Step two adds the thematic vowel (Pataḥ) and implies the silent shewa.
3. Step three adds the 1cs pronominal suffix of the perfect as memorized in the Qal. The syllabic ending makes explicit the implicit silent shewa.

2. Pu"al imperfect 1cs שׁבר

1.	Boxes:	□▣□יְ (Pu"al)	יְשֻׁבּר
2.	Colors:	A/A	יְשֻׁבַּר
3.	Qal stem:	אֶשְׁבֹּר	אֲשֻׁבַּר
	Answer:		אֲשֻׁבַּר

1. Step one derives the boxes from the stem name Pu"al: Dagesh Forte in the second root letter, a Qibbuṣ under the first root letter, and a Yod, representing all the imperfect preformatives, with a vocal shewa (because in the open pro-pretonic position).
2. Step two adds the thematic vowel (Pataḥ).
3. Step three adds the 1cs preformative of the Qal imperfect (א). The 1cs preformative (Alef) of the imperfect takes a Ḥatef-Pataḥ.

3. Hithpa"ēl participle ms שׁבר

1.	Boxes:	□▣□מִתְ (Hithpa"ēl)	מִתְשַׁבּר » מִשְׁתַּבּר[3]
2.	Colors:	Green	מִשְׁתַּבֵּר
3.	Qal stem:	שֹׁבֵר	______
	Answer:		מִשְׁתַּבֵּר

1. Step one derives the boxes from the stem name Hithpa"ēl: Dagesh Forte in the second root letter, a Pataḥ under the first root letter, and the הִתְ syllabic preformative, מִתְ in the participle.
2. Step two adds the green (Ṣere) thematic vowel.
3. Step three adds nothing because there are no preformative or sufformative elements from the Qal.

23.4. Parsing the Intensive Stems

Parsing is a process of elimination. Try to eliminate possibilities with each step.

---

[3] Note the transposition of שׁ and ת. Adjust the boxes of the Hithpa"ēl with verbs beginning with certain letters: with the sibilants ס, שׂ, שׁ, the reflexive ת of the prefix הת transposes with the sibilant: *הִתְשַׁמֵּר » הִשְׁתַּמֵּר. With the sibilant צ, the ת transposes, and the ת partially assimilates to a ט: *הִתְצַדֵּק » *הִצְתַּדֵּק » הִצְטַדֵּק. With the dentals ד, ט, ת, and the נ, the ת of the prefix often assimilates fully: *הִתְטַהֵר » הִטַּהֵר, *הִתְנַבֵּא » הִנַּבֵּא.

The three steps are the same as when creating the forms (23.2).

1. קַטְּלִי

1.	Boxes:	□▣□	Pi"ēl imperative, infinitive construct, absolute.
2.	Colors:	_____	Eliminates 2ms, 2fp imperative and infinitives
3.	Qal stem:	קַטְּלִי	Eliminates all forms except imperative 2fs
	Answer:	Pi"ēl imperative 2fs of קטל	

1. Step one identifies the boxes: Pi"ēl imperative, infinitive absolute, or construct, which eliminates all other possbilities.
2. Step two eliminates the imperative 2ms, 2fp and infinitives forms because they do not have vocal shewa.
3. Step three is the Qal stem. The form must be an imperative because the infinitives do not end in Ḥireq-Yod. The 2fs imperative ends in Ḥireq-Yod, thus eliminating imperative 2mp.

2. קֻטַּלְתֶּן

1.	Boxes:	□▣□	Pu"al perfect
2.	Colors:	A (A/A)	Eliminates forms with vocalic endings (vocal shewa): 3fs, 3cp
3.	Qal stem:	קֻטַּלְתֶּן	Eliminates all forms except perfect 2fp
	Answer:	Pu"al perfect 2fp of קטל	

1. Step one identifies the boxes: Pu"al perfect.
2. Step two eliminates forms with vocal shewa: 3fs, 3cp.
3. Step three confirms the perfect conjugation and eliminates all forms except the perfect 2fp.

3. הִתְקַטֵּל

1.	Boxes:	□▣□הִתְ	Hithpa"ēl perfect, imperative, infinitive absolute, or infinitive construct
2.	Colors:	green (A-ē/Ē-a)	Eliminates all perfects except 3ms and all imperatives except 2ms
3.	Qal stem:		_____
	Answer:	Hithpa"ēl perfect 3ms, imperative 2ms, infinitive absolute, or infinitive construct of קטל	

1. Step one identifies all the possible boxes.
2. Step two, a green thematic vowel, eliminates all perfects except 3ms and all imperatives except 2ms.
3. Step three is without Qal preformatives or sufformatives.

23.5. The Meaning of the Intensive Stems

These stems are traditionally called intensive because the doubling of the second root letter intensifies the action in some way. The intensive stems, of course, also have other meanings.

1. Pi"ēl
    1. Intensive:

Qal	Pi"ēl
שָׁבַר to break	שִׁבֵּר to smash
צָחַק to laugh	צִחֵק to laugh to scorn, to mock

The action may also be intensified by extending the action to many objects: קטל (Qal) to kill – קִטֵּל (Pi"ēl) to kill one after another, to massacre

2. Factitive (to make)

Qal	Pi"ēl
למד to learn	to make learn (to teach)
אבד to perish, disappear	to make someone perish, disappear
קדשׁ to be holy	to make holy

Many of these verbs are statives in the Qal; the Pi"ēl puts one into the state of the Qal. For instance, כבד – Qal: to be heavy, Pi"ēl: to put in a heavy state, or to make heavy

3. Denominative[4] (from the noun)
    דִּבֵּר to speak words (from the noun דָּבָר)
    כִּהֵן (Note the implicit Dagesh Forte in the ה) to act like a priest (from the noun כֹּהֵן)

2. Pu"al: The Pu"al is the passive of the Pi"ēl.
    1. Intensive: שׁבר – Pi"ēl: to smash, Pu"al: to be smashed
    2. Factitive: קדשׁ – Pi"ēl: to make holy, Pu"al: to be made holy

3. Hithpa"ēl: The Hithpa"ēl is the passive/reflexive of the Pi"ēl
    1. Intensive: הלל – Pi"ēl: to praise, Hithpa"ēl: to be praised (passive)
    2. Factitive: קדשׁ – Pi"ēl: to make holy, Hithpa"ēl: to make oneself holy (reflexive)

---

[4] Compare the English denominative verb "to phone (someone)."

Exercise Twenty-Three

I. Questions

1. What are the intensive stems?
2. What are the three steps to form the intensive stems?
3. Describe the adjustments (transpositions) necessary for the Hithpa"ēl.
4. Describe the process of parsing.
5. What are the three steps to parse the intensive stems?
6. What are the possible meanings of the Pi"ēl, Pu"al, and Hithpa"ēl?

II. Vocabulary

אֶ֫רֶז (*a*)	cedar	גדל	Qal: be great
יָהּ	shortened form of יהוה		Pi"ēl: make great, magnify
בקשׁ	Pi"ēl: seek	דרשׁ	Qal: seek
למד	Qal: learn	יַחְדָּו	all together, together
	Pi"ēl: make learn (teach)	ספר	Qal: count
נבא	Hithpa"ēl and Niph'al: prophesy		Pi"ēl: recount, declare (in detail)
הלל	Qal: boast	שׁבר	Qal: break
	Pi"ēl: praise		Pi"ēl: smash
	Hithpa"ēl: boast oneself,	לְבָנוֹן	Lebanon (הַלְּבָנוֹן with article)
	boast in (ב)	קדשׁ	Qal: be holy
פלל	Hithpa"ēl: pray		Pi"ēl: make holy
מלט	Pi"ēl: deliver, save		Hithpa"ēl: make oneself holy

III. Drills

1. Word Breakdown: In the following order: label every Dagesh Forte and Lene, Mappiq; vocal and silent shewa; Qames and Qames-Hatuf. Next, divide syllables labeling them open or closed. Then pronounce the words.

   בַּגַּיְא   אָזְלַת   וַיִּזְבְּחוּ   שָׁמֳרָתְ

2. Attach the following particles and translate all vocabulary words.
   Interrogative מה

   הָדָר   הַבַּיִת   חַלָּה

   Conjunctive ו

   בְּרָכָה   לַ֫יְלָה   אֱלֹהִים

Interrogative ה

אָמוֹר　　　בְּרָכָה　　　מָתְנַיִם

3. Attach the boxes and translate all vocabulary words. List all steps.
   1. ms construct עָמָל
   2. fs construct צְדָקָה
   3. ms construct כֶּסֶף (*a*)

4. Attach the boxes with suffixes and translate all vocabulary words. List all steps.

   Singular Nouns
   1. 1cs צַוָּאר
   2. 2fp מֶלֶךְ (*a*)

   Plural Nouns

   3. 3mp שְׂבָכָה
   4. 2ms יֶלֶד (*a*)

5. Attach the suffixes to the prepositions and translate.
   1. 3ms מִן
   2. 2fs לְ
   3. 3ms עִם
   4. 3mp תַּחַת

6. Verbs: List the three steps and the final answer and translate.

   (1) Boxes
   (2) Colors
   (3) Qal Stem
   Final Answer

   1. Create

   Pi"ēl
   1. Perfect 3ms דבר
   2. Participle fs (T-form) קדשׁ
   3. Infinitive absolute שׁבר
   4. Cohortative plural קדשׁ

   Pu"al

   5. Cohortative 1cs קדשׁ
   6. Perfect 3cp בקשׁ
   7. Participle mp שׁבר
   8. Imperfect 3ms (+Vav-consecutive) בקשׁ

   Hithpa"ēl

   9. Imperative 2ms פלל
   10. Perfect 3ms הלך
   11. Participle fp נבא

12. Infinitive absolute קדשׁ

2. Parse: Give the three steps (eliminating forms in each step) and all possible final answers and translate all vocabulary words.

1.	שַׁבֵּר	5.	הִתְקַטֵּל
2.	קַטֵּל	6.	נִסְתַּתְּרָה
3.	קֻטְּלוּ	7.	מְשֻׁבָּרוֹת
4.	מְקַטְּלֵי	8.	מִסְתַּכְּלִים

7. Translation

1. וְהָיוּ הַדְּבָרִים הָאֵלֶּה אֲשֶׁר אָנֹכִי אֹמֵר לְךָ הַיּוֹם עַל־לְבָבֶךָ וְלִמַּדְתָּ אֹתָם
לְבָנֶיךָ וְלִבְנֵי־בָנֶיךָ וְדִבַּרְתָּ עֲלֵיהֶם בְּבֵיתְךָ וּבְדַרְכֶּךָ׃

2. גַּדְּלוּ יהוה אִתִּי וְהַלְלוּ שְׁמוֹ יַחְדָּו׃

3. קוֹל יהוה שֹׁבֵר הָעֵצִים וַיהוה מְשַׁבֵּר אֶת־אַרְזֵי הַלְּבָנוֹן׃

4. אָמַר יהוה אֶל־הַנָּבִיא בֶּן־אָדָם אֲנִי שֹׁלֵחַ אֹתְךָ אֶל־בְּנֵי־יִשְׂרָאֵל הִנָּבֵא עֲלֵיהֶם
בְּשֵׁם־יהוה וְדִבַּרְתָּ אֲלֵיהֶם הַדָּבָר הַכָּתוּב בְּסִפְרִי׃

5. דִּרְשׁוּ יהוה וְעֻזּוֹ בַּקְּשׁוּ פָנָיו תָּמִיד׃

6. צִוָּה יהוה אֶת־מֹשֶׁה קַבֵּץ אֶת־רָאשֵׁי בְּנֵי־יִשְׂרָאֵל וְאָמַרְתָּ אֲלֵיהֶם הִתְקַדְּשׁוּ
אַתָּה וְהָעָם כִּי מָחָר אָנֹכִי יֹרֵד עַל־הָהָר וְדִבַּרְתִּי לְךָ וְלָעָם׃

7. כֹּה אָמַר יהוה קִרְבוּ אֵלַי שִׁמְעוּ זֹאת אֲנִי הוּא אֲנִי הוּא קְדוֹשׁ יִשְׂרָאֵל דְּבָרִי
עֹמֵד לְעוֹלָם׃

Chapter 24
The Causatives: Hiph'îl, Hoph'al

24.1. Introduction: This chapter, assuming and building on chapter 22, focuses on the forming, parsing, and meaning of the causative stems: Hiph'îl, Hoph'al.

24.2. Forming the Causative Stems – Hiph'îl, Hoph'al.

To form the causative stems properly, follow the same three steps of 23.2.

1. Memorize the boxes by spelling the stems properly (22.2 and 22.3). Remember the Hiph'îl is mostly an Haph'îl except in the perfect.

	Hiph'îl (Haph'îl)	**Hoph'al**
Perfect	הִ□ְ□□	הָ□ְ□□
Imperfect	יַ□ְ□□	יָ□ְ□□
Imperative	הַ□ְ□□	
Infinitive	הַ□ְ□□	
Participle	מַ□ְ□□	מָ□ְ□□

2. Memorize the thematic vowels: *the Hiph'îl never reduces thematic vowels.*

	Hiph'îl (Haph'îl)	**Hoph'al**
Perfect/Imperfect-Imperative	A-î/Î-ē	A/A
Infinitive Absolute	Ē	–
Infinitive Construct	Î	–
Participle	Î	Ā

The lower case "i" in the perfect (A-î/) stands for all third person forms. In the Hiph'îl, there are four special "Ṣere forms": the Ṣere thematic vowel occurs in (1) the jussive third (and second) person singular forms, (2) the Vav-consecutive of the third person singular forms, (3) the imperative 2ms, and (4) the infinitive absolute. *Memorize these special "Ṣere forms."*

3. Know the Qal stem thoroughly: especially, the preformative and sufformative elements of the root.

24.3. Examples of Forming the Causative Stems

1. Hiph'îl perfect 3cp of קטל
   1. Boxes: הִ□ְ□□ (Hiph'îl) — הִקְטל
   2. Colors: A-î/Î-ē — הִקְטִיל
   3. Qal stem: קָטְלוּ — הִקְטִילוּ

   Answer: הִקְטִילוּ

1. Step one derives the boxes from the stem name Hiph'îl: a preformative ה with a Ḥireq, followed by a silent shewa under the first root letter.
2. Step two adds the thematic vowel (Ḥireq-Yod for all third persons in the Hiph'îl perfect).
3. Step three adds the 3cp pronominal ending of the perfect, as memorized in the Qal. *In the Hiph'îl, thematic vowels never reduce.*

2. Hiph'îl imperative 2ms of קטל

1.	Boxes:	□□□ְהַ (Haph'îl)	הַקְטל
2.	Colors:	a special "Ṣere form" (24.2.2)	הַקְטֵל
3.	Qal stem:	קְטֹל	
	Answer:		הַקְטֵל

1. Step one derives the boxes from the stem name Haph'îl.
2. Step two adds the thematic vowel: Ṣere, a memorized form.
3. Step three adds nothing because the Qal is without preformatives or sufformatives.

3. Hoph'al imperfect 1cp of קטל

1.	Boxes:	□□□ְיָ	יָקְטל
2.	Colors:	A/A	יָקְטַל
3.	Qal stem:	נִקְטֹל	נָקְטַל
	Answer:		נָקְטַל

1. Step one derives the boxes from the stem name Hoph'al: a preformative ה with a Qameṣ-Ḥatuf, followed by a silent shewa under the first root letter.
2. Step two adds the thematic vowel (Pataḥ).
3. Step three adds the 1cp pronominal prefix of the imperfect, as memorized in the Qal.

24.4. Parsing the Causative Forms

Parsing is a process of elimination. Try to eliminate possibilities with each step.

1. תַּקְטֵלְנָה

1.	Boxes:	□□□ְיַ	Hiph'îl imperfect
2.	Colors:	Ē (A-î/Î-ē)	Eliminates all imperfects except 2fp, 3fp
3.	Qal stem:	תִּקְטֹלְנָה	2fp, 3fp
	Answer:	Hiph'îl imperfect 2fp or 3fp of קטל	

1. Step one identifies the boxes of the Hiph'îl (Haph'îl) imperfect, which eliminates all other possibilities.
2. Step two eliminates all imperfect forms except 2fp, 3fp.
3. Step three confirms step two.

2. הַקְטִיל

1.	Boxes:	□□□הַ	Hiph'îl imperative, infinitive construct, or infinitive absolute
2.	Colors:	green (Ḥireq-Yod – A-î/Î-ē)	Eliminates imperative 2ms, 2fp, and infinitive absolute
3.	Qal stem:	קְטִל	Eliminates imperative 2fs, 2mp
	Answer:	Hiph'îl infinitive construct of קטל	

1. Step one identifies the boxes of the Hiph'îl imperative or infinitives.
2. Step two eliminates the imperative 2ms, 2fp and the infinitive absolute.
3. Step three eliminates the imperative 2fs, 2mp.

3. מָקְטָלִים

1.	Boxes:	□□□מָ	Hoph'al participle
2.	Colors:	red (irreducible long)	Hoph'al participle
3.	Qal stem:	קְטָלִים	Eliminates all participles except masculine plural
	Answer:	Hoph'al participle mp of קטל	

1. Step one identifies the boxes as a Hoph'al participle.
2. Step two confirms step one.
3. Step three eliminates all participles except masculine plural.

24.5. The Meaning of the Causative Stems

Both the Hiph'îl and the Hoph'al are causative in meaning. Of course, not every Hiph'îl verb will be translated with "cause" – הִשְׁלִיךְ to throw, cast, for instance.

1. Hiph'îl
   1. Transitive (with direct object) – הִכְשִׁיל אֶת־הָאָדָם he caused the man to stumble.
   2. Intransitive (without direct object): this is also called the inner causative: the subject is also the object – הִשְׁמִין he caused (himself) to become fat, he became fat.

2. Hoph'al: The passive of the Hiph'îl.
   הִפְקִיד Hiph'îl: to cause (someone) to be an overseer; הָפְקַד Hoph'al: he was caused to be an overseer, he was made an overseer.

Exercise Twenty-Four

I. Questions

1. What are the causative stems?
2. When is a Hiph'îl a Hiph'îl? When is a Hiph'îl a Haph'îl?
3. What are the three steps for creating the causative stems?
4. What are the special "Ṣere forms" of the Hiph'îl?
5. Do Hiph'îl thematic vowels reduce?
6. What are the three steps to parse the causative stems?
7. What is the meaning of the Hiph'îl and Hoph'al?

II. Vocabulary

מַמְלָכָה	kingdom (construct מַמְלֶכֶת [*a*])
אַבְנֵר	Abner
בֶּטֶן (*i*)	womb
בָּבֶל	Babylon
פקד	Qal: pay attention to, observe, visit, appoint Niph'al: passive of Qal Hiph'îl: set (over), cause (one) to be an overseer, entrust
יצב	Hithpa"ēl (only): station oneself, take one's stand
אבד	Qal: perish, die, vanish Pi"ēl: make perish (destroy), make die (kill), make vanish
שׁמד	Niph'al: be annihilated, exterminated Hiph'îl: annihilate, exterminate
פֶּה	mouth
אֹזֶן (*o*)	ear
שׁחת	Niph'al: be marred, spoiled, corrupted Pi"ēl: spoil, ruin, destroy Hiph'îl: spoil, ruin, destroy, corrupt, act corruptly
שׁכם	Hiph'îl (only): rise early, make an early start
שׁלך	Hiph'îl: throw, cast (down, away, off)
סגר	Qal: shut Niph'al: be closed, shut Pi"ēl: deliver up (make closed up) Hiph'îl: deliver up, close up
כשׁל	Qal: stumble Hiph'îl: cause to stumble
שׂכל	Qal: be wise Hiph'îl: give attention to, ponder, have insight, give insight, act wisely, have success

III. Drills

1. Word Breakdown: In the following order: label every Dagesh Forte and Lene, Mappiq; vocal and silent shewa; Qameṣ and Qameṣ-Ḥatuf. Next, divide syllables labeling them open or closed. Then pronounce the words.

   הִשְׁתַּמֵּר　　　תִּשְׁבְּרֻ֫נוּ　　　גָּלוּי　　　וַיֵּ֫בְךְּ

2. Attach the following particles and translate all vocabulary words.
   Article

   חֵ֫שֶׁק　　　חָמוֹץ　　　הָבְנִי

   Preposition כ

   הָאֲדָמָה　　　הֵרָיוֹן　　　יְרוּשָׁלַ֫יִם

   Preposition מִן

   הָרָן　　　זֶ֫בַח　　　מוֹרֶה

3. Attach the boxes and translate all vocabulary words. List all steps.
   1. mp absolute　חָכָם
   2. mp construct　קֶ֫בֶר (*i*)
   3. fs construct　אַלְמָנָה

4. Attach the boxes with suffixes and translate all vocabulary words. List all steps.

   Singular Nouns
   1. 2mp　פֹּ֫עַל (*o*)
   2. 3ms　מְזִמָּה

   Plural Nouns
   3. 3fp　חֶ֫רֶב (*a*)
   4. 1cs　חָצִיר

5. Attach the boxes with suffixes to the prepositions and translate.
   1. 2ms　תַּ֫חַת
   2. 3mp　לְפָנִים
   3. 2fp　כ
   4. 3fs　אֵת (direct object)

6. Verb
   1. Create: List the three steps, the final answer, and translate.
      Hiph'îl
      1. Imperfect 2fs זכר
      2. Imperative 2ms כנס
      3. Participle fs שׁמד

4. Jussive 3ms סתר

Hoph'al

5. Perfect 3fs סתר
6. Imperfect 3fs (+Vav-consecutive) קדשׁ
7. Cohortative sg. מלך

Pi"ēl

8. Imperfect 3ms (+Vav-consecutive) קדשׁ
9. Infinitive construct שׁבר

Pu"al

10. Imperfect 2fp בקשׁ
11. Perfect 1cp קדשׁ

Hithpa"ēl

12. Infinitive construct צדק
13. Perfect 3cp שׁדל

2. Parse: Give the three steps (eliminating forms in each step) and all possible answers, and translate all vocabulary words.

1.	הַבְדֵּל	5.	תִּנַּבֵּא
2.	אָקְדַּשׁ	6.	נַזְכִּירָה
3.	הַקְדִּישִׁי	7.	הָשְׁמַדְתִּי
4.	בִּקְשׁוּ	8.	מַכְנִיסָה

7. Translation

1. אָמַר יהוה לְיִרְמְיָהוּ הַיּוֹם הַזֶּה הִפְקַדְתִּי אֹתְךָ לְנָבִיא עַל־הַגּוֹיִם וְעַל־הַמַּמְלָכוֹת
לְדַבֵּר מִשְׁפָּטַי וְלִכְתֹּב דְּבָרָי׃

2. וְהָיָה כִּי יְדַבֵּר יְהוֹשֻׁעַ אֲלֵיכֶם לַעֲבֹר אֶת־הַיַּרְדֵּן וְנָתַן יהוה מַלְכֵיהֶם בְּיָדְךָ
וְאִבַּדְתֶּם אֶת־שְׁמָם מִתַּחַת הַשָּׁמָיִם לֹא יִתְיַצֵּב אִישׁ בְּפָנֶיךָ עַד אֲשֶׁר אִבַּדְתֶּם אֹתָם׃

3. אָמַר דָּוִד אֶל־אַבְנֵר הֲלֹא אִישׁ אַתָּה וּמִי כָמוֹךָ בְּיִשְׂרָאֵל וְלָמָּה לֹא שָׁמַרְתָּ
אֶל־אֲדֹנֶיךָ הַמֶּלֶךְ כִּי בָא אִישׁ לְהַשְׁחִית אֶת־הַמֶּלֶךְ אֲדֹנֶיךָ׃

4. וַיַּשְׁכֵּם אֲבִימֶ֫לֶךְ בַּבֹּ֫קֶר וַיִּקְרָא לְכָל־עֲבָדָיו וַיְדַבֵּר אֶת־כָּל־הַדְּבָרִים הָאֵ֫לֶּה
בְּאָזְנֵיהֶם וַיִּתְפַּלְלוּ אֶל־יהוה וַיִּשְׁמַע יהוה אֶת־תְּפִלָּתָם׃

5. עָלֶ֫יךָ הָשְׁלַ֫כְתִּי יהוה כִּי מִבֶּ֫טֶן אִמִּי אֵלִי אָתָּה׃

6. שִׂפְתֵי[1] כֹהֵן יִשְׁמְרוּ דַ֫עַת וְתוֹרָה יְבַקְשׁוּ מִפִּיהוּ כִּי מַלְאַךְ יהוה צְבָאוֹת הוּא
וְאַתֶּם הִכְשַׁלְתֶּם רַבִּים בַּתּוֹרָה׃

---

[1] Feminine dual plural construct of שָׂפָה.

CHAPTER 25
THE REFLEXIVE/PASSIVE NIPH‘AL

25.1. Introduction: This chapter, assuming and building on chapter 22, focuses on the forming, parsing, and meaning of the Niph‘al.

25.2. Forming the Niph‘al

To form the Niph‘al properly, follow the same three steps in 23.2 and 24.2.

1. Memorize the boxes by properly spelling the stem for the perfect and participle (22.2 and 22.3).[1]

	Niph‘al
Perfect	נִ□□□
Imperfect	יִ⊡ָ□□
Imperative	הִ⊡ָ□□
Infinitive	נִ□□□/הִ⊡ָ□□
Participle	נִ□□□

For the infinitives, two options exist. נִ□□□ for the infinitive absolute only and הִ⊡ָ□□ for the infinitive absolute or infinitive construct.

2. Memorize the thematic vowels.

Perfect/Imperfect-Imperative	A/Ē-a
Infinitive Absolute	Ō
Infinitive Construct	Ē
Participle	Ā

3. Know the Qal stem thoroughly: especially, the preformative and sufformative elements on the root.

25.3. Examples of Forming the Niph‘al

1. Niph‘al perfect 2mp of קטל

1.	Boxes:	נִ□□□ (Niph‘al)	נִקְטל
2.	Colors:	A/Ē-a	נִקְטַל
3.	Qal stem:	קְטַלְתֶּם	נִקְטַלְתֶּם
	Answer:		נִקְטַלְתֶּם

[1] For the Niph‘al, the boxes are difficult to memorize because the Nun of the Niph‘al assimilates to the first root letter in the imperfects, imperatives, infinitive construct, and one option of the infinitive absolute.

1. Step one derives the boxes from the stem name Niph'al: a preformative נ with a Ḥireq, followed by a silent shewa under the first root letter.
2. Step two adds the thematic vowel (Pataḥ).
3. Step three adds the 2mp pronominal ending of the perfect, as memorized in the Qal.

2. Niph'al imperative 2fs of קטל

1.	Boxes:	הִ◙ָ□□	הִקָּטל
2.	Colors:	A/Ē-a	הִקָּטֵל
3.	Qal stem:	קִטְלִי	הִקָּטֵלִי
	Answer:		הִקָּטְלִי

1. Step one is the boxes memorized. A preformative ה with a Ḥireq precedes a Dagesh Forte in the first root letter and a Qameṣ under the first root letter. The word "Niph'al" only helps with the Dagesh Forte (the נ of the Niph'al) in the first root letter.
2. Step two adds the thematic vowel (Ṣere).
3. Step three adds the vocalic ending of the imperative 2fs (Ḥireq-Yod), thus reducing the thematic vowel (originally a Ḥireq) to a vocal shewa.

25.4. Parsing the Niph'al

Parsing is a process of elimination. Try to eliminate possibilities with each step.

1. נִקְטָל

1.	Boxes:	נִ□ְ□□	Niph'al perfect or participle, Qal imperfect 1cs
2.	Colors:	Red (irreducible long)	Eliminates all perfect forms, Qal imperfect 1cs
3.	Qal stem:	קָטֵל or קָטוּל	_____
	Answer:	Niph'al participle ms of קטל	

1. Step one identifies the boxes as a Niph'al perfect, participle, or Qal imperfect 1cs.
2. Step two eliminates the perfect (perfect 3ms pausal would be נִקְטָ֑ל, with Athnaḥ or Silluq), and Qal imperfect 1cs.
3. Step three eliminates nothing because the Qal furnishes only preformatives or suffformatives.

2. תִּקָּטֵל

1.	Boxes:	יִ◙ָ□□	Niph'al imperfect
2.	Colors:	A/Ē-a	Eliminates 2fp, 3fp

3. Qal stem: תִּקְטֹל Eliminates all except imperfect 2ms or 3fs
   Answer: Niph'al imperfect 2ms or 3fs of קטל

   1. Step one identifies the boxes as a Niph'al imperfect.
   2. Step two identifies the thematic vowel as a Niph'al imperfect and eliminates 2fp, 3fp forms.
   3. Step three eliminates all forms except the 2ms or 3fs.

25.5. The Meaning of the Niph'al

The Niph'al is the reflexive or passive of the Qal.

1. Reflexive

	Qal	**Niph'al**
שׁמר	to guard	to guard oneself
סתר	to hide	to hide oneself

2. Passive

	Qal	**Niph'al**
קבר	to bury	to be buried
ילד	to bear, bring forth	to be born

Exercise Twenty-Five

I. Questions

1. Write the boxes for the Niph'al. Why are these boxes difficult to learn?
2. Describe the three steps to form and to parse the Niph'al.
3. What are the meanings of the Niph'al?

II. Vocabulary

עַמּוֹן	Ammon
לֵוִי	Levi
נְאֻם	utterance, declaration
שְׁאֵרִית	(abs. and const.) remainder, remnant
לחם	Niph'al: fight
שׁבע	Niph'al: put oneself under oath, swear Hiph'îl: cause to swear, adjure
שׁמר	Qal: keep Niph'al: keep oneself, take heed, be careful
פֶּן	lest
שׁאר	Niph'al: be left over, remain Hiph'îl: cause (something or someone) to be left over, spare
נחם	Niph'al: be sorry, repent, suffer grief, be comforted Pi"ēl: comfort, console
שׂרף	Qal: burn Niph'al: be burned
סתר	Niph'al: hide oneself, be hid Hiph'îl: hide, conceal

III. Drills

1. Word Breakdown: In the following order: label every Dagesh Forte and Lene, Mappiq; vocal and silent shewa; Qameṣ and Qameṣ-Ḥatuf. Next, divide syllables labeling them open or closed. Then pronounce the words.

   כָּל־חָכְמָתָם   בַּנְּחָלִים   כָּשְׁלָה   מֵעֲוֹנֹתֵיהֶם

2. Attach the following particles and translate all vocabulary words.
   Interrogative מה

   רָבִיב   הֵרוֹן   חָרָשׁ

   Conjunctive ו

   יִדְּעֹנִי   אֲרָמִית   יְבֶ֫מֶת

   Interrogative ה

   תְּחִנָּה   עֲיָם   שָׁאַ֫לְתִּי

3. Attach the boxes and translate all vocabulary words. List all steps.
   1. ms construct נַ֫עַר (*a*)
   2. fs construct מַשָּׂאָה
   3. ms absolute חֶ֫רֶשׁ (*a*)

4. Attach the boxes with suffixes and translate all vocabulary words. List all steps.
   Singular Nouns
   1. 2ms נַ֫עַר (*a*)

   Plural Nouns
   2. 2fp מַלְבֵּן

5. Attach the suffixes to the prepositions and translate.
   1. 1cs לְמַ֫עַן
   2. 3fp מִן
   3. 2mp אֵת (direct object)
   4. 1cp אֶל

6. Verbs
   1. Create: List the three steps, the final answer, and translate.
      Niph‘al
      1. Infinitive absolute שׁפך
      2. Participle mp לחם
      3. Infinitive construct סתר
      4. Cohortative sg. קטל
      5. Imperfect 3fp שׁמד

Pi“ēl

6. Participle mp דבר
7. Imperative 2mp בקשׁ

Pu“al

8. Participle ms שׁבר
9. Perfect 3ms בקשׁ

Hithpa“ēl

10. Imperative 2fp פלל
11. Imperfect 3ms (+Vav-consecutive) הלך

Hiph‘îl

12. Perfect 3cp שׁחת
13. Imperative 2fp קדשׁ

Hoph‘al

14. Imperfect 1cp קהל
15. Perfect 3cp שׁלך

2. Parse: Give all possible answers, and translate all vocabulary words.

1.	שִׁבַּ֫רְתִּי	5.	יִשָּׁמְדוּן
2.	נִקְטַל	6.	הִקָּטֵל
3.	הִקָּטֹל	7.	הַסְתֵּר
4.	מַשְׁמִידוֹת	8.	נִשְׁפָּכָה

7. Translation

1. נִלְחַם יוֹאָב בְּעִיר בְּנֵי־עַמּוֹן וַיִּשְׁלַח אֶל־דָּוִד מַלְאָכִים לֵאמֹר נִלְכְּדָה הָעִיר וּבָאֵשׁ תִּשָּׂרֵף׃
2. אָמַר מֹשֶׁה אֶל־הָעָם נָתַן יהוה לָכֶם אֶת־הָאָרֶץ אֲשֶׁר נִשְׁבַּע לַאֲבוֹתֵיכֶם׃
3. וְעַתָּה הִשָּׁמְרוּ לָכֶם פֶּן־תִּשְׁכְּחוּ אֶת־יְהוָה אֲשֶׁר עָשָׂה עִמָּכֶם חֶסֶד וְעִם־בְּנֵיכֶם׃
4. יִקְרְאוּ אֶל־יהוֹה וַיהוָה יַסְתִּיר אֶת־פָּנָיו מֵהֶם בָּעֵת הַהִיא כִּי לֹא קִדְּשׁוּ אֶת־שְׁמוֹ הַגָּדוֹל׃

5. וַיִּנָּחֵם יהוה כִּי הִמְלִיךְ אֶת־שָׁאוּל לְמֶלֶךְ עַל־כָּל־יִשְׂרָאֵל וְלֹא אָדָם הוּא
לְהִנָּחֵם׃

6. לָכֵן כֹּה אָמַר יהוה עַל־אַנְשֵׁי הָעִיר הַהִיא עַל־הַמְבַקְשִׁים אֶת־נֶפֶשׁ הַנָּבִיא
עַל־הָאֹמְרִים אֵלָיו לֹא תִנָּבֵא בְּשֵׁם יְהוָה׃

7. בַּיָּמִים הָהֵם הַגּוֹיִם יְבַקְשׁוּ אֶת־יְהוָה וּשְׁאֵרִית עַמּוֹ תִּקָּבֵץ יַחְדָּו׃

CHAPTER 26
THE RELATIVE CLAUSE
CIRCUMSTANTIAL CLAUSES
COMPARATIVE-SUPERLATIVE

26.1. Introduction: This chapter examines the syntax of the relative clause, the circumstantial clause, and the comparative-superlative.

26.2. Relative Clause

A relative clause *relates* a clause to another word (the antecedent). A relative clause modifies a substantive like an adjective or functions as a substantive (10.10). The relative particle אֲשֶׁר usually introduces relative clauses, but sometimes, especially in poetry, the אֲשֶׁר can be omitted (Psalm 34:9), as in English: "This is the book which I wrote" or "This is the book I wrote."

1. Syntax of the relative clause
   1. Frequently, a relative clause describes or modifies a substantive (10.10).
      הָעֵץ אֲשֶׁר בְּתוֹךְ הַגָּן – The tree which (is) in the midst of the garden.
      The noun "tree" (the antecedent of the relative clause) is defined or described as the tree "which is in the midst of the garden." The relative clause modifies the word "tree."

   2. Sometimes the relative clause acts like a noun (10.10, substantive use of the relative clause), functioning usually as a direct object.
      וַאֲשֶׁר הוּא עֹשֶׂה יהוה מַצְלִיחַ – And that which he was doing, the Lord was prospering.
      The relative clause, "and that which he was doing," is the direct object of the participle מַצְלִיחַ. The accusative marker אֵת (Micah 6:1) may precede a relative clause functioning as a direct object.

2. Retrospective Pronouns and Adverbs
   The relative pronoun, probably a mere connecting link in Hebrew, often used pronouns and adverbs to define more closely the relation of the relative clause to its antecedent. In English, these retrospective pronouns and adverbs are superfluous.
   1. Retrospective Pronouns (frequent before an adjective, a participle, or a negative sentence)
      1. Subject
         כָּל־רֶמֶשׂ אֲשֶׁר הוּא חַי – Every creeping thing which it (is) alive.
         The retrospective pronoun (הוּא) occurs before the adjective חַי. The retrospective pronoun "looks back" to the antecedent "every creeping

(thing)." English omits the retrospective pronoun: "Every creeping thing that is living."

2. Genitive (possessive pronoun)
הָאִישׁ אֲשֶׁר לֹא־תִשְׁמַע לְשֹׁנוֹ – The man who you will not hear his tongue (language).
The retrospective pronoun (3ms suffix on לְשֹׁנוֹ), a possessive pronoun, makes the relative clause possessive: "The man whose language you will not hear." The 3ms suffix "looks back" to "the man."

3. Object
אֲנִי יוֹסֵף אֲשֶׁר מְכַרְתֶּם אֹתִי – I am Joseph whom you sold me.
The retrospective pronoun (אֹתִי) "looks back" to "Joseph." English omits the retrospective pronoun – "I am Joseph whom you sold."

2. Retrospective Adverbs שָׁם, שָׁמָּה, מִשָּׁם
   1. שָׁם:
      The adverb שָׁם more closely defines the relation of the relative clause to its antecedent.
      הַמָּקוֹם אֲשֶׁר אַתָּה שָׁם – The place which you (are) there = The place where you are.
      The retrospective adverb שָׁם combines with אֲשֶׁר to mean "where." The adverb שָׁם "looks back" on הַמָּקוֹם.

   2. שָׁמָּה:
      הַמָּקוֹם אֲשֶׁר אַתָּה בָא שָׁמָּה – The place which you are coming to there = The place where you are coming.
      אֲשֶׁר ... שָׁמָּה = where, to which

   3. מִשָּׁם:
      הַמָּקוֹם אֲשֶׁר אַתָּה יֹצֵא מִשָּׁם – The place which you are going out from there = The place from which you are going out.
      אֲשֶׁר ... מִשָּׁם = from which

26.3. Circumstantial Clauses

Circumstantial clauses express the circumstances under which the action of the verb happens. English expresses these clauses by dependent clauses or phrases. Circumstantial clauses are adverbial, modifing the (main) verb by answering the questions: how? when? where? why? to what extent?

1. Vav + noun (pronoun) followed by a participle

   A Vav connected to a noun (pronoun) followed by a participle frequently introduces a circumstantial clause.

   וַתִּתְפַּלֵּל חַנָּה לִפְנֵי־יהוה וְעֵלִי שֹׁמֵר אֶת־פִּיהָ – And (then) Hannah prayed before the Lord while (as) Eli was watching her mouth.

   The circumstantial clause – וְעֵלִי שֹׁמֵר אֶת־פִּיהָ – furnishes the circumstances under which the action of the verb happens: "While (as) Eli was watching her mouth" is the circumstances under which "Hannah prayed." This circumstantial clause modifies the main verb, answering the question – when? "Hannah prayed," when? "while Eli was watching her mouth."

   The Vav-consecutive construction expresses a different meaning.

   וַתִּתְפַּלֵּל חַנָּה לִפְנֵי־יהוה וַיִּשְׁמֹר עֵלִי אֶת־פִּיהָ – And then Hannah prayed before the Lord and then Eli watched her mouth.

   The second clause is an independent clause that continues the story: "Hannah prayed before the Lord and then Eli watched her mouth."

2. Vav + noun followed by noun(s)

   בָּנָה מִגְדָּל וְרֹאשׁוֹ בַשָּׁמַיִם – He built a tower and its top (is) in the heavens = He built a tower *with* its top in the heavens.

   This circumstantial clause וְרֹאשׁוֹ בַשָּׁמַיִם answers the question – How? "He built the tower," how? "*with* its top in the heavens."

26.4. Comparative and Superlative

Hebrew lacks comparative and superlative forms (smaller, smallest).

1. Comparative
   1. Hebrew commonly expresses the comparative with an adjective (or stative verb) followed by the מִן of comparison.

      מַה־מָּתוֹק מִדְּבַשׁ – What is sweet (apart) from honey? = What is sweeter than honey?
   2. Hebrew expresses the correlative comparatives – greater-less – by a definite adjective הַגָּדוֹל: the greater (Gen 1:16).

2. Superlatives
   1. With adjective:
      1. Simple definite adjective –הַקָּטָן the small(est)
      2. Definite attributive adjective – בְּנוֹ הַקָּטָן His son, the small one = his youngest son.
      3. Adjective (without article) as the first member of a construct package.

         קְטַן בָּנָיו – The small (one) of his sons = the youngest of his sons.

2. With nouns:

   A construct package with two nouns of the same word, with the last word of the package in the plural, expresses the superlative.

   שִׁיר הַשִּׁירִים – The song of songs = the most excellent song.

EXERCISE TWENTY-SIX

I. Questions

1. Define a relative clause.
2. What are the two main functions of a relative clause?
3. What are retrospective pronouns and adverbs? When do retrospective pronouns frequently occur?
4. How do you translate relative clauses with retrospective pronouns as the subject, object, or genitive? How should the retrospective adverbs – שָׁם, מִשָּׁם, and שָׁמָּה – be translated in relative clauses?
5. Define a circumstantial clause.
6. List two kinds of circumstantial clauses (Vav + ... etc.).
7. How does Hebrew commonly express the comparative? The correlative comparative?
8. List the ways that adjectives and nouns express the superlative.

II. Vocabulary

אֲרָם	Aram	יִשַׁי	Jesse
רִבְקָה	Rebecca	כָּל־, כֹּל	all (with suffix כֻּלּוֹ)
מאס	reject, despise	גְּבוּל	boundary, territory
צלח	Qal: be successful	אֹכֶל (*a*), אָכְלָה	food
	Hiph'îl: succeed, prosper, cause	קָטֹן, קָטָן	(adj.) small, little, young
	to be successful	טָהוֹר	(adj.) clean
שָׂדֶה	field	מוֹעֵד	appointed time, place, meeting

III. Drills

1. Word Breakdown: In the following order: label every Dagesh Forte and Lene, Mappiq; vocal and silent shewa; Qameṣ and Qameṣ-Ḥatuf. Next, divide syllables labeling them open or closed. Then pronounce the words.

מִמֶּנּוּ   אֳנִיּוֹת   שָׁמְרֵנִי   מִגְרָשֶׁהָ

2. Attach the following particles and translate all vocabulary words.
   Article

   עָצָב חִתִּי מִצְרִי

   Preposition ב

   הַגּוֹיִם חָכְמָה יְלֵל

   Interrogative ה

   אֲסַרְתִּי דִּבֵּר עַם

3. Attach the boxes and translate all vocabulary words. List all steps.
   1. mp construct דֶּלֶת (*a*)
   2. fs construct מִצְוָה
   3. fp construct מַשָּׂאָה
   4. mp absolute מֶלֶךְ (*a*)

4. Attach the boxes with suffixes and translate all vocabulary words. List all steps.

   Singular Nouns
   1. 3ms מֶלֶךְ (*a*)
   2. 1cp אֲדָמָה

   Plural Nouns
   3. 2fs קֹדֶשׁ (*o*)
   4. 1cs תְּפִלָּה

5. Attach the suffixes to the prepositions and translate.
   1. 2ms לְמַעַן
   2. 3mp אֶל
   3. 2mp מִן
   4. 1cs עִם

6. Verb
   1. Create: List the three steps, the final answer, and translate.

      Pi"ēl
      1. Participle mp absolute בקשׁ

      Pu"al
      2. Perfect 2mp בקשׁ
      3. Participle fp construct דבר

      Hithpa"ēl
      4. Imperative 2fs קטל
      5. Perfect 3ms שׁבר

Hiph'îl
6. Imperfect 3ms (+Vav-consecutive) שׁמד
7. Infinitive construct מלך
8. Imperative 2mp פשׁט

Hoph'al
9. Imperfect 3fs כנס
10. Imperfect jussive 3ms שׁמד

Niph'al
11. Imperative 2fp שׁמר
12. Infinitive construct קטל

2. Parse: Give the three steps (eliminating forms in each step) and all possible answers, and translate all vocabulary words.

1.	נִקְטֹל	5.	הַמְלִיךְ
2.	תִּתְקַדְּשִׁי	6.	תַּקְהֵלְנָה
3.	מְבֻקָּשָׁה	7.	יַקְטֵל
4.	תִּצְטַדְּקִי	8.	הַמְבַקְשִׁים

7. Translation

1. הָלַךְ עֶ֫בֶד אַבְרָהָם אֲרָמָה וְכָל־טוּב אֲדֹנָיו בְּיָדוֹ וְשָׁם מָצָא אֶת־רִבְקָה וַיִּשְׁאַל
אֹתָהּ בַּת־מִי אָתְּ׃
2. בָּא אֶל־הָעִיר וְרִבְקָה יֹשֶׁבֶת עַל־עָ֫יִן וַיְדַבֵּר לָהּ וַיִּשְׂמַח שִׂמְחָה גְדוֹלָה כִּי עָשָׂה
יְהוָה עִמּוֹ חֶסֶד׃
3. נָתַן יהוה לָ֫נוּ מִכָּל־הַבְּהֵמָה הַטְּהוֹרָה לְאָכְלָה וְהַבְּהֵמָה אֲשֶׁר לֹא טְהוֹרָה הִיא
לֹא נָתַן לָ֫נוּ אֹתָהּ׃
4. גַּם מִן־אַרְצָם יָצְאוּ וִידֵיהֶם עַל־רֹאשָׁם כִּי מָאַס יהוה אֹתָם וְלֹא הִצְלִיחַ דַּרְכָּם׃
5. נָתַן אַבְרָהָם לִפְנֵיהֶם לֶ֫חֶם וָ֫יַיִן אֲשֶׁר־עָשָׂה אֹתָם וְהוּא עֹמֵד עֲלֵיהֶם תַּ֫חַת הָעֵץ׃
6. שָׁאַל שְׁמוּאֵל אֶת־יִשַׁי הֲבֵן אַחֵר לָךְ וַיְדַבֵּר יִשַׁי אֶל־שְׁמוּאֵל לֵאמֹר לִי בֵּן אַחֵר
דָּוִד קָטֹן בָּנָי׃
7. וַיְהִי בַבֹּ֫קֶר כִּי יָצָא יְהוֹנָתָן אֶל־הַשָּׂדֶה לְמוֹעֵד דָּוִד וְנַ֫עַר עִמּוֹ קָטֹן עֲבָדָיו׃

CHAPTER 27
ATTACHING PRONOMINAL SUFFIXES TO THE VERB: THE PERFECT

27.1. Introduction

Hebrew can express a pronominal direct object in two ways: with the definite direct object marker (accusative marker אֵת) with a pronominal suffix or with the pronominal suffix directly attached to a verb. Sections 27.2-27.5 specifically apply to the Qal perfect, and generally to the Pi"ēl perfect and Hiph'îl perfect (27.6).

27.2. Proto-Hebrew Forms of the Perfect

Learn the Proto-Hebrew forms of the perfect for forming and for parsing verbal forms with suffixes.

1. Pataḥs were the original vowels under the first and second root letters in all standard verbs – *קַטַל. In stative verbs, third person verbs restore the original Ḥireq under the second root letter (*אַהִב), other persons have Pataḥ like the standard verb.

2. 2fs קָטַלְתְּ (originally *קַטַלְתִּ): Hebrew dropped final short vowels and lengthened the Pataḥ under the first root letter in the open pretonic position: קָטַלְתְּ. When attaching suffixes to the 2fs form, restore and lengthen the Ḥireq to Ḥireq-Yod (*קַטַלְתִּי, compare Biblical Aramaic 2fs קְטַלְתִּי) and attach the suffixes directly to the verb.[1] Now the 1cs and the 2fs perfects with pronominal suffixes are identical – context distinguishes the forms.
   2fs perfect with 3ms suffix (also 1cs perfect with 3ms suffix) – קְטַלְתִּיהוּ

3. 3fs קָטְלָה (originally *קַטַלַת): Like the feminine noun (תּוֹרָה « *תּוֹרַת), the 3fs perfect originally ended in ת◌. Restore the original feminine form *קַטַלַת and attach suffixes to the original form.
   3fs perfect with a 1cs suffix – קְטָלַתְנִי

4. 2mp קְטַלְתֶּם (originally *קַטַלְתּוּ, compare Biblical Aramaic 2mp קְטַלְתּוּן): When attaching suffixes, restore the original form and attach suffixes directly to the verb.
   2mp perfect with a 1cs suffix – קְטַלְתּוּנִי

27.3. Accent and Vowel Reduction Patterns

1. Accent
   1. All third persons (3ms, 3fs, 3cp) accent the third root letter (R_3).

[1] Without connecting vowels, see 14.2.1; 27.4.

3ms perfect with 3ms suffix – שְׁמָר֫וֹ (exception: 3ms verb with a 2ms suffix שְׁמָרְךָ֫ which does not accent R_3 but the 2ms suffix)
3fs perfect with 1cs suffix – שְׁמָרַ֫תְנִי
3cp perfect with 3ms suffix – שְׁמָר֫וּהוּ

2. All other persons accent on the pronominal element of the verb – ת or נ:
1cs perfect with 2ms suffix שְׁמַרְתִּ֫יךָ
1cp perfect with 2ms suffix שְׁמַרְנ֫וּךָ

2. Vowel Reduction Pattern
The Qal perfect with suffixes follows the *noun reduction pattern* (6.3).

27.4. Attaching Suffixes

	Suffixes attached directly to the verb[2]	Suffixes attached with connecting vowels to the verb
1cs	נִי	□ַ֫נִי
2ms	ךָ	□ְךָ֫
2fs	ךְ	□ֵ֫ךְ (or □֫□ֵךְ with a 3fs verb)
3ms	הוּ	□֫וֹ
3fs	הָ	□ָ֫ה
1cp	נוּ	□ָ֫נוּ
2mp	כֶ֫ם	□ְכֶ֫ם
2fp	כֶ֫ן	□ְכֶ֫ן
3mp	ם	□ָ֫ם (or □֫□ַם with a 3fs verb)
3fp	ן	□ָ֫ן (or □֫□ַן with a 3fs verb)

Note the 1cs ending is נִי instead of □ִי. In the left column, the 3ms and 3fs suffixes are הוּ and הָ instead of וֹ and □ָה (14.5.3). In the right column, the 2fs box with Ṣere follows the noun boxes; the 1cp box with Qameṣ follows the suffixes with the prepositions (14.2.1). Of course, the accent rules of 27.3.1 concerning third person verbs (especially 3fs verbs) take precedent sometimes over the accents with the boxes in the right column.

1. General Principles
   1. Verbs ending in an historic long vowel (1cs, 1cp, 3cp, and 2fs, 2mp; 27.2.4) and the 3fs verb with syllabic suffixes attach pronominal suffixes directly to the verb, without connecting vowels:

[2] The suffixes may be syllabic, which are open syllables: 1cs, 2ms, 3ms, 3fs, 1cp, or the suffixes may be alphabetic, which closes a syllable: 2fs, 3mp, 3fp.

3cp perfect with 1cs suffix – שְׁמָר֫וּנִי
3fs perfect with 1cs suffix – שְׁמָרַ֫תְנִי

2. The remaining verbs (2ms, 3ms, and the 3fs with alphabetic suffixes) require connecting vowels:
   2ms perfect with 1cs suffix קְטַלְתַּ֫נִי
   3fs perfect with 2fs suffix קְטָלָ֫תֶךְ

2. Specific Problems
   1. 3fs verb: The original Pataḥ under the third root letter (*קְטַלְתְּ the implicit silent shewa becomes explicit, before suffixes that directly attach – קְטָלַ֫תְנִי 3fs perfect with 1cs suffix) lengthens to Qameṣ in open syllables (with alphabetic suffixes: 2fs, 3mp, 3fp). 3fs perfect with 2fs suffix – קְטָלָ֫תֶךְ
   2. 2ms verb: The connecting vowel of the suffixes replaces the original Pataḥ under the pronominal ת (*קְטַלְתַּ): 2ms perfect with a 3fs suffix – קְטַלְתָּהּ.

3. Contracted or Assimilated Forms
   1. 3ms suffix
      1. With the 1cs perfect, two forms are possible – קְטַלְתִּ֫יהוּ and the contracted form – קְטַלְתִּיו. In the contracted form, the ה drops between vowels and then the Shureq becomes a Vav.
      2. With the 3fs perfect, the ה of the suffix assimilates to the feminine ת of the verb – *קְטָלַ֫תְהוּ » קְטָלַ֫תּוּ.
   2. 3fs suffix with the 3fs perfect: The ה of the suffix assimilates to the feminine ת of the verb – *קְטָלַ֫תְהָ » קְטָלַ֫תָּה. (The final ה is phony.)

27.5. Attaching Pronominal Suffixes to the Perfect

1. Follow four steps
   1. Restore the proto-form of the perfect (27.2): bring back the original Pataḥs (or the Ḥireq thematic vowel in the stative verb 3ms) under the first and second root letters and the original forms of the 2fs, 3fs, and 2mp.
   2. Attach the appropriate suffix box (27.4) and establish accent (27.3.1): according to the verb, choose the suffix that attaches to the verb directly or indirectly with connecting vowels. Third person verbs accent the third root letter (3ms verb with 2ms suffix is the exception); other persons accent the pronominal ת or נ of the verb.
   3. Work the rules of syllables (27.3.2): Qal perfects with pronominal suffixes follow *the noun reduction pattern* (6.3).
   4. Adjust for specific problems (27.4.2):
      1. The 3fs verb lengthens the original Pataḥ under the R_3 letter in an open syllable.

2. The connecting vowel of the suffix replaces the original Pataḥ under the pronominal ת in the 2ms.
3. Contraction: 3ms suffix with 1cs, 3fs verbs; 3fs suffix with a 3fs verb.

2. Examples
   1. 3fs perfect with 2ms suffix קטל
      1. Restore the proto-form of the verb: קַטַלַתְ.
         The restored feminine ending has an implicit silent shewa (footnote 3-6).
      2. Attach the appropriate suffix and establish the accent: קַטַלַתְךָ.
         The suffix directly attaches, with implicit silent becoming explicit – the shewa is actually medial. Third person verbs accent R_3.
      3. Work the rules of syllables: קְטָלַתְךָ (6.3.2; 6.3.5).
      4. Adjust for specific problems: None
         Answer: קְטָלַתְךָ

   2. 1cs perfect with 3ms suffix קטל
      1. Restore the proto-form of the verb: קַטַלְתִּי.
      2. Attach the appropriate suffix and establish the accent: קַטַלְתִּיהוּ (27.3.1).
         The 1cs perfect, with its historic long Ḥireq-Yod, attaches suffixes directly to the verb (27.4.1).
      3. Work the rules of syllables: קְטַלְתִּיהוּ (6.3.3; 6.3.5).
      4. Adjust for specific problems.
         The suffix may contract: The ה drops between vowels and the final Shureq becomes a Vav: קְטַלְתִּיו.
         Answer: קְטַלְתִּיהוּ or קְטַלְתִּיו

27.6. Derived Stems: Pi"ēl and Hiph'îl Perfect[3]

1. Pi"ēl (and Hithpa"ēl): The Pi"ēl is like the Qal perfect (27.2; 27.5), with a notable exception: *in an open pretonic syllable, the thematic vowel reduces to vocal shewa (verb reduction pattern)*.
   Pi"ēl perfect 3ms with 1cs suffix – בִּקְשַׁנִי
   Pi"ēl perfect 3ms with 2ms suffix: The thematic vowel reduces in the open pretonic position – *בִּקְשְׁךָ. The shewa fight produces a Segol – בִּקֶשְׁךָ – to avoid consecutive shewas.

2. Hiph'îl: The Hiph'îl is like the Qal perfect (27.2; 27.5), with a notable exception: *the thematic vowels never reduce in the Hiph'îl* because the thematic vowel is either historic long or short in a closed unaccented syllable.

[3] Pronominal suffixes rarely occur with the Niph'al, Pu"al, or Hoph'al.

Hiph'îl perfect 3ms with 1cs suffix – הִשְׁלִיכַ֫נִי
Hiph'îl perfect 1cp with 2ms suffix – הִשְׁלַכְנ֫וּךָ

27.7. Parsing Forms with Pronominal Suffixes

1. Five steps
    1. Identify boxes (if there is no box, the form is Qal).
    2. Identify proto-forms (restore every Qameṣ and vocal shewa to Pataḥ; Ṣere to Ḥireq) and the root (and any Qal preformatives or sufformative characteristics).
    3. Identify the suffix.
    4. Look for the accented syllable and the vowel reduction pattern.
    5. Adjust for specific problems.

2. Example
    קְטָלַ֫תָּה
    1. Identify boxes: There is no box – the form is a Qal.
    2. Identify the proto-form: *קַטַלַתְ 3fs perfect.
    3. Identify the suffix: The suffix is not readily identified; the form is probably contracted or assimilated.
    4. The accent and the reduction pattern: This confirms the 3fs form.
    5. Adjust for specific problems: The Dagesh Forte in the restored feminine ת indicates an assimilated form. The possibilities are: 3ms or 3fs suffix on a 3fs perfect (27.4.2; 27.4.3). The 3fs suffix הָ explains the form better than the masculine suffix הוּ (27.4.3). The 3ms suffix on a 3fs perfect would be קְטָלַ֫תּוּ. The ה of the suffix assimilated to the ת of the 3fs. Then a phony ה was added to read the long Qameṣ under the ת.
    Answer: Qal perfect 3fs with 3fs suffix.

See appendix VI, pages 300-301 for the paradigm of strong verb with pronominal suffixes

Exercise Twenty-Seven

I. Questions

1. What are the original vowels under the first and second root letters of a standard verb and stative verb in the perfect?
2. What is the proto-form of the perfect 3fs, 2fs, 2mp?
3. Where is the accent on the perfect with pronominal suffixes?
4. What is the reduction pattern of the Qal perfect with pronominal suffixes?
5. What are the two ways in which pronominal suffixes attach to the perfect?

6. Discuss the specific problems of attaching pronominal suffixes to the 3fs and 2ms perfect.
7. Which pronominal suffixes contract? With which verbs do they contract?
8. Describe the steps for attaching pronominal suffixes.
9. What is the reduction pattern of the Pi"ēl perfect?
10. Discuss the special problem of the 2ms suffix on the Pi"ēl perfect 3ms.
11. Discuss the reduction pattern of the Hiph'îl perfect.
12. Describe the steps for parsing forms with pronominal suffixes.

II. Vocabulary

מֶרְכָּבָה	chariot	רֶ֫כֶב (*i*)	chariots (collective)
מַטֶּה	staff, tribe	חֶרְפָּה	reproach, disgrace
חֲמוֹר	(male) donkey	כפר	Pi"ēl: cover over; make propitiation
מַחֲנֶה	camp, army		
גֶּ֫פֶן (*a*)	vine	עָוֺן	iniquity, guilt, punishment
זֶ֫רַע (*a*)	seed, offspring	רכב	Qal: mount, ride
קֶ֫רֶב (*i*)	(preposition) middle of בְּקֶ֫רֶב in the middle of		Hiph'îl: cause to mount, cause to ride

III. Drills

1. Word Breakdown: In the following order: label every Dagesh Forte and Lene, Mappiq; vocal and silent shewa; Qameṣ and Qameṣ-Ḥatuf. Next, divide syllables labeling them open or closed. Then pronounce the words.

   הָיְתָה   לַיְלָה

2. Attach the following particles and translate all vocabulary words.
   Interrogative מה

   עָרִיץ   הַדָּבָר

   Preposition ל

   יְדֵיהֶם   אֲדָמָה

   Preposition מן

   חֶרְפָּה   עִם

3. Attach the boxes and translate all vocabulary words. List all steps.
   1. fp construct מִלְחָמָה
   2. mp construct עָמָל

4. Attach the boxes with suffixes and translate all vocabulary words. List all steps.

   Singular Nouns
   1. 3fp בֶּגֶד (*i*)
   2. 2fs תּוּשִׁיָּה

   Plural Nouns
   3. 1cp צְדָקָה
   4. 2fp קֹדֶשׁ (*o*)

5. Attach the suffixes to the prepositions and translate.
   1. 1cs תַּחַת
   2. 2ms מִן
   3. 1cp בְּ
   4. 3fp אֵת (direct object)

6. Verbs
   1. Create: List the three steps, the final answer, and translate.
      1. Pi"ēl participle fs construct בקשׁ
      2. Pu"al imperfect 1cp שׁבר
      3. Hithpa"ēl imperative 2fp שׁמר
      4. Hiph'îl perfect 3cp קהל
      5. Niph'al perfect 3fs לחם

   2. Parse: Give all possible answers: list all steps, and translate all vocabulary words.
      1. מְקַטֶּלֶת
      2. הִסְתַּתְּרוּ
      3. שִׁבַּרְתְּ
      4. קְטוּלֵי
      5. אֶקְטְלָה

7. Attach pronominal suffixes to the perfect: List the four steps.
   1. 1cs suffix on the 3ms Qal of קטל
   2. 2ms suffix on the 3fs Qal of אהב (A-ē/A)
   3. 1cp suffix on the 2ms Qal of קטל
   4. 3fs suffix on the 2fs Qal of שׁמר
   5. 3mp suffix on the 3fs Qal of רדף
   6. 3ms suffix on the 1cs Qal of קטל
   7. 1cs suffix on the 2mp Qal of רדף
   8. 3fs suffix on the 3fs Qal of קטל
   9. 1cp suffix on the 3cp Qal of שׁמר
   10. 3fp suffix on the 1cp Qal of אהב (A-ē/A)
   11. 3ms suffix on the 2ms Pi"ēl of בקשׁ
   12. 2ms suffix on the 1cs Hiph'îl of קטל

8. Parse: List the steps, and translate all vocabulary words.

1.	קְטָלוֹ	6.	קְטַלְתַּנִי
2.	קִטְלוּנִי	7.	בִּקְשָׁתֶךְ
3.	רְדַפְתִּינוּ	8.	שְׁמַרְתּוּהוּ
4.	הִקְטִילָם	9.	שְׁמָרָנוּ
5.	שְׁמָרַתּוּ	10.	הִמְלִיכַתְנִי

9. Translation

1. שִׁמְעוּ אֶת־הַדָּבָר אֲשֶׁר דִּבֶּר יהוה עֲלֵיכֶם בֵּית יִשְׂרָאֵל יהוה אֱלֹהִים אֱמֶת
הוּא אֱלֹהִים חַיִּים וּמֶלֶךְ עוֹלָם׃
2. אָמַר הַנָּבִיא יְהוָה כִּפֵּר עֲוֺנֵנוּ וְחֶרְפָּתֵנוּ אַל תִּזְכֹּר אֱלֹהִים׃
3. צִוָּה יְהוֹשֻׁעַ אֶת־רָאשֵׁי הָעָם לֵאמֹר עִבְרוּ בְּקֶרֶב הַמַּחֲנֶה וַאֲמַרְתֶּם אֲלֵיהֶם
מָחָר אַתֶּם עֹבְרִים אֶת־הַיַּרְדֵּן הַזֶּה׃
4. וְאֶת־שְׁלֹמֹה בֶּן־דָּוִד הִמְלִיכוֹ יהוה עַל־כָּל־יִשְׂרָאֵל וְהָעָם כִּבְּדוֹ׃
5. קְדוֹשָׁיו לְעוֹלָם נִשְׁמָרוּ וְזֶרַע רְשָׁעִים נִכְרָת׃
6. עִבְדוּ אֶת־יהוה בְּשִׂמְחָה כִּי יְהוָה הוּא אֱלֹהִים הוּא עָשָׂה אֹתָנוּ וְלוֹ אֲנָחְנוּ׃

CHAPTER 28
ATTACHING PRONOMINAL SUFFIXES TO THE VERB: THE IMPERFECT, IMPERATIVE, AND INFINITIVE CONSTRUCT

28.1. Introduction: As in the perfect, pronominal suffixes can attach directly to the imperfect, imperative, and infinitive construct (The participle attaches the pronominal suffixes of nouns and adjectives [Chapters 12 and 13] and has the *reduction pattern of verbs*, 17.3.3; 19.2.1, participle mp with 3fs suffix – יֹשְׁבֶ֫יהָ).

28.2. The Imperfect

1. Proto-forms: In the imperfect, only the proto-forms of the thematic vowels are important:

Thematic Vowel	Proto-Form (short vowel)
Ḥolem	Qameṣ-Ḥatuf
Ṣere	Ḥireq
Pataḥ	Pataḥ

2. Accent and Vowel Reduction Pattern
    1. Accent
        1. The 2mp and 2fp suffixes (כֶם, כֶן) always take the accent. The 2ms suffix (ךָ) takes the accent except with verbs ending in an historic long vowel: 3mp imperfect with 2ms suffix – יִקְטְל֫וּךָ.
        2. All other forms accent the R_3 letter: 3ms imperfect with 1cs suffix – יִקְטְלֵ֫נִי.
    2. Vowel reduction patterns:
        1. Ḥolem/Ṣere: Original Qameṣ-Ḥatuf and Ḥireq thematic vowels *reduce* to vocal shewa in open pretonic syllables: *the verb reduction pattern* (17.3.3).
           3ms imperfect with 1cs suffix – יִקְטְלֵ֫נִי
        2. Pataḥ: Pataḥ thematic vowels *lengthen* to Qameṣ in open pretonic syllables: *the noun reduction pattern* (6.3).
           3ms imperfect with 1cs suffix – יִלְבָּשֵׁ֫נִי

3. Attaching Suffixes and Boxes

	Suffixes attached directly to verb	Boxes attached to verb with connecting vowels	Boxes attached to verb with connecting vowels and energic Nun
1cs	נִי	□ֵ֫נִי	□ֶ֫נִּי
2ms	ךָ	□ְךָ	□ֶ֫ךָּ
2fs	ךְ	□ֵ֫ךְ	
3ms	הוּ	□ֵ֫הוּ	□ֶ֫נּוּ
3fs	הָ	□ֶ֫הָ or □ָהּ	□ֶ֫נָּה
1cp	נוּ	□ֵ֫נוּ	□ֶ֫נּוּ
2mp	כֶ֫ם	□ְכֶ֫ם	
2fp	כֶ֫ן	□ְכֶ֫ן	
3mp	ם	□ֵ֫ם	
3fp	ן	□ֵ֫ן	

1. General Principles
   1. Left column: Verbs ending in an historic long vowel (2fs, 2mp, 3mp) attach the suffixes directly to the verb: 3mp imperfect with 3ms suffix – יִקְטְל֫וּהוּ.

   2. Middle column: Other verbs attach suffixes to the verb with a box and connecting vowel: 3ms imperfect with 3ms suffix – יִקְטְלֵ֫הוּ.

   3. Right column: A variant form of the middle column has an energic Nun, which gave energy (emphasis) to the verb, but it is usually, or at least sometimes, without emphasis in the Old Testament. The energic Nun assimilates to the suffixes of the 1cs, 2ms, and 1cp:
      1cs *□ֶ֫נְנִי » □ֶ֫נִּי – יִקְטְלֶ֫נִּי 3ms imperfect with 1cs suffix (energic)
      The ה of the suffix assimilates to the energic Nun in the 3ms and 3fs:
      3ms *□ֶ֫נְהוּ » □ֶ֫נּוּ – יִקְטְלֶ֫נּוּ 3ms imperfect with 3ms energic suffix
      Occasionally, the energic Nun does not assimilate: Qal imperfect 3ms with 3ms with energic Nun – יְעַבְרֶ֫נְהוּ.

2. Specific Problems
   1. Qameṣ-Ḥatuf: When attached to verbs with connecting vowels (middle column), the 2ms, 2mp, and 2fp suffixes shift the accent to the end of the word. The original Qameṣ-Ḥatuf remains in a closed unaccented syllable: 3ms imperfect with 2ms suffix – יִקְטָלְךָ֫ (no Metheg).

2. Pataḥ: Pataḥ thematic vowels lengthen to Qameṣ in open pretonic syllables: 3ms imperfect with 2ms suffix – יִלְבָּשְׁךָ (Metheg).

4. Attaching Suffixes and Boxes to the Imperfect
   1. Follow four steps (27.5).
      1. Restore the proto-vowel of the thematic vowel (28.2.1).
      2. Attach appropriate suffix/box (28.2.3) and establish the accent (28.2.2.1).
      3. Work the rules of syllables (28.2.2.2).
      4. Adjust for specific problems (28.2.3.2).

   2. Examples
      1. 3ms suffix with a 3fs imperfect of קטל (A/Ō)
         1. The proto-vowel is Qameṣ-Ḥatuf: תִּקְטָל.
         2. Attach the appropriate box ◌ֵהוּ (middle column) and establish the accent: תִּקְטָלֵהוּ.
         3. Work the *verb reduction pattern*: תִּקְטְלֵהוּ.
         4. Adjust for specific problems: None.
         Answer: תִּקְטְלֵהוּ

      2. 3fs suffix with a 2fs imperfect of לבשׁ (A-ē/A)
         1. The proto-vowel is Pataḥ: תִּלְבַּשִׁי.
         2. Attach the appropriate suffix הָ and establish the accent: תִּלְבַּשִׁיהָ.
         3. Work the *noun reduction pattern*: תִּלְבָּשִׁיהָ.
         4. Adjust for specific problems: None.
         Answer: תִּלְבָּשִׁיהָ

28.3. Imperative

The imperative generally follows the imperfect: accenting the third root letter, reducing Ḥolem and Ṣere thematic vowels, lengthening Pataḥ thematic vowels, and attaching the same suffixes/boxes.

1. Proto-form
   1. Qameṣ-Ḥatuf thematic vowel
      1. 2ms: The proto-form of the 2ms imperative with suffixes is *קָטְלְ.[1]
      2ms imperative with 1cs suffix: קָטְלֵנִי

      2. 2fs and 2mp: The proto-form of the 2fs and 2mp imperative with suffixes is *קְטָל[2] (Qameṣ-Ḥatuf). With suffixes, these forms reduce the Qameṣ-Ḥatuf in the open pretonic position, ensuring a shewa fight.

---

[1] The emphatic imperative (קָטְלָה 18.4.2) has the same proto-form – *קָטְלְ.

*קָטְלִיהוּ » *קְטְלִיהוּ » קִטְלִיהוּ 2fs imperative with 3ms suffix
The Qameṣ-Ḥatuf reduces to medial shewa in the 2fs, 2mp forms, so the third root letter, if a B^{ə}gad K^{ə}fat letter, does not receive Dagesh Lene: 2fs with a 1cs suffix – עִבְדִינִי (medial, political shewa).

2. Pataḥ Thematic Vowel: Pataḥ thematic vowels have a single proto-form (*שְׁלַח). The Pataḥ thematic vowel, as in the imperfect, lengthens to Qameṣ in the open pretonic position.

שׁלח (A/A)	2ms + 1cs suffix	שְׁלָחֵנִי
	2fs + 1cs suffix	שְׁלָחִינִי
	2mp + 1cs suffix	שְׁלָחוּנִי

2. Attaching the Suffixes and Boxes to the Imperative
Follow the same four steps (as the imperfect, 28.2.4).
Example: 2ms imperative with 3ms suffix of קטל (A/Ō)
   1. Restore the proto-form of the verb (28.3.1): 2ms with suffixes – קָטְלְ.
   2. Attach appropriate box (28.2.3), ◌ֵהוּ and establish the accent – קָטְלֵהוּ.
      Most imperfect/imperative forms accent R_3 (28.2.2).
   3. Work the rules of syllables: קָטְלֵהוּ (6.3.3).
   4. Adjust for specific problems: None.
      Answer: קָטְלֵהוּ

28.4. Infinitive Construct

1. Proto-form
The infinitive construct, like the imperative, varies the vowel of the proto-forms between R_1 and R_2 or between R_2 and R_3.
   1. *קָטְלְ: This is the usual proto-form of the infinitive construct with suffixes.
      קָטְלוֹ Killing him or his killing (context decides)

   2. *קְטָל: This is a variant proto-form of the infinitive construct with 2ms, 2mp, and 2fp suffixes: infinitive construct with 2ms suffix – קְטָלְךָ.
      *קְטָל is also the proto-form of the infinitive construct without suffixes: קְטֹל.

2. Attaching Suffixes
Being a verbal noun, the infinitive construct *takes the pronominal suffixes of the singular noun/adjective* (12.2 left column).
   1. General principles

[2] The imperative 2ms form קְטֹל (without suffixes) has the same proto-form: *קְטָל.

1. The suffixes usually attach to the proto-form: *קָטְלְ (28.4.1); קָטְלוֹ infinitive construct with 3ms suffix.
2. Translate the infinitive construct with suffixes: קָטְלוֹ his killing (or) killing him. Context determines the appropriate choice.

2. Specific problems
   1. 1cs:
      The 1cs suffix has a variant box □ִי or □ֵנִי. These forms frequently distinguish meaning – קָטְלִי my killing, קָטְלֵנִי killing me.
   2. 2ms and 2mp:
      Variant forms exist:

	*קָטְלְ	*קְטָל
2ms	קָטְלְךָ	קְטָלְךָ
2mp	קָטְלְכֶם	קְטָלְכֶם

Translate: "your killing" or "killing you," context determines.

3. Attaching the Boxes
   Follow the same four steps (28.2.4; 28.3.2)
   Example: infinitive construct with 1cp suffix עבד
   1. Restore proto-form (28.4.1): עָבְדְ.
   2. Attach appropriate box (12.2; 28.4.2) and establish the accent (follow the accent of the boxes in 12.2 left column) □ֵנוּ: עָבְדְנוּ.
   3. Work the rules of syllables (6.3.3): עָבְדֵנוּ.
      No Dagesh Lene in R_3 (28.3.1 medial shewa)
   4. Adjust for specific problems: None.
      Answer: עָבְדֵנוּ

28.5. Derived Stems: Pi"ēl and Hiph'îl

1. Pi"ēl (Hithpa"ēl)
   1. The Imperfect and the Imperative
      These reduce the thematic vowel with an attached pronominal suffix.
      Imperfect 3ms with 1cs suffix: יְבַקְשֵׁנִי
      Imperfect 3ms with 2ms suffix: יְבַקֶּשְׁךָ (27.6.1)
      Imperative 2ms with 3ms suffix: בַּקְשֵׁהוּ (footnote 4-5)
   2. Infinitive Construct
      The Pi"ēl infinitive construct takes *suffixes of the nouns* (like the Qal, 12.2 left column) and reduces the thematic vowel.
      Infinitive construct with 3ms suffix: בַּקְשׁוֹ (Compare with the imperative 2ms with 3ms suffix: בַּקְשֵׁהוּ.)

Infinitive construct with 2ms suffix: בַּקֶּשְׁךָ (27.6.1)

2. Hiph'îl: *The Hiph'îl never reduces thematic vowels.*
   1. Imperfect:
      Imperfect 3ms with 1cs suffix: יַמְלִיכֵנִי
      Imperfect 3mp with 3ms suffix: יַמְלִיכוּהוּ

   2. Imperative: Without a pronominal suffix, the 2ms imperative is a "Ṣere form," הַקְטֵל; with a pronominal suffix, the 2ms imperative takes Ḥireq-Yod for the thematic vowel: הַמְלִיכֵנִי 2ms imperative with 1cs suffix.

   3. Infinitive Construct: The Hiph'îl infinitive construct takes *pronominal suffixes of the noun* (12.2 left column).
      Infinitive construct with 3ms suffix – הַמְלִיכוֹ

   Attaching suffixes to the Pi"ēl, Hithpa"ēl, and Hiph'îl is identical to the Qal (28.4.3). *The Hiph'îl never reduces thematic vowels.*

28.6. Parsing Forms with Pronominal Suffixes

Follow 27.7.1.

1. Process:
   1. Identify boxes (if there is no box, the form is Qal).
   2. Identify the proto-form and the root (and Qal preformatives or sufformatives).
   3. Identify the suffix.
   4. Identify the accented syllable and the reduction pattern.
   5. Adjust for specific problems.

2. Example
   קָטְלוֹ
   1. Identify the box.
      There is no box, the form is Qal.
   2. The restored proto-form: *קְטֹל.
      The imperative 2ms or infinitive construct
   3. Identify the suffix.
      3ms suffix of the noun suffixes (28.4.2.); therefore, the form is an infinitive construct with a 3ms suffix.
   4. Accented syllable and reduction pattern: Not applicable.
   5. Adjust for specific problems.
      Infinitive constructs take the suffixes of the nouns.
      Answer: Qal infinitive construct with 3ms suffix.

EXERCISE TWENTY-EIGHT

I. Questions

1. Give the proto-forms of the thematic vowels of the imperfect.
2. Where does the accent occur in the imperfect?
3. Describe the vowel reduction patterns of the imperfect.
4. What is the energic Nun?
5. Discuss the specific problem of attaching a 2ms, 2mp, or 2fp suffix to a 3ms imperfect verb.
6. Describe the attaching of suffixes/boxes to the imperfect.
7. Describe the proto-form of the imperative with A/Ō verbs. Give the proto-form for קטל of the Qal imperative 2ms with suffix, and the Qal imperative 2fs with suffix.
8. Describe the proto-form of the imperative with A/A verbs.
9. Describe the attaching of suffixes/boxes to the imperative.
10. Describe the proto-forms of the infinitive construct.
11. Which suffixes have two forms with the infinitive construct?
12. Give the options for translating קָטְלוֹ.
13. The infinitive construct takes which suffixes?
14. Discuss the Hiph'îl imperative 2ms with and without a pronominal suffix.
15. Discuss the parsing of the imperfect, imperative, and infinitive construct with pronominal suffixes.

II. Vocabulary

גִּבּוֹר	warrior, mighty man	רֶ֫גֶל (*a*)	(f) foot
יַעֲקֹב	Jacob	כַּף	(f) palm (of hand), sole (of foot)
מִדְיָן	Midian		(כַּפִּי with suffix)
מִדְיָנִי	Midianite	שֶׁ֫מֶן (*a*)	oil
שֵׁ֫בֶט (*i*)	rod, staff, tribe	מִנְחָה	gift, offering
בּוֹר	pit		

III. Drills

1. Word Breakdown: In the following order: label every Dagesh Forte and Lene, Mappiq; vocal and silent shewa; Qameṣ and Qameṣ-Ḥatuf. Next, divide syllables labeling them open or closed. Then pronounce the words.

יִקְטָלְךָ   בַּגִּלְגָּל

2. Attach the following particles and translate all vocabulary words.
   Article

   רֶ֫כֶב   חָזָק

   Preposition כּ

   יהוה   חָכְמָה

   Interrogative ה

   שָׁמַר   חֵ֫לֶק

3. Attach the boxes and translate all vocabulary words. List all steps.
   1. mp construct עֶ֫בֶד (*a*)   2. mp construct כּוֹכָב

4. Attach the boxes with suffixes and translate all vocabulary words. List all steps.

   Singular Nouns   Plural Nouns

   1. 3ms עֶ֫בֶד (*a*)   2. 2fs תּוֹרָה

5. Attach the suffixes to the prepositions and translate.
   1. 3mp כּ   2. 3ms אֵל

6. Verb
   1. Create: list the three steps, the final answer, and translate.

      Pi"ēl
      1. Infinitive Absolute בקשׁ

      Hithpa"ēl
      2. Participle mp Absolute קטל

      Hiph'îl
      3. Imperative 2ms שׁמד

      Niph'al
      4. Imperfect 2fp כתב

   2. Parse: Give all possible answers. List all steps, and translate.
      1. אָהֵב   4. כִּבֵּד
      2. קְטַנִּי   5. כֻּתַּב

3. הַשְׁמֵד   6. מַשְׁלָה

7. Attach pronominal suffixes to the perfect: List the four steps.
   1. 1cp suffix on the 3ms Qal of שׁמר
   2. 3ms suffix on the 3cp Qal of קטל
   3. 2ms suffix on the 3ms Pi"ēl of בקשׁ

8. Attach pronominal suffixes to the imperfect: List the four steps.
   1. 3ms suffix (energic) on the 3ms Qal of קטל (A/Ō)
   2. 2mp suffix on the 1cs Qal of לבשׁ (A/A)
   3. 1cp suffix on the 3ms Pi"ēl of בקשׁ

9. Attach pronominal suffixes to the imperative: List the four steps.
   1. 1cs suffix on the 2mp Qal of שׁמר (A/Ō)
   2. 1cp suffix on the 2ms Hiph'îl of מלך
   3. 1cs suffix on the 2ms Qal of לבשׁ (A/A)

10. Attach pronominal suffixes to the infinitive construct: List the four steps and all possible answers.
    1. 3ms suffix on the Qal infinitive construct of קטל
    2. 2ms suffix on the Pi"ēl infinitive construct of בקשׁ
    3. 3ms suffix on the Hiph'îl infinitive construct of שׁמר

11. Parse: List the steps, and translate all vocabulary words.

1.	יִשְׁמְרֶךָּ	5.	תִּקְטָלְךָ
2.	הַמְלִיכוּנִי	6.	הַשְׁמִירֵנִי
3.	שְׁמָרַתּוּ	7.	קְטָלוֹ
4.	בַּקְּשֵׁנִי	8.	שָׁמְרוֹ

12. Translation
    1. צַדִּיק אֹהֵב מִשְׁפָּט תּוֹרַת אֱלֹהָיו בְּלִבּוֹ׃
    2. וַיְהִי כִשְׁמֹעַ אֶת־דִּבְרֵי אִשְׁתּוֹ אֲשֶׁר דִּבְּרָה אֵלָיו לֵאמֹר כַּדְּבָרִים הָאֵלֶּה עָשָׂה
    לִי עַבְדֶּךָ וַיִּרְדֹּף אַחֲרֵי עַבְדּוֹ כָּל־הַלָּיְלָה׃
    3. וַיְהִי בִּימֵי שְׁפֹט הַשֹּׁפְטִים וַיְהִי רָעָב בָּאָרֶץ וַיְקַבֵּץ שְׁמוּאֵל אֶת־כָּל־יִשְׂרָאֵל
    יְרוּשָׁלַיְמָה לִשְׁאֹל בַּיהוָה׃
    4. מִן־חַטָּאוֹת שָׁמְרֵנִי יְהוָה אַל תִּמְשָׁלְנָה בִּי׃
    5. מִשְׁפְּטֵי יהוה אֱמֶת בְּשָׁמְרָם בְּרָכָה גְּדוֹלָה׃

Morphological Principles: Weak Verbs

CHAPTER 29
OVERVIEW OF THE WEAK VERB
R_1-GUTTURAL (PE GUTTURAL) VERBS

29.1. Introduction and Overview of the Weak Verb

The weak verb (22.1) is the Mount Everest of Hebrew. Learn it thoroughly and you will conquer the most challenging mountain of Hebrew. Weak verbs classify into ten categories:

1. R_1-Guttural עבד
2. R_1-Alef Special Cases אמר
3. R_2-Guttural ברך
4. R_3-Guttural שלח
5. R_3-Alef מלא
6. R_1-Nun נפל
7. R_1-Vav/Yod ישב
8. R_2-Vav/Yod קום
9. R_3-Vav/Yod גלה (« גלו or גלי)
10. Geminate Verbs סבב

Doubly weak verbs are also possible: חטא – R_1-Guttural and R_3-Alef.

Forming and parsing weak verbs (boxes, colors, Qal, 23.3) usually affect the boxes (or the first syllable in the Qal imperfect) or the colors (or the thematic vowel in the Qal), and sometimes, both the boxes and the colors. The boxes affect the beginning (or the first syllable) of a word; the colors, the end of the word (or the last syllable). R_1 and some R_2 weaknesses affect the first syllable; R_3 weaknesses, the second syllable.

Weak verbs classified by affected syllable.

Boxes (first syllable)	**Colors** (second or rarely third syllable)	**Boxes and Colors** (all syllables)
R_1-Guttural	R_3-Guttural	R_1-Alef Special Cases
R_2-Guttural	R_3-Alef	R_2-Vav/Yod
R_1-Nun	R_3-Vav/Yod	Geminate Verbs
R_1-Vav/Yod		

In the weak verbs, the intensive stems are most regular; the Niph'al, Hiph'îl, and Hoph'al are generally regular; and the Qal is nuts. Mastering the strong verb (chapters 22-25) is essential for understanding the weak verb.

The first weak verb, the R_1-Guttural verb, has a guttural for the first root letter – עזב. R_1-Guttural verbs affect the boxes and frequently the first syllable of the Qal.

29.2. Weaknesses or Infirmities of R₁-Guttural Verbs

1. Dagesh Forte: Gutturals (including ר) will not take Dagesh Forte (5.7.2).
2. Vocal shewa: Gutturals (excluding ר) will not take a simple vocal shewa, but only a composite shewa (5.7.1).
3. Silent shewa:
    1. Gutturals (excluding ר) often take a composite shewa even in the silent shewa position (footnote 5-2).
    2. Gutturals taking a silent shewa often affect (change) the preceding preformative vowel.

29.3. Strong Areas of the R_1-Guttural Verbs

When the R_1-Guttural has a vowel under it and is not in a position to take a Dagesh Forte, the R_1-Guttural verbs are "strong."

The strong areas include:

Pi"ēl, Pu"al, Hithpa"ēl,
Qal perfect (except for 2mp, 2fp)
Qal imperative 2fs, 2mp (עִבְדִי, עִבְדוּ)[1]
Qal participle active, Qal participle passive (ms)
Qal infinitive absolute

If the composite shewa in the vocal shewa position is considered strong, then most of the Qal would be "strong."

Qal perfect (All)
Qal imperative (All)
Qal participle active and passive
Qal infinitive absolute and construct

29.4. Remedy for the Infirmity of Dagesh Forte

The weakness of the Dagesh Forte occurs only in the Niph'al imperfect, imperative, and infinitive absolute and construct. In strong verbs, the Nun of the Niph'al assimilates in the imperfect, imperative, and infinitives (22.3.2 and footnote 25-1); however, R_1-Guttural verbs reject Dagesh Forte and lengthen the preceding Ḥireq to Ṣere[2] (Compare 7.2.2).

Strong verb	יִשָּׁמֵר « יִנְשָׁמֵר*
R_1-Guttural verb	יֵעָזֵב « יִנְעָזֵב*

---

[1] These forms are strong like שִׁמְרִי, שִׁמְרוּ. One expects *עֲבְדוּ, *עֲבְדִי after the shewa fight, but the Ḥireq is an exception to the shewa rule (3.2.2).

[2] Rarely, R_1-Gutturals may have an implicit Dagesh Forte – וַיֶּחָלְקֵם. (Compare 7.2.2)

29.5. Remedy for the Infirmity of Vocal Shewa

Instead of receiving a simple vocal shewa, R_1-Gutturals take composite shewa (5.7.1), usually Ḥatef-Pataḥ. Ḥatef-Segol is usual in the Qal imperative 2ms and infinitive construct of R_1-Alef verbs.

Strong verb:	כְּתֹב
R_1-Guttural verb:	עֲזֹב
R_1-Guttural (א):	אֱמֹר

29.6. Remedy for the Infirmity of the Guttural Rejecting Silent Shewa (see 29.9)

1. Niph'al, Hiph'îl, Hoph'al
    1. Pataḥ: Forms taking a Pataḥ under a preformative (Hiph'îl imperfect, imperative, infinitives, and participle) retain the Pataḥ under the preformative and take a Ḥatef-Pataḥ under the R_1-Guttural.

Strong verb:	יַקְטִיל	R_1 P[3]
R_1-Guttural verb:	יַעֲבִיר	G_1 P[4]

    2. Ḥireq/Segol: Forms taking a Ḥireq under a preformative (Niph'al perfect, infinitive absolute, participle; Hiph'îl perfect) change the preformative vowel to Segol and take a Ḥatef-Segol under the R_1-Guttural.

Strong verb:	נִקְטַל	R_1 P
R_1-Guttural verb:	נֶעֱזַב	G_1 P

    3. Qameṣ-Ḥatuf: Forms taking a Qameṣ-Ḥatuf under a preformative (Hoph'al) retain the Qameṣ-Ḥatuf under the preformative and take a Ḥatef-Qameṣ-Ḥatuf under the R_1-Guttural.

Strong verb:	הָקְטַל	R_1 P
R_1-Guttural verb:	נָעֳזַב	G_1 P

2. Qal Imperfect

    The Qal imperfect takes Segol or Pataḥ for the preformative vowel (and the corresponding Ḥatef shewa for the R_1-Guttural).

    1. Segol
        1. All first common singular (1cs) forms: G_1 אֶ » אֶעֱבֹר
        2. All verbs, stative and standard, with a Pataḥ thematic vowel (/A): G_1 P » יֶאֱהַב
        3. All standard, R_1-Alef verbs (/Ō) R_1-א: א P » יֶאֱסֹר

---

[3] R_1 represents the first root letter; P represents "preformative."

[4] G_1 represents a guttural in the first root position.

2. Pataḥ
   1. Standard verbs (/Ō) that are 𝔊₁-ה, ח, ע: יַעֲבֹר (𝔊₁ P̱)
   2. Standard verbs (/Ō) 𝔊₁-א that are non-pausal (for pausal forms, see 6.5.3) forms with vocalic endings (יַאַחְרוּ) and most forms with pronominal suffixes (יַאַסְרֵנִי).

29.7. Remedy for the Infirmity of the Silent Shewa (see 29.9)

R_1-Gutturals sometimes retain silent shewa, but the preformative vowel changes as if the composite shewa had replaced the silent shewa.

Niph'al perfect 3ms: נֶחְבָּא (instead of *נִחְבָּא) as if from *נֶחֱבָא
Qal imperfect 3ms: יַחְתֹּם (instead of *יִחְתֹּם) as if from *יַחֲתֹם

With forms that retain silent shewa, work the form with the composite shewa and then restore the silent shewa: *יַחֲתֹם » יַחְתֹּם.

Remember: All these remedies are general – there are exceptions.

29.8. Final Considerations (17.3.3; 18.2.3)

1. With vocalic endings, thematic vowels reduce, leaving consecutive vocal shewas – *יַעֲזֹבוּ » *יַעֲזְבוּ. The composite shewa under the R_1-Guttural becomes the vowel of composite shewa – *יַעֲזְבוּ » יַעַזְבוּ. The shewa under the second root letter, a medial (political) shewa, leaves the Bᵊgad Kᵊfat in the third root position without Dagesh Lene – יַעַזְבוּ.

2. Pronominal Suffixes with the Imperfect of R_1-Guttural Verbs
   Most imperfects of R_1-Guttural verbs have Pataḥs for the preformative and R_1, יַאַסְרֵנוּ, but sometimes Segols are possible נֶאֶסָרְךָ.

29.9. Summary of Adjustments to the Boxes (Summary of 29.6; 29.7)

Because a guttural in the R_1-position affects the vowels under the preformative and the R_1-letter, adjust the boxes slightly:

1. Hiph'îl

	Strong Verb	**R_1-Guttural with Silent Shewa**	**R_1-Guttural with Composite Shewa**
Perfect	הִ□ְ□□	הֶ□ְ□□	הֶ□ֱ□□
Imperfect	יַ□ְ□□	יַ□ְ□□	יַ□ֲ□□
Imperative	הַ□ְ□□	הַ□ְ□□	הַ□ֲ□□
Infinitive	הַ□ְ□□	הַ□ְ□□	הַ□ֲ□□
Participle	מַ□ְ□□	מַ□ְ□□	מַ□ֲ□□

2. Hoph'al

	Strong Verb and R_1-Guttural with Silent Shewa	**R_1-Guttural with Composite Shewa**
Perfect	הָ□ְ□□	הָ□ֳ□□
Imperfect	יָ□ְ□□	יָ□ֳ□□
Participle	מָ□ְ□□	מָ□ֳ□□

3. Niph'al

	Strong Verb	**R_1-Guttural with Silent Shewa**	**R_1-Guttural with Composite Shewa**
Perfect	נִ□ְ□□	נֶ□ְ□□	נֶ□ֱ□□
Imperfect	יִ⊡ָ□□	יֵ□ָ□□	יֵ□ָ□□
Imperative	הִ⊡ָ□□	הֵ□ָ□□	הֵ□ָ□□
Infinitive	הִ⊡ָ□□/נִ□ְ	הֵ□ָ□□/נֶ□ְ	הֵ□ָ□□/נֶ□ֱ
Participle	נִ□ְ□□	נֶ□ְ□□	נֶ□ֱ□□

4. Qal Imperfect: Although the Qal imperfect does not have boxes, note the following patterns.

	Strong Verb	**R_1-Guttural with Silent Shewa**	**R_1-Guttural with Composite Shewa**
Imperfect	יִ□ְ	יֶ□ְ or יַ□ְ For the proper option, see 29.6.2.	יֶ□ֱ or יַ□ֲ For the proper option, see 29.6.2.

29.10. Forming the Qal in Weak Verbs

Follow three steps:

1. Write the form as a strong verb.
2. Identify the weakness: especially the area of the verb affected (R_1, R_2, R_3 or thematic vowels).
3. Make the proper adjustments (from steps one and two).

29.11. Forming R_1-Guttural Verbs

Follow the three steps for working strong verbs (23.2), and adjust the boxes when necessary.

Examples of forming R_1-Guttural verbs

1. Hiph'îl Perfect 1cs עבר
   1. Boxes: הִ□ְ□□ » הֶ□ֱ□□   הֶעֱבר
   2. Colors: A-i/I-e   הֶעֱבַר
   3. Qal stem: קָטַ֫לְתִּי   הֶעֱבַ֫רְתִּי

   Answer: הֶעֱבַרְתִּי
   1. Step one applies the boxes adjusted for R_1-Guttural: הִ□ְ□□ » הֶ□ֱ□□ (or הַ□ֲ□□).
   2. Step two adds the thematic vowel (A/).
   3. Step three adds the Qal sufformative תִּי.

2. Qal Imperfect 2ms עבר (A/Ō)
   1. Write the form as a strong verb: תִּעְבֹר.
   2. Identify the weakness: R_1-Guttural – ע; R_1 and the preformative are affected.
   3. Make adjustments: the Qal imperfect has two possibilities: Segol or Pataḥ. R_1-ע (A/Ō) verbs take Pataḥ (unless 1cs, 29.6.2.2).

   Answer: תַּעֲבֹר

29.12. Parsing the Qal in Weak Verbs

Follow three steps:

1. Eliminate boxes or colors.
2. Identify the Qal preformatives and sufformatives.
3. Identify the weakness of the verb (R_1, R_2, R_3 or thematic vowels).

29.13. Parsing R_1-Guttural Verbs

The steps are like the strong verbs (23.4).[5]

1. Boxes (adjusted)
2. Colors
3. Qal stem (preformatives / sufformatives)

Remember your verb will have three root letters (for now).

Examples

1. הֶעֱבַ֫רְתִּי
   1. Boxes: □□□ֶה » □□□ְה — Hiph'îl perfect
   2. Colors: A (A-î/Î-ē) — Eliminate all third persons: 3ms, 3fs, 3cp.
   3. Qal stem: קָטַ֫לְתִּי — Eliminate all except Hiph'îl perfect 1cs.

   Answer: Hiph'îl perfect 1cs

2. עֲבֹר
   1. Eliminate boxes or colors (of derived stems): The thematic vowel (Ḥolem) suggests the Qal.
   2. Qal stem – קְטֹל: Qal imperative 2ms or infinitive construct
   3. Weakness of the verb: The verb is a R_1-Guttural (ע), making a Ḥatuf-Pataḥ necessary under R_1.

   Answer: Qal imperative 2ms or infinitive construct

3. יַעְבֹר
   1. Boxes (?): — Hiph'îl imperfect □□□ְיַ or Qal pattern □ְיַ (29.9)
   2. Colors: Ḥolem — Eliminate the Hiph'îl imperfect and vocalic endings of the Qal imperfect.

   Now switch to the Qal steps (29.12).

   1. Eliminate boxes or colors: — The colors eliminate the boxes of the Hiph'îl.
   2. Qal stem: יִקְטֹל — Qal imperfect 3ms
   3. Weakness: The R_1-Guttural, although taking the silent shewa, changes the usual preformative vowel Ḥireq to Pataḥ.[6]

---

[5] Context is the fourth step when reading the Hebrew Old Testament. Context determines the correct parsing of identical forms: קְטֹל imperative 2ms or infinitive construct – context decides.

[6] More accurately, the original Pataḥ remains (footnote 36-7).

R_1-GUTTURAL (PE GUTTURAL) VERBS

	Qal	Niph'al	Pi"ēl	Pu"al	Hithpa"ēl	Hiph'îl	Hoph'al
Perfect	Strong 29.3 (or G in 2mp, 2fp)	G נֶ (G נְ) 29.6.1	Strong 29.3			G הֶ (G הֶ) 29.6.1	G P (G P) 29.6.1
Imperfect	1cs G אֶ Stative G P R_1-א אֹ P R_1-ה, ח, ע Non-1cs and non-stative forms G P (exception: vocalic, non-pausal or with suffixes G P)	Dagesh rejection: Ḥireq becomes Ṣere 29.4				G P (G P) 29.6.1	
Imperative	Vocal shewa position: G » R_1-ה, ח, ע; אֱ » R_1-א 2fs, 2mp are strong 29.5						
Infinitive Construct	G for R_1-א G for R_1-ה, ח, ע 29.5						
Infinitive Absolute	Strong 29.3	□הֵ or □נֶ					
Participle Active		G נֶ (G נְ) 29.6.1					
Participle Passive	G 29.5						

Note: For the corresponding color chart, see page 351

QAL IMPERFECT (29.6.2)

		Standard (/Ō)							Stative (/A) 29.6.2 or Standard with Pataḥ thematic vowels	
		R₁-א 29.6.2	R₁-ה 29.6.2		R₁-ח 29.6.2		R₁-ע 29.6.2			
			Composite Shewa	Silent Shewa	Composite Shewa	Silent Shewa	Composite Shewa	Silent Shewa	Composite Shewa	Silent Shewa
1cs 29.6.2		אֶאֱסֹר	אֶהֱרֹג	אֶהְדֹּף	אֶחֱלֹף	אֶחְתֹּם	אֶעֱזֹב	אֶעְשֹׂר	אֶאֱמַץ	אֶחְסַר
2ms		תֶּאֱסֹר	תַּהֲרֹג	תַּהְדֹּף	תַּחֲלֹף	תַּחְתֹּם	תַּעֲזֹב	תַּעְשֹׂר	תֶּאֱמַץ	תֶּחְסַר
3ms		יֶאֱסֹר	יַהֲרֹג	יַהְדֹּף	יַחֲלֹף	יַחְתֹּם	יַעֲזֹב	יַעְשֹׂר	יֶאֱמַץ	יֶחְסַר
2fs	Non-pausal 29.6.2	תַּאַסְרִי 29.6.2	תַּהַרְגִי	תַּהְדְּפִי	תַּחַלְפִי	תַּחְתְּמִי	תַּעַזְבִי	תַּעְשְׂרִי	תֶּאֶמְצִי	תֶּחְסְרִי
	Pausal 6.5.3	תֶּאֱסֹרִי	תַּהֲרֹגִי	תַּהְדֹּפִי	תַּחֲלֹפִי	תַּחְתֹּמִי	תַּעֲזֹבִי	תַּעְשֹׂרִי	תֶּאֱמָצִי	תֶּחְסָרִי
2/3fp	Pausal and Non-pausal	תֶּאֱסֹרְנָה	תַּהֲרֹגְנָה	תַּהְדֹּפְנָה	תַּחֲלֹפְנָה	תַּחְתֹּמְנָה	תַּעֲזֹבְנָה	תַּעְשֹׂרְנָה	תֶּאֱמַצְנָה	תֶּחְסַרְנָה

Chart courtesy of Isaac Jerusalmi

Note: Usually, suffixed forms are like vocalic, non-pausal forms – יַאַסְרֵ֫נוּ.

Note: For the corresponding color chart, see page 352

Exercise Twenty-Nine

I. Questions

1. Define a weak verb. What are the weak letters?
2. What syllable does an R_1 weakness affect? What syllable does an R_3 weakness affect?
3. In the weak verb, what stems are regular, generally regular, and most difficult?
4. Describe the weaknesses of the R_1-Guttural verbs.
5. What part of the verb is affected in R_1-Guttural verbs?
6. In what areas are R_1-Guttural verbs completely strong?
7. Where does the Dagesh Forte problem occur? How is it solved?
8. Where does the vocal shewa problem occur? How is it solved?
9. Where does the silent shewa problem occur? How is it solved?
10. When do Qal imperfects follow the Segol pattern and when do they follow the Pataḥ pattern for the preformatives?
11. When the R_1-Gutturals retain the silent shewa under an R_1-Guttural letter, how does this affect the preformative vowel?
12. What further complication occurs when the Qal imperfect has a vocalic ending?
13. With a guttural in the R_1 position, how are the boxes adjusted? How is the Qal imperfect adjusted?
14. Describe the forming and the parsing of weak verbs.
15. Describe the forming and the parsing of weak verbs in the Qal.

II. Vocabulary

ברך — Qal: bless
Pi"ēl: bless, pronounce a blessing on

אמן — Niph'al: make firm, sure, establish
Hiph'îl: trust, believe (sometimes with בּ, to believe in)

חשׁב — Qal: think, account, plan, reckon, impute
Niph'al: passive of Qal
Pi"ēl: think upon, plan, derive, reckon

חרם — Hiph'îl: devote to the ban, exterminate, destroy
Hoph'al: passive of Hiph'îl

אסר — Qal: bind, tie, imprison
Niph'al: passive of Qal

אסף — Qal: gather, collect
Niph'al: passive of Qal

חָפֵץ — Qal: delight in, take pleasure (with בּ)

חזק — Qal: be strong, be firm, prevail
Pi"ēl: put in a strong state, make strong
Hiph'îl: cause to be strong, seize, take hold (with בּ)

אֱמֶת — truth (with 3ms suffix אֲמִתּוֹ, root אמן)

חַיִל — strength, mighty man, ability, army, wealth

חָצֵר	settlement, enclosure	עזר	Qal: help, aid
נַחֲלָה	inheritance		Niph'al: passive of Qal

III. Drills

1. Word Breakdown: In the following order: label every Dagesh Forte and Lene, Mappiq; vocal and silent shewa; Qameṣ and Qameṣ-Ḥatuf. Next, divide syllables labeling them open or closed. Then pronounce the words.

   מִצִּיּוֹן　　　　יָדַע

2. Attach the following particles and translate all vocabulary words.
   Interrogative מה

   חָזוֹן　　　　הֵם

   Preposition ב

   אֱמֶת　　　　תְּהוֹם

3. Attach the boxes and translate all vocabulary words: list all steps.
   1. mp construct נַעַר (*a*)
   2. fs construct מִלְחָמָה

4. Attach the boxes with suffixes and translate all vocabulary words: list all steps.

   Singular Nouns
   1. 3ms מִלְחָמָה
   2. 3mp בֹּשֶׁת (*o*)

   Plural Nouns
   3. 2ms גַּנָּב
   4. 1cp קֹדֶשׁ (*o*)

5. Attach the suffixes to the prepositions and translate.
   1. 2fs לְ
   2. 1cp מִן
   3. 3ms לְמַעַן
   4. 3mp אֵת (with)

6. Verbs
   1. Create: List all steps, the final answer, then translate all vocabulary words.
      Qal
      1. Imperfect 3mp אזר (A/Ō)
      2. Imperfect 3fs (shewa) חסר (A/A)
      3. Imperfect 2ms (shewa) הדף (A/Ō)
      4. Imperfect 2ms +1cp suffix אסף (A/Ō)
      5. Infinitive construct +2ms suffix עמד (A/Ō)

Hiph'îl
6. Participle mp absolute אכל
7. Imperfect 3ms +Vav-consecutive עמד
8. Imperative 2mp +1cs suffix עבר

Hoph'al
9. Perfect 3cp עמד

Niph'al
10. Imperfect 3fp אדר

2. Parse: Give all possible answers. List all steps, then translate all vocabulary words.

1.	יַחְתֹּם	6.	חֲזַק
2.	יַעְמְדוּן	7.	הַעֲבִידֵ֫הוּ
3.	יַעֲמֵד	8.	וַיֶּהֶרְסֶ֫הָ
4.	נַעֲמֹד	9.	יַעַבְרֶ֫נְהוּ
5.	הָעָזְבָה	10.	הַעֲמֵד

7. Translation

1. אָמַ֗ר בָּרוּךְ יהוה אֱלֹהֵי אֲדֹנִ֔י אַבְרָהָ֔ם אֲשֶׁר לֹא עָזַב חַסְדּוֹ וַאֲמִתּ֖וֹ מֵעִם אֲדֹנִ֑י׃
2. הֶאֱמִ֖ן בַּיהוָ֑ה וַיַּחְשְׁבֶ֥הָ לּ֖וֹ צְדָקָֽה׃
3. וַיַּעְזְרֵ֥ם יהוָ֗ה וַיְמַלְּטֵם מֵרְשָׁעִ֑ים כִּי יהוָ֖ה בְּקִרְבָּֽם׃
4. וּנְתָנָם יהוה אֱלֹהֶ֛יךָ לְפָנֶ֖יךָ וְאִבַּדְתָּ֑ם הַחֲרֵם תַּחֲרִים אֹתָם לֹא תִכְרֹת לָהֶ֛ם
בְּרִ֖ית׃
5. כִּי עַם קָדוֹשׁ אַתָּה לַיהוָ֖ה אֱלֹהֶ֑יךָ בְּךָ בָּחַר יהוה אֱלֹהֶ֗יךָ לוֹ לְעַ֣ם
מִכֹּל הָעַמִּים אֲשֶׁ֖ר עַל־פְּנֵי הָאֲדָמָֽה׃
6. קָרָא יוֹסֵף בְּקוֹל גָּד֖וֹל אִסְר֥וּהוּ וַיַּאַסְר֖וּהוּ לְעֵינֵיהֶֽם׃

CHAPTER 30
R_1- GUTTURAL א (PE ALEF)
SPECIAL CASES
אמר, אכל, אבד, אפה, אבה, (אחז)

30.1. Introduction: R_1-Guttural א (special cases) present unique problems only in the Qal imperfect.[1] Elsewhere, the verbs are like other R_1-Guttural verbs. The verbs with these problems are אמר, אכל, אבד, אפה, אבה[2] (and occasionally אחז, and other verbs rarely). R_1-Guttural א (special cases) affects the preformative vowel (and R_1) and the thematic vowel.

30.2. Weaknesses or Infirmities of R_1-Guttural א Verbs (Special Cases)

The R_1-Guttural א quiesces and changes:

1. The preformative vowel (ā » ō)
2. The thematic vowel (various dissimilations)

30.3. Remedy for the Preformative Vowel

1. 1cs

   *אַאְכָל ('a'kol) » *אַאכָל » *אָאכָל » *אֹאכָל » *אֹכָל
   1 2 3 4 5

   The original form (1) of the 1cs quiesces the second Alef (2) (the Alef of the root) and lengthens the original Pataḥ to Qameṣ (3). The Qameṣ becomes Ḥolem (ā » ō) (4), and the quiesced Alef drops (5).

2. All other forms

   *יַאְכָל (ya'kol) » *יַאכָל » *יָאכָל[3] » *יֹאכָל Qal Imperfect 3ms
   1 2 3 4

   All other forms follow the same steps as the 1cs, except the quiesced Alef is retained in spelling (4).

30.4. Remedy for the Thematic Vowel

The thematic vowel dissimilates from the vowel of the preformative.

*אֹכָל ('ōkol) » אֹכַל ('ōkal) Qal imperfect 1cs
1 2

---

[1] The Qal infinitive construct of אמר with ל preposition is also a problem: the Alef quiesces, and the Segol under the ל preposition lengthens to Ṣere by compensation – *לֶאֱמֹר » *לֵאמֹר » לֵאמֹר (8.2.5).

[2] The weak verbs אפה and אבה are doubly weak: the first syllable follows the remedies of 30.3; the last syllable follows chapter 37.

[3] Compare the first syllable of וַיָּאצֶל (Num 11:25).

The Qameṣ-Ḥatuf (1) dissimilates from the Ḥolem of the preformative and becomes a Pataḥ (2).

Various dissimilations are possible (See chart at the end of the chapter.):[4]

1. In regular (that is, forms without Vav-consecutive וַ◙), non-pausal forms, the Qameṣ-Ḥatuf becomes Pataḥ: תֹּאמַר.
2. In regular, pausal forms, the Qameṣ-Ḥatuf becomes Ṣere: תֹּאמֵ֑ר.
3. In Vav-consecutive (וַ◙), non-pausal forms, the Qameṣ-Ḥatuf becomes
   1. Segol (For אמר, note the shift of accent, see footnote 20-1: וַתֹּ֫אמֶר.)
   2. Pataḥ (For אכל and 1cs of אמר, note the accent does not shift: וַתֹּאכַ֫ל, וָאֹמַ֫ר.)
4. In Vav-consecutive (וַ◙), pausal forms, the Qameṣ-Ḥatuf becomes Pataḥ: וַתֹּאמַ֑ר, וַתֹּאכַ֑ל.

30.5. Forming R_1-Guttural א Verbs (Special Cases)

1. Replace the preformative vowel with Ḥolem. For the 1cs, quiesce the initial Alef and drop the R_1-Guttural א of the root.
2. Dissimilate the thematic vowel according to 30.4.

   Example: Qal imperfect 3ms pausal of אמר
   1. יֹאמָר (Qameṣ-Ḥatuf)
   2. יֹאמֵ֑ר (30.4.2)

30.6. Parsing R_1-Guttural א Verbs (Special Cases)

Follow the same steps in 29.12.

Example

וַיֹּ֫אמֶר

1. Eliminate boxes or colors: There are no boxes
2. Qal (preformatives/sufformatives): Imperfect 3ms
   The Vav-consecutive with the pointing וַ◙ also indicates an imperfect.
3. Weakness: The preformative Ḥolem comes from the queisced Alef; the Segol is the dissimilated vowel (30.4.3).
   Answer: Qal imperfect 3ms + Vav-consecutive of אמר

30.7. אכל with Pronominal Suffixes

Only אכל takes pronominal suffixes in the Qal imperfect in R_1 Guttural א verbs (special cases). The original thematic vowel (Qameṣ-Ḥatuf) will always reduce with pronominal suffixes (28.2.2):

יֹאכְלֶ֫נּוּ Qal imperfect 3ms +3ms energic ending.

---

[4] The 2fp, 3fp forms always take Pataḥ.

DISSIMILATION OF THEMATIC VOWELS (30.4)
אמר, אכל, אבד, (אחז)

	Regular (without Vav-consecutive וַ▣)	Vav-Consecutive וַ▣
Non-pausal	יֹאמַר יֹאכַל יֹאבַד (יֹאחֵז) 30.4.1	וַיֹּ֫אמֶר וַיֹּ֫אחֶז וַיֹּאכַל (וָאֹמַר 1cs only) 30.4.3
Pausal	יֹאמֵ֑ר יֹאכֵ֑ל יֹאבֵ֑ד 30.4.2	וַיֹּאמַ֑ר וַיֹּאכַ֑ל 30.4.4

□ַ (□ֵ) 30.4.1	□ֶ/□ַ 30.4.3
□ֵ 30.4.2	□ַ 30.4.4

Notes:

1. Bracketed words are exceptions.
2. אבד never occurs with Vav-consecutive (וַ▣).
3. יֹאחֵז/יֹאחַז (30.4.1) is like the regular, pausal form (30.4.2; 30.4.3) – וַיֹּ֫אחֶז.
4. אבה, אפה – Third weak verbs (chapter 37) do not dissimilate thematic vowels.
5. Imperfect 2, 3fp forms always take Pataḥ.

Note: For the corresponding color chart, see page 353

Exercise Thirty

I. Questions

1. List the verbs that are special cases R_1-Guttural א.
2. Where do the unique problems of R_1-Guttural א occur? How are these verbs treated elsewhere?
3. What part of the verb is affected in R_1-Guttural א special cases?
4. Describe the two weaknesses of these verbs.
5. Discuss the remedies for these two weaknesses and trace the development of the 1cs and the 2ms.
6. What are the various dissimilation possibilities for the thematic vowel?
7. Which forms always take Pataḥ?
8. Discuss the forming and the parsing of these verbs.
9. Which verb takes pronominal suffixes? Which reduction pattern does it follow?

II. Vocabulary

אַךְ	only, surely, but	מְלָאכָה	work
אַ֫יִל	ram	דּוֹר	(pl. דֹּרוֹת) generation
פְּלִשְׁתִּי	Philistine	הפך	Qal: turn, turn over, overthrow
פתח	Qal: open		Niph'al: reflexive of Qal
	Niph'al: be opened, loosened	אחז	Qal: grasp, take hold of
	Pi"ēl: loosen, free, open		(frequently with ב or
פֶּ֫תַח (*i*)	opening, gate, entrance		accusative)
לְבַד	alone (with suffix, לְבַדִּי; with	חוּץ	(noun) the outside, street
	מִן: מִלְּבַדִּי besides, apart from)	ערך	Qal: arrange in order
נֶ֫גֶד (*e*)	before, in front of, opposite to	אבה	to be willing, to consent
	(with suffix נֶגְדִּי)	אפה	to bake

III. Drills

1. Word Breakdown: In the following order: label every Dagesh Forte and Lene, Mappiq; vocal and silent shewa; Qameṣ and Qameṣ-Ḥatuf. Next, divide syllables labeling them open or closed. Then pronounce the words.

   אֹיְבַי   הִסַּבֶּ֫ינָה

2. Attach the following particles and translate all vocabulary words.
   Article

   הֶבֶל   צַדִּיק

Preposition ל

שְׁמוֹ עֲרָבִי

Interrogative ה

הָיָה מְלִיצָה

3. Attach the boxes and translate all vocabulary words. List all steps.
   1. mp absolute סֵ֫פֶר (*i*) 2. fp absolute חֲפַרְפָּרָה

4. Attach the boxes with suffixes and translate all vocabulary words. List all steps.

Singular Nouns	Plural Nouns
1. 1cs חֹ֫רֶף (*o*)	3. 3ms תְּנוּבָה
2. 2mp נַ֫עַר (*a*)	4. 1cs נָחָשׁ

5. Attach the suffixes to the prepositions and translate.

1. 1cs עַל	3. 2mp מִן
2. 2fs אֵ֫ת (direct object)	4. 3ms אַחַר

6. Verbs
   1. Create: List all steps and the final answer.
      Qal
      1. Imperfect 3ms +3ms suffix (energic) אכל
      2. Imperative 2ms אכל
      3. Imperfect 1cs אבד
      4. Imperfect 3fs +Vav-consecutive אמר
      5. Imperfect 1cp (pausal) אבד
      6. Imperfect 2ms +Vav-consecutive (pausal) אכל
      7. Imperfect 3fs חזק (A/A)
      8. Imperative 2fs חלף (A/Ō)
      9. Perfect 3ms +1cs suffix הרג

      Niph'al
      10. Perfect 3ms (shewa – that is, maintain silent shewa under R_1-א) אדר

   2. Parse: Give all possible answers. List all steps.

1. חֲרוּצִים	6. וַתֹּאכַ֫לְנָה
2. יֹאמַר	7. יִמְנָעֵ֫נִי
3. הַעֲבִיר֫וּנִי	8. וַ֫יֹּאמֶר

4.	אֱכֹל	9.	הֵאָסְרוּ
5.	אָסְפְּכֶם	10.	תָּעֳמַדְנָה

7. Translation

1. וַיַּהֲפֹךְ אֶת־הֶעָרִים הָאֵלֶּה וְאֵת כָּל־הַכִּכָּר וְאֵת כָּל־יֹשְׁבֵי הֶעָרִים׃
2. וַיַּשְׁכֵּם אַבְרָהָם בַּבֹּקֶר אֶל־הַמָּקוֹם אֲשֶׁר עָמַד שָׁם אֶת־פְּנֵי־יְהוָה׃
3. וַיֹּאמֶר הַמַּלְאָךְ לְדָוִד וְאֹחֵז בְּשָׁאוּל וָאֶהֶרְגֵהוּ וַיְדַבֵּר דָּוִד אֶל־נְעָרָיו וַיַּהַרְגוּהוּ׃
4. פִּי־צַדִּיק יְדַבֵּר חָכְמָה וּלְשׁוֹן רְשָׁעִים תִּכָּרֵת׃
5. דִּבֶּר שָׁאוּל אֶל־עֲבָדָיו לֵאמֹר דַּבֵּר אֶל־דָּוִד הִנֵּה חָפֵץ בְּךָ הַמֶּלֶךְ וְכָל־עֲבָדָיו
   אֲהֵבוּךָ וַיְדַבְּרוּ עַבְדֵי־שָׁאוּל בְּאָזְנֵי דָוִד אֶת־הַדְּבָרִים הָאֵלֶּה׃
6. יְהוָֹה בַּבֹּקֶר תִּשְׁמַע קוֹלִי בַּבֹּקֶר אֶעֱרָךְ־לְךָ דְּבָרָי׃

CHAPTER 31
R_2-GUTTURAL (AYIN GUTTURAL) VERBS

31.1. Introduction: Guttural problems usually involve the Dagesh Forte and shewa (5.7.1; 5.7.2). For R_2-Guttural verbs, the Dagesh Forte problem is limited to the intensive stems, the Pi"ēl, Pu"al, and Hithpa"ēl; whereas, the shewa problem occurs whenever the thematic vowel reduces under the R_2-Guttural (31.5). R_2-Guttural verbs primarily affect the boxes.

31.2. Weaknesses or Infirmities of R_2-Guttural Verbs

1. Dagesh Forte: Gutturals (including ר) will not take Dagesh Forte (5.7.2). This problem is limited to the intensives: Pi"ēl, Pu"al, and Hithpa"ēl.
2. Vocal shewa: Gutturals reject simple vocal shewa and take a composite shewa (almost always □ֲ Ḥatef-Pataḥ).

31.3. Strong Areas of R_2-Guttural Verbs

All stems outside the intensives are virtually strong with a Ḥatef-Pataḥ (□ֲ) for a reduced thematic vowel.

31.4. Remedies for the Infirmity of the Dagesh Forte

(1) The R_2-Guttural rejects the Dagesh Forte, and the preceding short vowel lengthens by compensation (compare 7.2.2), or (2) the R_2-Guttural implies the Dagesh Forte (compare 7.2.2).

1. The R_2-Guttural rejects the Dagesh Forte, and the preceding short vowel lengthens.

Strong Verb		R_2-Guttural Verb: Dagesh rejected (Boxes adjusted)	
□▣□ִ	קִדֵּשׁ	□□□ֵ	בֵּרֵךְ
□▣□ַ	קַדֵּשׁ	□□□ָ	בָּרֵךְ
□▣□ֻ	קֻדַּשׁ	□□□ֹ	בֹּרַךְ

2. The Guttural implies the Dagesh Forte

Strong Verb		R_2-Guttural Verb: Dagesh rejected (Boxes adjusted)	
□▣□ִ	קִדֵּשׁ	□□□ִ	נִחֵם
□▣□ַ	קַדֵּשׁ	□□□ַ	נַחֵם
□▣□ֻ	קֻדַּשׁ	□□□ֻ	נֻחַם

The following chart indicates when the Dagesh Forte is rejected or implied. These are general patterns – there are exceptions:

R: Rejects Dagesh Forte with compensatory lengthening
I : Implies Dagesh Forte

	Pi“ēl	Pu“al	Hithpa“ēl
א	R	R	R
ה	I	R	I
ח	I	I	I
ע	I	R	I
ר	R	R	R

Chart courtesy of Isaac Jerusalmi

31.5. Remedy for the Infirmity of the Vocal Shewa

The thematic vowel reduced, the R_2-Guttural takes a Ḥatef-Pataḥ (◌ֲ).
Strong verb: קִדְּשׁוּ
R_2-Guttural verb: מֵאֲנוּ

31.6. Final Considerations

1. In the Qal imperfect-imperative of R_2-Guttural verbs, almost all thematic vowels are Pataḥ (/A).
   Qal imperfect 3ms: יִבְחַר
   Qal imperative 2ms: בְּחַר

2. In R_2-Guttural verbs, the Qal imperative and the Qal infinitive construct differ. In most paradigms, such as the strong verb, they are identical: קְטֹל – Qal imperative 2ms or Qal infinitive construct.

	Qal Imperative	Qal Infinitive
2ms	בְּחַר	בְּחֹר
2fs	בַּחֲרִי (« *בְּחְרִי Two vocal shewas: R_1 takes corresponding short vowel.)	בָּחֳרִי[1] (with 1cs suffix)
2mp	בַּחֲרוּ (pausal בְּחָ֫רוּ)	
2fp	בְּחַ֫רְנָה	

31.7. Forming and Parsing R_2-Guttural Verbs

Follow 29.10-29.13. Like R_1-Guttural verbs, adjust the boxes for R_2-Guttural verbs. Examples:

1. Pi"ēl Imperative 2ms ברך
   1. Boxes: □▣□ » □□□ בָּרֵךְ « *בַּרֵּךְ
   2. Colors: A-ē/Ē בָּרֵךְ
   3. Qal: קְטֹל

      Answer: בָּרֵךְ

      In step one, R_2-ר rejects the Dagesh Forte and lengthens the Pataḥ to Qameṣ, 31.4.

2. נֻחַם
   1. Boxes: □□□ » □▣□ Pu"al perfect
   2. Color: A/A Pu"al perfect (excluding 3fs, 3cp)
   3. Qal: קָטַל Pu"al perfect 3ms

      Answer: Pu"al perfect 3ms of נחם

      In step one, R_2-ח implies the Dagesh Forte, so the Qibbuṣ remains.

[1] בָּחֳרִי comes from *בָּחְרִי: the guttural rejects the simple vocal shewa and takes a composite shewa that echoes the Qameṣ-Ḥatuf. Compare 29.6.1; 16:4 פָּעֳלִי.

R_2-GUTTURAL (AYIN GUTTURAL) VERBS

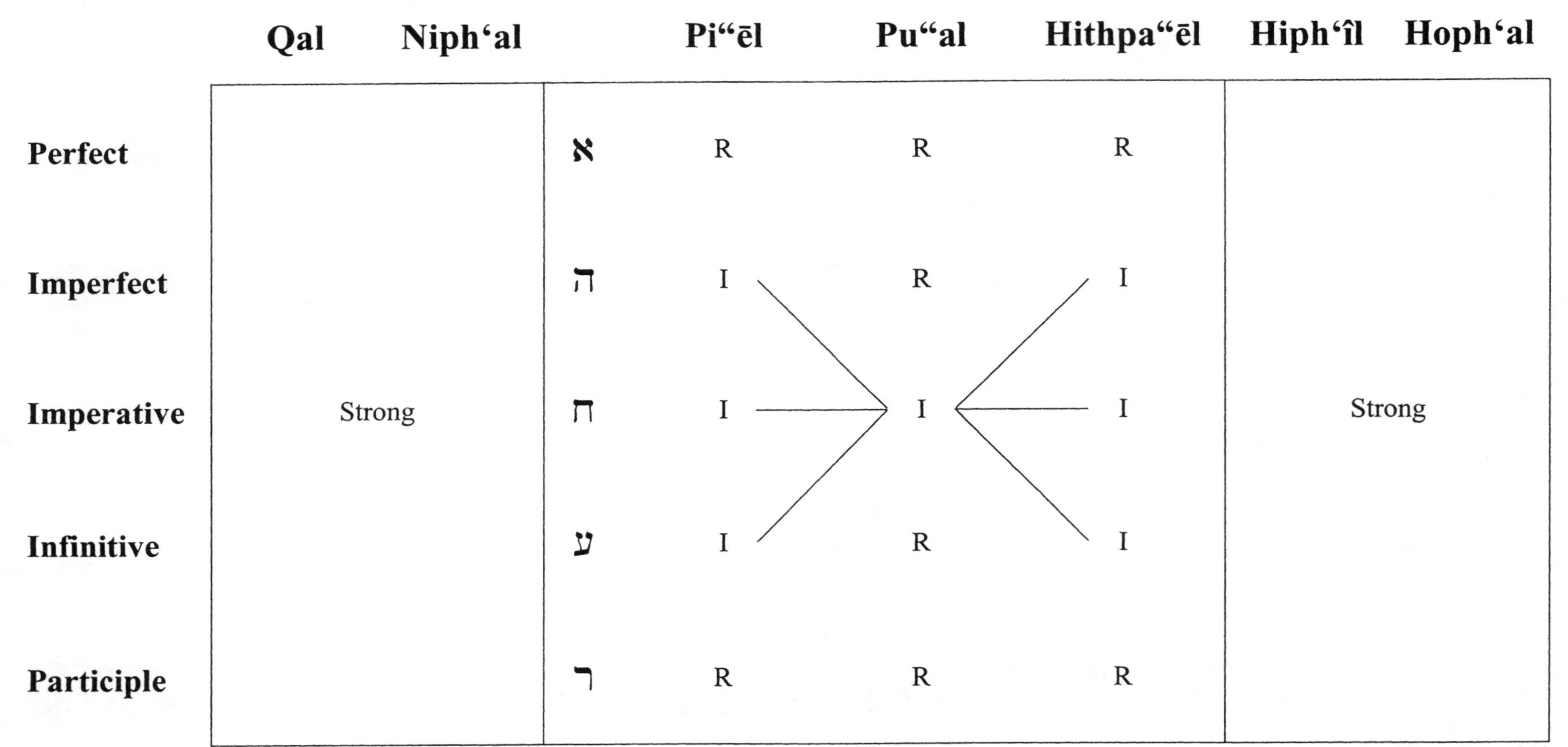

	Qal	Niph'al		Pi"ēl	Pu"al	Hithpa"ēl	Hiph'îl	Hoph'al
Perfect			א	R	R	R		
Imperfect			ה	I	R	I		
Imperative	Strong		ח	I	I	I	Strong	
Infinitive			ע	I	R	I		
Participle			ר	R	R	R		

Chart courtesy of Isaac Jerusalmi

R: Rejects Dagesh Forte with compensatory lengthening

I: Implies Dagesh Forte

Note: For the corresponding color chart, see page 354

EXERCISE THIRTY-ONE

I. Questions

1. What part of the verb is primarily affected in R_2-Guttural verbs?
2. Describe the weaknesses of R_2-Guttural verbs. Which conjugations are affected by these weaknesses?
3. Discuss the remedies for these weaknesses.
4. When is the Dagesh Forte rejected or implied? Reproduce the chart for rejected or implied Dagesh.
5. What is the thematic vowel for nearly all R_2-Guttural verbs in the imperfect-imperative of the Qal?
6. How does the thematic vowel differ between the imperative and the infinitive construct of R_2-Guttural verbs?
7. Discuss the forming and the parsing of R_2-Guttural verbs.

II. Vocabulary

זְרוֹעַ	arm
חָזָק	(adj.) strong, hard, mighty
גאל	Qal: redeem, act as a kinsman redeemer Niph‘al: reflexive and passive of Qal
בער	Qal: burn, consume Pi“ēl: make burn (kindle), consume, destroy Pu“al: passive of Pi“ēl Hiph‘îl: cause to burn (kindle), burn up, destroy
טָהֵר	Qal: be clean (ceremonially or morally) Pi“ēl: put in a clean state, cleanse, purify Hithpa“ēl: reflexive of Pi“ēl
פעל	Qal: do, make
צעק	Qal: cry, cry out, call Niph‘al: passive of Qal זעק is the same word
שׁרת	Pi“ēl: minister, serve (participle: minister, officer)
כבס	Pi“ēl: wash clothes (by treading) poetically – wash or cleanse a soul
רָצוֹן	favor, will, pleasure, acceptance
חֵמָה	heat, wrath, anger
כעס	Qal: be vexed, angry, irritated Pi“ēl: put in a vexed condition, anger Hiph‘îl: vex, anger, provoke anger

III. Drills

1. Word Breakdown: In the following order: label every Dagesh Forte and Lene, Mappiq; vocal and silent shewa; Qameṣ and Qameṣ-Ḥatuf. Next, divide syllables labeling them open or closed. Then pronounce the words.

יָמָיו   בִּתָּהּ

2. Attach the following particles and translate all vocabulary words.
Interrogative מה

עָב   מֶ֫לֶךְ

Conjunctive ו

בָּכָה   יְשִׁימוֹן

Preposition מן

פְּתִי   יְתוּר

3. Attach the boxes and translate all vocabulary words. List all steps.
1. fs construct חֲפַרְפָּרָה   2. mp construct חָמָס

4. Attach the boxes with suffixes and translate all vocabulary words. List all steps.

Singular Nouns
1. 3fp צְדָקָה
2. 2mp פֹּ֫עַל (*o*)

Plural Nouns
3. 2ms סֵ֫פֶר (*i*)
4. 2fs מִפְקָד

5. Attach the suffixes to the prepositions and translate.
1. 1cp אֵת (with)
2. 3mp ב
3. 3ms כ
4. 3mp תַּ֫חַת

6. Verbs
1. Create: List all steps and the final answer.
Qal
1. Imperfect 2fs אמר
2. Emphatic imperative כעס
3. Perfect 2fs +3fs suffix שׁמר
4. Imperfect 2mp בהל
5. Infinitive construct דחף
6. Imperfect 1cs +Vav-consecutive אמר

Pi"ēl
7. Imperfect 3ms +2ms suffix ברך
8. Imperative 2ms +1cs suffix טהר
9. Infinitive construct +1cp טהר

Pu"al
10. Perfect 1cp ברך

Hiph'îl
11. Perfect 2mp אכל

Niph'al
12. Participle ms הרג

2. Parse: Give all possible answers.

1.	בֹּעֲרָה	7.	אֹכְלָה
2.	תְּשַׂחֵק	8.	מְאָסָם
3.	מְבֹעֶרֶת	9.	חִלְּפוּ
4.	בַּחֲרֵי	10.	הִצְטָרֵךְ
5.	יְבָרֲכֵם	11.	כִּעֲסַתָּה
6.	טִהֲרוּ	12.	יֹאחֵז

7. Translation

1. לָכֵן אֱמֹר לִבְנֵי־יִשְׂרָאֵל אֲנִי יְהוָה וְגָאַלְתִּי אֶתְכֶם בִּזְרוֹעַ חֲזָקָה וּבְמִשְׁפָּטִים גְּדוֹלִים׃
2. לָכֵן כֹּה־אָמַר אֲדֹנָי יהוה הִנֵּה אַפִּי וַחֲמָתִי אֶל־הַמָּקוֹם הַזֶּה עַל־הָאָדָם וְעַל־הַבְּהֵמָה וְעַל־עֵץ הַשָּׂדֶה וְעַל־פְּרִי הָאֲדָמָה וּבָעֲרָה וְאָכְלָה כָּאֵשׁ׃
3. בָּרְכוּ יהוה כָּל־צְבָאָיו מְשָׁרְתָיו פֹּעֲלֵי רְצוֹנוֹ׃
4. וַיֹּאמֶר שְׁמוּאֵל אֶל־שָׁאוּל מָאַסְתָּ אֶת־דְּבַר יְהוָה וַיִּמְאָסְךָ יהוה מִמְּלֹךְ עַל־יִשְׂרָאֵל׃
5. אֵלֶיךָ צָעֲקוּ וְנִמְלָטוּ בְּךָ בָּטְחוּ וְלֹא־יָרְאוּ׃
6. עָשָׂה אַחְאָב אֶת־הָרַע בְּעֵינֵי־יְהוָה וַיַּכְעֵס אֶת־יהוה אֱלֹהֵי יִשְׂרָאֵל מִכֹּל מַלְכֵי יִשְׂרָאֵל אֲשֶׁר הָיוּ לְפָנָיו׃
7. כַּבְּסֵנִי מֵעֲוֹנִי וּמֵחַטָּאתִי טַהֲרֵנִי׃ כִּי פְּשָׁעַי אֲנִי יָדַעְתִּי וְחַטָּאתִי נֶגְדִּי תָמִיד׃

CHAPTER 32
R_3-GUTTURAL (LAMED GUTTURAL) VERBS (EXCLUDING א AND ר)

32.1. Introduction: Because gutturals prefer a Pataḥ under them or before them (5.7.3), R_3-Guttural verbs pressure thematic vowels (especially Ṣere/Ḥireq) to become Pataḥ. If the R_3-Guttural fails to conform the thematic vowel to Pataḥ, the R_3-Guttural takes a Furtive Pataḥ (5.7.3). R_3-Guttural verbs affect the thematic vowels (colors).

32.2. Weakness or Infirmity of R_3-Guttural Verbs

R_3-Guttural verbs prefer a Pataḥ or Qameṣ thematic vowel.

32.3. Strong Areas of R_3-Guttural Verbs

All conjugations with Pataḥ or (Qameṣ) thematic vowels are like the strong verb:
Pu"al and Hoph'al – A/A
Niph'al perfect, imperfect-imperative – A/(Ē)-a
Pi"ēl perfect – A-(ē)/
Hithpa"ēl perfect, imperfect-imperative 2, 3fp – A-(ē)/(Ē)-a
Hiph'îl – A-(î)/(Î-ē)

32.4. Remedies for the Infirmity of the R_3-Gutturals

1. Finite Verbal Forms (Perfect, Imperfect, Imperative)
   1. Ṣere (originally Ḥireq) thematic vowels
      1. In non-pausal forms, Ṣere thematic vowels become Pataḥ.

	Strong Verb	**R_3-Guttural Verb**
Pi"ēl perfect 3ms	קִטֵּל	בִּקַּע
Hithpa"ēl imperfect 3ms	יִתְקַטֵּל	יִתְבַּקַּע

      2. In pausal forms, restore Ṣere thematic vowels and place a Furtive Pataḥ before the R_3-Guttural if it ends the word (5.7.4).

	Non-pausal	**Pausal**
Pi"ēl perfect 3ms	בִּקַּע	בִּקֵּעַ
Hithpa"ēl imperfect 3ms	יִתְבַּקַּע	יִתְבַּקֵּעַ
Hithpa"ēl imperfect 3mp	יִתְבַּקְּעוּ[1]	יִתְבַּקֵּעוּ[1]

[1] The R_3-Guttural is without Furtive Pataḥ because the R_3-Guttural does not end the word.

2. Ḥireq-Yod thematic vowels (Hiph'îl[2]) withstand the pressure of the R_3-Guttural and take a Furtive Pataḥ.

	Strong Verb	R_3-Guttural Verb
Hiph'îl perfect 3ms	הִקְטִיל	הִשְׁמִיעַ

2. Non-Finite Forms (infinitive absolute, infinitive construct, participles – active and passive)
In both pausal and non-pausal forms, the non-finite forms retain the usual thematic vowels, and the R_3-Guttural takes a Furtive Pataḥ (occasionally, the Ṣere thematic vowel becomes Pataḥ).

	Strong Verb	R_3-Guttural Verb
Qal infinitive construct	קְטֹל	שְׁלֹחַ
Qal participle active ms	קֹטֵל	שֹׁלֵחַ
Qal participle passive ms	קָטוּל	שָׁלוּחַ
Pi"ēl infinitive construct (exception)	קַטֵּל	(Gen 8:10) שַׁלַּח

32.5. Final Considerations

1. Like the R_2-Guttural verbs (31.6.1), almost all R_3-Guttural verbs have Pataḥ for the thematic vowel in the Qal imperfect-imperative (/A).[3]

Qal imperfect 3ms	יִשְׁלַח
Qal imperative 2ms	שְׁלַח

2. In all T-form participles, the R_3-Guttural changes the Segols into Pataḥs (5.7.3).

	Strong Verb	R_3-Guttural Verb
Qal participle active fs T-form	קֹטֶ֫לֶת	שֹׁלַ֫חַת

3. R_3-Gutturals in the silent shewa position take the silent shewa, not a composite shewa like R_1-Guttural verbs (29.6).

	Strong Verb	R_3-Guttural Verb
Qal perfect 1cs	קָטַ֫לְתִּי	שָׁלַ֫חְתִּי

---

[2] In the Hiph'îl, three of the four special Ṣere forms (jussive third person singular, Vav-consecutive third person singular, and the imperative 2ms) and the imperfect-imperative 2fp, 3fp change the Ṣere to Pataḥ because of the R_3-Guttural (32.4.1). The Hiph'îl infinitive absolute, a non-finite form, usually keeps the Ṣere.

[3] As in R_2-Guttural verbs, the Qal imperative 2ms and the infinitive construct differ: שְׁלַח imperative 2ms; שְׁלֹחַ infinitive construct, 31.6.2.

4. In all conjugations, the perfect 2fs form (without pronominal suffixes) adds a Pataḥ under the R_3-Guttural. (Compare the Segolate nouns with gutturals: *נַעְרְ » נַ֫עַר 15.2; 16.3.)

	Strong Verb	**R_3-Guttural Verb**
Qal perfect 2fs	קָטַלְתְּ	שָׁלַ֫חַתְּ[4]
Pi"ēl perfect 2fs	קִטַּלְתְּ	שִׁלַּ֫חַתְּ

32.6. Forming and Parsing R_3-Guttural Verbs (29.10-29.13)

These verbs primarily affect the thematic vowels (colors).

Examples:

1. Niph'al imperfect 3ms שׁלח
   1. Boxes: יִ▣□□ יִשָּׁלֵח
   2. Colors: A/Ē-a (» A/A) יִשָּׁלַח (32.4.1)
   3. Qal: יִקְטֹל יִשָּׁלַח

      Answer: יִשָּׁלַח

2. נְשַׁלַּח
   1. Boxes: יְ□▣□ Pi"ēl imperfect
   2. Colors: A/A (A-ē/Ē) Pi"ēl imperfect (excluding 2fs, 2mp, 3mp)
   3. Qal: נִקְטֹל Pi"ēl imperfect 1cp שׁלח

      Answer: Pi"ēl imperfect 1cp שׁלח

      The R_3-ח changes the Ṣere to Pataḥ, 32.4.1.

[4] This is a very rare exception of a vowel preceding a Dagesh Lene.

R$_3$-GUTTURAL (LAMED GUTTURAL) VERBS

FINITE FORMS (E » A: ṢERE » PATAḤ, 32.4.1)

The Hebrew world goes Red

	Qal	Niph'al	Pi"ēl	Pu"al	Hithpa"ēl	Hiph'îl	Hoph'al	
Perfect		A/Ē-a » A/A	A-ē/Ē » A/A	A/A remains A/A	A-ē/Ē-a » A/A	A-î/Î-ē » A-î/Î-a (In jussive, Vav-consecutive and imperative 2ms forms ē » a)	A/A remains A/A	In pausal forms, the usual thematic vowel is retained and the R$_3$-Guttural receives a Furtive Pataḥ
Imperfect	Pataḥ 32.5.1							
Imperative								

NON-FINITE FORMS (32.4.2)

Infinitive Absolute	Usual thematic vowels are retained, and the R$_3$-Guttural receives a Furtive Pataḥ (an occasional exception of Ṣere » Pataḥ)	Pausal and Non-Pausal forms
Infinitive Construct		
Participle		

Note: For the corresponding color chart, see page 355

R_3-Guttural (Lamed Guttural) Verbs (32.4)

	Non-Pausal	**Pausal**
Finite Forms (Perfect, Imperfect, Imperative)	Ṣere becomes Pataḥ; Ḥireq-Yod takes Furtive Pataḥ 32.4.1	Ṣere thematic vowel restored, and Furtive Pataḥ added when necessary 32.4.1
Non-Finite Forms (Infinitives and Participles)	Pausal and Non-Pausal: Thematic vowels retained, and Furtive Pataḥ added when necessary 32.4.2	

Chart courtesy of Isaac Jerusalmi

Note: For the corresponding color chart, see page 356

EXERCISE THIRTY-TWO

I. Questions

1. List the four characteristics of gutturals (chapter 5) and identify the characteristic most important for R_3-Guttural verbs.
2. What part of the word do these verbs affect?
3. What is the weakness of R_3-Guttural verbs?
4. What is a Furtive Pataḥ? When does it occur?
5. What areas of the R_3-Guttural verbs are like strong verbs?
6. Define finite verbal forms and non-finite verbal forms.
7. Discuss the remedies for the weakness of R_3-Guttural verbs.
8. What is the thematic vowel for almost all Qal imperfect-imperatives?
9. Does the R_3-Guttural reject silent shewa like R_1-Guttural verbs?
10. Discuss how R_3-Gutturals affect the T-form participles.
11. Which perfect form behaves like a Segolate noun? Write and describe the form.
12. Describe the forming and the parsing of R_3-Guttural verbs. Discuss the step where the weakness occurs.

II. Vocabulary

שׂבע	Qal: be satisfied, be in excess Hiph'îl: cause to be satisfied, satisfy	בקע	Qal: split, break open or through Niph'al: passive of Qal Pi"ēl: split into pieces
יָמִין	the right, right hand, right side, south	שְׂמֹאל/שְׂמֹאול	the left, left side, left hand, north
רָעֵב	Qal: be hungry (compare the noun רָעָב hunger, famine)	משׁח	Qal: anoint (compare מָשִׁיחַ anointed one)
אֱלִישָׁע	Elisha	יֵהוּא	Jehu
זרע	Qal: sow, scatter seed Niph'al: be sown, be fruitful	שׁוֹפָר	horn, ram's horn
		בלע	Qal: swallow, engulf Pi"ēl: swallow up, confound, destroy
תקע	Qal: thrust, drive, clap, blow (horn) Niph'al: passive of Qal	פרשׂ	Qal: spread (out) Niph'al: be scattered, spread out
קָהָל	assembly, congregation		

III. Drills

1. Word Breakdown: In the following order: label every Dagesh Forte and Lene, Mappiq; vocal and silent shewa; Qameṣ and Qameṣ-Ḥatuf. Next, divide syllables labeling them open or closed. Then pronounce the words.

לֶאֱסָרְךָ   יָחֳכַם

2. Attach the following particles and translate all vocabulary words.

Article

חָדָשׁ　　　הָדָר

Preposition כ

יְצָקָה　　　אֱלֹהִים

Interrogative ה

אָמַרְתָּ　　　יְצָקָה

3. Attach the boxes and translate all vocabulary words. List all steps.

1. mp construct קֹדֶשׁ (*o*)
2. mp construct חָדָשׁ
3. dual absolute פַּעַם (*a*)
4. fs construct פְּעֻלָּה

4. Attach the boxes with suffixes and translate all vocabulary words. List all steps.

Singular Nouns

1. 1cs פַּחֳדָּה
2. 3ms פֹּעַל (*o*)

Plural Nouns

3. 3mp חָדָשׁ
4. 2fs מַעֲרָצָה

5. Attach the suffixes to the prepositions and translate.

1. 2ms מִן
2. 3ms לְמַעַן
3. 2fp אֶל
4. 3fs לְ

6. Verbs

1. Create: List all steps, the final answer, then translate all vocabulary words.

Qal

1. Imperative 2ms סעד
2. Imperfect 3ms +3ms suffix אסף
3. Participle mp +3fs suffix אכל
4. Participle fs (t) זרע
5. Imperfect 2ms +Vav-consecutive (pausal) אכל

Pi"ēl

6. Imperfect 1cs (Pausal) שׁלח

Hiph'îl

7. Imperative 2ms שׂבע

8. Imperfect 1cp +3fs (energic) +Vav-consecutive בקע
9. Jussive 3fs בטח

Niph'al
10. Imperative 2ms (pausal) שׁבע

2. Parse: Give all possible answers.

1.	זִרְחִי	6.	הַעֲמִידוּ
2.	הִשְׁבַּעְתָּנוּ	7.	וַיְבָרֶךְ
3.	יְבַהֵל	8.	אֹכְלוֹת
4.	בְּטוֹחַ	9.	אֹמַר
5.	יַאַסְפֵנִי	10.	שָׁמֵעַ

7. Translation

1. הַדָּבָר אֲשֶׁר הָיָה אֶל־יִרְמְיָהוּ מֵאֵת יהוה בַּיָּמִים הָהֵם אֶזְרַע אֶת־בֵּית יִשְׂרָאֵל וְאֶת־בֵּית יְהוּדָה זֶרַע אָדָם וְזֶרַע בְּהֵמָה׃
2. וַיְהִי בְּדַבֵּר מֹשֶׁה אֵת כָּל־הַדְּבָרִים הָאֵלֶּה וַתִּבָּקַע הָאֲדָמָה אֲשֶׁר תַּחְתֵּיהֶם׃ וַתִּפְתַּח הָאָרֶץ אֶת־פִּיהָ וַתִּבְלַע אֹתָם וְאֶת־בָּתֵּיהֶם וְאֵת כָּל־הָאָדָם אֲשֶׁר לָהֶם׃
3. אִם יִתָּקַע שׁוֹפָר בְּעִיר וְעָם לֹא יִרְאוּ אִם תִּהְיֶה רָעָה בְּעִיר וַיהוה לֹא עָשָׂה׃
4. דִּרְשׁוּ יהוה וְעֻזּוֹ בַּקְּשׁוּ פָנָיו תָּמִיד׃ הוּא יהוה אֱלֹהֵינוּ בְּכָל־הָאָרֶץ מִשְׁפָּטָיו׃
5. וַיַּעֲמֹד שְׁלֹמֹה לִפְנֵי מִזְבַּח יהוה נֶגֶד כָּל־קְהַל יִשְׂרָאֵל וַיִּפְרֹשׂ כַּפָּיו הַשָּׁמָיְמָה׃ וַיֹּאמַר יהוה אֱלֹהֵי יִשְׂרָאֵל אֵין־כָּמוֹךָ אֱלֹהִים בַּשָּׁמַיִם וּבָאָרֶץ שֹׁמֵר הַבְּרִית וְהַחֶסֶד לַעֲבָדֶיךָ הַהֹלְכִים לְפָנֶיךָ בְּכָל־לִבָּם׃

Chapter 33
R_3-Alef (Lamed Alef) Verbs

33.1. Introduction: R_3-Alef verbs prefer Ṣere in the perfect (contrast the R_3-Guttural which prefers Pataḥ) and regularly lengthen Pataḥ thematic vowels to Qameṣ because the R_3-Alef quiesces in the silent shewa position. R_3-Alef verbs primarily affect the thematic vowels (colors).

33.2. Weaknesses or Infirmities of R_3-Alef verbs

1. R_3-Alef quiesces in the silent shewa position (5.8 and footnote 5-3) and lengthens preceding short vowels.
2. The R_3-Alef usually replaces Pataḥ with Ṣere in many perfects.

33.3. Strong Areas of R_3-Alef Verbs

Outside the perfect, R_3-Alef verbs are virtually strong verbs, with Pataḥ thematic vowels usually lengthening to Qameṣ.

33.4. Remedies for the Infirmity of the R_3-Alef Verbs

1. R_3-Alef quiesces: The R_3-Alef, in the silent shewa position, quiesces, and the thematic vowel, if short (Pataḥ, Ḥireq), lengthens by compensation (to Qameṣ, Ṣere).

   Qal perfect 1cs *מָצַאְתִּי » *מָצַאתִּי » *מָצַאתִי » מָצָ֫אתִי
   1 2 3 4

   The reconstructed strong form (1) quiesces the Alef in the silent shewa position (2), thus opening the syllable and omitting the Dagesh Lene in the ת (3). The Pataḥ lengthens by compensation to Qameṣ (4).

   Similarly, at the end of the word the R_3-Alef quiesces in the silent shewa position, and the preceding thematic vowel, if Pataḥ, lengthens to Qameṣ.

	Strong Verb	**R_3-Alef Verb**
Pu"al imperfect 3ms	*יְקֻטַּל(ְ)	*יְמֻצַּא(ְ) » *יְמֻצַּא » יְמֻצָּא
		1 2 3

   The reconstructed strong form (1) quiesces the R_3-Alef in the implied silent shewa position (2), and the Pataḥ lengthens to Qameṣ (3).

2. Perfects
   1. Mixed conjugations:
      Those conjugations with a Pataḥ, Ṣere, or Ḥireq-Yod in the perfect are mixed conjugations: Qal stative A-ē/ , Pi"ēl A-ē/ , Hithpa"ēl A-ē/ , Hiph'îl A-î/ . In the perfect of R_3-Alef verbs, mixed conjugations become pure conjugations: Ē/ in the Qal stative, Pi"ēl, Hithpa"ēl; Ē-î/ in the Hiph'îl.

			Strong Verb			**R$_3$-Alef Verb**
Qal stative	A-ē/	3ms	כָּבֵד	Ē/	3ms	מָלֵא
		1cs	כָּבַ֫דְתִּי		1cs	מָלֵ֫אתִי
Pi"ēl	A-ē/	3ms	קִטֵּל	Ē/	3ms	מִצֵּא
		1cs	קִטַּ֫לְתִּי		1cs	מִצֵּ֫אתִי
Hithpa"ēl	A-ē/	3ms	הִתְקַטֵּל	Ē/	3ms	הִתְמַצֵּא
		1cs	הִתְקַטַּ֫לְתִּי		1cs	הִתְמַצֵּ֫אתִי
Hiph'îl	A-î/	3ms	הִקְטִיל	Ē-î/	3ms	הִמְצִיא
		1cs	הִקְטַ֫לְתִּי		1cs	הִמְצֵ֫אתִי

2. Pure conjugations:
   Those conjugations with only Pataḥ in the perfect are pure conjugations: Niph'al A/ , Pu"al A/ , Hoph'al A/ . In the perfect of the R$_3$-Alef verbs, pure conjugations become mixed: Ē-ā/ in the Niph'al, Pu"al, Hoph'al.

			Strong Verb			**R$_3$-Alef Verb**
Niph'al	A/	3ms	נִקְטַל	Ē-ā/	3ms	נִמְצָא
		1cs	נִקְטַ֫לְתִּי		1cs	נִמְצֵ֫אתִי
Pu"al	A/	3ms	קֻטַּל	Ē-ā/	3ms	מֻצָּא
		1cs	קֻטַּ֫לְתִּי		1cs	מֻצֵּ֫אתִי

3. Qal Perfect (standard verb):
   The Alef quiesces, and the Pataḥ lengthens to Qameṣ.

		Strong Verb		**R$_3$-Alef Verb**
Qal standard	3ms	קָטַל	3ms	מָצָא
	1cs	קָטַ֫לְתִּי	1cs	מָצָ֫אתִי

33.5. Final Considerations

1. Outside the perfect, thematic vowels are regular (like strong verbs).

2. Like R_2-Guttural and R_3-Guttural verbs, R_3-Alef verbs in the Qal imperfect-imperative take Pataḥ (lengthened to Qameṣ) thematic vowels.[1]

	R_3-Guttural Verb		R_3-Alef Verb	
Qal imperfect	3ms	יִשְׁלַח	3ms	יִמְצָא

3. All 2, 3fp imperfect-imperative forms of all conjugations quiesce the Alef and take Segol for a thematic vowel (analogy to R_3-Vav/Yod verbs).

	Strong Verb		R_3-Alef Verb	
Qal imperfect	2fp	תִּקְטֹלְנָה	2fp	תִּמְצֶאנָה
Hiph'îl imperfect	2fp	תַּקְטֵלְנָה	2fp	תַּמְצֶאנָה

4. All T-form participles quiesce the Alef and lengthen the preceding Segol to Ṣere.
   *מֹצֶאֶת » *מֹצֶאת » מֹצֵאת
   1 2 3
   The reconstructed strong form (1) quiesces the Alef (2) and lengthens Segol to Ṣere (3). (Compare *לֶאֱלֹהִים » *לֶאלֹהִים » לֵאלֹהִים and footnote 30-2.)

33.6. Forming and Parsing R_3-Alef Verbs (29.10-29.13)

Examples:

1. Pi"ēl perfect 2ms מלא
   1. Boxes: □▣□ מִלֵּא
   2. Colors: A-ē/Ē (» Ē/Ē) מִלֵּא
   3. Qal: קָטַלְתָּ מִלֵּאתָ « *מִלֵּאְתָּ

   The R_3-Alef quiesces in the silent shewa position (33.4.1).

   Answer: מִלֵּאתָ

2. הִמְצֵאתֶם
   1. Boxes: הִ□□□ Hiph'îl perfect
   2. Colors: Ē-î/Î-ē (A-î/Î-ē) Hiph'îl perfect (excluding 3ms, 3fs, 3cp)
   3. Qal: קְטַלְתֶּם Hiph'îl perfect 2mp, the Alef quiesces in silent shewa position.

   Answer: Hiph'îl perfect 2mp מצא

[1] See 32.5.1; 31.6.2.

R_3-Alef (Lamed Alef) Verbs

The Hebrew world goes Green

	Qal (Standard)	Qal (Stative)	Niph'al	Pi"ēl	Pu"al	Hithpa"ēl	Hiph'îl	Hoph'al	
Perfect 33.4.2	A » Ā	A-ē » Ē	A » Ē-ā	A-ē » Ē	A » Ē-ā	A-ē » Ē	A-î » Ē-î	A » Ē-ā	"Greening Effect"
Imperfect	/Ā 33.5.2		All other thematic vowels are like strong verbs except, (1) When R_3-Alef ends the word, the Alef quiesces, and the short thematic vowel (Pataḥ) lengthens (33.4.1) (2) All 2, 3fp imperfect-imperative forms quiesce the Alef and take Segol for the thematic vowel (33.5.3).						
Imperative									
Infinitive Absolute									
Infinitive Construct									
Participle	All T-form participles quiesce the R_3-Alef and lengthen preceding Segol to Ṣere: מֹצֵאת 33.5.4.								

Notes: R_3-Alef in the silent shewa position (also at the end of the word) quiesces, and the preceding vowel, if short, lengthens.

Note: For the corresponding color chart, see page 357

EXERCISE THIRTY-THREE

I. Questions

1. What part of the verb is affected in R_3-Alef verbs?
2. Contrast the thematic vowel preferences of the R_3-Guttural verbs and of the perfect of the R_3-Alef verbs.
3. What are the weaknesses of R_3-Alef verbs?
4. When are the R_3-Alef verbs virtually like strong verbs?
5. Discuss the remedies for the infirmities of R_3-Alef verbs.
6. What are pure conjugations in the perfect? What are mixed conjugations in the perfect? Where do they occur?
7. How do R_3-Alef verbs affect thematic vowels outside of the perfect?
8. What is the thematic vowel of R_3-Alef verbs in the Qal imperfect-imperative? What other weak verbs have the same thematic vowel?
9. What is the thematic vowel for the 2, 3fp imperfect-imperative of all conjugations of R_3-Alef verbs?
10. Discuss T-form participles in R_3-Alef verbs. How do they differ from strong verbs?
11. Describe the forming and the parsing of R_3-Alef verbs.

II. Vocabulary

מִשְׁכָּן	dwelling place, tabernacle
נָחָשׁ	snake
חָמָס	violence, wrong
פַּר	bull
פָּרָה	cow
צָפוֹן	north
רֹב	multitude, abundance
רֵעַ	friend
שׁכן	Qal: dwell, settle (in a tent) Pi"ēl: make settle, establish
פלא	Niph'al: be (or do) extraordinary (things), be (or do) wonderful (things) Hiph'îl: do wondrously, marvellously
טמא	Qal: be (or become) unclean, defiled Niph'al: defile oneself, be defiled Pi"ēl: put in an unclean state, defile, pronounce unclean Hithpa"ēl: put oneself in an unclean state, defile oneself
רפא	Qal: heal Niph'al: passive of Qal Pi"ēl: heal
מָלֵא	Qal: be full, fill Niph'al: passive of Qal Pi"ēl: put in a full state, fill, fulfill, wholly devote to

III. Drills

1. Word Breakdown: In the following order: label every Dagesh Forte and Lene, Mappiq; vocal and silent shewa; Qameṣ and Qameṣ-Ḥatuf. Next, divide syllables labeling them open or closed. Then pronounce the words.

   וַתִּגְבַּהּ　　　　גָּבְהָא

2. Attach the following particles and translate all vocabulary words.

   Interrogative מה

   עָרִיץ　　　　סְפֹרָה

   Conjunctive ו

   נְדוּד　　　　כַּוָּן

   Preposition מן

   מַלְאָךְ　　　　חֹשֶׁב

3. Attach the boxes and translate all vocabulary words. List all steps.
   1. fs construct נַחֲלָה
   2. fp absolute נַחֲלָה
   3. mp absolute נַעַר (*a*)
   4. mp construct מַבָּט

4. Attach the boxes with suffixes and translate all vocabulary words. List all steps.

   Singular Nouns
   1. 2ms פְּקֻדָּה
   2. 2fs עָוֹן

   Plural Nouns
   3. 3ms פִּקּוּד
   4. 2mp קֹדֶשׁ (*o*)

5. Attach the suffixes to the prepositions and translate.
   1. 3fs עַל
   2. 1cp תַּחַת
   3. 2fs ב
   4. 3ms את (direct object)

6. Verbs
   1. Create: List all steps and the final answer.

      Qal
      1. Imperfect 1cs +Vav-consecutive אמר
      2. Imperfect 2fp מלא
      3. Imperfect 3ms +1cs שלח
      4. Imperative 2ms +3mp קטל (A/Ō)

5. Imperfect 1cp שׂנא
6. Imperfect 1cp (shewa) חשׁך (A/A)
7. Imperative 2ms חטא

Pi"ēl
8. Infinitive construct שׂמח
9. Participle fs (t) טמא

Hiph'îl
10. Perfect 1cs פלא
11. Imperfect 3ms +Vav-consecutive מצא

Hoph'al
12. Perfect 3ms מצא

2. Parse: Give all possible answers.

1.	יִמְצָאֻוּנְהָ	7.	מֵחֲטֹא
2.	יִתְהַלָּכ֑וּן	8.	חָטָאת
3.	יַחֲרִימָהּ	9.	נֶחֱטָא
4.	תַּמְצֶאנָה	10.	מְצְאָה
5.	יַחְשְׁבֵנִי	11.	טַמַּאֲכֶם
6.	יַשְׁלַח	12.	מֹלֵאת

7. Translation

1. וַתִּשָּׁחֵת הָאָרֶץ לִפְנֵי הָאֱלֹהִים וַתִּמָּלֵא הָאָרֶץ חָמָס׃
2. עָשָׂה שְׁלֹמֹה הָרַע בְּעֵינֵי־יהוָה וְלֹא מִלֵּא אַחֲרֵי יהוָה כְּדָוִד אָבִיו׃
3. וְלֹא תְטַמֵּא אֶת־הָאָרֶץ אֲשֶׁר אַתֶּם יֹשְׁבִים בָּהּ אֲשֶׁר אֲנִי שֹׁכֵן בְּתוֹכָהּ כִּי אֲנִי
יהוה שֹׁכֵן בְּתוֹךְ בְּנֵי יִשְׂרָאֵל׃
4. וַיִּתְפַּלֵּל אַבְרָהָם אֶל־הָאֱלֹהִים וַיִּרְפָּא אֱלֹהִים אֶת־אֲבִימֶלֶךְ וְאֶת־אִשְׁתּוֹ׃
5. הַלְלוּ יהוה בְּכָל־לִבְּךָ סַפְּרוּ כָּל־נִפְלְאוֹתָיו תָּמִיד׃
6. וַיֹּאמֶר אֶל־הָאִשָּׁה אַף כִּי אָמַר אֱלֹהִים לֹא תֹאכְלוּ מִכֹּל־עֵץ הַגָּן׃ וַתֹּאמֶר
הָאִשָּׁה אֶל־הַנָּחָשׁ מִפְּרִי עֵץ־הַגָּן נֹאכֵל וּמִפְּרִי הָעֵץ אֲשֶׁר בְּתוֹךְ־הַגָּן אָמַר
אֱלֹהִים לֹא תֹאכְלוּ מִמֶּנּוּ׃
7. שִׂנְאוּ רָע וְאֶהֱבוּ טוֹב וּמִלֵּאתֶם אֶת־אֲשֶׁר דִּבַּרְתִּי׃

Chapter 34
R_1-Nun (Pe Nun) Verbs

34.1. Introduction: R_1-Nun in the silent shewa position frequently assimilates to the following consonant. When the R_1-Nun assimilates, only two root letters remain. Similarly, the following weak verbs (chapters 35-38) normally retain two root letters. R_1-Nun verbs affect the boxes and often the first syllable of the Qal.

34.2. Weaknesses or Infirmities of R_1-Nun Verbs

1. R_1-Nuns in the silent shewa position are unstable.
2. R_1-Nuns in the vocal shewa position of the Qal imperative and infinitive construct are frequently unstable.

34.3. Strong Areas of the R_1-Nun Verbs

1. With a vowel under the R_1-Nun, the R_1-Nun is stable (like strong verbs): Pi"ēl, Pu"al, Hithpa"ēl, Niph'al imperfect, imperative, infinitives, Qal perfect, participles, infinitive absolute.
   Pi"ēl imperfect 3ms יְנַצֵּל

2. In the vocal shewa position, R_1-Nun is often stable: Qal perfect 2mp, 2fp, Qal imperative 2ms, 2fp (sometimes) and infinitive construct (sometimes).
   Qal perfect 2mp נְפַלְתֶּם

3. In the silent shewa position, R_1-Nun may be stable if R_2 is a guttural letter.
   Hiph'îl perfect 3ms הִנְחִיל

34.4. Remedies for the Infirmities of the R_1-Nun Verbs

1. Nun Assimilates: R_1-Nuns in the silent shewa position assimilate[1] to the following consonant.
   R_3 R_2 יִנְ » R_3 R_2 R_2 יִ » R_3 $R_{1\&2}$ יִ

   Qal imperfect 3ms יִפֹּל » יִפְפֹּל* » יִנְפֹּל*
   Niph'al perfect 3ms נִגַּשׁ » נִגְגַּשׁ* » נִנְגַּשׁ*
   Hiph'îl perfect 3ms הִפִּיל » הִפְפִּיל* » הִנְפִּיל*
   Hoph'al (Huph'al[2]) perfect 3ms הֻפַּל » הֻפְפַּל* » הֻנְפַּל*

---

[1] See 9.2.1 and footnote 9-1.

[2] Hoph'al frequently becomes a Huph'al when the following letter has a Dagesh Forte: הָשְׁמַר, but הֻפַּל.

The Hiph'îl, Hoph'al, Niph'al perfect, participle, and Qal imperfect assimilate the R_1-Nun.

2. Nun disappears (AWOL): In verbs with Pataḥ or Ṣere (not Ḥolem) thematic vowels in the Qal imperative and infinitive construct, the R_1-Nun disappears (goes AWOL). The form without the R_1-Nun may reflect an original biliteral root.

	Orange	Red	Green (only נתן)
	(A/Ō)	(A/A)	(A/Ē)
Qal Imperfect (Assimilation)	יִפֹּל	יִגַּשׁ	יִתֵּן
Qal Imperative	נְפֹל	גַּשׁ (Dagesh Lene)	תֵּן (Dagesh Lene)
Qal Infinitive Construct	נְפֹל	*גַּשְׁתְּ » *גֶּשֶׁת » גֶּשֶׁת (*i*)	*תִּתְּ » *תִּנְתְּ » תֵּת (*i*)
3ms suffix	נָפְלוֹ	גִּשְׁתּוֹ	תִּתּוֹ
with לְ	לִנְפֹּל	לָגֶשֶׁת	לָתֵת

1. Orange: Verbs with Ḥolem thematic vowels are like strong verbs in the Qal imperative and infinitive construct.

2. Red: Verbs with Pataḥ thematic vowels are without the Nun in the Qal imperative and the infinitive construct (AWOL). If the second root letter is a Bᵊgad Kᵊfat letter, it (גַּשׁ) takes a Dagesh Lene (Dagesh Forte cannot begin a word, 4.3.5.). The Qal infinitive construct adds a ת to the end of the word and imitates the Segolate pattern (15.2).

3. Green: Verbs with a Ṣere thematic vowel are without the Nun in the Qal imperative and infinitive construct (AWOL). When the Nun disappears in the Qal imperative, the second root letter (ת) takes a Dagesh Lene. The Qal infinitive construct adds a ת to the end of the word, but before the Segolate process begins, the added ת assimilates the R_3-Nun of the root, producing the final form – תֵּת (a hovering Dagesh representing the R_3-Nun, which lands with pronominal suffixes: 3ms תִּתּוֹ. The Ṣere occurs under the first letter in closed accented syllables [6.3.1], and (the original) Ḥireq occurs in closed unaccented syllables [6.3.3]).

34.5. Final Considerations

1. נתן: The R_3-Nun may also assimilate in the silent shewa position.
   Qal perfect 1cs *נָתַנְתִּי » נָתַתִּי (Review קְטַנּוּ [21.3.2])

2. לקח: In the Qal imperfect, imperative, and infinitive construct, לקח acts like a R_1-Nun verb – לקח » *נקח.
   - Qal imperfect 3ms יִקַּח
   - Qal imperative 2ms קַח
   - Qal infinitive construct (לָ)קַחַת[3]

   In other conjugations, לקח is regular:
   - Niph'al perfect 3ms נִלְקַח

3. נשׂא: Note the irregular infinitive construct:
   - Qal imperfect 3ms יִשָּׂא
   - Qal imperative 2ms שָׂא
   - Qal infinitive construct (לָ)שֵׂאת or שְׂאֵת

34.6. Forming and Parsing R_1-Nun Verbs (29.10-29. 13)

R_1-Nun verbs frequently affect the boxes.

Examples:

1. Hiph'îl perfect 1cs נפל
   1. Boxes: הִ□□□ » הִ▣□ הִנְפַל » הִפַּל (34.4.1)
   2. Colors: A-î/Î-ē הִפַּל
   3. Qal: קָטַלְתִּי הִפַּלְתִּי
      Answer: הִפַּלְתִּי

2. Qal infinitive construct נגשׁ (A/A)
   1. Strong form: נְגַשׁ (?)
   2. Identify weakness: R_1-Nun verb (A/A)
   3. Adjustments: The Qal infinitive construct loses the R_1-Nun, adds a ת to the end of the word, and imitates the Segolate pattern.
      *נְגַשׁ (?) » *גַּשׁ » *גַּשְׁתְּ » *גַּשֶׁת » גֶּשֶׁת
      Answer: גֶּשֶׁת

[3] In the Qal infinitive construct, לקח follows the נַעַר (16.2.2) Segolate pattern. The Segols become Pataḥ under the influence of the R_3-Guttural (5.7.3).

3. נִגָּשׁ

    1. Boxes: □▣נִ = □□□ְנִ or □▣□ִ — Niph‘al perfect/participle, Pi“ēl perfect, or Qal imperfect
    2. Colors: Qameṣ — Niph‘al participle ms absolute
    3. Qal: קֹטֵל or קָטוּל — ________

    Answer: Niph‘al participle ms absolute נִגָּשׁ

    The second step eliminates the Pi“ēl perfect, the Qal imperfect, and the Niph‘al perfect.

R_1-NUN (PE NUN) VERBS

<table>
<tr><th></th><th colspan="3">Qal</th><th>Niph‘al</th><th>Pi“ēl</th><th>Pu“al</th><th>Hithpa“ēl</th><th>Hiph‘îl</th><th>Hoph‘al</th></tr>
<tr><td>Perfect</td><td colspan="3">Strong
34.3.1</td><td>Assimilation
34.4.1</td><td colspan="3" rowspan="6">Strong
34.3.1</td><td colspan="2" rowspan="6">Assimilation
34.4.1</td></tr>
<tr><td>Imperfect</td><td colspan="3">Assimilation
34.4.1</td><td rowspan="4"></td></tr>
<tr><td>Imperative</td><td>(Orange)
Strong
34.3.2</td><td>(Red)
Nun goes
AWOL
34.4.2</td><td>(Green)
Nun goes
AWOL
34.4.2</td></tr>
<tr><td>Infinitive Absolute</td><td colspan="3">Strong
34.3.1</td></tr>
<tr><td>Infinitive Construct</td><td>(Orange)
Strong
34.3.2</td><td>(Red)
Nun goes
AWOL Plus
Tav (Segolate)
34.4.2</td><td>(Green)
Nun goes
AWOL Plus
Tav (Segolate)
34.4.2</td></tr>
<tr><td>Participle</td><td colspan="3">Strong
34.3.1</td><td>Assimilation
34.4.1</td></tr>
</table>

Note: For the corresponding color chart, see page 358

EXERCISE THIRTY-FOUR

I. Questions

1. What part of the word is frequently affected in R_1-Nun verbs?
2. Describe the weaknesses of R_1-Nun verbs.
3. When are R_1-Nun verbs like strong verbs?
4. Discuss the remedies for the weaknesses.
5. What is assimilation? When does it occur with R_1-Nun verbs?
6. When does the R_1-Nun disappear?
7. When does a Hoph'al become a Huph'al (at least sometimes)?
8. Discuss the Segolate process in R_1-Nun verbs. Where does it occur?
9. Discuss the special considerations for the following verbs: נתן, לקח, נשׂא.
10. Describe the forming and the parsing of R_1-Nun verbs.

II. Vocabulary

נסע	Qal: (pull up, out) set out, journey, depart Hiph'îl: causative of Qal
קֶ֫דֶם	before, front, east
נצח	Pi"ēl: act as a leader, overseer
נֵ֫צַח (*i*)	eminence, glory, perpetuity
זָכָר	male, man
שׁקר	Pi"ēl: act falsely, lie (compare שֶׁ֫קֶר)
אִשֶּׁה	(construct singular אִשֵּׁה, construct plural אִשֵּׁי) offering by fire, fire offering
נגד	Hiph'îl: declare, tell Hoph'al: passive of Hiph'îl
יֵ֫שַׁע (*i*)	salvation, deliverance
מֵעִים	(The word only occurs in the plural.) internal organs; inward parts
(ו)יסד	Qal: establish, found Niph'al: passive, reflexive of the Qal Pi"ēl: establish, found Pu'al: passive of Pi"ēl
נגע	Qal: touch (usually with ב), reach, strike Hiph'îl: cause to touch, reach, arrive, approach
נצל	Niph'al: deliver oneself, be delivered Hiph'îl: take away, deliver (from)

III. Drills

1. Word Breakdown: In the following order: label every Dagesh Forte and Lene, Mappiq; vocal and silent shewa; Qameṣ and Qameṣ-Ḥatuf. Next, divide syllables labeling them open or closed. Then pronounce the words.

לָיְלָה   הַשָּׂאטִים

2. Attach the following particles and translate all vocabulary words.
   Article

   הֲמִלָּה　　　מַהֲמֹרָה

   Preposition ב

   יְמָנִי　　　כִּבְשָׂה

   Interrogative ה

   עָגוּר　　　נְפִלִים

3. Attach the boxes and translate all vocabulary words. List all steps.
   1. ms construct בָּכָל
   2. fp absolute מִבְדָּלָה
   3. mp construct אֹהֶל (*o*)
   4. fs construct זְוָעָה

4. Attach the boxes with suffixes and translate all vocabulary words. List all steps.
   Singular Nouns
   1. 3ms מֶלֶךְ (*a*)
   2. 3mp כֶּסֶל (*i*)

   Plural Nouns
   3. 2fs זְוָעָה
   4. 1cs מַמְלָכָה

5. Attach the suffixes to the prepositions and translate.
   1. 2fs מִן
   2. 1cp אֶל
   3. 2mp כ
   4. 2fp אֵת (with)

6. Verbs
   1. Create: Give the steps and the final answer.
      Qal
      1. Imperative 2ms +3ms (energic) לקח
      2. Imperfect 3ms +2ms נתן (A/Ē)
      3. Imperative 2fp נתן (A/Ē)
      4. Infinitive construct לקח
      5. Emphatic imperative נגשׁ (A/A)
      6. Imperfect 3ms +Vav-consecutive אכל
      7. Imperfect 1cp נגף (A/Ō)

      Hiph'îl
      8. Imperfect 3ms +3mp suffix נצל
      9. Perfect 2fs נחל

H*u*ph'al
10. Imperfect 2mp נגד

Niph'al
11. Perfect 1cp לקח
12. Imperfect 3mp +Vav-consecutive נחם

2. Parse: Give all possible answers.

1.	קְחָה	7.	נְשֵׂאת
2.	נִסְעָה	8.	קַח
3.	נִתַּתָּ	9.	לָטַעַת
4.	שְׂאֵת	10.	יַגֵּשׁ
5.	וְהַנִּדָּחָה	11.	יִשְׂאוּ
6.	גְּשׁוּ	12.	יִטְּשֵׁנוּ

7. Translation

1. וַיִּבְחַר־לוֹט אֶת־כָּל־כִּכַּר הַיַּרְדֵּן וַיִּסַּע לוֹט מִקֶּדֶם סְדֹמָה׃ אַבְרָהָם יָשַׁב
בְּאֶרֶץ־כְּנָעַן וְלוֹט יָשַׁב בְּעָרֵי הַכִּכָּר׃

2. וַיֹּאמֶר אֵלָיו שְׁמוּאֵל קָרַע יהוה אֶת־מַמְלֶכֶת יִשְׂרָאֵל מֵעָלֶיךָ הַיּוֹם וּנְתָנָהּ
לְרֵעֲךָ הַטּוֹב מִמֶּךָּ׃ וְגַם נֵצַח יִשְׂרָאֵל לֹא יְשַׁקֵּר וְלֹא יִנָּחֵם כִּי לֹא אָדָם הוּא
לְהִנָּחֵם׃ וַיֹּאמֶר חָטָאתִי עַתָּה כַּבְּדֵנִי נָא נֶגֶד זִקְנֵי־עַמִּי וְנֶגֶד יִשְׂרָאֵל׃

3. שִׁמְעוּ־זֹאת בֵית־יַעֲקֹב הַנִּקְרָאִים בְּשֵׁם יִשְׂרָאֵל וּמִמְּעֵי יְהוּדָה יָצָאוּ הַנִּשְׁבָּעִים
בְּשֵׁם יהוה וּבֵאלֹהֵי יִשְׂרָאֵל יַזְכִּירוּ לֹא בֶאֱמֶת וְלֹא בִצְדָקָה׃ אַף יָדִי
יָסְדָה אֶרֶץ וִימִינִי פֵּרְשָׁה שָׁמָיִם קֹרֵא אֲנִי אֲלֵיהֶם יַעַמְדוּ יַחְדָּו׃ הִקָּבְצוּ כֻלְּכֶם
וּשֲׁמָעוּ מִי בָהֶם הִגִּיד אֶת־אֵלֶּה׃

CHAPTER 35
R_1-VAV AND YOD (PE VAV/YOD) VERBS

35.1. Introduction: R_1-Yod (original Vav)

R_1-Yod verbs represent two verbs: R_1-Yod (original Vav) and R_1-Yod (original Yod). R_1-Yod (original Vav) Verbs retain the original Vav in Niph'al, Hiph'îl, Hoph'al, and Hithpa"ēl. In the other conjugations (Pi"ēl, Pu"al, and some Qal forms) a Yod replaces the original Vav. R_1-Yod (Vav) verbs primarily obscure the boxes and frequently the first syllable of the Qal.

35.2. Weaknesses or Infirmities of R_1-Yod (original Vav)

1. Forms retaining the original Vav (Niph'al, Hiph'îl, and Hoph'al) usually contract the original Vav with the preceding short vowel.
2. The original Vav disappears in the Qal imperfect, imperative, and the infinitive construct, probably reflecting an original biliteral root (34.4.2).

35.3. Strong Areas of R_1-Yod (original Vav) Verbs

1. The original Vav remains in the:
   Niph'al imperfect, imperative, infinitive (with the box □□▣ָהִ), and Hithpa"ēl (sometimes)

   Niph'al imperfect 3ms יִוָּלֵד

2. Forms replacing the original Vav with a Yod are virtually strong:
   Qal perfect, participles, infinitive absolute

   Qal perfect 3ms יָשַׁב

   Pi"ēl, Pu"al, and Hithpa"ēl (sometimes)

   Pu"al perfect 3ms יֻלַּד

35.4. Remedies for the Infirmities of the R_1-Yod (original Vav) Verbs

1. Forms retaining the original Vav usually contract the Vav with the preceding short vowel:
   1. Hoph'al » Hûph'al: uw » ū *הֻוְשַׁב » הוּשַׁב perfect 3ms
   2. Hiph'îl » Haph'îl (The Hiph'îl is a Haph'îl throughout the paradigm in R_1-Yod [original Vav] verbs): aw » ô *הַוְשִׁיב » הוֹשִׁיב perfect 3ms
   3. Niph'al » Naph'al (The Niph'al is a Naph'al in the perfect, participle, and one infinitive absolute option [□□□נִ]): aw » ô *נַוְעַץ » נוֹעַץ perfect 3ms

2. The original Vav disappears in the Qal imperfect, imperative and infinitive construct.
   1. Imperfect: The original Vav disappears, and the preformative Ḥireq lengthens to Ṣere by compensation.
      Qal Imperfect 3ms *יִוְשַׁב » *יֵשַׁב » יֵשֵׁב

   2. Imperative: The imperative drops the Vav (AWOL like R_1-Nun verbs, 34.4.3).

		R_1-Yod (Vav)	R_1-Nun
Qal Imperative	2ms	*וְשֵׁב » שֵׁב	תֵּן
	2fs	שְׁבִי	תְּנִי
	2mp	שְׁבוּ	תְּנוּ
	2fp	שֵׁבְנָה	תֵּנָּה

   3. Infinitive Construct: The infinitive construct drops the Vav (AWOL), adds ת, and imitates the Segolate pattern (like R_1-Nun verbs, 34.4.2).

      R_1-Yod (Vav): *וְשֵׁב » *שֵׁב » *שֵׁבְתְּ » *שֵׁבֶת » שֶׁבֶת (*i*) 1cs suffix שִׁבְתִּי
      R_1-Nun: *נְגַשׁ » *גַּשׁ » *גַּשְׁתְּ » *גַּשֶׁת » גֶּשֶׁת (*i*) 1cs suffix גִּשְׁתִּי

      With a pronominal suffix, R_1-Yod (original Vav) verbs take Ḥireq under the first letter: שִׁבְתִּי (ישׁב). R_1-Yod (Vav)/R_3-Guttural verbs take Pataḥ under the first letter: דַּעְתִּי (ידע) Qal infinitive construct with 1cs suffix.

35.5. Final Considerations

1. In R_1-Yod (original Vav) verbs, the thematic vowels for the Qal are A/Ē-a: יָשַׁב/יֵשֵׁב – שֵׁב. Verbs ending in an R_3-Guttural change the thematic vowels to A/A: יָדַע/יֵדַע – דַּע.

2. A Vav-Consecutive (וַ◘) with the imperfect retracts the accent in the Qal, Hiph'îl, and (sometimes) Niph'al when the final syllable is closed, and the penult is an open syllable with a long vowel (footnote 20-1). Because the final syllable is closed and unaccented, the Ṣere shortens to Segol.

		Imperfect	With Vav-Consecutive (וַ◘)
Qal	3ms	יֵשֵׁב	וַיֵּשֶׁב
Hiph'îl (jussive)	3ms	יוֹשֵׁב	וַיּוֹשֶׁב
Niph'al	3ms	יִוָּלֵד	וַיִּוָּלֶד
Qal	3mp	יֵשְׁבוּ	וַיֵּשְׁבוּ (The accent does not retract because the final syllable is open.)

3. הלך also acts like an R_1-Yod (Vav) verb outside the perfect, participle, and infinitive absolute.

Qal perfect 3ms	הָלַךְ
Qal imperfect 3ms	יֵלֵךְ
Qal imperative 2ms	לֵךְ
Qal infinitive construct	לֶכֶת (*e*) with 1cs לֶכְתִּי
Hiph'îl perfect 3ms	הוֹלִיךְ

35.6. Introduction: R_1-Yod (original Yod)

The R_1-Yod (original Yod) verbs (frequently יבשׁ, יטב, ילל, ימן, ינק, יעץ, ישׁר) occur in the Qal and Hiph'îl. Like the R_1-Yod (Vav) verbs, the R_1-Yod (original Yod) verbs obscure the box pattern.

35.7. Weaknesses or Infirmities of R_1-Yod (original Yod) Verbs

1. Hiph'îl: The R_1-Yod contracts with the preceding short vowel.
2. Qal: In the silent shewa position (in the imperfect), the Yod quiesces.

35.8. Strong Areas of the R_1-Yod (original Yod) Verbs

R_1-Yod (original Yod) verbs are like strong verbs in the Qal perfect, imperative, infinitives, and participles.

35.9. Remedies for the Infirmities of the R_1-Yod (original Yod) Verbs

1. Hiph'îl » Haph'îl (The original R_1-Yod contracts with the preceding short vowel: ay » ê, 11.10.1.)

   Hiph'îl perfect 3ms *הַיְטִיב » הֵיטִיב

   Hiph'îl imperfect 3ms *יַיְטִיב » יֵיטִיב with Vav-consecutive וַיֵּיטֶב

   Hiph'îl imperative 2ms *הַיְטֵב » הֵיטֵב

2. Qal (imperfect): The original R_1-Yod quiesces to form the vowel Ḥireq-Yod, compare 8.2.2 and footnote 8-2.

   Qal imperfect 3ms *יִיְטַב » יִיטַב

35.10. Final Consideration: R_1-Yod (original Yod) verbs are A/A (stative) in the Qal.

35.11. Introduction: Mixed Forms

There are two mixed forms: (1) a few verbs follow both R_1-Yod (original Vav) and R_1-Yod (original Yod) patterns, and (2) R_1-Yod / R_2-Ṣade verbs frequently follow R_1-Nun patterns.

35.12. Verbs Partly R_1-Yod (original Vav) and Partly R_1-Yod (original Yod): ירא and ירשׁ

1. ירא

	R_1-Yod (Vav)	R_1-Yod (Yod)
Qal imperfect 3ms		יִירָא
Qal imperative 2ms		יְרָא
Qal infinitive construct		(irregular) יִרְאָה
Niph'al imperfect 3ms	יִוָּרֵא	

ירא follows R_1-Yod (Yod) pattern in the Qal and the R_1-Yod (Vav) pattern in the Niph'al.

2. ירשׁ

	R_1-Yod (Vav)	R_1-Yod (Yod)
Qal imperfect		יִירַשׁ
Qal imperative 2ms	רֵשׁ	
Qal infinitive construct	רֶ֫שֶׁת (*i*)	
Niph'al imperfect 3ms	יִוָּרֵשׁ	
Hiph'îl perfect 3ms	הוֹרִישׁ	

ירשׁ follows R_1-Yod (Yod) pattern in the Qal imperfect and R_1-Yod (Vav) pattern elsewhere.

35.13. Verbs R_1-Yod/R_2-Ṣade (יצג, יצע, יצת, and frequently יצק, יצר, but excluding יצא)

These verbs sometimes act like R_1-Nun verbs: the Yod may assimilate to the following Ṣade when the R_1-Yod is in the silent shewa position (34.4.1). Moreover, in the Qal imperative and infinitive construct, the R_1-Yod may disappear (34.4.2).

Qal imperfect 1cs — (יִפֹּל « יִנְפֹּל*) אֶצֹּק « אֶיְצֹק*
Qal imperative 2ms — יְצֹק (נְפֹל) or צַק[1] (גַּשׁ)
Qal infinitive construct — צֶ֫קֶת (גֶּ֫שֶׁת)
Hiph'îl imperfect 3mp — יַצִּ֫יקוּ « יַיְצִיקוּ*

[1] Note the change in the thematic vowel from Ḥolem to Pataḥ (both irregular and irritating).

35.14. The Irregular Verb יָכֹל (Ō/A)

The Qal stative verb יָכֹל (Ō/A) (to be able, prevail) has an irregular Qal imperfect: יוּכַל (3ms).

35.15. Forming and Parsing R_1-Yod Verbs (29.10-29.13)

1. Hiphʿîl imperative 2mp ישׁע

1.	Boxes:	הַ□ְ□□ » הוֹ□□	הוֹשׁע « *הַוְשׁע (35.4.1)
2.	Colors:	A-î/Î-ē	הוֹשִׁיע
3.	Qal:	שִׁמְרוּ	הוֹשִׁיעוּ
	Answer:	הוֹשִׁיעוּ	

2. Qal imperfect 3ms יטב (י)
   1. Strong form: יִקְטֹל » יִיְטב
   2. Weakness: The R_1-Yod (Yod) verbs affect the boxes or the first syllable of the Qal. Moreover, all R_1-Yod (Yod) verbs have a Pataḥ thematic vowel in the Qal.
   3. Adjustments: R_1-Yod quiesces in the silent shewa position and forms a Ḥireq-Yod – *יִיְטב » *יִיטב (35.9.2).
      The thematic vowel is Pataḥ (35.10): יִיטַב.
      Answer: יִיטַב

3. הוֹשַׁע

1.	Boxes:	הוֹ□□ » הַ□ְ□□ (הַ□ְ□)	Hiphʿîl perfect, imperative, infinitives
2.	Colors:	A-î/Î-ē; with R_3-Guttural A-î/Î-a and most Ṣere forms (a) (24.2.2; 32.4)	Hiphʿîl imperative 2ms, 2fp infinitive absolute (irregular)
3.	Qal:	שְׁמֹר or שָׁמוֹר	Hiphʿîl imperative 2ms or infinitive absolute (irregular)
	Answer:	Hiphʿîl imperative 2ms of ישׁע	

R_1-YOD (ORIGINAL PE VAV) VERBS (35.1-5)

	Qal	Niph'al » Naph'al	Pi"ēl Pu"al Hithpa"ēl	Hiph'îl » Haph'îl	Hoph'al
Perfect	Strong: Yod replaces Vav 35.3.2	aw » ô *נַוְשַׁב » נוֹשַׁב 35.4.1.3			
Imperfect	Impf./Impv. have thematic vowels /Ē-a. Impf. drops Vav and lengthens preceding Ḥireq to Ṣere 35.4.2	Strong with Vav retained by Dagesh Forte יִוָּשֵׁב 35.3.1	Strong (In Pi"ēl, Pu"al, the original Vav becomes Yod; Hithpa"ēl sometimes retain Vav; sometimes it becomes Yod) 35.3.2	aw » ô *הַוְשִׁיב » הוֹשִׁיב *יַוְשִׁיב » יוֹשִׁיב etc. 35.4.1	uw » û *יֻוְשַׁב » יוּשַׁב etc. 35.4.1
Imperative	Drops Vav (like R_1-Nun green/red) 35.4.2				
Infinitive Construct	Drops Vav, adds ת and forms Segolate patterns (like R_1-Nun green/red) 35.4.2				
Infinitive Absolute	Strong: Yod replaces Vav 35.3.2				
Participle		aw » ô *נַוְשָׁב » נוֹשָׁב 35.4.1			*מֻוְשָׁב » מוּשָׁב

הלך is a R_1-Yod (Vav) verb in the Qal imperfect, imperative, infinitive construct, and the Hiph'îl. Elsewhere, it is regular – הֹלֵךְ Qal participle masculine singular absolute, יִתְהַלֵּךְ Hithpa"ēl imperfect 3ms (35.5.3).

Note: For the corresponding color chart, see page 359

	R₁-Yod (Original Yod) (35.6-10)		Mixed Forms				Irregular Form
			ירא 35.12.1		ירש 35.12.2		יכל (Ō/A) 35.14
	Qal	**Haph'îl (« Hiph'îl)**	**Qal R_1-Yod (Yod)**	**Derived Conjugations R_1-Yod (Vav)**	**Qal R_1-Yod (Yod)**	**Derived Conjugations R_1-Yod (Vav)**	**Qal**
Perfect	Strong 35.8.		יָרֵא		יָרַשׁ	Niph'al perf. 3ms נוֹרַשׁ	יָכֹל 3ms
Imperfect	Yod in silent shewa position quiesces: short Ḥireq lengthens to Ḥireq-Yod 35.9.2		יִירָא		יִירַשׁ	Hiph'îl impf. 3ms יוֹרִישׁ	יוּכַל Imperfect 3ms
Imperative	All impf./impv. has Pataḥ for thematic vowels 35.10	ay » ê Perf. 3ms הֵיטִיב » הַיְטִיב* 35.9.1	יְרָא	Niph'al perf. 3ms נוֹרָא Niph'al impf. 3ms יִוָּרֵא	R_1-Yod (Vav) רֵשׁ		
Infinitive Absolute	Strong 35.8		Strong		Strong		
Infinitive Construct			יִרְאָה/יְרֹא*		R_1-Yod (Vav) רֶשֶׁת		
Participle			Strong		Strong		

*irregular

Note: For the corresponding color chart, see page 360

Exercise Thirty-Five

I. Questions

1. What part of the word is affected in R_1-Vav and Yod verbs?
2. What are the two R_1-Yod verbs?
3. Describe the weaknesses of the R_1-Yod (Vav) verbs.
4. When are R_1-Yod (Vav) verbs like strong verbs?
5. Discuss the remedies for the weaknesses of R_1-Yod (Vav) verbs.
6. Describe the changes in the names of the conjugations: Niph'al, Hiph'îl, and Hoph'al. What do they become in R_1-Yod (Vav) verbs?
7. How are R_1-Yod (Vav) verbs similar to R_1-Nun verbs in the Qal?
8. What are the thematic vowels in the Qal of R_1-Yod (Vav) verbs? What are the thematic vowels of R_1-Yod (Vav) / R_3-Guttural verbs?
9. Explain the changes that the Vav-consecutive (וַ◻) makes to the imperfect. When and where do these changes occur?
10. How is הלך associated with R_1-Yod (Vav) verbs?
11. Describe the weaknesses of the R_1-Yod (Yod) verbs.
12. When do these weaknesses occur?
13. When are the R_1-Yod (Yod) verbs like strong verbs?
14. Discuss the remedies for these weaknesses.
15. What are the thematic vowels in the Qal of R_1-Yod (Yod) verbs?
16. Discuss the mixed forms ירא and ירשׁ: when do they act like R_1-Yod (Vav) verbs and when do they act like R_1-Yod (Yod) verbs?
17. R_1-Yod / R_2-Ṣade verbs are like which weak verb?
18. How is the stative verb יָכֹל (Ō/A) irregular?
19. Discuss the parsing and the forming of R_1-Yod verbs.

II. **Vocabulary**: R_1-Yod (original Yod) verbs are marked with (י); consider all other R_1-Yod verbs as original Vav.

יסף	Qal: add Niph'al: be added, joined Hiph'îl: add (יסף means "again" or "more" when followed by an infinitive or another verb – וַיֹּסֶף ... וַיִּקַּח And he added and took = he took again)	חדל	Qal: cease, come to an end, desist, fail
		מטר	Hiph'îl: rain, cause rain to fall
		יצר	Qal: form, fashion, plan, foreordain (participle: one who forms, a potter) Niph'al: passive of Qal
יכח	Hiph'îl: decide, judge, reprove, correct, convict	יעץ (י)	Qal: advise, counsel Niph'al: consult together, exchange counsel

יטב	Qal: be good, be pleasing Hiph'îl: do good (to), deal well (with), do thoroughly	מָטָר	rain
		עֵצָה	counsel, advice
		נָתָן	Nathan
ישׁע	Niph'al: be freed, saved Hiph'îl: free, save, deliver, liberate	בַּת־שֶׁ֫בַע	Bathsheba
		ירשׁ	Qal: take possession of, dispossess Hiph'îl: cause to possess or inherit, cause to dispossess
יָכֹל (Ō/A)	Qal: be able, have power, prevail, endure		

III. Drills

1. Word Breakdown: In the following order: label every Dagesh Forte and Lene, Mappiq; vocal and silent shewa; Qameṣ and Qameṣ-Ḥatuf. Next, divide syllables labeling them open or closed. Then pronounce the words.

   רָנִּי   נָגוּעַ

2. Attach the following particles and translate all vocabulary words.
   Interrogative מה

   רָחָב   פִּנָּה

   Conjunctive ו

   פָּרַח   רְחֹבוֹת

   Preposition מן

   כָּלָה   הַמֶּ֫לֶךְ

3. Attach the boxes and translate all vocabulary words.
   1. mp construct צַדִּיק
   2. fp construct מִבְדָּלָה
   3. ms construct פֹּ֫עַל (*o*)
   4. fs construct יָשָׁר

4. Attach the boxes with suffixes and translate all vocabulary words. List all steps.

   Singular Nouns
   1. 3ms מִשְׁפָּח
   2. 1cs עֲבֹת

   Plural Nouns
   3. 3mp פֹּ֫עַל (*o*)
   4. 2ms שֹׁ֫רֶשׁ (*o*)

5. Attach the suffixes to the prepositions and translate.
   1. 2mp אתּ (direct object)
   2. 3mp אַחַר
   3. 3fs ב
   4. 3mp עִם

6. Verbs
   1. Create: List all steps and the final answer.

      Qal
      1. Infinitive construct ירד
      2. Imperfect 1cs +2ms +Vav-consecutive ידע
      3. Imperfect 3ms +Vav-consecutive ירד
      4. Participle mp +3fs ישׁב
      5. Perfect 1cs +3ms (Ō/A) יכל
      6. Infinitive construct ידע
      7. Imperfect 1cs יטב (י)

      Hiph'îl
      8. Imperfect 3ms +Vav-consecutive נגע
      9. Perfect 2ms יצא
      10. Imperative 2ms +1cs ידע
      11. Imperfect 3mp +2fs יעל
      12. Perfect 2fs יטב (י)

      Hoph'al
      13. Perfect 3fs ילד

      Niph'al
      14. Imperative 2fp יתר

   2. Parse: Give all possible answers.
      1. הוֹדַע
      2. דַּע
      3. רֶ֫דֶת
      4. יֵיטֵב
      5. תּוֹרֵ֫דְנָה
      6. הֵיטַ֫בְנוּ
      7. הוֹצֵא
      8. יָבֹשׁ
      9. דַּעְתְּךְ
      10. יוּכְלוּ
      11. לִדְתָּהּ
      12. יְלָ֫דַתּוּ
      13. אֲיסִירֵם
      14. יוֹעַצְתּוֹ

7. Translation

1. וְעַתָּה יהוה אֱלֹהֵי יִשְׂרָאֵל שְׁמֹר לְעַבְדְּךָ דָוִד אָבִי אֵת אֲשֶׁר דִּבַּרְתָּ לּוֹ לֵאמֹר
לֹא־יִכָּרֵת לְךָ אִישׁ מִלְּפָנַי יֹשֵׁב עַל־כִּסֵּא יִשְׂרָאֵל רַק אִם יִשְׁמְרוּ בָנֶיךָ
אֶת־דַּרְכָּם לָלֶכֶת לְפָנַי כַּאֲשֶׁר הָלַכְתָּ לְפָנָי׃ וְעַתָּה אֱלֹהֵי יִשְׂרָאֵל יֵאָמֶן נָא
דְּבָרְךָ אֲשֶׁר דִּבַּרְתָּ לְעַבְדְּךָ דָּוִד אָבִי׃

2. וְנָתַתִּי אֶת־זַרְעֲךָ כַּעֲפַר הָאָרֶץ אֲשֶׁר אִם יוּכַל אִישׁ לְסַפֵּר אֶת עֲפַר הָאָרֶץ
גַּם־זַרְעֲךָ יִסָּפֵר׃

3. רָאָה פַרְעֹה כִּי־חָדַל הַמָּטָר וַיֹּסֶף לַחֲטֹא וַיַּכְבֵּד לִבּוֹ הוּא וַעֲבָדָיו׃ וַיֶּחֱזַק
לֵב פַּרְעֹה וְלֹא שִׁלַּח אֶת־בְּנֵי יִשְׂרָאֵל כַּאֲשֶׁר דִּבֶּר יהוה בְּיַד־מֹשֶׁה׃

4. וַיֹּאמֶר נָתָן אֶל־בַּת־שֶׁבַע אֵם שְׁלֹמֹה לֵאמֹר הֲלֹא שָׁמַעַתְּ כִּי מָלַךְ אֲדֹנִיָּהוּ
וַאֲדֹנֵינוּ דָוִד לֹא יָדָע׃ וְעַתָּה לְכִי אִיעָצֵךְ נָא עֵצָה וּמַלְּטִי אֶת־נַפְשֵׁךְ
וְאֶת־נֶפֶשׁ בְּנֵךְ שְׁלֹמֹה׃

CHAPTER 36
R_2-VAV AND YOD (AYIN VAV/YOD) VERBS

36.1. Introduction: There are two "collapsed" verbs: R_2-Vav (Yod) verbs and Geminate verbs (chapter 38). Geminate verbs collapse R_3 into R_2; R_2-Vav (Yod) verbs quiesce the R_2-Vav (Yod), and the verb collapses R_3 and R_1, now united by a thematic vowel. The preformative vowel, usually connected to R_1 (R_3R_2 $\underset{:}{R}_1$Ᵽ$_v$), is now in an open syllable with R_2-Vav (Yod) verbs (R_3R_1 Ᵽ$_v$). For "collapsed" verbs, the Pi"ēl, Pu"al, and Hithpa"ēl stems are usually replaced by Pôlēl, Pôlal and Hithpôlēl stems.[1]

36.2. Weaknesses or Infirmities of R_2-Vav (Yod) Verbs

R_2-Vav (Yod) is very unstable and quiesces (or contracts), "collapsing" the verb.

36.3. Strong Areas of R_2-Vav (Yod) Verbs: None[1]

36.4. Remedies for the Infirmities of R_2-Vav (Yod) Verbs

1. Hoph'al/Hûph'al: The R_2-Vav (Yod) verbs in the Hoph'al become an R_1-Vav (Yod) verb (*קום » *וקם, 35.4.1 uw » û).

Perfect 3ms	הוּקַם
Imperfect 3ms	יוּקַם
Participle ms absolute	מוּקָם

2. Hiph'îl
   1. General observations
      1. Preformative vowels:[2] I (Ḥireq) – in the perfect and the participle; A – in the imperfect, the imperative, and the infinitive.
      2. Thematic vowel uniting R_1 to R_3: Î – Ḥireq-Yod (or Ṣere in the Ṣere forms).
   2. Specific observations
      1. Perfect: Vocalic endings attach directly to R_3; syllabic suffixes (17.3.3) unite to R_3 with a connecting Ḥolem-Vav, sometimes written defectively as Ḥolem.

---

[1] Occasionally, a strong Pi"ēl, Pu"al, and Hithpa"ēl form is found. The Pôlēl, Pôlal and Hithpôlēl insert Ḥolem between R_1 and R_2 and unite R_2 and R_3 with Pataḥ or Ṣere. See the R_2-Vav/Yod verb paradigm in appendix VI.

[2] All preformative vowels lengthen or reduce as necessary. As with the strong verbs, the Hiph'îl has a preformative ה in the perfect, imperative and infinitive; in the imperfect and participle, the ה is supplanted (footnote 22-3).

Vocalic endings (and 3ms)		Syllabic suffixes[3] (with connecting Ḥolem [-Vav])	
3ms	הֵקִים	1cs	(הֱ)הֲקִימֹ֫תִי
3fs	הֵקִ֫ימָה	2fs	(הֱ)הֲקִימֹת
3cp	הֵקִ֫ימוּ	2mp	(הֱ)הֲקִימֹתֶם

2. Imperfect: Note the "Ṣere forms." The Vav-consecutive third person forms retract the accent (35.5.2), reducing the Ṣere to Segol in a closed unaccented syllable.

3ms	יָקִים
2fp, 3fp	תָּקֵ֫מְנָה
3ms Jussive	יָקֵם
3ms Vav-Consecutive	וַיָּ֫קֶם

3. Imperative/Infinitive:

Imperative 2ms and infinitive absolute	הָקֵם
Imperative 2fs	הָקִ֫ימִי
Infinitive construct	הָקִים

4. Participle: The participle (analogous to first syllable of the R_1-Yod verb, מֵיטִיב, 35.9.1) has a Ḥireq preformative.

ms	מֵקִים
fs absolute	מְקִימָה

3. Niph'al (» Naph'al in the perfect/participle)
   1. General observations
      1. Preformative vowel:[4] A – in the perfect/participle (Naph'al); I (Ḥireq) – in all other conjugations.
      2. Thematic vowel uniting R_1 to R_3: Ô – Ḥolem-Vav (defectively, Ḥolem)
   2. Specific observations
      1. Perfect: Vocalic endings attach directly to R_3; consonantal suffixes unite to R_3 with a connecting Ḥolem (-Vav). The thematic vowel

[3] Other (rare) forms analogous to the strong verb for the consonantal suffixes have Pataḥ as the thematic vowel and are without the connecting Ḥolem – הֵקַ֫מְתִּי (1cs).

[4] The Niph'al preformative letters, like the strong verb, are נ in the perfect and participle; ה in the imperative and infinitive. The imperfect has the אֵיתָן letters.

Ḥolem (-Vav) may dissimilate to Shureq when followed by the connecting Ḥolem (-Vav).

Vocalic endings (and 3ms)		Syllabic suffixes (with connecting Ḥolem [-Vav]) with dissimilation	
3ms	נָקוֹם	1cs	נְקוּמֹתִי
3fs	נָקֽוֹמָה	2fs	נְקוּמֹת
3cp	נָקֽוֹמוּ	2mp	נְקוּמֹתֶם

2. Imperfect, Imperative, Infinitive: These forms assimilate the Nun of Niph'al in R_1.

Imperfect 3ms	יִקּוֹם « *יִנְקוֹם
Imperative 2ms and infinitive absolute/construct	הִקּוֹם

3. Participle: (Naph'al)

ms	נָקוֹם
fs absolute	נְקוֹמָה

4. Qal
   1. General observations
      1. Preformative vowels (imperfect only):[5]
         Standard verbs: A[6]
         Stative verbs: A for A-ē/Û verbs; Ḥireq for Ô/Ô verbs

      2. Thematic vowels:[7]
         Standard verbs: A-ā/Û (R_2-Vav) and A-ā/Î (R_2-Yod)
         Stative verbs: A-ē/Û and Ô/Ô

   2. Specific observations
      1. Perfect: The smaller case letter of the thematic vowel stands for all third person verbs.

	Standard Verb	**Stative Verbs**	
	A-ā/	A-ē/	Ô/
3ms	קָם	מֵת	בּוֹשׁ

[5] The preformative vowels will not be supplied for forming the verbs. The אֵיתָן letters are the preformative letters in the Qal.

[6] The Pataḥ, the original preformative vowel of most standard verbs (still retained in R_1-Guttural verbs), changed later to Ḥireq: יִשְׁמֹר (attenuation).

[7] Thematic vowels will be supplied for forming the verbs.

3fs	קָ֫מָה	מֵ֫תָה	בּ֫וֹשָׁה
3cp	קָ֫מוּ	מֵ֫תוּ	בּ֫וֹשׁוּ
1cs	קַ֫מְתִּי	מַ֫תִּי[8]	בּ֫וֹשְׁתִּי
2mp	קַמְתֶּם	מַתֶּם[8]	בּוֹשְׁתֶּם

2. Imperfect: The 2fp, 3fp connect R_3 to the suffix with Segol-Yod, which always takes the accent. The jussive 3ms has a Ḥolem (R_2-Vav) or Ṣere (R_2-Yod) thematic vowel. In the Vav-consecutive (3ms, 3fs), the accent retracts, and the thematic vowel, Ḥolem or Ṣere, reduces in a closed unaccented syllable. בּוֹשׁ has Ḥolem-Vav throughout the imperfect.

	Standard Verbs		Stative Verbs	
	/Û (R_2-Vav)	/Î (R_2-Yod)	/Û	/Ô
3ms	יָקוּם	יָשִׂים	יָמוּת	יֵבוֹשׁ
2fp, 3fp	תְּקוּמֶ֫ינָה	תְּשִׂימֶ֫ינָה	תְּמוּתֶ֫ינָה	תְּבוֹשֶׁ֫ינָה
Jussive 3ms	יָקֹם	יָשֵׂם	יָמֹת	יֵבוֹשׁ
Vav-consecutive 3ms	וַיָּ֫קָם	וַיָּ֫שֶׂם	וַיָּ֫מָת	וַיֵּבוֹשׁ
Vav-consecutive 3mp	וַיָּ֫קוּמוּ	וַיָּ֫שִׂימוּ	וַיָּ֫מוּתוּ	וַיֵּ֫בוֹשׁוּ

3. Imperative: Form these by removing the preformative. Note the exceptional 2fp.

	Standard Verbs		Stative Verbs	
	/Û	/Î	/Û	/Ô
2ms	קוּם	שִׂים	מוּת	בּוֹשׁ
2fs	ק֫וּמִי	שִׂ֫ימִי	מ֫וּתִי	בּ֫וֹשִׁי
2mp	ק֫וּמוּ	שִׂ֫ימוּ	מ֫וּתוּ	בּ֫וֹשׁוּ
2fp	קֹ֫מְנָה	-----	-----	בּ֫וֹשְׁנָה

4. Infinitive

1. Absolute[9]

קוֹם	שׂוֹם	מוֹת	בּוֹשׁ

2. Construct

קוּם	שִׂים	מוּת	בּוֹשׁ

---

[8] מַ֫תִּי and מַתֶּם are contracted from *מַ֫תְתִּי and *מַתְתֶּם.

[9] The form is may be analogous to the last syllable of the strong verb: כָּתוֹב.

5. Participle: The masculine singular is identical to the perfect 3ms

ms	קָם	שָׂם	מֵת	בּוֹשׁ
fs	קָמָה	שָׂמָה	מֵתָה	בּוֹשָׁה

36.5. Accent

1. Normally, the thematic vowel uniting R_3 and R_1 takes the accent.[10]

Qal perfect 1cs קַמְתִּי

Qal perfect 3fs קָמָה

An exception is the Qal imperfect 2fp, 3fp when the Segol-Yod takes the accent תְּשׁוּבֶינָה.

2. The participles accent the end of the word (except with pronominal suffixes).

Qal ms קָם

Qal fs קָמָה (contrast with the Qal perfect 3fs קָמָה)

Niph'al ms נָקוֹם

Niph'al fs נְקוֹמָה

3. In the perfect of the Niph'al and Hiph'îl, the connecting Ḥolem (-Vav) takes the accent (except the 2mp, 2fp suffixes, which always take the accent).

Hiph'îl perfect 1cs (הֱ)הֲקִימֹתִי

Hiph'îl perfect 2mp (הֱ)הֲקִימֹתֶם

4. Pronominal suffixes shift the accent down the word (27.3.1 and 28.2.2).

Qal perfect 3cp +2ms שָׂמוּךָ

Hiph'îl perfect 1cs +3mp הֲבִיאוֹתִים

36.6. The R_2-Vav / R_3-Alef Verb בוא

This verb is doubly weak: R_2-Vav / R_3-Alef.

1. Qal: Note the quiesced Alef in all forms except the 3fs, 3cp, 2fp, 3fp (chapter 33).

1. Perfect	3ms	בָּא		1cs	בָּאתִי
	3fs	בָּאָה		2mp	בָּאתֶם
	3cp	בָּאוּ			

[10] The Hoph'al, following the R_1-Yod (Vav) verb, takes the normal accent pattern: תּוּקַמְתִּי.

2. Imperfect 3ms יָבוֹא (defectively יָבֹא)
   2fp תְּבוֹאֶינָה

   Vav-consecutive 3ms וַיָּבוֹא (The Alef quiesces, and the accent does not retract, footnote 20-1.)

3. Imperative 2ms בּוֹא

4. Infinitive absolute/construct בּוֹא

5. Participle

   ms בָּא

   mp בָּאִים

2. Hiph'îl

1. Perfect: Outside the third persons, two forms exist (36.4.2 and footnote 36-3)

   2ms הֵבֵאתָ Alef quiesced, see footnote 36-3, or

   (הֱ)הֲבִיאֹתָ Alef is alive and well, with connecting Ḥolem (-Vav).

   3ms הֵבִיא

   3fs הֵבִיאָה

   3cp הֵבִיאוּ

2. Imperfect

   3ms יָבִיא

   Jussive 3ms יָבֵא

   Vav-consecutive 3ms (Alef quiesced with no retraction of stress) וַיָּבֵא

3. Imperative

   2ms הָבֵא

   2fs הָבִיאִי

4. Infinitives

   Absolute הָבֵא

   Construct הָבִיא

5. Participle

ms מֵבִיא

fs absolute מְבִיאָה

36.7. Forming and Parsing R_2-Vav (Yod) Verbs

1. Forming

Although the boxes are obscured, the preformatives of the boxes are still visible (footnotes 36-2 and 36-4). Nevertheless, replace the first step of boxes with "preformative vowel." Retain, of course, the preformative with the "preformative vowel." Replace colors with the "thematic vowel uniting R_1 and R_3." Add a fourth step for the accent and rules of syllables. In forming these verbs, remove the R_2-Vav/Yod and collapse the form in the first step. A fifth step may be necessary if a Vav-consecutive is added.

Example: Hiph'îl imperfect 2mp קוּם

1. Preformative vowel with implied boxes: Pataḥ יַקם
2. Thematic vowel uniting R_1 and R_3: Ḥireq-Yod יַקִים
3. Qal imperfect 2mp (Strong Verb): תִּשְׁמְרוּ תַּקִימוּ
4. Accent and rules of syllables for the preformative vowel: תָּקִ֫ימוּ

Answer: תָּקִ֫ימוּ

1. Step one: The form is collapsed, and the preformative Pataḥ is placed under an imperfect preformative.
2. Step two: The thematic vowel, Ḥireq-Yod, connects R_1 to R_3.
3. Step three: The Qal preformative/sufformative is added.
4. Step four: Establish the accent (36.5) and lengthen the Pataḥ under the preformative to Qameṣ (6.3.2).

2. Parsing: If the usual parsing steps are unsuccessful (29.10-29.13), the form has probably collapsed (R_2-Vav [Yod] or Geminate form).

Examples:

תָּקוּם

1.	Preformative vowel: Qameṣ (« Pataḥ)	Niph'al perfect, participle, Hiph'îl imperfect, imperative, infinitive, Qal imperfect
2.	Thematic vowel uniting R_1 and R_3: Shureq	Qal imperfect
3.	Qal: תִּשְׁמֹר	2ms, 3fs
4.	Accent and rules of syllables:	________

Answer: Qal imperfect 2ms, 3fs of קוּם

1. Step one: The Qameṣ probably reflects an original Pataḥ.

2. Step two: The thematic vowel uniting R_1 and R_3 eliminates all forms except Qal imperfect.
3. Step three: Eliminate all Qal imperfects except 2ms and 3fs.
4. Step four: This step confirms the answer.

קַמְתְּ

1. Preformative vowel: None	
2. Thematic vowel uniting R_3 and R_1: Pataḥ	Qal perfect
3. Qal: קָטַלְתְּ	2fs
4. Accent and rules of syllables:	
Answer: Qal perfect 2fs of קוּם	

1. Step one: The verb does not have a preformative letter (אֵיתָן letters, or נ, ה, מ).
2. Step two: The Pataḥ indicates a Qal perfect (A-ā/ or A-ē/).
3. Step three: The perfect suffix תְּ indicates a 2fs.
4. Step four: This step confirms the answer.

R_2-Vav/Yod (Ayin Vav/Yod) Verbs

		Qal 36.4.4				**(Niph‘al »)** **Naph‘al** 36.4.3	**Hiph‘îl** 36.4.2		**Hoph‘al** 36.4.1
Preformative Vowels		A		A or I		A (Perfect, Participle) or I	I (Perfect, Participle) or A		
		Standard		Stative					
Thematic vowels		A-ā/Û	A-ā/Î	A-ē/Û	Ô/Ô	Ô	Î (Ē)		
		(R_2-Vav)	(R_2-Yod)				Ḥireq-Yod	Pataḥ	R_2-Vav
Perfect	3ms	קָם	שָׂם	מֵת	בּוֹשׁ	נָקוֹם	הֵקִים		verbs
	3fs	קָ֫מָה	שָׂ֫מָה	מֵ֫תָה	בּ֫וֹשָׁה		הֵקִ֫ימָה		become
	3cp	קָ֫מוּ	שָׂ֫מוּ	מֵ֫תוּ	בּ֫וֹשׁוּ		הֵקִ֫ימוּ		R_1-Vav
	1cs	קַ֫מְתִּי	שַׂ֫מְתִּי	מַ֫תִּי	בֹּ֫שְׁתִּי	נְקוּמֹ֫תִי	(הֱ)הֲקִימֹ֫תִי	הֲקַ֫מְתִּי	verbs
Imperfect	3ms	יָקוּם	יָשִׂים	יָמוּת	יֵבוֹשׁ	יִקּוֹם	יָקִים		הוּקַם
Jussive	3ms	יָקֹם	יָשֵׂם	יָמֹת	יֵבוֹשׁ		יָקֵם		Perfect 3ms
Vav-Consecutive	3ms	וַיָּ֫קָם	וַיָּ֫שֶׂם	וַיָּ֫מָת	וַיֵּבוֹשׁ		וַיָּ֫קֶם		
Imperative	2ms	קוּם	שִׂים	מוּת	בּוֹשׁ	הִקּוֹם	הָקֵם		
Infinitive	Absolute	קוֹם	שׂוֹם	מוֹת	בּוֹשׁ	הִקּוֹם	הָקֵם		
	Construct	קוּם	שִׂים	מוּת	בּוֹשׁ	הִקּוֹם	הָקִים		
Participle	ms	קָם	שָׂם	מֵת	בּוֹשׁ	נָקוֹם	מֵקִים		
	fs	קָמָה	שָׂמָה	מֵתָה	בּוֹשָׁה	נְקוֹמָה	מְקִימָה		

Note: For the corresponding color chart, see page 381.

R_2-Vav/Yod (Ayin Vav/Yod) Verbs

בּוֹא

		Qal (Ā/Ō) 36.6.1			Hiph'îl (Green) 36.6.2			
Perfect	3ms	בָּא	1cs	בָּ֫אתִי	3ms	הֵבִיא	1cs:	הֵבֵ֫אתִי/(הֱ)הֱבִיאֹ֫תִי
	3fs	בָּ֫אָה	2mp	בָּאתֶם	3fs	הֵבִ֫יאָה		
	3cp	בָּ֫אוּ			3cp	הֵבִ֫יאוּ		
Imperfect	3ms	יָבֹא				יָבִיא		
Jussive	3ms	יָבֹא				יָבֵא		
Vav-Consecutive	3ms	וַיָּבוֹא				וַיָּבֵא		
Imperative	2ms	בּוֹא				הָבֵא		
Infinitive	Absolute	בּוֹא				הָבֵא		
	Construct	בּוֹא				הָבִיא		
Participle	ms	בָּא				מֵבִיא		
	fs	בָּאָה				מְבִיאָה		

Note: For the corresponding color chart, see page 362

Exercise Thirty-Six

I. Questions

1. What are "collapsed" verbs?
2. How does the R_2-Vav (Yod) verb "collapse," and what is the result of the collapse? (What is the weakness of the R_2-Vav [Yod] verb?)
3. What are the strong areas of R_2-Vav (Yod) verbs?
4. How do R_2-Vav (Yod) verbs behave in the Hoph'al/Hûph'al?
5. What are the "thematic vowels uniting R_1 and R_3" for the Hiph'îl, Niph'al, and Qal?
6. What are the "preformative vowels" of the Hiph'îl, Niph'al, and Qal?
7. How are vocalic endings attached to the Niph'al and Hiph'îl perfect? How are the syllabic suffixes connected? What additional complication occurs in the Niph'al when syllabic suffixes are attached? What is the other option the Hiph'îl has in the perfect instead of the connecting Ḥolem (-Vav) forms?
8. Discuss the complications of the Qal and Hiph'îl 3ms imperfect Vav-consecutive forms.
9. The Qal participles are identical to what other form?
10. How are R_2-Vav (Yod) verbs accented?
11. Discuss the weaknesses of the verb בוא (especially Qal imperfect 3ms, imperfect 3ms Vav-consecutive, Hiph'îl perfect, imperfect 3ms Vav-consecutive).
12. Discuss the forming and the parsing of R_2-Vav (Yod) verbs.

II. Vocabulary

שׁוּב Qal: turn back, return, go back, come back (with another verb = again: to return and do = to do again)
Hiph'îl: cause to return, bring back

מוּת Qal: die
Hiph'îl: cause to die, kill
Hoph'al: passive of Hiph'îl

בְּכוֹר firstborn

מאן Pi"ēl: refuse, reject

בְּתוּלָה virgin

נטשׁ Qal: leave, forsake, permit
Niph'al: passive of Qal

קוּם Qal: arise, stand up, stand
Hiph'îl: cause to rise, arise, cause to stand, erect, raise up

סוּר Qal: turn aside, depart
Hiph'îl: cause to turn aside, depart, remove, take away

שִׂים Qal: put, place, set, ordain

נוּס Qal: flee
Hiph'îl: cause to flee

חָלָל slain, pierced, fatally wounded

גִּלְבֹּעַ Gilboa

דבק Qal: cling, stick to, cleave
Hiph'îl: cause to cling, stick to

III. Drills

1. Word Breakdown: In the following order: label every Dagesh Forte and Lene, Mappiq; vocal and silent shewa; Qameṣ and Qameṣ-Ḥatuf. Next, divide syllables labeling them open or closed. Then pronounce the words.

   בְּאָזְנָי   נְטוּיוֹת

2. Attach the following particles and translate all vocabulary words.
   Article

   עָשׂוֹר   רִצְפָּה

   Preposition לְ

   קַ֫חַת   יְשׁוּעָה

   Interrogative הֲ

   עַלִּיז   נַ֫חַת

3. Attach the boxes and translate all vocabulary words: list all steps.
   1. ms construct כֶּ֫סֶל (*i*)
   2. Dual absolute נְחֹ֫שֶׁת (*u*)
   3. fs construct מַצֵּבָה
   4. fp absolute נַעֲרָה

4. Attach the boxes with suffixes and translate all vocabulary words: list all steps.
   Singular Nouns
   1. 3fs עֲדָבָה
   2. 2ms עָוֹן

   Plural Nouns
   3. 2fp נֶ֫גַע (*i*)
   4. 3ms מַמְלָכָה

5. Attach the suffixes to the prepositions and translate.
   1. 2ms לְ
   2. 2fs לְמַ֫עַן
   3. 2mp אֵת (direct object)
   4. 1cs עַל

6. Verbs
   1. Create: List all steps and the final answer.
      Qal
      1. Infinitive absolute מוּת
      2. Perfect 3cp קוּם (A-ā/)
      3. Imperative 2mp דִּין
      4. Imperfect 3ms +Vav-consecutive סוּר (A-ā/Û)

5. Imperfect 3ms בּוֹשׁ (Ô/Ô)
6. Imperfect 3ms קוּם (A-ā/Û)

Hiph'îl
7. Perfect 3ms +1cs מוּת
8. Participle ms נוּף
9. Imperative 2ms +1cs + conjunctive Vav קוּם
10. Perfect 1cs בּוֹא
11. Jussive 3ms נוּעַ
12. Imperfect 3ms +3ms +Vav-consecutive מוּת

Hoph'al
13. Imperfect 3ms שִׁית

Niph'al
14. Imperative 2ms כּוּן

2. Parse: Give all possible answers.

1.	וַהֲקֵמֹתוֹ	8.	מְקִימָהּ
2.	תָּרֹם	9.	הֲרִימֹתָ
3.	יְעֹורוּ	10.	נְשׁוֹב
4.	נָפֹוצוּ	11.	תְּקוּמֶינָה
5.	מַתֶּן	12.	הָבֵא
6.	בָּאֲתְנוּ	13.	קְרוּאֶיהָ
7.	הֵבֵאתִי	14.	תֵּבוֹשׁ

7. Translation

1. וַיֹּאמֶר יהוה אֶל־מֹשֶׁה בְּמִדְיָן לֵךְ שֻׁב מִצְרָיִם כִּי מֵתוּ כָּל־הָאֲנָשִׁים הַמְבַקְשִׁים
אֶת־נַפְשֶׁךָ׃ וַיִּקַּח מֹשֶׁה אֶת־אִשְׁתּוֹ וְאֶת־בָּנָיו וַיַּרְכִּבֵם עַל־הַחֲמֹר וַיָּשָׁב אַרְצָה
מִצְרָיִם וַיִּקַּח מֹשֶׁה אֶת־מַטֵּה הָאֱלֹהִים בְּיָדוֹ׃ וַיֹּאמֶר יהוה אֶל־מֹשֶׁה אֱמֹר
אֶל־פַּרְעֹה כֹּה אָמַר יהוה בְּנִי בְכֹרִי יִשְׂרָאֵל׃ וָאֹמַר אֵלֶיךָ שַׁלַּח אֶת־בְּנִי
וַתְּמָאֵן לְשַׁלְּחוֹ הִנֵּה אָנֹכִי הֹרֵג אֶת־בִּנְךָ בְּכֹרֶךָ׃

2. שִׁמְעוּ אֶת־הַדָּבָר הַזֶּה אֲשֶׁר אָנֹכִי נֹשֵׂא עֲלֵיכֶם בֵּית יִשְׂרָאֵל׃ נָפְלָה לֹא
תוֹסִיף קוּם בְּתוּלַת יִשְׂרָאֵל נִטְּשָׁה עַל־אַדְמָתָהּ אֵין מְקִימָהּ׃

3. וְשַׂמְתִּי עֵינִי עֲלֵיהֶם לְטוֹבָה וַהֲשִׁבֹתִים עַל־הָאָרֶץ הַזֹּאת וְנָתַתִּי לָהֶם לֵב
לָדַעַת אֹתִי וְשָׁבוּ אֵלַי בְּכָל־לִבָּם כִּי אֲנִי יהוה וְהָיוּ־לִי לְעָם׃

4. וּפְלִשְׁתִּים נִלְחֲמוּ בְּיִשְׂרָאֵל וַיָּנֻס אִישׁ־יִשְׂרָאֵל מִפְּנֵי פְּלִשְׁתִּים וַיִּפְּלוּ חֲלָלִים
בְּהַר הַגִּלְבֹּעַ וַיַּדְבְּקוּ פְלִשְׁתִּים אַחֲרֵי שָׁאוּל וְאַחֲרֵי בָּנָיו׃

CHAPTER 37
R$_3$-VAV AND YOD (LAMED VAV/YOD) VERBS

37.1. Introduction: Traditionally, grammarians designate R$_3$-Vav/Yod verbs as R$_3$-He or Lamed He verbs from the Qal perfect 3ms – גָּלָה. This designation, however, is inaccurate: genuine R$_3$-He verbs are R$_3$-Guttural verbs ending in a He and Mappiq (תָּמַהּ, גָּבַהּ). Verbs ending with a He (in the Qal perfect 3ms) without a Mappiq are actually R$_3$-Vav/Yod verbs (שׁלה » *שׁלו; עשׂה » *עשׂי or *עשׂו). There are remnants of the R$_3$-Vav/Yod, such as שָׁלַוְתִּי and the Qal passive participle בָּנוּי. R$_3$-Vav (Yod) verbs primarily affect the thematic vowels (colors).

37.2. Weakness or Infirmity of R$_3$-Vav/Yod Verbs

R$_3$-Vav/Yod verbs contract or quiesce, obscuring the thematic vowel.

37.3. Strong Areas of R$_3$-Vav/Yod Verbs

		Strong	R$_3$-Vav/Yod
1.	Qal passive participle	שָׁמוּר	בָּנוּי
2.	Perfect 1cs (rare)	שָׁמַרְתִּי	שָׁלַוְתִּי

37.4. Remedies for the Infirmities of R$_3$-Vav/Yod Verbs

Remedies for these verbs apply to all the stems: Qal, Niph'al, Pi"ēl, and so forth. The remedies, therefore, will follow the conjugations: perfect, imperfect, imperative, infinitives, and participles.

1. Perfect
   1. All third persons have the following endings:

	Ending	Qal	Pi"ēl
3ms	□ָה	בָּנָה	גִּלָּה
3fs	□ְתָה	בָּנְתָה	גִּלְּתָה
3cp	□וּ	בָּנוּ	גִּלּוּ

The 3ms and 3cp endings attach directly to R$_2$; in the 3fs, the original feminine marker ת is retained (compare the original feminine ת in the feminine construct – תּוֹרַת, footnote 11-3). Occasionally, pausal forms retain the original Yod in the 3cp in pause – חָסָיוּ, נָטָיוּ.

   2. All other persons preserve the original Yod, contracted or quiesced as Ḥireq-Yod or Ṣere-Yod:[1]

---

[1] These are general patterns; there are exceptions. Those conjugations with Ṣere-Yod may take Ḥireq-Yod; those conjugations with Ḥireq-Yod may take Ṣere-Yod.

1. Ḥireq-Yod in the Qal, Pi“ēl, Hithpa“ēl, and Hiph‘îl

   Qal perfect 1cs בָּנִ֫יתִי (« *בָּנַ֫יְתִי Compare 8.2.2.)

   Pi“ēl perfect 1cs גִּלִּ֫יתִי (« *גִּלַּ֫יְתִי Compare 8.2.2.)

2. Ṣere-Yod in the Niph‘al, Pu“al, and Hoph‘al

   Niph‘al perfect 1cs נִגְלֵ֫יתִי (« *נִגְלַ֫יְתִי Compare 11.10.1.)

   Pu“al perfect 1cs גֻּלֵּ֫יתִי (« *גֻּלַּ֫יְתִי Compare 11.10.1.)

2. Imperfect

1. Non-endings (18.2.3) end in ◌ֶה[2]

   Qal imperfect 3ms יִבְנֶה

   Niph‘al imperfect 3ms יִגָּלֶה

2. Vocalic endings (18.2.3) attach directly to R_2[3]

   Qal imperfect 3mp יִפְנוּ

   Hiph‘îl imperfect 3mp יַרְבּוּ

3. Syllabic endings (18.2.3) maintain the original Yod by contraction

   Qal imperfect 2, 3fp *תִּגְלַיְנָה « *תִּגְלֵינָה « תִּגְלֶ֫ינָה

   1 2 3

   The original form (1) contracts, ay » ê (2), and the Ṣere becomes Segol because of the final Qameṣ (3) (12.2.3).[4]

4. Jussive and Vav-consecutive forms: these forms remove the ending ◌ֶה, forming a consonantal cluster, which may imitate the Segolate process (15.2) in the Qal and Hiph‘îl.

   1. Qal

	Imperfect	Jussive	Vav-Consecutive
3ms	יִגְלֶה	יִגְל	וַיִּגְל

---

[2] The original form may have been *יִבְנַי » *יִבְנֵי » יִבְנֶה.

[3] *יִבְנַיוּ » *יִבְנַוּ » יִבְנוּ (ayû » aû » û)

[4] This Segol spreads to R_3-Alef, R_2-Vav/Yod, and Geminate verbs: תִּמְצֶ֫אנָה, תְּקוּמֶ֫ינָה, תְּסֻבֶּ֫ינָה.

In the Qal jussive and Vav-consecutive, four forms are theoretically possible:

Ḥireq	Ṣere
יִגְל	יֵגְל
יִ֫גֶל	יֵ֫גֶל (compare סֵ֫פֶר [*i*])

2. Hiph'îl

	Imperfect	Jussive	Vav-Consecutive
3ms	יַגְלֶה	יַגְל	וַ֫יֶּגֶל / וַיַּגְל

In the Hiph'îl jussive and Vav-consecutive, two forms are theoretically possible:

Pataḥ	Segol
יַגְל	יֶ֫גֶל (compare מֶ֫לֶךְ [*a*])

3. Other Conjugations[5]

		Imperfect	Jussive	Vav-Consecutive
1.	Niph'al 3ms	יִגָּלֶה	*יִגָּל	וַיִּגָּל
2.	Pi"ēl 3ms	יְגַלֶּה	יְגַל	וַיְגַל
3.	Pu"al 3ms	יְגֻלֶּה	*יְגֻל	וַיְגֻל
4.	Hithpa"ēl 3ms	יִתְגַּלֶּה	יִתְגַּל	וַיִּתְגַּל
5.	Hoph'al 3ms	יָגְלֶה	*יָגְל	וַיָּגְל

3. Imperatives
   1. Non-endings (18.2.3) ends in ◌ֵה

      Qal imperative 2ms　　בְּנֵה

      Piel imperative 2ms　　כַּלֵּה

   2. Vocalic endings (2fs, 2mp) attach directly to R_2

      Qal imperative 2fs　　בְּנִי

      Hiph'îl imperative 2fs　　הַרְבִּי

[5] The asterisked forms are reconstructed. For the jussive and Vav-consecutive of the Pi"ēl, Pu"al, and Hithpa"ēl, a hovering Dagesh occurs over R_2 – יְגַל (footnote 4-6).

3. Syllabic ending (2fp) maintains the original Yod by contraction (37.4.2).
   Qal imperative 2fp בְּנֶ֫ינָה
   Hiph'îl imperative 2fp הַגְלֶ֫ינָה

4. Infinitives
   1. Infinitive absolute ends:
      1. ֹה◌ in the Qal, Niph'al, Pi"ēl, and Pu"al
         Qal infinitive absolute בָּנֹה

      2. ֵה◌ in the Hiph'îl, Hoph'al, and Hithpa"ēl
         Hiph'îl infinitive absolute הַגְלֵה

   2. Infinitive construct ends in וֹת◌:
      Qal infinitive construct בְּנוֹת
      Pi"ēl infinitive construct כַּלּוֹת

5. Participles
   1. Active
      1. The masculine singular absolute ends in ֶה◌
         Qal participle ms בֹּנֶה

      2. The noun endings of the feminine singular, feminine plural, and masculine plural attach directly to R_2.

		Qal	Pi"ēl
Participle active	mp	בֹּנִים	מְכַלִּים
	fs	בֹּנָה	מְכַלָּה
	fp	בֹּנוֹת	מְכַלּוֹת

      3. The feminine singular T-form ends in ֵית◌ (from ֶ֫יֶת◌). The Yod quiesces, and the Segol under R_2 lengthens to Ṣere (compare the R_3-Alef Verb מֹצֵאת 33.5.4).

	R_3-Vav/Yod	R_3-Alef
Qal participle fs (T-form)	בֹּנֵית	מֹצֵאת

2. Passive: The R_3-Yod is consonantal like a strong verb.

		R_3-Vav/Yod	Strong
Qal participle passive	ms	בָּנוּי	שָׁמוּר
	fs	בְּנוּיָה	שְׁמוּרָה
	mp	בְּנוּיִם	שְׁמוּרִים
	fp	בְּנוּיוֹת	שְׁמוּרוֹת

37.5. Attaching Pronominal Suffixes to R_3-Vav/Yod Verbs

1. Perfect
   1. In the 3ms, suffixes attach to R_2:

      Qal perfect 3ms +3ms גָּלָהוּ

   2. Other forms follow the strong pattern of attaching to the pronominal endings.

      Qal perfect 3fs +1cs גָּלַתְנִי
      Qal perfect 1cs +2ms גְּלִיתִיךָ
      Qal perfect 3cp +1cs גָּלוּנִי

2. Imperfect/Imperative: these attach suffixes directly to vocalic endings or to R_2.

   Qal imperfect 3ms +1cs יִגְלֵנִי
   Qal imperfect 3mp +1cs יִגְלוּנִי
   Qal imperative 2ms +1cs גְּלֵנִי
   Qal imperative 2fs +1cs גְּלִינִי

3. Infinitive construct

   Qal infinitive construct +3ms בְּנוֹתוֹ

4. Participles

   Qal participle active ms +1cs גֹּלֵנִי

37.6. Forming and Parsing R_3-Vav/Yod Verbs

For these verbs, the boxes are regular. Replace the colors (and sometimes the Qal) with the endings for the R_3-Vav/Yod verbs. The Qal preformatives and sufformatives are essentially the same.

1. Hiph'îl perfect 3fs גלה
   1. Boxes: □□□הִ הִגלה
   2. Ending □תָה הִגְלְתָה
   3. Qal: שָׁמְרָה, but the second step also replaces the Qal

The boxes are regular. Replace the colors (and the Qal) with the ending.
Answer: הִגְלַתָה

2. מְכַלֶּה
   1. Boxes: מְ□ַ□ּ□ Pi"ēl participle
   2. Ending: □ֶה Masculine singular absolute
   3. Qal: שֹׁמֵר ________

   The boxes and the ending indicate a Pi"ēl participle masculine singular absolute of כלה

   Answer: Pi"ēl participle masculine singular absolute of כלה

37.7. Nouns Derived from R_3-Yod (Vav) Roots

1. שָׂדֶה: The proto-form was שַׂדַי, which contracted to שָׂדֶה in the absolute and שְׂדֵה in the construct. See appendix three for this noun with suffixes.

2. פְּרִי: The proto-form was *פַּרְי, which became *פַּרִי by adding the secondary vowel (15.2) Ḥireq. The form then became פְּרִי. In suffixed forms, the original Pataḥ under R_1 becomes Ḥireq or Segol in closed unaccented syllables, פִּרְיִי. See כְּלִי in appendix three.

R_3-Vav/Yod (Lamed Vav/Yod) Verbs

Perfect 37.4.1	3's 3ms ◌ָה בָּנָה 3fs ◌ְתָה בָּנְתָה 3cp ◌וּ בָּנוּ Other forms preserve Yod: Ḥireq-Yod: Qal, Pi"ēl, Hithpa"ēl, Hiph'îl Ṣere-Yod: Niph'al, Pu"al, Hoph'al Qal 1cs בָּנִ֫יתִי Niph'al 1cs נִגְלֵ֫יתִי
Imperfect 37.4.2	(1) Without ending ◌ֶה : Qal 3ms יִבְנֶה (2) Vocalic endings directly connect to R_2: Qal 3mp יִבְנוּ 2fs תִּבְנִי (3) Syllabic ending 2, 3fp ◌ֶ֫ינָה : Qal 3fp תִּבְנֶ֫ינָה Jussive, Vav-consecutive forms drop the ending ◌ֶה and may have Segolatization Qal יִגֶל, יִגֶל, יִגֶל, יִגֶל (סֵ֫פֶר [*i*]) Hiph'îl יַגֶל, יֶגֶל (מֶ֫לֶךְ [*a*])
Imperative 37.4.3	(1) 2ms ◌ֵה גְּלֵה (2) Vocalic endings 2fs, 2mp connect directly to R_2 בְּנִי, בְּנוּ (3) Syllabic ending 2fp ◌ֶ֫ינָה גְּלֶ֫ינָה
Infinitive Absolute 37.4.4	(1) ◌ֹה in Qal, Niph'al, Pi"ēl, Pu"al: Qal בָּנֹה (2) ◌ֵה in Hiph'îl, Hoph'al, Hithpa"ēl: Hiph'îl הַגְלֵה
Infinitive Construct 37.4.4	◌וֹת Qal בְּנוֹת
Participle 37.4.5	Qal Active ms ◌ֶה בֹּנֶה fs ◌ָה בֹּנָה T-Form בֹּנִית mp ◌ִים בֹּנִים fp ◌וֹת בֹּנוֹת
	Qal Passive ms בָּנוּי fs בְּנוּיָה The Yod is consonantal like a strong verb mp בְּנוּיִם fp בְּנוּיוֹת

Note: For the corresponding color chart, see page 363

Exercise Thirty-Seven

I. Questions

1. How are R_3-Vav/Yod verbs traditionally designated?
2. What part of the verb is affected in R_3-Vav (Yod) verbs?
3. What is the infirmity of R_3-Vav/Yod verbs?
4. When are R_3-Vav/Yod verbs like strong verbs?
5. Discuss the endings for the perfect, imperfect, imperative, infinitives, and participles.
6. Discuss the possible forms for the jussive (3ms) and the Vav-consecutive (3ms) forms (especially in the Qal and Hiph‘îl). Also describe how these forms are "derived" from the imperfect 3ms.
7. Discuss how pronominal suffixes attach to R_3-Vav/Yod verbs.
8. Describe the forming and the parsing of R_3-Vav/Yod verbs.

II. Vocabulary

בַּ֫עַד (*a*)	(construct בְּעַד separation) away from, behind, through, about, on behalf of	נֶ֫גֶב (*e*)	south, Negev region
חָיָה	Qal: live, have life Pi"ēl: preserve alive, revive Hiph‘îl: cause to be alive (preserve alive), revive	גור	Qal: sojourn, journey, dwell for a time
רבה	Qal: be or become many, numerous, great	כלה	Qal: be complete, come to an end, fail, finish, fulfill Pi"ēl: make an end of, finish, complete
גלה	Qal: uncover (with אֹ֫זֶן (*o*) to uncover the ear = to reveal) Niph‘al: reflexive and passive of the Qal: uncover oneself Pi"ēl: uncover, reveal Hiph‘îl: cause to depart, take into exile	פנה	Qal: turn, face Hiph‘îl: cause to face, turn
		תעה	Qal: wander about, go astray, err Hiph‘îl: cause to wander, mislead
		כסה	Pi"ēl: cover, clothe, conceal, overwhelm Hithpa"ēl: reflexive of the Pi"ēl, to cover oneself

III. Drills

1. Word Breakdown: In the following order: label every Dagesh Forte and Lene, Mappiq; vocal and silent shewa; Qameṣ and Qameṣ-Ḥatuf. Next, divide syllables labeling them open or closed. Then pronounce the words.

וַתְּצַוּוּ   הָרִאשֹׁנוֹת

2. Attach the following particles and translate all vocabulary words.

Preposition כ

אֱלֹהִים　　　אֱסֹף

Conjunctive ו

הֲדֹם　　　מַבּוּל

Preposition מִן

יִצְחָק　　　מִכְמָס

3. Attach the boxes and translate all vocabulary words. List all steps.
   1. mp absolute בָּדָל　　　2. mp construct קֹדֶשׁ (*o*)

4. Attach the boxes with suffixes and translate all vocabulary words. List all steps.

	Singular Nouns		Plural Nouns
1.	3fp כֶּסֶל (*i*)	3.	1cp סֵפֶר (*i*)
2.	3ms דָּבָר	4.	2ms אֲדָמָה

5. Attach the suffixes to the prepositions and translate.

1.	2mp תַּחַת	3.	3fs כ
2.	3ms אֵל	4.	2fs את (with)

6. Verbs
   1. Create: List all steps and the final answer.

      Qal
      1. Imperfect 3ms עלה
      2. Participle passive ms גלה
      3. Imperfect 3ms +Vav-consecutive עשׂה
      4. Perfect 1cs מות (A-ē)
      5. Imperfect 2ms אמר
      6. Participle active ms absolute נגה

      Pi"ēl
      7. Infinitive construct +3mp כלה
      8. Perfect 3ms +3ms צוה

Hiph'îl

9. Jussive 3ms גלה
10. Imperfect 3ms נכה
11. Imperfect 3ms עלה

Niph'al

12. Imperfect 2fp אפה
13. Perfect 3fs קום
14. Imperfect 2ms חבא

2. Parse: Give all possible answers.

1.	כִּלַּתּוּ	8.	צַוּוּ
2.	פְּדוּיֵי	9.	וַיַּךְ
3.	רָאָה	10.	גִּשְׁתִּי
4.	הֶהָמֵת	11.	הֵיטַבְנוּ
5.	וַיֶּגֶל	12.	יֵרֵד
6.	וַיִּפְתְּ	13.	וַיָּשֶׁב
7.	וַיֵּרָא	14.	קָמָה

7. Translation: Genesis 20:1-8

v. 1	קָדֵשׁ	Kedesh
	שׁוּר	Shur
	גְּרָר	Gerar
v. 6	מֵחֲטוֹ	Irregular infinitive construct of חטא + מן – from sinning

CHAPTER 38
GEMINATE ($R_2R_3 = R_2R_2$; DOUBLE AYIN) VERBS

38.1. Introduction: Geminate (twin) verbs have the same letter for R_2 and R_3: סבב, קלל. Geminate verbs frequently collapse R_3 into R_2. This collapsing obscures the boxes and shifts the thematic vowel[1] to unite R_2 to R_1, leaving the preformative vowel now in an open pretonic (or pro-pretonic) syllable.

38.2. General Weakness or Infirmity of Geminate Verbs

Geminate verbs tend to collapse R_3 into R_2: סבב » סֹ(ּ)ב.

38.3. Strong Areas of Geminate Verbs

1. Qal perfect third persons (sometimes)

   3ms סָבַב

   3fs סָבְבָה

   3cp סָבְבוּ

2. Qal participles

   Active ms סֹבֵב

   Passive ms סָבוּב

3. Qal infinitives

   Absolute סָבוֹב

   Construct סְבֹב

38.4. General Remedies Applying to all Conjugations

1. When the verb collapses, the thematic vowel shifts and unites R_2 to R_1. The preformative vowel, now in an open pretonic syllable, lengthens.

   *יַסְבֹב » *יַסֹב » יָסֹב

   1 2 3

   The original form (1) collapses and shifts the thematic vowel between R_2 and R_1 (2), and the original Pataḥ, in an open pretonic syllable, lengthens to Qameṣ (3).

[1] The Pôlēl, Pôlal, and Hithpôlēl replace the Pi"ēl, Pu"al, and Hithpa"ēl (usually), see footnote 36-1.

2. If the verb collapses and the R_2 ends the word, a hovering Dagesh represents R_3. If R_2 does not end the word, the hovering Dagesh lands.[2]

		Strong	Collapsed
Perfect	3ms	סָבַב	סַב
	3cp	סָבְבוּ	סַבּוּ

3. Syllabic suffixes (17.3.3; 18.2.3) require a connecting vowel (36.4.2) to unite the suffix to the root.
   1. Perfect: □וֹ Qal perfect 2ms סַבּוֹתָ
   2. Imperfect/Imperative: □ֶי Qal imperfect 2, 3fp תְּסֻבֶּינָה

4. Accent (compare 36.5)
   1. Normally, the shifted thematic vowel uniting R_2 to R_1 takes the accent.
      Qal perfect 3cp סַבּוּ
      Qal imperfect 3mp יָסֹבּוּ

   2. Participles accent the end of the word.
      Niph'al participle fs absolute נְסַבָּה
      Hiph'îl participle fs absolute מְסִבָּה

   3. The connecting vowels of consonantal suffixes take the accent (except the 2mp, 2fp suffixes of the perfect, which always take the accent).
      Qal perfect 1cs סַבּוֹתִי
      Qal perfect 2mp סַבּוֹתֶם

   4. Pronominal suffixes shift the accent (usually over R_2).
      Qal imperfect 3ms +3ms (energic ending) יְסֻבֶּנּוּ

38.5. Specific Remedies

1. Hoph'al
   1. General observations
      1. Preformative vowel: Û (the first syllable follows the R_1-Vav [Yod] pattern: *הָסַב » *הֻוְסַב » *הוּסַב)
      2. Thematic vowels: A/A

[2] Compare the geminate noun *עַם (עמם) with a 1cs suffix: עַמִּי.

2. Specific observations: The Hoph'al follows the general remedies (38.4): collapsing the original form (1) (and creating a hovering Dagesh at the end of a word) and shifting the thematic vowel to unite R_1 to R_2 (2).
   1. Perfect

      3ms *הוּסַבַב (1) » הוּסַבּ (2)

      3fs הוּסַבָּה

      2ms הוּסַבּוֹתָ

   2. Imperfect

      3ms *יוּסַבַב (1) » יוּסַבּ (2)

      3mp יוּסַבּוּ

      2, 3fp תּוּסַבֶּינָה

   3. Participle

      3ms *מוּסַבַב (1) » מוּסַבּ (2)

      3fs מוּסַבָּה — The Qameṣ reduces to Pataḥ in a closed unaccented syllable.

2. Hiph'îl
   1. General observations:
      1. Preformative vowel:[3] I (Ḥireq) – perfect and participle; A – imperfect, imperative, and infinitive.
      2. Thematic vowels: Ē (reducible to Ḥireq in closed unaccented syllables)

   2. Specific observations: The Hiph'îl follows the general remedies (38.4) (except the two alternate forms of the imperfect: transposed gemination forms and doubly geminated forms). The original form (1) collapses, shifting the Ṣere thematic vowel and creating a hovering Dagesh (2). The preformative vowel lengthens in the open pretonic position (3) and reduces in the open pro-pretonic position (4).
      1. Perfect

         3ms *הִסְבֵב (1) » *הִסֵבּ (2) » הֵסֵבּ (3)

         3fs הֵסֵבָּה

         2ms הֲסִבּוֹתָ (4)

[3] Like the strong verb, the Hiph'îl has a preformative ה in the perfect, imperative, and infinitive; in the imperfect and participle, the ה is supplanted.

2. Imperfect: The imperfect has three possible forms (theoretically)
   1. Normal Gemination $R_2R_2R_1$: These follow the general remedies (38.4.).

      3ms *יַסְבֵב (1) » *יַסֵּב (2) » יָסֵב (3)
      3mp יָסֵבּוּ
      2, 3fp תְּסִבֶּינָה (4)
      Jussive 3ms יָסֵב
      Vav-consecutive 3ms וַיָּסֶב Accent retracts (35.5.2).
      3mp וַיָּסֵבּוּ

   2. Transposition (Metathesis) of Gemination[4]
      $R_2R_2R_1$ » $R_2R_1R_1$: These do not follow the general remedies (38.4).

      3ms *יַסְבֵב » *יַסְּסֵב » יַסֵּב
      3mp יַסֵּבּוּ
      Vav-consecutive 3ms וַיַּסֵּב

   3. Double gemination $R_2R_2R_1$ » $R_2R_2R_1R_1$:

      3mp יַסֵּבּוּ
      Vav-consecutive 3mp וַיַּסֵּבּוּ

3. Imperative: Derive the imperatives from the imperfects (normal gemination).

   2ms *הַסְבֵב » *הַסֵּב » הָסֵב
   2fs הָסֵבִּי
   2mp הָסֵבּוּ
   2fp הֲסִבֶּינָה

4. Infinitive absolute and construct – *הַסְבֵב » *הַסֵּב » הָסֵב

5. Participle: This form is analogous to R_1-Yod (original Yod) verbs in the first syllable מֵ.

	Geminate	R_1-Yod (Yod)
ms	מֵסֵב	מֵיטִיב[5]
fs	מְסִבָּה	

[4] This is the usual pattern of Aramaic.

[5] Also compare the R_2-Vav/Yod Hiph'îl participle: מֵקִים.

3. Niph‘al (« Naph‘al)
   1. General observations[6]
      1. Preformative vowel: A – in the perfect and participle (Naph‘al); I (Ḥireq) – in the imperfect, imperative, and infinitive.
      2. Thematic vowels: A/A

   2. Specific observations: The Niph‘al follows the general remedies (38.4). The original forms (1) collapse, creating a hovering Dagesh and shifting the thematic vowel (2). The preformative vowel (Pataḥ) lengthens (3) or reduces (4) as necessary.
      1. Perfect and Participle

Perfect	3ms	*נַסְבַב (1) » *נַסַב (2) » נָסַב (3)
	3fs	נָסַבָּה
	2ms	נְסַבּוֹתָ (4)
Participle	ms	*נַסְבָב (1) » *נַסָב (2) » נָסָב (3)
	mp	נְסַבִּים (4)

      2. Imperfect, Imperative, and Infinitive

Imperfect	3ms	*יִנְסַבַב (1) » *יִסַּבַב (2) » יִסַּב
	3mp	יִסַּבּוּ
	2, 3fp	תִּסַּבֶּינָה
Vav-consecutive	3ms	וַיִּסַּב
Imperative	2ms	*הִנְסַבַב (1) » *הִסַּבַב (2) » הִסַּב
	2fs	הִסַּבִּי
Infinitive	absolute	*הִנְסַבוֹב (1) » *הִסַּבוֹב (2) » הִסּוֹב
	construct	*הִנְסַבֵב (1) » *הִסַּבֵב (2) » הִסֵּב

Note the Ḥolem-Vav of the absolute and the Ṣere of the construct.

6 There are exceptions to these general observations: חלל (pollute, defile) is Niph‘al, not a Naph‘al, נִחַל (perfect 3ms), and the thematic vowels are A/A or A/Ē. Like the strong verb, the preformative is נ for the perfect and participle, ה for the imperative, infinitive, and an אֵיתָן letter for the imperfect.

4. Qal
   1. General observations
      1. Preformative vowels (imperfect only): A – with standard verbs; I – with stative verbs, transposed geminated forms, and doubly geminated forms.
      2. Thematic vowels: A/Ō with standard verbs, A/A with stative verbs.

   2. Specific observations: The Qal follows the Hiph'îl (38.5.2).
      1. Perfect: The third person verbs *may* be strong or collapsed; all other persons collapse.

	Strong	**Collapsed**	**Collapsed (Stative)**
3ms	סָבַב	סַב	קַל
3fs	סָבְבָה	סַבָּה	קַלָּה
3cp	סָבְבוּ	סַבּוּ	קַלּוּ

All other persons collapse:

1cs	סַבּוֹתִי	קַלּוֹתִי
2ms	סַבּוֹתָ	קַלּוֹתָ
2mp	סַבּוֹתֶם	קַלּוֹתֶם

      2. Imperfect
         1. Normal Gemination: These follow the general remedies (38.4). Note the Pataḥ and Ḥireq preformative vowels.

	Standard (A/Ō)	**Stative (A/A)**
3ms	*יַסְבֹב » יָסֹב	יֵקַל
3mp	יָסֹבּוּ	יֵקַלּוּ
2, 3fp	תְּסֻבֶּינָה	תְּקַלֶּינָה
Jussive 3ms	יָסֹב	יֵקַל
Vav-consecutive 3ms	וַיָּסָב[7] (35.5.2)	וַיֵּקַל
Vav-consecutive 3mp	וַיָּסֹבּוּ	וַיֵּקַלּוּ

         2. Transposition (Metathesis) of Gemination: $R_2R_2R_1$ » $R_2R_1R_1$ These do not follow the general remedies, see footnote 38-4. Note the Ḥireq preformative vowel.

3ms	*יִסְבֹב » *יִסְסֹב » יִסֹּב
3mp	יִסְּבוּ

[7] Note the Qameṣ-Ḥatuf in the closed unaccented syllable.

2, 3fp	תִּסֹּבְנָה
Jussive 3ms	יִסֹּב
Vav-consecutive 3ms	וַיִּסֹּב

3. Imperative: Remove the preformative element of normal geminated forms.
   2ms (תָּסֹב) » סֹ(ּ)ב
   2fs סֹבִּי
   2mp סֹבּוּ
   2fp סֻבֶּינָה

4. Participles and infinitive are like strong verbs (38.3.2).

38.6. Final Considerations

1. Transposed gemination is possible in the Qal, Niph‘al, Hiph‘îl, and Hoph‘al.
2. Geminate verbs have many "mixed" forms with R_2-Vav/Yod Verbs: Niph‘al imperfect 2mp תָּבֹזּוּ (בזז). The Ḥolem is from the R_2-Vav/Yod verbs (see 36.4.3).

38.7. Forming and Parsing Geminate Verbs (compare 36.7)

1. Forming: Because "collapsed" verbs obscure the boxes, replace the boxes with "preformative vowel." Replace colors with "thematic vowel." The Qal remains the same, but add a fourth step for other general remedies (38.4). Assume the collapse of the verb and the hovering Dagesh (unless the form is strong [38.3]) at the first step. Examples:
   1. Hiph‘îl cohortative sg. סבב
      1. Preformative vowel: Pataḥ — יַס(ּ)ב
      2. Thematic vowel: Ṣere — יַסֵ(ּ)ב
      3. Qal: אֶקְטְלָה — אַסֵבָּה
      4. Other remedies: Accent and rules of syllables (38.4.4; 6.3.2) — אָסֵבָּה

      Answer: אָסֵבָּה

      1. Step one: Put the preformative vowel Pataḥ (38.5.2.1.1) under an imperfect preformative.
      2. Step two: Unite R_2 and R_1 with a Ṣere thematic vowel (38.5.2.1.2).
      3. Step three: Add the Qal preformatives and sufformatives. The hovering Dagesh lands because ◌ָה ends the word.

4. Step four: Establish the accent (38.4.4.1) and lengthen the Pataḥ preformative vowel in the pretonic open position to Qameṣ (6.3.2).

2. Qal perfect 2ms סבב

1.	Preformative vowel: None	סב(ּ)
2.	Thematic vowel: A	סַב(ּ)
3.	Qal: קָטַ֫לְתָּ	סַבּתָ
4.	Other general remedies: Connecting vowel (38.4.3.), accent, and rules of syllables	סַבֹּ֫תָ

Answer: סַבֹּ֫תָ

1. Step one: There is no preformative in the Qal perfect.
2. Step two: Standard verbs are A/Ō.
3. Step three: Add the Qal suffix תָ and land the hovering Dagesh.
4. Step four: Add the Ḥolem to connect the Geminate verb with its consonantal suffix. Establish the accent (38.4.4), and leave the Pataḥ under R_1 unchanged in a closed unaccented syllable (6.3.3).

2. Parsing: If the usual parsing method is unsuccessful 29.10-29.13, the form has probably collapsed: R_2-Vav (Yod) or Geminate Verb.
Example: נְסַבִּ֫ים

1.	Preformative vowel: It is obscured, but the preformative is נ.	Niph'al perfect, participle, Qal imperfect, Hiph'îl imperfect
2.	Thematic vowel: Pataḥ	Eliminate Hiph'îl
3.	Qal: The ending ִים is a participle ending – קֹטְלִים	Eliminate all forms except Niph'al participle mp absolute
4.	Other general remedies: The accent at the end of the word also indicates a participle (38.4.4.2).	

Answer: Niph'al participle mp absolute of סבב

1. Step one: The preformative vowel is reduced, but the preformative נ furnishes the options.
2. Step two: The Pataḥ eliminates the Hiph'îl option because the Hiph'îl would have a Ṣere.
3. Step three: The participle ending □ִים indicates the Niph'al participle mp absolute.
4. Step four: The accent at the end of word confirms the answer.

$R_2R_3=R_2R_2$ Geminate (Ayin-Ayin: Double Ayin) Verbs

	Qal 38.5.4	Niph‘al 38.5.3	Hiph‘îl 38.5.2	Hoph‘al 38.5.1
Preformative vowels / **Thematic vowels**	A (Standard), I (Transposed): A/Ō; I (Stative): A/A	A – Perfect, Participle; I – Imperfect, Imperative, Infinitive A/A	I - Perfect, Participle; A - Imperfect, Imperative, Infinitive Ē/Ē	Û A/A
Perfect	Third persons Strong / Collapsed / Stative 3ms סָבַב / סַב / קַל 3fs סָבְבָה / סַבָּה / קַלָּה 3cp סָבְבוּ / סַבּוּ / קַלּוּ 1cs — / סַבּוֹתִי / קַלּוֹתִי	Niph‘al » Naph‘al A/A		R_1-Vav in the first syllable הוּסַב
Imperfect	Two imperfect forms (theoretically) 1. Normal Gemination (Stative): יָסֹב יָסֹבּוּ יֵקַלּוּ 2. Transposed Gemination יִסֹּב		Three imperfect forms (theoretically) 1. Normal Gemination: יָסֵב יָסֵבּוּ 2. Transposed Gemination יַסֵּב 3. Doubled Gemination יַסֵּבּוּ	
Imperative	ms סֹב, mp סֹבּוּ fs סֹבִּי, fp סֻבֶּינָה			
Infinitive Absolute	(strong) סָבוֹב	הִסּוֹב		
Infinitive Construct	סֹב (or strong סְבֹב)	הִסֵּב		
Participle	(strong) סֹבֵב	נָסָב נְסַבָּה	ms מֵסֵב (R_1-Yod analogy) fs מְסִבָּה	

General Notes:

1. Transposed gemination is possible in all stems (38.6.1).
2. There are numerous analogies to R_2-Vav/Yod verbs (38.6.2).
3. The Pi“ēl, Pu“al, and Hithpa“ēl are rare and like strong verbs (footnote 38-1 and 36-1).

Note: For the corresponding color chart, see page 364

Exercise Thirty-Eight

I. Questions

1. Describe a Geminate verb.
2. How does the Geminate verb collapse? How does this affect a preformative?
3. What is the general weakness of the Geminate verb?
4. Where are the strong areas of the Geminate verb?
5. What are the four general remedies of the Geminate verb?
6. What are the preformative vowels of the Qal (imperfect), Niph‘al, Hiph‘îl and Hoph‘al? What are the thematic vowels for the same stems?
7. What weak verb is analogous to the first syllable of the Hoph‘al in the Geminate verb?
8. Discuss the various imperfect options of the Hiph‘îl and Qal.
9. How are the imperatives formed in the Qal?
10. Geminate verbs are sometimes “mixed” with which weak verb?
11. Describe the forming and the parsing of Geminate verbs. How does it differ from other weak verbs? Which weak verbs are like the Geminate verbs in forming and parsing?

II. Vocabulary

רַק	only, surely
עמד	a longer form of עִם
שִׁפְחָה	female slave
אֶלֶף (*a*)	thousand, tribe(?), clan(?)
אָמָה	(with 1cs suffix אַמְהֹתִי) female slave, handmaid
ארר	Qal: curse
שׁדד	Qal: destroy, slay, devastate Pi“ēl: destroy, assault Pu“al: be destroyed
תמם	(Stative) Qal: be completed, finished, come to an end, cease Hiph‘îl: finish, complete, perfect
רנן	Qal: give a ringing cry Pi“ēl: same as Qal Hiph‘îl: same as Qal; cause a cry, give a ringing cry
שׁמם	Qal: be desolated, be appalled, awestruck Niph‘al: be desolated, be appalled Hiph‘îl: devastate, destroy
חנן	Qal: favor, be gracious to Niph‘al: be pitied Hithpa“ēl: seek favor
חתת	Qal: be shattered, broken, be dismayed Hiph‘îl: shatter, terrify
פרר	Hiph‘îl: break, frustrate, make ineffective Hoph‘al: passive of Hiph‘îl
רעע	(Stative) Qal: be evil, bad, be displeasing Hiph‘îl: do evil, hurt, injure

III. Drills

1. Word Breakdown: In the following order: label every Dagesh Forte and Lene, Mappiq; vocal and silent shewa; Qameṣ and Qameṣ-Ḥatuf. Next, divide syllables labeling them open or closed. Then pronounce the words.

   הַנָּכְרִיּוֹת   וְהִשְׁבַּתִּי

2. Attach the following particles and translate all vocabulary words.
   Preposition כ

   הָאֲדָמָה   יִלּוֹד

   Interrogative מה

   נָקִי   אָרַ֫בְתִּי

   Interrogative ה

   אָרַ֫בְתִּי   דֶּ֫רֶךְ

3. Attach the boxes and translate all vocabulary words. List all steps.
   1. ms construct נַ֫עַר (*a*)   2. fs construct אֲדָמָה

4. Attach the boxes with suffixes and translate all vocabulary words. List all steps.

   Singular Nouns
   1. 2fp עֶ֫בֶד (*a*)
   2. 1cs עֵדָה

   Plural Nouns
   3. 2ms לַ֫הַב (*a*)
   4. 1cp פְּקֻדָּה

5. Attach the suffixes to the prepositions and translate.
   1. 3fs מִן
   2. 3fs כ
   3. 2fp אֵת (with)
   4. 1cs אֶל

6. Verbs
   1. Create: list all steps and the final answer.
      Qal
      1. Imperfect 2ms (A/Ō) סבב
      2. Imperfect 2ms +Vav-consecutive (A/Ō) סבב
      3. Imperative 2mp (A/Ō) בזז
      4. Imperfect 3ms +Vav-consecutive (A/Ō) מדד
      5. Participle Active fs (T-form) גלה

6. Imperfect 3ms +1cs (A/Ō) חנן
7. Imperfect 3ms +Vav-consecutive (metathesis of gemination) (A/Ō) סבב

Hiph'îl

8. Imperfect 3ms +Vav-consecutive נוח
9. Perfect 3fs חלל
10. Jussive 3ms שׁוב
11. Imperfect 3ms +3mp +Vav-consecutive שׁמם
12. Imperfect 3ms +Vav-consecutive פרר
13. Participle ms absolute חלל

Hoph'al

14. Imperfect 2fp סבב

Niph'al

15. Imperative 2ms סבב

2. Parse: Give all possible answers.

1.	סַבּ֫וּנִי	8.	נָסָב
2.	אַחֵל	9.	יֵחַ֫תּוּ
3.	יִקַּ֫לּוּ	10.	יְשָׁלּ֫וּךְ
4.	הֲקִלּוֹתַ֫נִי	11.	יֹאפֶה
5.	יְפֵרֶ֫נּוּ	12.	הַטֵּה
6.	תְּחָנֵּם	13.	מוֹת
7.	תָּחֹ֫נּוּ	14.	יָשֹׁב

7. Translation: Genesis 20:9-18

v. 9 מַעֲשִׂים deeds, works

v. 13 הִתְעוּ read as הִתְעָה

APPENDIXES

Phonological Chart of Hebrew Consonants (Modern Hebrew Pronunciation)

	Plosive Voiceless	Plosive Voiced	Spirantic Voiceless	Spirantic Voiced	Silent
Labials	פּ	בּ, (מ)	פ	ב, ו	
Dentals	ט, ת, תּ	ד, דּ			
Palatals	כּ, ק	ג, גּ, י	כ		
Gutturals			ה, ח, (כ)		א, ע
Sibilants			ס, צ, שׂ, שׁ	ז	

Plosive: A sound produced by the complete stoppage and sudden release of breath. Also called "stops."

Spirantic: A sound produced by the passing by breath through the partially closed oral cavity.

Voiceless: A sound produced without the vibration (or with very little vibration) of the vocal cords.

Voiced: Sound produced by vibrating the vocal cords.

Labials: Sound formed mainly with the lips.

Dentals: Sounds formed with the tongue against or near the upper front teeth.

Palatals: Sounds formed with the middle of the tongue raised against or near the hard palate.

Gutturals: Sounds formed deep in the throat with the back of the tongue raised against or near the soft palate.

Sibilants: Hissing or "s" sounds.

The latteral ל, and the ר are semi-plosive, voiced sounds.

The nasal sounds נ and מ are voiced sounds formed by the passage of breath through the nose. The מ is also a labial.

Regular Nouns with Suffixes

Singular Absolute		סוּס	דָּבָר	תּוֹרָה	צְדָקָה
		(horse)	(word)	(law)	(righteousness)
Singular Construct		סוּס־	דְּבַר־	תּוֹרַת־	צִדְקַת־
Suffix	1cs	סוּסִי	דְּבָרִי	תּוֹרָתִי	צִדְקָתִי
	2ms	סוּסְךָ	דְּבָרְךָ	תּוֹרָתְךָ	צִדְקָתְךָ
	2fs	סוּסֵךְ	דְּבָרֵךְ	תּוֹרָתֵךְ	צִדְקָתֵךְ
	3ms	סוּסוֹ	דְּבָרוֹ	תּוֹרָתוֹ	צִדְקָתוֹ
	3fs	סוּסָהּ	דְּבָרָהּ	תּוֹרָתָהּ	צִדְקָתָהּ
	1cp	סוּסֵנוּ	דְּבָרֵנוּ	תּוֹרָתֵנוּ	צִדְקָתֵנוּ
	2mp	סוּסְכֶם	דְּבַרְכֶם	תּוֹרַתְכֶם	צִדְקַתְכֶם
	2fp	סוּסְכֶן	דְּבַרְכֶן	תּוֹרַתְכֶן	צִדְקַתְכֶן
	3mp	סוּסָם	דְּבָרָם	תּוֹרָתָם	צִדְקָתָם
	3fp	סוּסָן	דְּבָרָן	תּוֹרָתָן	צִדְקָתָן
Plural Absolute		סוּסִים	דְּבָרִים	תּוֹרוֹת	צְדָקוֹת
Plural Construct		סוּסֵי־	דִּבְרֵי־	תּוֹרוֹת־	צִדְקוֹת־
	1cs	סוּסַי	דְּבָרַי	תּוֹרוֹתַי	צִדְקוֹתַי
	2ms	סוּסֶיךָ	דְּבָרֶיךָ	תּוֹרוֹתֶיךָ	צִדְקוֹתֶיךָ
	2fs	סוּסַיִךְ	דְּבָרַיִךְ	תּוֹרוֹתַיִךְ	צִדְקוֹתַיִךְ
	3ms	סוּסָיו	דְּבָרָיו	תּוֹרוֹתָיו	צִדְקוֹתָיו
	3fs	סוּסֶיהָ	דְּבָרֶיהָ	תּוֹרוֹתֶיהָ	צִדְקוֹתֶיהָ
	1cp	סוּסֵינוּ	דְּבָרֵינוּ	תּוֹרוֹתֵינוּ	צִדְקוֹתֵינוּ
	2mp	סוּסֵיכֶם	דִּבְרֵיכֶם	תּוֹרוֹתֵיכֶם	צִדְקוֹתֵיכֶם
	2fp	סוּסֵיכֶן	דִּבְרֵיכֶן	תּוֹרוֹתֵיכֶן	צִדְקוֹתֵיכֶן
	3mp	סוּסֵיהֶם	דִּבְרֵיהֶם	תּוֹרוֹתֵיהֶם	צִדְקוֹתֵיהֶם
	3fp	סוּסֵיהֶן	דִּבְרֵיהֶן	תּוֹרוֹתֵיהֶן	צִדְקוֹתֵיהֶן

מֶ֫לֶךְ	סֵ֫פֶר	קֹ֫דֶשׁ	נַ֫עַר	נֵ֫צַח	פֹּ֫עַל
(king)	(book)	(holiness)	(lad)	(perpetuity)	(work)
*מַלְכְּ	*סִפְרְ	*קָדְשְׁ	*נַעֲרְ	*נִצְחְ	*פָּעְלְ
מַלְכִּי	סִפְרִי	קָדְשִׁי	נַעֲרִי	נִצְחִי	פָּעֳלִי
מַלְכְּךָ	סִפְרְךָ	קָדְשְׁךָ	נַעַרְךָ	נִצְחֲךָ	פָּעָלְךָ
מַלְכֵּךְ	סִפְרֵךְ	קָדְשֵׁךְ	נַעֲרֵךְ	נִצְחֵךְ	פָּעֳלֵךְ
מַלְכּוֹ	סִפְרוֹ	קָדְשׁוֹ	נַעֲרוֹ	נִצְחוֹ	פָּעֳלוֹ
מַלְכָּהּ	סִפְרָהּ	קָדְשָׁהּ	נַעֲרָהּ	נִצְחָהּ	פָּעֳלָהּ
מַלְכֵּ֫נוּ	סִפְרֵ֫נוּ	קָדְשֵׁ֫נוּ	נַעֲרֵ֫נוּ	נִצְחֵ֫נוּ	פָּעֳלֵ֫נוּ
מַלְכְּכֶם	סִפְרְכֶם	קָדְשְׁכֶם	נַעַרְכֶם	נִצְחֲכֶם	פָּעָלְכֶם
מַלְכְּכֶן	סִפְרְכֶן	קָדְשְׁכֶן	נַעַרְכֶן	נִצְחֲכֶן	פָּעָלְכֶן
מַלְכָּם	סִפְרָם	קָדְשָׁם	נַעֲרָם	נִצְחָם	פָּעֳלָם
מַלְכָּן	סִפְרָן	קָדְשָׁן	נַעֲרָן	נִצְחָן	פָּעֳלָן
מְלָכִים	סְפָרִים	קֳדָשִׁים	נְעָרִים	נְצָחִים	פְּעָלִים
מַלְכֵי־	סִפְרֵי־	קָדְשֵׁי־	נַעֲרֵי־	נִצְחֵי־	פָּעֳלֵי־
מְלָכַי	סְפָרַי	קֳדָשַׁי	נְעָרַי	נְצָחַי	פְּעָלַי
מְלָכֶ֫יךָ	סְפָרֶ֫יךָ	קֳדָשֶׁ֫יךָ	נְעָרֶ֫יךָ	נְצָחֶ֫יךָ	פְּעָלֶ֫יךָ
מְלָכַ֫יִךְ	סְפָרַ֫יִךְ	קֳדָשַׁ֫יִךְ	נְעָרַ֫יִךְ	נְצָחַ֫יִךְ	פְּעָלַ֫יִךְ
מְלָכָיו	סְפָרָיו	קֳדָשָׁיו	נְעָרָיו	נְצָחָיו	פְּעָלָיו
מְלָכֶ֫יהָ	סְפָרֶ֫יהָ	קֳדָשֶׁ֫יהָ	נְעָרֶ֫יהָ	נְצָחֶ֫יהָ	פְּעָלֶ֫יהָ
מְלָכֵ֫ינוּ	סְפָרֵ֫ינוּ	קֳדָשֵׁ֫ינוּ	נְעָרֵ֫ינוּ	נְצָחֵ֫ינוּ	פְּעָלֵ֫ינוּ
מַלְכֵיכֶם	סִפְרֵיכֶם	קָדְשֵׁיכֶם	נַעֲרֵיכֶם	נִצְחֵיכֶם	פָּעֳלֵיכֶם
מַלְכֵיכֶן	סִפְרֵיכֶן	קָדְשֵׁיכֶן	נַעֲרֵיכֶן	נִצְחֵיכֶן	פָּעֳלֵיכֶן
מַלְכֵיהֶם	סִפְרֵיהֶם	קָדְשֵׁיהֶם	נַעֲרֵיהֶם	נִצְחֵיהֶם	פָּעֳלֵיהֶם
מַלְכֵיהֶן	סִפְרֵיהֶן	קָדְשֵׁיהֶן	נַעֲרֵיהֶן	נִצְחֵיהֶן	פָּעֳלֵיהֶן

Irregular Nouns with Suffixes

Singular Absolute	אָב	אָח	אָחוֹת	בֵּן
	(father)	(brother)	(sister)	(son)
Singular Construct	אֲבִי־	אֲחִי־	אֲחוֹת־	בֶּן־
Suffix 1cs	אָבִי	אָחִי	אֲחֹתִי	בְּנִי
2ms	אָבִיךָ	אָחִיךָ	אֲחוֹתְךָ	בִּנְךָ
2fs	אָבִיךְ	אָחִיךְ	אֲחוֹתֵךְ	בְּנֵךְ
3ms	אָבִיו	אָחִיו	אֲחֹתוֹ	בְּנוֹ
3fs	אָבִיהָ	אָחִיהָ	אֲחֹתָהּ	בְּנָהּ
1cp	אָבִינוּ	אָחִינוּ	אֲחֹתֵנוּ	בְּנֵנוּ
2mp	אֲבִיכֶם	אֲחִיכֶם	אֲחוֹתְכֶם	
2fp	אֲבִיכֶן			
3mp	אֲבִיהֶם	אֲחִיהֶם	אֲחֹתָם	
3fp	אֲבִיהֶן			
Plural Absolute	אָבוֹת	אַחִים		בָּנִים
Plural Construct	אֲבוֹת־	אֲחֵי־		בְּנֵי־
1cs	אֲבֹתַי	אֶחָי	אַחְיוֹתַי	בָּנַי
2ms	אֲבֹתֶיךָ	אַחֶיךָ		בָּנֶיךָ
2fs		אַחַיִךְ	אֲחוֹתַיִךְ	בָּנַיִךְ
3ms	אֲבֹתָיו	אֶחָיו	אַחְיֹתָיו	בָּנָיו
3fs		אַחֶיהָ		בָּנֶיהָ
1cp	אֲבֹתֵינוּ	אַחֵינוּ		בָּנֵינוּ
2mp	אֲבֹתֵיכֶם	אֲחֵיכֶם	אֲחוֹתֵיכֶם	בְּנֵיכֶם
2fp				
3mp	אֲבֹתָם	אֲחֵיהֶם	אַחְיֹתֵיהֶם	בְּנֵיהֶם
3fp				בְּנֵיהֶן

Singular Absolute		בַּת	בַּ֫יִת	יוֹם	מַ֫יִם
		(daughter)	(house)	(day)	(water)
Singular Construct		בַּת־	בֵּית־	יוֹם־	מַי־
Suffix	1cs	בִּתִּי	בֵּיתִי		
	2ms	בִּתְּךָ	בֵּיתְךָ		
	2fs		בֵּיתֵךְ		
	3ms	בִּתּוֹ	בֵּיתוֹ	יוֹמוֹ	
	3fs	בִּתָּהּ	בֵּיתָהּ		
	1cp				
	2mp		בֵּיתְכֶם		
	2fp				
	3mp		בֵּיתָם	יוֹמָם	
	3fp				
Plural Absolute		בָּנוֹת	בָּתִּים	יָמִים	מַ֫יִם
Plural Construct		בְּנוֹת־	בָּתֵּי־	יְמֵי־	מֵי־ (מֵימֵי־)
	1cs	בְּנֹתַי		יָמַי	מֵימַי
	2ms	בְּנֹתֶ֫יךָ	בָּתֶּ֫יךָ	יָמֶ֫יךָ	מֵימֶ֫יךָ
	2fs	בְּנֹתַ֫יִךְ	בָּתַּ֫יִךְ	יָמַ֫יִךְ	
	3ms	בְּנֹתָיו		יָמָיו	מֵימָיו
	3fs	בְּנֹתֶ֫יהָ		יָמֶ֫יהָ	מֵימֶ֫יהָ
	1cp	בְּנֹתֵ֫ינוּ	בָּתֵּ֫ינוּ	יָמֵ֫ינוּ	מֵימֵ֫ינוּ
	2mp	בְּנֹתֵיכֶם	בָּתֵּיכֶם	יְמֵיכֶם	
	2fp				
	3mp	בְּנֹתֵיהֶם	בָּתֵּיהֶם	יְמֵיהֶם	מֵימֵיהֶם
	3fp				

(Irregular Nouns with Suffixes)

Singular Absolute	שֵׁם	פֶּה	(כֶּלִי) כְּלִי	שָׂדֶה
	(name)	(mouth)	(vessel)	(field)
Singular Construct	שֵׁם־, שֶׁם־	פִּי־	כְּלִי־	שְׂדֵה
Suffix 1cs	שְׁמִי	פִּי		שָׂדִי
2ms	שִׁמְךָ	פִּיךָ	כֶּלְיְךָ	שָׂדְךָ/שָׂדֶךָ
2fs	שְׁמֵךְ			
3ms	שְׁמוֹ	פִּיו (פִּיהוּ)		שָׂדֵהוּ
3fs	שְׁמָהּ	פִּיהָ		שָׂדָהּ
1cp	שְׁמֵנוּ	פִּינוּ		
2mp	שִׁמְכֶם	פִּיכֶם		
2fp				
3mp	שְׁמָם	פִּיהֶם		
3fp				
Plural Absolute	שֵׁמוֹת	(פִּיּוֹת)	כֵּלִים	
Plural Construct	שְׁמוֹת־		כְּלֵי־	
1cs			כֵּלַי	
2ms			כֵּלֶיךָ	שָׂדֶיךָ
2fs				
3ms			כֵּלָיו	
3fs			כֵּלֶיהָ	שְׂדֹתֶיהָ
1cp			כֵּלֵינוּ	שָׂדֵינוּ/שְׂדֹתֵינוּ
2mp			כְּלֵיכֶם	שְׂדוֹתֵיכֶם
2fp				
3mp	שְׁמוֹתָם		כְּלֵיהֶם	שְׂדֹתֵיהֶם/שְׂדֹתָם
3fp	שְׁמוֹתָן			

PREPOSITIONS WITH SUFFIXES

	ל	(עמם) עם	את
	(for, to)	(with)	(direct object marker)
1cs	לִי	עִמִּי	אֹתִי
2ms	לְךָ	עִמְּךָ	אֹתְךָ
2fs	לָךְ	עִמָּךְ	אֹתָךְ
3ms	לוֹ	עִמּוֹ	אֹתוֹ
3fs	לָהּ	עִמָּהּ	אֹתָהּ
1cp	לָנוּ	עִמָּנוּ	אֹתָנוּ
2mp	לָכֶם	עִמָּכֶם	אֶתְכֶם
2fp	לָכֶן	עִמָּכֶן	אֶתְכֶן
3mp	לָהֶם	עִמָּם/עִמָּהֶם	אֶתְהֶם/אֹתָם
3fp	לָהֶן	עִמָּהֶן	אֶתְהֶן/אֹתָן

	ב	(אתת) את	כ
	(in, with)	(with)	(like, as, according to)
1cs	בִּי	אִתִּי	כָּמוֹנִי
2ms	בְּךָ	אִתְּךָ	כָּמוֹךָ
2fs	בָּךְ	אִתָּךְ	כָּמוֹךְ
3ms	בּוֹ	אִתּוֹ	כָּמוֹהוּ
3fs	בָּהּ	אִתָּהּ	כָּמוֹהָ
1cp	בָּנוּ	אִתָּנוּ	כָּמוֹנוּ
2mp	בָּכֶם	אִתְּכֶם	כָּכֶם
2fp	בָּכֶן	אִתְּכֶן	כָּכֶן
3mp	בָּם/בָּהֶם	אִתְּהֶם	כְּמוֹהֶם
3fp	בָּהֶן	אִתְּהֶן	כְּמוֹהֶן

(Prepositions with Suffixes)

	Singular Suffixes		Plural Suffixes	
	מִן	אֵל	לִפְנֵי	אחר
	(from)	(to, unto)	(to the face of)	(after)
1cs	מִמֶּנִּי	אֵלַי	לְפָנַי	אַחֲרַי
2ms	מִמְּךָ	אֵלֶיךָ	לְפָנֶיךָ	אַחֲרֶיךָ
2fs	מִמֵּךְ	אֵלַיִךְ	לְפָנַיִךְ	אַחֲרַיִךְ
3ms	מִמֶּנּוּ	אֵלָיו	לְפָנָיו	אַחֲרָיו
3fs	מִמֶּנָּה	אֵלֶיהָ	לְפָנֶיהָ	אַחֲרֶיהָ
1cp	מִמֶּנּוּ	אֵלֵינוּ	לְפָנֵינוּ	אַחֲרֵינוּ
2mp	מִכֶּם	אֲלֵיכֶם	לִפְנֵיכֶם	אַחֲרֵיכֶם
2fp	מִכֶּן	אֲלֵיכֶן	לִפְנֵיכֶן	אַחֲרֵיכֶן
3mp	מֵהֶם	אֲלֵיהֶם	לִפְנֵיהֶם	אַחֲרֵיהֶם
3fp	מֵהֶן	אֲלֵיהֶן	לִפְנֵיהֶן	אַחֲרֵיהֶן

	(Segolate)		(Segolate)
	לְמַעַן	עַל	תחת
	(for the sake of)	(upon)	(under)
1cs	לְמַעֲנִי	עָלַי	תַּחְתַּי
2ms	לְמַעַנְךָ	עָלֶיךָ	תַּחְתֶּיךָ
2fs	לְמַעֲנֵךְ	עָלַיִךְ	תַּחְתַּיִךְ
3ms	לְמַעֲנוֹ	עָלָיו	תַּחְתָּיו
3fs	לְמַעֲנָהּ	עָלֶיהָ	תַּחְתֶּיהָ
1cp	לְמַעֲנֵנוּ	עָלֵינוּ	תַּחְתֵּינוּ
2mp	לְמַעַנְכֶם	עֲלֵיכֶם	תַּחְתֵּיכֶם
2fp	לְמַעַנְכֶן	עֲלֵיכֶן	תַּחְתֵּיכֶן
3mp	לְמַעֲנָם	עֲלֵיהֶם	(תַּחְתֵּיהֶם)תַּחְתָּם
3fp	לְמַעֲנָן	עֲלֵיהֶן	(תַּחְתֵּיהֶן)תַּחְתָּן

Hebrew Pronominal Suffixes

Person Gender Number	Independent Pronouns	Singular Nouns	Plural Nouns	Perfect: Directly attached	Perfect with connecting vowel	Imperfect / Imperative: Directly attached	Imperfect / Imperative with connecting vowel	Imperfect / Imperative with Energic Nun
1cs	אָנֹכִי/אֲנִי	□ִי	□ַי	□נִי	□ַנִי	□נִי	□ֵנִי	□ֶנִּי
2ms	אַתָּה	□ְךָ	□ֶיךָ	□ךָ	□ְךָ	□ךָ	□ְךָ	□ֶךָּ
2fs	אַתְּ	□ֵךְ	□ַיִךְ	□ךְ	□ֵךְ 3fs verb □□ֶךְ	□ךְ	□ֵךְ	
3ms	הוּא	□וֹ □הוּ	□ָיו	□הוּ	□וֹ	□הוּ	□ֵהוּ	□ֶנּוּ
3fs	הִיא	□ָהּ	□ֶיהָ	□הָ	□ָהּ	□הָ	□ֶהָ □ָהּ	□ֶנָּה
1cp	אֲנַחְנוּ	□ֵנוּ	□ֵינוּ	□נוּ	□ָנוּ	□נוּ	□ֵנוּ	□ֶנּוּ
2mp	אַתֶּם	□ְכֶם	□ֵיכֶם			□כֶם	□ְכֶם	
2fp	אַתֶּן	□ְכֶן	□ֵיכֶן			□כֶן	□ְכֶן	
3mp	הֵם/הֵמָּה	□ָם	□ֵיהֶם	□ם	□ָם 3fs verb □□ַם	□ם	□ֵם	
3fp	הֵן/הֵנָּה	□ָן	□ֵיהֶן	□ן	□ָן 3fs verb □□ַן	□ן	□ֵן	

Strong Verb

Perfect		Qal	Niph'al	Pi"ēl	Pu"al	Hithpa"ēl	Hiph'îl	Hoph'al
SG.	1C	קָטַלְתִּי	נִקְטַלְתִּי	קִטַּלְתִּי	קֻטַּלְתִּי	הִתְקַטַּלְתִּי	הִקְטַלְתִּי	הָקְטַלְתִּי
	2M	קָטַלְתָּ	נִקְטַלְתָּ	קִטַּלְתָּ	קֻטַּלְתָּ	הִתְקַטַּלְתָּ	הִקְטַלְתָּ	הָקְטַלְתָּ
	2F	קָטַלְתְּ	נִקְטַלְתְּ	קִטַּלְתְּ	קֻטַּלְתְּ	הִתְקַטַּלְתְּ	הִקְטַלְתְּ	הָקְטַלְתְּ
	3M	קָטַל	נִקְטַל	קִטֵּל	קֻטַּל	הִתְקַטֵּל	הִקְטִיל	הָקְטַל
	3F	קָטְלָה	נִקְטְלָה	קִטְּלָה	קֻטְּלָה	הִתְקַטְּלָה	הִקְטִילָה	הָקְטְלָה
PL.	1C	קָטַלְנוּ	נִקְטַלְנוּ	קִטַּלְנוּ	קֻטַּלְנוּ	הִתְקַטַּלְנוּ	הִקְטַלְנוּ	הָקְטַלְנוּ
	2M	קְטַלְתֶּם	נִקְטַלְתֶּם	קִטַּלְתֶּם	קֻטַּלְתֶּם	הִתְקַטַּלְתֶּם	הִקְטַלְתֶּם	הָקְטַלְתֶּם
	2F	קְטַלְתֶּן	נִקְטַלְתֶּן	קִטַּלְתֶּן	קֻטַּלְתֶּן	הִתְקַטַּלְתֶּן	הִקְטַלְתֶּן	הָקְטַלְתֶּן
	3C	קָטְלוּ	נִקְטְלוּ	קִטְּלוּ	קֻטְּלוּ	הִתְקַטְּלוּ	הִקְטִילוּ	הָקְטְלוּ

Imperfect		Qal	Niph'al	Pi"ēl	Pu"al	Hithpa"ēl	Hiph'îl	Hoph'al
SG.	1C	אֶקְטֹל	אֶקָּטֵל	אֲקַטֵּל	אֲקֻטַּל	אֶתְקַטֵּל	אַקְטִיל	אָקְטַל
	2M	תִּקְטֹל	תִּקָּטֵל	תְּקַטֵּל	תְּקֻטַּל	תִּתְקַטֵּל	תַּקְטִיל	תָּקְטַל
	2F	תִּקְטְלִי	תִּקָּטְלִי	תְּקַטְּלִי	תְּקֻטְּלִי	תִּתְקַטְּלִי	תַּקְטִילִי	תָּקְטְלִי
	3M	יִקְטֹל	יִקָּטֵל	יְקַטֵּל	יְקֻטַּל	יִתְקַטֵּל	יַקְטִיל	יָקְטַל
	3F	תִּקְטֹל	תִּקָּטֵל	תְּקַטֵּל	תְּקֻטַּל	תִּתְקַטֵּל	תַּקְטִיל	תָּקְטַל
PL.	1C	נִקְטֹל	נִקָּטֵל	נְקַטֵּל	נְקֻטַּל	נִתְקַטֵּל	נַקְטִיל	נָקְטַל
	2M	תִּקְטְלוּ	תִּקָּטְלוּ	תְּקַטְּלוּ	תְּקֻטְּלוּ	תִּתְקַטְּלוּ	תַּקְטִילוּ	תָּקְטְלוּ
	2F	תִּקְטֹלְנָה	תִּקָּטַלְנָה	תְּקַטֵּלְנָה	תְּקֻטַּלְנָה	תִּתְקַטַּלְנָה	תַּקְטֵלְנָה	תָּקְטַלְנָה
	3M	יִקְטְלוּ	יִקָּטְלוּ	יְקַטְּלוּ	יְקֻטְּלוּ	יִתְקַטְּלוּ	יַקְטִילוּ	יָקְטְלוּ
	3F	תִּקְטֹלְנָה	תִּקָּטַלְנָה	תְּקַטֵּלְנָה	תְּקֻטַּלְנָה	תִּתְקַטַּלְנָה	תַּקְטֵלְנָה	תָּקְטַלְנָה

	Qal	Niph'al	Pi"ēl	Pu"al	Hithpa"ēl	Hiph'îl	Hoph'al
Cohortative	אֶקְטְלָה	אֶקָּטְלָה	אֲקַטְּלָה	אֲקֻטְּלָה	אֶתְקַטְּלָה	אַקְטִילָה	
Jussive	יִקְטֹל	יִקָּטֵל	יְקַטֵּל	יְקֻטַּל	יִתְקַטֵּל	יַקְטֵל	יָקְטַל
With Vav-Consecutive	וַיִּקְטֹל	וַיִּקָּטֵל	וַיְקַטֵּל	וַיְקֻטַּל	וַיִּתְקַטֵּל	וַיַּקְטֵל	וַיָּקְטַל

Imperative		Qal	Niph'al	Pi"ēl	Pu"al	Hithpa"ēl	Hiph'îl	Hoph'al
SG.	2M	קְטֹל	הִקָּטֵל	קַטֵּל		הִתְקַטֵּל	הַקְטֵל	
	2F	קִטְלִי	הִקָּטְלִי	קַטְּלִי		הִתְקַטְּלִי	הַקְטִ֫ילִי	
PL.	2M	קִטְלוּ	הִקָּטְלוּ	קַטְּלוּ		הִתְקַטְּלוּ	הַקְטִ֫ילוּ	
	2F	קְטֹ֫לְנָה	הִקָּטַ֫לְנָה	קַטֵּ֫לְנָה		הִתְקַטַּ֫לְנָה	הַקְטֵ֫לְנָה	
Emphatic Imperative		קָטְלָה						

Participle		Qal	Niph'al	Pi"ēl	Pu"al	Hithpa"ēl	Hiph'îl	Hoph'al
ACT	MS	קֹטֵל		מְקַטֵּל			מַקְטִיל	
	MP	קֹטְלִים		מְקַטְּלִים			מַקְטִילִים	
	FS	קֹטְלָה קֹטֶ֫לֶת		מְקַטְּלָה מְקַטֶּ֫לֶת			מַקְטִילָה מַקְטֶ֫לֶת	
	FP	קֹטְלוֹת		מְקַטְּלוֹת			מַקְטִילוֹת	
PASS	MS	קָטוּל			מְקֻטָּל			מָקְטָל
	MP	קְטוּלִים			מְקֻטָּלִים			מָקְטָלִים
	FS	קְטוּלָה			מְקֻטָּלָה מְקֻטֶּ֫לֶת			מָקְטָלָה
	FP	קְטוּלוֹת			מְקֻטָּלוֹת			מָקְטָלוֹת
REFL	MS		נִקְטָל			מִתְקַטֵּל		
	MP		נִקְטָלִים			מִתְקַטְּלִים		
	FS		נִקְטָלָה נִקְטֶ֫לֶת			מִתְקַטְּלָה מִתְקַטֶּ֫לֶת		
	FP		נִקְטָלוֹת			מִתְקַטְּלוֹת		

Infinitive	Qal	Niph'al	Pi"ēl	Pu"al	Hithpa"ēl	Hiph'îl	Hoph'al
ABSOLUTE	קָטוֹל	נִקְטֹל הִקָּטֹל	קַטֹּל קַטֵּל	קֻטֹּל	הִתְקַטֵּל	הַקְטֵל	הָקְטֵל
CONSTRUCT	קְטֹל	הִקָּטֵל	קַטֵּל	קֻטַּל	הִתְקַטֵּל	הַקְטִיל	הָקְטַל

STRONG VERB WITH PRONOMINAL SUFFIXES

	Suffixes	1cs	2ms	2fs	3ms
Perfect	1cs	-----	קְטַלְתִּיךָ	קְטַלְתִּיךְ	קְטַלְתִּיהוּ קְטַלְתִּיו
	2ms	קְטַלְתַּנִי	-----	-----	קְטַלְתָּהוּ קְטַלְתּוֹ
	2fs	קְטַלְתִּינִי	-----	-----	קְטַלְתִּיהוּ
	3ms	קְטָלַנִי A-e/ שְׁכֵחַנִי	קְטָלְךָ	קְטָלֵךְ	קְטָלָהוּ קְטָלוֹ
	3fs	קְטָלַתְנִי	קְטָלַתְךָ	קְטָלָתֶךְ	קְטָלַתְהוּ קְטָלַתּוּ
	1cp	-----	קְטַלְנוּךָ	קְטַלְנוּךְ	קְטַלְנוּהוּ
	2mp	קְטַלְתּוּנִי	-----	-----	קְטַלְתּוּהוּ
	3cp	קְטָלוּנִי	קְטָלוּךָ אֲהֵבוּךָ	קְטָלוּךְ	קְטָלוּהוּ
Imperfect	3ms	/O יִקְטְלֵנִי /A יִלְבָּשֵׁנִי	יִקְטָלְךָ יִלְבָּשְׁךָ	יִקְטְלֵךְ יִלְבָּשֵׁךְ	יִקְטְלֵהוּ יִלְבָּשֵׁהוּ
	3ms +energic Nun	יִקְטְלֶנִּי	יִקְטְלֶךָּ	-----	יִקְטְלֶנּוּ
	3mp	יִקְטְלוּנִי	יִקְטְלוּךָ	יִקְטְלוּךְ	יִקְטְלוּהוּ /A יִגְאָלוּהוּ
Imperative	2ms	קָטְלֵנִי	-----	-----	קָטְלֵהוּ
(from an imperfect /A שְׁלָחֵנִי 2ms +1cs, שְׁמָעוּנִי 2mp +1cs)					
Infinitive		קָטְלִי קָטְלֵנִי	קָטְלְךָ כָּתְבְךָ	קָטְלֵךְ	קָטְלוֹ
Pi“ēl Perfect		קִטְּלַנִי	קִטֶּלְךָ	קִטְּלֵךְ	קִטְּלוֹ
Hiph‘îl Perfect		הִקְטִילַנִי	הִקְטִילְךָ	הִקְטִילֵךְ	הִקְטִילוֹ

3fs	1cp	2mp	2fp	3mp	3fp
קְטַלְתִּיהָ	-----	קְטַלְתִּיכֶם	-----	קְטַלְתִּים	קְטַלְתִּין
קְטַלְתָּהּ	קְטַלְתָּנוּ	-----	-----	קְטַלְתָּם	-----
קְטַלְתִּיהָ	קְטַלְתִּינוּ	-----	-----	קְטַלְתִּים	-----
קְטָלָהּ	קְטָלָנוּ	-----	-----	קְטָלָם A-e/ לְבֵשָׁם	קְטָלָן
קְטָלַתָּה	קְטָלַתְנוּ	-----	-----	קְטָלָתַם	-----
קְטַלְנוּהָ	-----	קְטַלְנוּכֶם	-----	קְטַלְנוּם	-----
-----	קְטַלְתּוּנוּ	-----	-----	-----	-----
קְטָלוּהָ	קְטָלוּנוּ	-----	-----	קְטָלוּם	קְטָלוּן
יִקְטְלֶהָ יִקְטְלָהּ יִלְבָּשֶׁהָ	יִקְטְלֵנוּ יִלְבָּשֵׁנוּ	יִקְטָלְכֶם	-----	יִקְטְלֵם	-----
יִקְטְלֶנָּה	יִקְטְלֶנּוּ	-----	-----	-----	-----
יִקְטְלוּהָ	יִקְטְלוּנוּ	יִקְטְלוּכֶם	-----	יִקְטְלוּם	-----
קָטְלֶהָ קָטְלָהּ	קָטְלֵנוּ	-----	-----	קָטְלֵם	-----
קָטְלָהּ	קָטְלֵנוּ	קְטָלְכֶם כָּתְבְכֶם	-----	קָטְלָם	קָטְלָן
קִטְלָהּ	קִטְלָנוּ	-----	-----	קִטְלָם	קִטְלָן
הִקְטִילָהּ	הִקְטִילָנוּ	הִקְטִילְכֶם	הִקְטִילְכֶן	הִקְטִילָם	הִקְטִילָן

R$_1$-GUTTURAL VERB

Perfect		Qal	Niph'al	Pi"ēl	Pu"al	Hithpa"ēl	Hiph'îl	Hoph'al
SG.	1C	עָמַדְתִי	נֶעֱמַדְתִי	עִמַדְתִי	עֻמַדְתִי	הִתְעַמַדְתִי	הֶעֱמַדְתִי	הָעֳמַדְתִי
	2M	עָמַדְתָ	נֶעֱמַדְתָ	עִמַדְתָ	עֻמַדְתָ	הִתְעַמַדְתָ	הֶעֱמַדְתָ	הָעֳמַדְתָ
	2F	עָמַדְתְ	נֶעֱמַדְתְ	עִמַדְתְ	עֻמַדְתְ	הִתְעַמַדְתְ	הֶעֱמַדְתְ	הָעֳמַדְתְ
	3M	עָמַד	נֶעֱמַד	עִמֵד	עֻמַד	הִתְעַמֵד	הֶעֱמִיד	הָעֳמַד
	3F	עָמְדָה	נֶעֶמְדָה	עִמְדָה	עֻמְדָה	הִתְעַמְדָה	הֶעֱמִידָה	הָעָמְדָה
PL.	1C	עָמַדְנוּ	נֶעֱמַדְנוּ	עִמַדְנוּ	עֻמַדְנוּ	הִתְעַמַדְנוּ	הֶעֱמַדְנוּ	הָעֳמַדְנוּ
	2M	עֲמַדְתֶם	נֶעֱמַדְתֶם	עִמַדְתֶם	עֻמַדְתֶם	הִתְעַמַדְתֶם	הֶעֱמַדְתֶם	הָעֳמַדְתֶם
	2F	עֲמַדְתֶן	נֶעֱמַדְתֶן	עִמַדְתֶן	עֻמַדְתֶן	הִתְעַמַדְתֶן	הֶעֱמַדְתֶן	הָעֳמַדְתֶן
	3C	עָמְדוּ	נֶעֶמְדוּ	עִמְדוּ	עֻמְדוּ	הִתְעַמְדוּ	הֶעֱמִידוּ	הָעָמְדוּ

Imperfect		Qal	Niph'al	Pi"ēl	Pu"al	Hithpa"ēl	Hiph'îl	Hoph'al
SG.	1C	אֶעֱמֹד	אֵעָמֵד	אֲעַמֵד	אֲעֻמַד	אֶתְעַמֵד	אַעֲמִיד	אָעֳמַד
	2M	תַעֲמֹד	תֵעָמֵד	תְעַמֵד	תְעֻמַד	תִתְעַמֵד	תַעֲמִיד	תָעֳמַד
	2F	תַעַמְדִי	תֵעָמְדִי	תְעַמְדִי	תְעֻמְדִי	תִתְעַמְדִי	תַעֲמִידִי	תָעָמְדִי
	3M	יַעֲמֹד	יֵעָמֵד	יְעַמֵד	יְעֻמַד	יִתְעַמֵד	יַעֲמִיד	יָעֳמַד
	3F	תַעֲמֹד	תֵעָמֵד	תְעַמֵד	תְעֻמַד	תִתְעַמֵד	תַעֲמִיד	תָעֳמַד
PL.	1C	נַעֲמֹד	נֵעָמֵד	נְעַמֵד	נְעֻמַד	נִתְעַמֵד	נַעֲמִיד	נָעֳמַד
	2M	תַעַמְדוּ	תֵעָמְדוּ	תְעַמְדוּ	תְעֻמְדוּ	תִתְעַמְדוּ	תַעֲמִידוּ	תָעָמְדוּ
	2F	תַעֲמֹדְנָה	תֵעָמַדְנָה	תְעַמֵדְנָה	תְעֻמַדְנָה	תִתְעַמַדְנָה	תַעֲמֵדְנָה	תָעֳמַדְנָה
	3M	יַעַמְדוּ	יֵעָמְדוּ	יְעַמְדוּ	יְעֻמְדוּ	יִתְעַמְדוּ	יַעֲמִידוּ	יָעָמְדוּ
	3F	תַעֲמֹדְנָה	תֵעָמַדְנָה	תְעַמֵדְנָה	תְעֻמַדְנָה	תִתְעַמַדְנָה	תַעֲמֵדְנָה	תָעֳמַדְנָה

	Qal	Niph'al	Pi"ēl	Pu"al	Hithpa"ēl	Hiph'îl	Hoph'al
Cohortative	אֶעֶמְדָה	אֵעָמְדָה	אֲעַמְדָה	אֲעֻמְדָה	אֶתְעַמְדָה	אַעֲמִידָה	אָעָמְדָה
Jussive	יַעֲמֹד	יֵעָמֵד	יְעַמֵד	יְעֻמַד	יִתְעַמֵד	יַעֲמֵד	יָעֳמַד
With Vav-Consecutive	וַיַּעֲמֹד	וַיֵּעָמֵד	וַיְעַמֵד	וַיְעֻמַד	וַיִּתְעַמֵד	וַיַּעֲמֵד	וַיָּעֳמַד

Imperative		Qal	Niph'al	Pi"ēl	Pu"al	Hithpa"ēl	Hiph'îl	Hoph'al
SG.	2M	עֲמֹד	הֵעָמֵד	עַמֵּד		הִתְעַמֵּד	הַעֲמֵד	
	2F	עִמְדִי	הֵעָֽמְדִי	עַמְּדִי		הִתְעַמְּדִי	הַעֲמִ֫ידִי	
PL.	2M	עִמְדוּ	הֵעָֽמְדוּ	עַמְּדוּ		הִתְעַמְּדוּ	הַעֲמִ֫ידוּ	
	2F	עֲמֹ֫דְנָה	הֵעָמַ֫דְנָה	עַמֵּ֫דְנָה		הִתְעַמֵּ֫דְנָה	הַעֲמֵ֫דְנָה	

Participle		Qal	Niph'al	Pi"ēl	Pu"al	Hithpa"ēl	Hiph'îl	Hoph'al
ACT	MS	עֹמֵד		מְעַמֵּד			מַעֲמִיד	
	MP	עֹמְדִים		מְעַמְּדִים			מַעֲמִידִים	
	FS	עֹמְדָה		מְעַמְּדָה			מַעֲמִידָה	
	FP	עֹמְדוֹת		מְעַמְּדוֹת			מַעֲמִידוֹת	
PASS	MS	עָמוּד			מְעֻמָּד			מָעֳמָד
	MP	עֲמוּדִים			מְעֻמָּדִים			מָעֳמָדִים
	FS	עֲמוּדָה			מְעֻמָּדָה			מָעֳמָדָה
	FP	עֲמוּדוֹת			מְעֻמָּדוֹת			מָעֳמָדוֹת
REFL	MS		נֶעֱמָד			מִתְעַמֵּד		
	MP		נֶעֱמָדִים			מִתְעַמְּדִים		
	FS		נֶעֱמָדָה			מִתְעַמְּדָה		
	FP		נֶעֱטָדוֹת			מִתְעַמְּדוֹת		

Infinitive	Qal	Niph'al	Pi"ēl	Pu"al	Hithpa"ēl	Hiph'îl	Hoph'al
ABSOLUTE	עָמוֹד	נַעֲמוֹד הֵעָמֹד	עַמֹּד עַמֵּד		הִתְעַמֵּד	הַעֲמֵד	הָעֳמֵד
CONSTRUCT	עֲמֹד	הֵעָמֵד	עַמֵּד		הִתְעַמֵּד	הַעֲמִיד	

R_1-ALEF VERB: SPECIAL CASES

Perfect		Qal	Niph'al	Pi"ēl	Pu"al	Hithpa"ēl	Hiph'îl	Hoph'al
SG.	1C	אָכַ֫לְתִי						
	2M	אָכַ֫לְתָ						
	2F	אָכַלְתְ						
	3M	אָכַל						
	3F	אָֽכְלָה						
PL.	1C	אָכַ֫לְנוּ						
	2M	אֲכַלְתֶם						
	2F	אֲכַלְתֶן						
	3C	אָֽכְלוּ						

Imperfect		Qal	Niph'al	Pi"ēl	Pu"al	Hithpa"ēl	Hiph'îl	Hoph'al
SG.	1C	אֹכַל						
	2M	תֹאכַל						
	2F	תֹאכְלִי						
	3M	יֹאכַל						
	3F	תֹאכַל						
PL.	1C	נֹאכַל						
	2M	תֹאכְלוּ						
	2F	תֹאכַ֫לְנָה						
	3M	יֹאכְלוּ						
	3F	תֹאכַ֫לְנָה						

	Qal	Niph'al	Pi"ēl	Pu"al	Hithpa"ēl	Hiph'îl	Hoph'al
Cohortative	אֹכְלָה						
Jussive	יֹאכַל						
With Vav-Consecutive	וַיֹּאכַל						

Imperative		Qal	Niph'al	Pi"ēl	Pu"al	Hithpa"ēl	Hiph'îl	Hoph'al
SG.	2M	אֱכֹל						
	2F	אִכְלִי						
PL.	2M	אִכְלוּ						
	2F	אֱכֹ֫לְנָה						

Participle		Qal	Niph'al	Pi"ēl	Pu"al	Hithpa"ēl	Hiph'îl	Hoph'al
ACT	MS	אֹכֵל						
	MP	אֹכְלִים						
	FS	אֹכְלָה						
	FP	אֹכְלוֹת						
PASS	MS	אָכוּל						
	MP	אֲכוּלִים						
	FS	אֲכוּלָה						
	FP	אֲכוּלוֹת						
REFL	MS							
	MP							
	FS							
	FP							

Infinitive	Qal	Niph'al	Pi"ēl	Pu"al	Hithpa"ēl	Hiph'îl	Hoph'al
ABSOLUTE	אָכוֹל						
CONSTRUCT	אֲכֹל לֶאֱכֹל						

R_2-GUTTURAL VERB

Perfect		Qal	Niph‘al	Pi“ēl	Pu“al	Hithpa“ēl	Hiph‘îl	Hoph‘al
SG.	1C	שָׁחַטְתִּי	נִשְׁחַטְתִּי	בֵּרַכְתִּי	בֹּרַכְתִּי	הִתְבָּרַכְתִּי	הִשְׁחַטְתִּי	הָשְׁחַטְתִּי
	2M	שָׁחַטְתָּ	נִשְׁחַטְתָּ	בֵּרַכְתָּ	בֹּרַכְתָּ	הִתְבָּרַכְתָּ	הִשְׁחַטְתָּ	הָשְׁחַטְתָּ
	2F	שָׁחַטְתְּ	נִשְׁחַטְתְּ	בֵּרַכְתְּ	בֹּרַכְתְּ	הִתְבָּרַכְתְּ	הִשְׁחַטְתְּ	הָשְׁחַטְתְּ
	3M	שָׁחַט	נִשְׁחַט	בֵּרַךְ	בֹּרַךְ	הִתְבָּרֵךְ	הִשְׁחִיט	הָשְׁחַט
	3F	שָׁחֲטָה	נִשְׁחֲטָה	בֵּרֲכָה	בֹּרֲכָה	הִתְבָּרֲכָה	הִשְׁחִיטָה	הָשְׁחֲטָה
PL.	1C	שָׁחַטְנוּ	נִשְׁחַטְנוּ	בֵּרַכְנוּ	בֹּרַכְנוּ	הִתְבָּרַכְנוּ	הִשְׁחַטְנוּ	הָשְׁחַטְנוּ
	2M	שְׁחַטְתֶּם	נִשְׁחַטְתֶּם	בֵּרַכְתֶּם	בֹּרַכְתֶּם	הִתְבָּרַכְתֶּם	הִשְׁחַטְתֶּם	הָשְׁחַטְתֶּם
	2F	שְׁחַטְתֶּן	נִשְׁחַטְתֶּן	בֵּרַכְתֶּן	בֹּרַכְתֶּן	הִתְבָּרַכְתֶּן	הִשְׁחַטְתֶּן	הָשְׁחַטְתֶּן
	3C	שָׁחֲטוּ	נִשְׁחֲטוּ	בֵּרֲכוּ	בֹּרֲכוּ	הִתְבָּרֲכוּ	הִשְׁחִיטוּ	הָשְׁחֲטוּ

Imperfect		Qal	Niph‘al	Pi“ēl	Pu“al	Hithpa“ēl	Hiph‘îl	Hoph‘al
SG.	1C	אֶשְׁחַט	אֶשָּׁחֵט	אֲבָרֵךְ	אֲבֹרַךְ	אֶתְבָּרֵךְ	אַשְׁחִיט	אָשְׁחַט
	2M	תִּשְׁחַט	תִּשָּׁחֵט	תְּבָרֵךְ	תְּבֹרַךְ	תִּתְבָּרֵךְ	תַּשְׁחִיט	תָּשְׁחַט
	2F	תִּשְׁחֲטִי	תִּשָּׁחֲטִי	תְּבָרֲכִי	תְּבֹרֲכִי	תִּתְבָּרֲכִי	תַּשְׁחִיטִי	תָּשְׁחֲטִי
	3M	יִשְׁחַט	יִשָּׁחֵט	יְבָרֵךְ	יְבֹרַךְ	יִתְבָּרֵךְ	יַשְׁחִיט	יָשְׁחַט
	3F	תִּשְׁחַט	תִּשָּׁחֵט	תְּבָרֵךְ	תְּבֹרַךְ	תִּתְבָּרֵךְ	תַּשְׁחִיט	תָּשְׁחַט
PL.	1C	נִשְׁחַט	נִשָּׁחֵט	נְבָרֵךְ	נְבֹרַךְ	נִתְבָּרֵךְ	נַשְׁחִיט	נָשְׁחַט
	2M	תִּשְׁחֲטוּ	תִּשָּׁחֲטוּ	תְּבָרֲכוּ	תְּבֹרֲכוּ	תִּתְבָּרֲכוּ	תַּשְׁחִיטוּ	תָּשְׁחֲטוּ
	2F	תִּשְׁחַטְנָה	תִּשָּׁחַטְנָה	תְּבָרֵכְנָה	תְּבֹרַכְנָה	תִּתְבָּרֵכְנָה	תַּשְׁחֵטְנָה	תָּשְׁחַטְנָה
	3M	יִשְׁחֲטוּ	יִשָּׁחֲטוּ	יְבָרֲכוּ	יְבֹרֲכוּ	יִתְבָּרֲכוּ	יַשְׁחִיטוּ	יָשְׁחֲטוּ
	3F	תִּשְׁחַטְנָה	תִּשָּׁחַטְנָה	תְּבָרֵכְנָה	תְּבֹרַכְנָה	תִּתְבָּרֵכְנָה	תַּשְׁחֵטְנָה	תָּשְׁחַטְנָה

	Qal	Niph‘al	Pi“ēl	Pu“al	Hithpa“ēl	Hiph‘îl	Hoph‘al
Cohortative	אֶשְׁחֲטָה	אֶשָּׁחֲטָה	אֲבָרֲכָה	אֲבֹרֲכָה	אֶתְבָּרֲכָה	אַשְׁחִיטָה	אָשְׁחֲטָה
Jussive	יִשְׁחַט	יִשָּׁחֵט	יְבָרֵךְ	יְבֹרַךְ	יִתְבָּרֵךְ	יַשְׁחֵט	יָשְׁחַט
With Vav-Consecutive	וַיִּשְׁחַט	וַיִּשָּׁחֵט	וַיְבָרֶךְ	וַיְבֹרַךְ	וַיִּתְבָּרֵךְ	וַיַּשְׁחֵט	וַיָּשְׁחַט

Imperative		Qal	Niph'al	Pi"ēl	Pu"al	Hithpa"ēl	Hiph'îl	Hoph'al
SG.	2M	שְׁחַט	הִשָּׁחֵט	בָּרֵךְ		הִתְבָּרֵךְ	הַשְׁחֵט	
	2F	שַׁחֲטִי	הִשָּׁחֲטִי	בָּרֲכִי		הִתְבָּרֲכִי	הַשְׁחִיטִי	
PL.	2M	שַׁחֲטוּ	הִשָּׁחֲטוּ	בָּרֲכוּ		הִתְבָּרֲכוּ	הַשְׁחִיטוּ	
	2F	שְׁחַטְנָה	הִשָּׁחַטְנָה	בָּרֵכְנָה		הִתְבָּרֵכְנָה	הַשְׁחֵטְנָה	

Participle		Qal	Niph'al	Pi"ēl	Pu"al	Hithpa"ēl	Hiph'îl	Hoph'al
ACT	MS	שֹׁחֵט		מְבָרֵךְ			מַשְׁחִיט	
	MP	שֹׁחֲטִים		מְבָרֲכִים			מַשְׁחִיטִים	
	FS	שֹׁחֲטָה		מְבָרֲכָה			מַשְׁחִיטָה	
	FP	שֹׁחֲטוֹת		מְבָרֲכוֹת			מַשְׁחִיטוֹת	
PASS	MS	שָׁחוּט			מְבֹרָךְ			מָשְׁחָט
	MP	שְׁחוּטִים			מְבֹרָכִים			מָשְׁחָטִים
	FS	שְׁחוּטָה			מְבֹרָכָה			מָשְׁחָטָה
	FP	שְׁחוּטוֹת			מְבֹרָכוֹת			מָשְׁחָטוֹת
REFL	MS		נִשְׁחָט			מִתְבָּרֵךְ		
	MP		נִשְׁחָטִים			מִתְבָּרֲכִים		
	FS		נִשְׁחָטָה			מִתְבָּרֲכָה		
	FP		נִשְׁחָטוֹת			מִתְבָּרֲכוֹת		

Infinitive	Qal	Niph'al	Pi"ēl	Pu"al	Hithpa"ēl	Hiph'îl	Hoph'al
ABSOLUTE	שָׁחוֹט	נִשְׁחוֹט הִשָּׁחֹט	בָּרֵךְ		הִתְבָּרֵךְ	הַשְׁחֵט	
CONSTRUCT	שְׁחֹט	הִשָּׁחֵט	בָּרֵךְ		הִתְבָּרֵךְ	הַשְׁחִיט	

R$_3$-GUTTURAL VERB

Perfect		Qal	Niph'al	Pi"ēl	Pu"al	Hithpa"ēl	Hiph'îl	Hoph'al
SG.	1C	שָׁלַחְתִּי	נִשְׁלַחְתִּי	שִׁלַּחְתִּי	שֻׁלַּחְתִּי	הִשְׁתַּלַּחְתִּי	הִשְׁלַחְתִּי	הָשְׁלַחְתִּי
	2M	שָׁלַחְתָּ	נִשְׁלַחְתָּ	שִׁלַּחְתָּ	שֻׁלַּחְתָּ	הִשְׁתַּלַּחְתָּ	הִשְׁלַחְתָּ	הָשְׁלַחְתָּ
	2F	שָׁלַחַתְּ	נִשְׁלַחַתְּ	שִׁלַּחַתְּ	שֻׁלַּחַתְּ	הִשְׁתַּלַּחַתְּ	הִשְׁלַחַתְּ	הָשְׁלַחַתְּ
	3M	שָׁלַח	נִשְׁלַח	שִׁלַּח	שֻׁלַּח	הִשְׁתַּלַּח	הִשְׁלִיחַ	הָשְׁלַח
	3F	שָׁלְחָה	נִשְׁלְחָה	שִׁלְּחָה	שֻׁלְּחָה	הִשְׁתַּלְּחָה	הִשְׁלִיחָה	הָשְׁלְחָה
PL.	1C	שָׁלַחְנוּ	נִשְׁלַחְנוּ	שִׁלַּחְנוּ	שֻׁלַּחְנוּ	הִשְׁתַּלַּחְנוּ	הִשְׁלַחְנוּ	הָשְׁלַחְנוּ
	2M	שְׁלַחְתֶּם	נִשְׁלַחְתֶּם	שִׁלַּחְתֶּם	שֻׁלַּחְתֶּם	הִשְׁתַּלַּחְתֶּם	הִשְׁלַחְתֶּם	הָשְׁלַחְתֶּם
	2F	שְׁלַחְתֶּן	נִשְׁלַחְתֶּן	שִׁלַּחְתֶּן	שֻׁלַּחְתֶּן	הִשְׁתַּלַּחְתֶּן	הִשְׁלַחְתֶּן	הָשְׁלַחְתֶּן
	3C	שָׁלְחוּ	נִשְׁלְחוּ	שִׁלְּחוּ	שֻׁלְּחוּ	הִשְׁתַּלְּחוּ	הִשְׁלִיחוּ	הָשְׁלְחוּ

Imperfect		Qal	Niph'al	Pi"ēl	Pu"al	Hithpa"ēl	Hiph'îl	Hoph'al
SG.	1C	אֶשְׁלַח	אֶשָּׁלַח	אֲשַׁלַּח	אֲשֻׁלַּח	אֶשְׁתַּלַּח	אַשְׁלִיחַ	אָשְׁלַח
	2M	תִּשְׁלַח	תִּשָּׁלַח	תְּשַׁלַּח	תְּשֻׁלַּח	תִּשְׁתַּלַּח	תַּשְׁלִיחַ	תָּשְׁלַח
	2F	תִּשְׁלְחִי	תִּשָּׁלְחִי	תְּשַׁלְּחִי	תְּשֻׁלְּחִי	תִּשְׁתַּלְּחִי	תַּשְׁלִיחִי	תָּשְׁלְחִי
	3M	יִשְׁלַח	יִשָּׁלַח	יְשַׁלַּח	יְשֻׁלַּח	יִשְׁתַּלַּח	יַשְׁלִיחַ	יָשְׁלַח
	3F	תִּשְׁלַח	תִּשָּׁלַח	תְּשַׁלַּח	תְּשֻׁלַּח	תִּשְׁתַּלַּח	תַּשְׁלִיחַ	תָּשְׁלַח
PL.	1C	נִשְׁלַח	נִשָּׁלַח	נְשַׁלַּח	נְשֻׁלַּח	נִשְׁתַּלַּח	נַשְׁלִיחַ	נָשְׁלַח
	2M	תִּשְׁלְחוּ	תִּשָּׁלְחוּ	תְּשַׁלְּחוּ	תְּשֻׁלְּחוּ	תִּשְׁתַּלְּחוּ	תַּשְׁלִיחוּ	תָּשְׁלְחוּ
	2F	תִּשְׁלַחְנָה	תִּשָּׁלַחְנָה	תְּשַׁלַּחְנָה	תְּשֻׁלַּחְנָה	תִּשְׁתַּלַּחְנָה	תַּשְׁלַחְנָה	תָּשְׁלַחְנָה
	3M	יִשְׁלְחוּ	יִשָּׁלְחוּ	יְשַׁלְּחוּ	יְשֻׁלְּחוּ	יִשְׁתַּלְּחוּ	יַשְׁלִיחוּ	יָשְׁלְחוּ
	3F	תִּשְׁלַחְנָה	תִּשָּׁלַחְנָה	תְּשַׁלַּחְנָה	תְּשֻׁלַּחְנָה	תִּשְׁתַּלַּחְנָה	תַּשְׁלַחְנָה	תָּשְׁלַחְנָה

	Qal	Niph'al	Pi"ēl	Pu"al	Hithpa"ēl	Hiph'îl	Hoph'al
Cohortative	אֶשְׁלְחָה	אֶשָּׁלְחָה	אֲשַׁלְּחָה	אֲשֻׁלְּחָה	אֶשְׁתַּלְּחָה	אַשְׁלִיחָה	אָשְׁלְחָה
Jussive	יִשְׁלַח	יִשָּׁלַח	יְשַׁלַּח	יְשֻׁלַּח	יִשְׁתַּלַּח	יַשְׁלַח	יָשְׁלַח
With Vav-Consecutive	וַיִּשְׁלַח	וַיִּשָּׁלַח	וַיְשַׁלַּח	וַיְשֻׁלַּח	וַיִּשְׁתַּלַּח	וַיַּשְׁלַח	וַיָּשְׁלַח

Imperative		Qal	Niph'al	Pi"ēl	Pu"al	Hithpa"ēl	Hiph'îl	Hoph'al
SG.	2M	שְׁלַח	הִשָּׁלַח	שַׁלַּח		הִשְׁתַּלַּח	הַשְׁלַח	
	2F	שִׁלְחִי	הִשָּׁלְחִי	שַׁלְּחִי		הִשְׁתַּלְּחִי	הַשְׁלִיחִי	
PL.	2M	שִׁלְחוּ	הִשָּׁלְחוּ	שַׁלְּחוּ		הִשְׁתַּלְּחוּ	הַשְׁלִיחוּ	
	2F	שְׁלַחְנָה	הִשָּׁלַחְנָה	שַׁלַּחְנָה		הִשְׁתַּלַּחְנָה	הַשְׁלַחְנָה	

Participle		Qal	Niph'al	Pi"ēl	Pu"al	Hithpa"ēl	Hiph'îl	Hoph'al
ACT	MS	שֹׁלֵחַ		מְשַׁלֵּחַ			מַשְׁלִיחַ	
	MP	שֹׁלְחִים		מְשַׁלְּחִים			מַשְׁלִיחִים	
	FS	שֹׁלְחָה		מְשַׁלְּחָה			מַשְׁלִיחָה	
	FP	שֹׁלְחוֹת		מְשַׁלְּחוֹת			מַשְׁלִיחוֹת	
PASS	MS	שָׁלוּחַ			מְשֻׁלָּח			מָשְׁלָח
	MP	שְׁלוּחִים			מְשֻׁלָּחִים			מָשְׁלָחִים
	FS	שְׁלוּחָה			מְשֻׁלָּחָה			מָשְׁלָחָה
	FP	שְׁלוּחוֹת			מְשֻׁלָּחוֹת			מָשְׁלָחוֹת
REFL	MS		נִשְׁלָח			מִשְׁתַּלֵּחַ		
	MP		נִשְׁלָחִים			מִשְׁתַּלְּחִים		
	FS		נִשְׁלָחָה			מִשְׁתַּלְּחָה		
	FP		נִשְׁלָחוֹת			מִשְׁתַּלְּחוֹת		

Infinitive	Qal	Niph'al	Pi"ēl	Pu"al	Hithpa"ēl	Hiph'îl	Hoph'al
ABSOLUTE	שָׁלוֹחַ	נִשְׁלוֹחַ הִשָּׁלֹחַ	שַׁלֵּחַ		הִשְׁתַּלֵּחַ	הַשְׁלֵחַ	הָשְׁלֵחַ
CONSTRUCT	שְׁלֹחַ	הִשָּׁלֵחַ	שַׁלֵּחַ		הִשְׁתַּלֵּחַ	הַשְׁלִיחַ	

R_3-ALEF VERB

Perfect		Qal	Niph'al	Pi"ēl	Pu"al	Hithpa"ēl	Hiph'îl	Hoph'al
SG.	1C	מָצָאתִי	נִמְצֵאתִי	מִצֵּאתִי	מֻצֵּאתִי	הִתְמַצֵּאתִי	הִמְצֵאתִי	הֻמְצֵאתִי
	2M	מָצָאתָ	נִמְצֵאתָ	מִצֵּאתָ	מֻצֵּאתָ	הִתְמַצֵּאתָ	הִמְצֵאתָ	הֻמְצֵאתָ
	2F	מָצָאת	נִמְצֵאת	מִצֵּאת	מֻצֵּאת	הִתְמַצֵּאת	הִמְצֵאת	הֻמְצֵאת
	3M	מָצָא	נִמְצָא	מִצֵּא	מֻצָּא	הִתְמַצֵּא	הִמְצִיא	הֻמְצָא
	3F	מָצְאָה	נִמְצְאָה	מִצְּאָה	מֻצְּאָה	הִתְמַצְּאָה	הִמְצִיאָה	הֻמְצְאָה
PL.	1C	מָצָאנוּ	נִמְצֵאנוּ	מִצֵּאנוּ	מֻצֵּאנוּ	הִתְמַצֵּאנוּ	הִמְצֵאנוּ	הֻמְצֵאנוּ
	2M	מְצָאתֶם	נִמְצֵאתֶם	מִצֵּאתֶם	מֻצֵּאתֶם	הִתְמַצֵּאתֶם	הִמְצֵאתֶם	הֻמְצֵאתֶם
	2F	מְצָאתֶן	נִמְצֵאתֶן	מִצֵּאתֶן	מֻצֵּאתֶן	הִתְמַצֵּאתֶן	הִמְצֵאתֶן	הֻמְצֵאתֶן
	3C	מָצְאוּ	נִמְצְאוּ	מִצְּאוּ	מֻצְּאוּ	הִתְמַצְּאוּ	הִמְצִיאוּ	הֻמְצְאוּ

Imperfect		Qal	Niph'al	Pi"ēl	Pu"al	Hithpa"ēl	Hiph'îl	Hoph'al
SG.	1C	אֶמְצָא	אֶמָּצֵא	אֲמַצֵּא	אֲמֻצָּא	אֶתְמַצֵּא	אַמְצִיא	אֻמְצָא
	2M	תִּמְצָא	תִּמָּצֵא	תְּמַצֵּא	תְּמֻצָּא	תִּתְמַצֵּא	תַּמְצִיא	תֻּמְצָא
	2F	תִּמְצְאִי	תִּמָּצְאִי	תְּמַצְּאִי	תְּמֻצְּאִי	תִּתְמַצְּאִי	תַּמְצִיאִי	תֻּמְצְאִי
	3M	יִמְצָא	יִמָּצֵא	יְמַצֵּא	יְמֻצָּא	יִתְמַצֵּא	יַמְצִיא	יֻמְצָא
	3F	תִּמְצָא	תִּמָּצֵא	תְּמַצֵּא	תְּמֻצָּא	תִּתְמַצֵּא	תַּמְצִיא	תֻּמְצָא
PL.	1C	נִמְצָא	נִמָּצֵא	נְמַצֵּא	נְמֻצָּא	נִתְמַצֵּא	נַמְצִיא	נֻמְצָא
	2M	תִּמְצְאוּ	תִּמָּצְאוּ	תְּמַצְּאוּ	תְּמֻצְּאוּ	תִּתְמַצְּאוּ	תַּמְצִיאוּ	תֻּמְצְאוּ
	2F	תִּמְצֶאנָה	תִּמָּצֶאנָה	תְּמַצֶּאנָה	תְּמֻצֶּאנָה	תִּתְמַצֶּאנָה	תַּמְצֶאנָה	תֻּמְצֶאנָה
	3M	יִמְצְאוּ	יִמָּצְאוּ	יְמַצְּאוּ	יְמֻצְּאוּ	יִתְמַצְּאוּ	יַמְצִיאוּ	יֻמְצְאוּ
	3F	תִּמְצֶאנָה	תִּמָּצֶאנָה	תְּמַצֶּאנָה	תְּמֻצֶּאנָה	תִּתְמַצֶּאנָה	תַּמְצֶאנָה	תֻּמְצֶאנָה

	Qal	Niph'al	Pi"ēl	Pu"al	Hithpa"ēl	Hiph'îl	Hoph'al
Cohortative	אֶמְצְאָה	אֶמָּצְאָה	אֲמַצְּאָה	אֲמֻצְּאָה	אֶתְמַצְּאָה	אַמְצִיאָה	אֻמְצְאָה
Jussive	יִמְצָא	יִמָּצֵא	יְמַצֵּא	יְמֻצָּא	יִתְמַצֵּא	יַמְצֵא	יֻמְצָא
With Vav-Consecutive	וַיִּמְצָא	וַיִּמָּצֵא	וַיְמַצֵּא	וַיְמֻצָּא	וַיִּתְמַצֵּא	וַיַּמְצֵא	וַיֻּמְצָא

Imperative		Qal	Niph'al	Pi"ēl	Pu"al	Hithpa"ēl	Hiph'îl	Hoph'al
SG.	2M	מְצָא	הִמָּצֵא	מַצֵּא		הִתְמַצֵּא	הַמְצֵא	
	2F	מִצְאִי	הִמָּצְאִי	מַצְּאִי		הִתְמַצְּאִי	הַמְצִיאִי	
PL.	2M	מִצְאוּ	הִמָּצְאוּ	מַצְּאוּ		הִתְמַצְּאוּ	הַמְצִיאוּ	
	2F	מְצֶאנָה	הִמָּצֶאנָה	מַצֶּאנָה		הִתְמַצֶּאנָה	הַמְצֶאנָה	

Participle		Qal	Niph'al	Pi"ēl	Pu"al	Hithpa"ēl	Hiph'îl	Hoph'al
ACT	MS	מֹצֵא		מְמַצֵּא			מַמְצִיא	
	MP	מֹצְאִים		מְמַצְּאִים			מַמְצִיאִים	
	FS	מֹצְאָה מֹצֵאת		מְמַצְּאָה			מַמְצִיאָה	
	FP	מֹצְאוֹת		מְמַצְּאוֹת			מַמְצִיאוֹת	
PASS	MS	מָצוּא			מְמֻצָּא			מֻמְצָא
	MP	מְצוּאִים			מְמֻצָּאִים			מֻמְצָאִים
	FS	מְצוּאָה			מְמֻצָּאָה			מֻמְצָאָה
	FP	מְצוּאוֹת			מְמֻצָּאוֹת			מֻמְצָאוֹת
REFL	MS		נִמְצָא			מִתְמַצֵּא		
	MP		נִמְצָאִים			מִתְמַצְּאִים		
	FS		נִמְצָאָה			מִתְמַצְּאָה		
	FP		נִמְצָאוֹת			מִתְמַצְּאוֹת		

Infinitive	Qal	Niph'al	Pi"ēl	Pu"al	Hithpa"ēl	Hiph'îl	Hoph'al
ABSOLUTE	מָצוֹא	נִמְצֹא הִמָּצֹא	מַצֹּא		הִתְמַצֵּא	הַמְצֵא	
CONSTRUCT	מְצֹא	הִמָּצֵא	מַצֵּא		הִתְמַצֵּא	הַמְצִיא	

R₁-NUN VERB

Perfect		Qal			Niph'al	*Pi"ēl	Hiph'îl	Hoph'al
SG.	1C	נָפַלְתִּי	נָגַשְׁתִּי	נָתַתִּי	נִגַּשְׁתִּי	נִגַּשְׁתִּי	הִגַּשְׁתִּי	הֻגַּשְׁתִּי
	2M	נָפַלְתָּ	נָגַשְׁתָּ	נָתַתָּ	נִגַּשְׁתָּ	נִגַּשְׁתָּ	הִגַּשְׁתָּ	הֻגַּשְׁתָּ
	2F	נָפַלְתְּ	נָגַשְׁתְּ	נָתַתְּ	נִגַּשְׁתְּ	נִגַּשְׁתְּ	הִגַּשְׁתְּ	הֻגַּשְׁתְּ
	3M	נָפַל	נָגַשׁ	נָתַן	נִגַּשׁ	נִגֵּשׁ	הִגִּישׁ	הֻגַּשׁ
	3F	נָֽפְלָה	נָֽגְשָׁה	נָֽתְנָה	נִגְּשָׁה	נִגְּשָׁה	הִגִּישָׁה	הֻגְּשָׁה
PL.	1C	נָפַלְנוּ	נָגַשְׁנוּ	נָתַנּוּ	נִגַּשְׁנוּ	נִגַּשְׁנוּ	הִגַּשְׁנוּ	הֻגַּשְׁנוּ
	2M	נְפַלְתֶּם	נְגַשְׁתֶּם	נְתַתֶּם	נִגַּשְׁתֶּם	נִגַּשְׁתֶּם	הִגַּשְׁתֶּם	הֻגַּשְׁתֶּם
	2F	נְפַלְתֶּן	נְגַשְׁתֶּן	נְתַתֶּן	נִגַּשְׁתֶּן	נִגַּשְׁתֶּן	הִגַּשְׁתֶּן	הֻגַּשְׁתֶּן
	3C	נָֽפְלוּ	נָֽגְשׁוּ	נָֽתְנוּ	נִגַּשְׁנוּ	נִגַּשְׁנוּ	הִגִּישׁוּ	הֻגְּשׁוּ

Imperfect		Qal			Niph'al	Pi"ēl	Hiph'îl	Hoph'al
SG.	1C	אֶפֹּל	אֶגַּשׁ	אֶתֵּן	אֶנָּגֵשׁ	אֲנַגֵּשׁ	אַגִּישׁ	אֻגַּשׁ
	2M	תִּפֹּל	תִּגַּשׁ	תִּתֵּן	תִּנָּגֵשׁ	תְּנַגֵּשׁ	תַּגִּישׁ	תֻּגַּשׁ
	2F	תִּפְּלִי	תִּגְּשִׁי	תִּתְּנִי	תִּנָּֽגְשִׁי	תְּנַגְּשִׁי	תַּגִּישִׁי	תֻּגְּשִׁי
	3M	יִפֹּל	יִגַּשׁ	יִתֵּן	יִנָּגֵשׁ	יְנַגֵּשׁ	יַגִּישׁ	יֻגַּשׁ
	3F	תִּפֹּל	תִּגַּשׁ	תִּתֵּן	תִּנָּגֵשׁ	תְּנַגֵּשׁ	תַּגִּישׁ	תֻּגַּשׁ
PL.	1C	נִפֹּל	נִגַּשׁ	נִתֵּן	נִנָּגֵשׁ	נְנַגֵּשׁ	נַגִּישׁ	נֻגַּשׁ
	2M	תִּפְּלוּ	תִּגְּשׁוּ	תִּתְּנוּ	תִּנָּֽגְשׁוּ	תְּנַגְּשׁוּ	תַּגִּישׁוּ	תֻּגְּשׁוּ
	2F	תִּפֹּלְנָה	תִּגַּשְׁנָה	תִּתֵּנָּה	תִּנָּגַשְׁנָה	תְּנַגֵּשְׁנָה	תַּגֵּשְׁנָה	תֻּגַּשְׁנָה
	3M	יִפְּלוּ	יִגְּשׁוּ	יִתְּנוּ	יִנָּֽגְשׁוּ	יְנַגְּשׁוּ	יַגִּישׁוּ	יֻגְּשׁוּ
	3F	תִּפֹּלְנָה	תִּגַּשְׁנָה	תִּתֵּנָּה	תִּנָּגַשְׁנָה	תְּנַגֵּשְׁנָה	תַּגֵּשְׁנָה	תֻּגַּשְׁנָה

	Qal			Niph'al	Pi"ēl	Hiph'îl	Hoph'al
Cohortative	אֶפְּלָה	אֶגְּשָׁה	אֶתְּנָה	אֶנָּֽגְשָׁה	אֲנַגְּשָׁה	אַגִּישָׁה	אֻגְּשָׁה
Jussive	יִפֹּל	יִגַּשׁ	יִתֵּן	יִנָּגֵשׁ	יְנַגֵּשׁ	יַגֵּשׁ	יֻגַּשׁ
With Vav-Consecutive	וַיִּפֹּל	וַיִּגַּשׁ	וַיִּתֵּן	וַיִּנָּגֵשׁ	וַיְנַגֵּשׁ	וַיַּגֵּשׁ	וַיֻּגַּשׁ

*Pu"al and Hithpa"ēl follow the same pattern.

Imperative		Qal			Niph'al	Pi"ēl	Hiph'îl	Hoph'al
SG.	2M	נְפֹל	גַּשׁ	תֵּן	הִנָּגֵשׁ	נַגֵּשׁ	הַגֵּשׁ	
	2F	נִפְלִי	גְּשִׁי	תְּנִי	הִנָּגְשִׁי	נַגְּשִׁי	הַגִּישִׁי	
PL.	2M	נִפְלוּ	גְּשׁוּ	תְּנוּ	הִנָּגְשׁוּ	נַגְּשׁוּ	הַגִּישׁוּ	
	2F	נְפֹלְנָה	גַּשְׁנָה	תֵּנָּה	הִנָּגַשְׁנָה	נַגֵּשְׁנָה	הַגֵּשְׁנָה	

Participle		Qal	Niph'al	Pi"ēl	Hiph'îl	Hoph'al
ACT	MS	נֹגֵשׁ		מְנַגֵּשׁ	מַגִּישׁ	
	MP	נֹגְשִׁים		מְנַגְּשִׁים	מַגִּישִׁים	
	FS	נֹגְשָׁה		מְנַגְּשָׁה	מַגִּישָׁה	
	FP	נֹגְשׁוֹת		מְנַגְּשׁוֹת	מַגִּישׁוֹת	
PASS	MS	נָגוּשׁ				מֻגָּשׁ
	MP	נְגוּשִׁים				מֻגָּשִׁים
	FS	נְגוּשָׁה				מֻגָּשָׁה
	FP	נְגוּשׁוֹת				מֻגָּשׁוֹת
REFL	MS		נִגָּשׁ			
	MP		נִגָּשִׁים			
	FS		נִגָּשָׁה			
	FP		נִגָּשׁוֹת			

Infinitive	Qal			Niph'al	Pi"ēl	Hiph'îl	Hoph'al
ABSOLUTE	נָפוֹל	נָגוֹשׁ	נָתוֹן	נִגּוֹשׁ	נַגֹּשׁ נַגֵּשׁ	הַגֵּשׁ	הֻגֵּשׁ
CONSTRUCT	נְפֹל	גֶּשֶׁת	תֵּת	הִנָּגֵשׁ	נַגֵּשׁ	הַגִּישׁ	הֻגַּשׁ

R$_1$-YOD/VAV VERB

Perfect		R$_1$-VAV Qal	Niph‘al	Hiph‘îl	Hoph‘al	R$_1$-YOD Qal	Hiph‘îl
SG.	1C	יָשַׁבְתִּי	נוֹשַׁבְתִּי	הוֹשַׁבְתִּי	הוּשַׁבְתִּי	יָטַבְתִּי	הֵיטַבְתִּי
	2M	יָשַׁבְתָּ	נוֹשַׁבְתָּ	הוֹשַׁבְתָּ	הוּשַׁבְתָּ	יָטַבְתָּ	הֵיטַבְתָּ
	2F	יָשַׁבְתְּ	נוֹשַׁבְתְּ	הוֹשַׁבְתְּ	הוּשַׁבְתְּ	יָטַבְתְּ	הֵיטַבְתְּ
	3M	יָשַׁב	נוֹשַׁב	הוֹשִׁיב	הוּשַׁב	יָטַב	הֵיטִיב
	3F	יָשְׁבָה	נוֹשְׁבָה	הוֹשִׁיבָה	הוּשְׁבָה	יָטְבָה	הֵיטִיבָה
PL.	1C	יָשַׁבְנוּ	נוֹשַׁבְנוּ	הוֹשַׁבְנוּ	הוּשַׁבְנוּ	יָטַבְנוּ	הֵיטַבְנוּ
	2M	יְשַׁבְתֶּם	נוֹשַׁבְתֶּם	הוֹשַׁבְתֶּם	הוּשַׁבְתֶּם	יְטַבְתֶּם	הֵיטַבְתֶּם
	2F	יְשַׁבְתֶּן	נוֹשַׁבְתֶּן	הוֹשַׁבְתֶּן	הוּשַׁבְתֶּן	יְטַבְתֶּן	הֵיטַבְתֶּן
	3C	יָשְׁבוּ	נוֹשְׁבוּ	הוֹשִׁיבוּ	הוּשְׁבוּ	יָטְבוּ	הֵיטִיבוּ

Imperfect		Qal	Niph‘al	Hiph‘îl	Hoph‘al	Qal		Hiph‘îl
SG.	1C	אֵשֵׁב	אִוָּשֵׁב	אוֹשִׁיב	אוּשַׁב	אִירַשׁ	אִיטַב	אֵיטִיב
	2M	תֵּשֵׁב	תִּוָּשֵׁב	תּוֹשִׁיב	תּוּשַׁב	תִּירַשׁ	תִּיטַב	תֵּיטִיב
	2F	תֵּשְׁבִי	תִּוָּשְׁבִי	תּוֹשִׁיבִי	תּוּשְׁבִי	תִּירְשִׁי	תִּיטְבִי	תֵּיטִיבִי
	3M	יֵשֵׁב	יִוָּשֵׁב	יוֹשִׁיב	יוּשַׁב	יִירַשׁ	יִיטַב	יֵיטִיב
	3F	תֵּשֵׁב	תִּוָּשֵׁב	תּוֹשִׁיב	תּוּשַׁב	תִּירַשׁ	תִּיטַב	תֵּיטִיב
PL.	1C	נֵשֵׁב	נִוָּשֵׁב	נוֹשִׁיב	נוּשַׁב	נִירַשׁ	נִיטַב	נֵיטִיב
	2M	תֵּשְׁבוּ	תִּוָּשְׁבוּ	תּוֹשִׁיבוּ	תּוּשְׁבוּ	תִּירְשׁוּ	תִּיטְבוּ	תֵּיטִיבוּ
	2F	תֵּשַׁבְנָה	תִּוָּשַׁבְנָה	תּוֹשֵׁבְנָה	תּוּשַׁבְנָה	תִּירַשְׁנָה	תִּיטַבְנָה	תֵּיטֵבְנָה
	3M	יֵשְׁבוּ	יִוָּשְׁבוּ	יוֹשִׁיבוּ	יוּשְׁבוּ	יִירְשׁוּ	יִיטְבוּ	יֵיטִיבוּ
	3F	תֵּשַׁבְנָה	תִּוָּשַׁבְנָה	תּוֹשֵׁבְנָה	תּוּשַׁבְנָה	תִּירַשְׁנָה	תִּיטַבְנָה	תֵּיטֵבְנָה

	Qal	Niph‘al	Hiph‘îl	Hoph‘al	Qal		Hiph‘îl
Cohortative	אֵשְׁבָה	אִוָּשְׁבָה	אוֹשִׁיבָה	אוּשְׁבָה	אִירְשָׁה	אִיטְבָה	אֵיטִיבָה
Jussive	יֵשֵׁב	יִוָּשֵׁב	יוֹשֵׁב	יוּשַׁב	יִירַשׁ	יִיטַב	יֵיטֵב
With Vav-Consecutive	וַיֵּשֶׁב	וַיִּוָּשֵׁב	וַיּוֹשֶׁב	וַיּוּשַׁב	וַיִּירַשׁ	וַיִּיטַב	וַיֵּיטֶב

Imperative		Qal	Niph'al	Hiph'îl	Hoph'al	Qal	Hiph'îl
SG.	2M	שֵׁב	הִוָּשֵׁב	הוֹשֵׁב			הֵיטֵב
	2F	שְׁבִי	הִוָּשְׁבִי	הוֹשִׁיבִי			הֵיטִיבִי
PL.	2M	שְׁבוּ	הִוָּשְׁבוּ	הוֹשִׁיבוּ			הֵיטִיבוּ
	2F	שֵׁבְנָה	הִוָּשַׁבְנָה	הוֹשֵׁבְנָה			הֵיטֵבְנָה

Participle		Qal	Niph'al	Hiph'îl	Hoph'al	Qal	Hiph'îl
ACT	MS	יֹשֵׁב		מוֹשִׁיב		יֹטֵב	מֵיטִיב
	MP	יֹשְׁבִים		מוֹשִׁיבִים		יֹטְבִים	מֵיטִיבִים
	FS	יֹשְׁבָה יֹשֶׁבֶת		מוֹשִׁיבָה		יֹטְבָה	מֵיטִיבָה
	FP	יֹשְׁבוֹת		מוֹשִׁיבוֹת		יֹטְבוֹת	מֵיטִיבוֹת
PASS	MS	יָשׁוּב			מוּשָׁב	יָטוּב	
	MP	יְשׁוּבִים			מוּשָׁבִים	יְטוּבִים	
	FS	יְשׁוּבָה			מוּשָׁבָה	יְטוּבָה	
	FP	יְשׁוּבוֹת			מוּשָׁבוֹת	יְטוּבוֹת	
REFL	MS		נוֹשָׁב				
	MP		נוֹשָׁבִים				
	FS		נוֹשָׁבָה				
	FP		נוֹשָׁבוֹת				

Infinitive	Qal	Niph'al	Hiph'îl	Hoph'al	Qal	Hiph'îl
ABSOLUTE	יָשׁוֹב		הוֹשֵׁב		יָטוֹב	הֵיטֵב
CONSTRUCT	שֶׁבֶת	הִוָּשֵׁב	הוֹשִׁיב	הוּשַׁב	יְטֹב	הֵיטִיב

R₂-YOD/VAV VERB

		R₂-VAV						R₂-YOD
Perfect		Qal	Niph'al	Hiph'îl	Hoph'al	*Pô'ēl*	*Pô'al*	Qal
SG.	1C	קַ֫מְתִּי	נְקוּמ֫וֹתִי	הֲקִימ֫וֹתִי	הוּקַ֫מְתִּי	קוֹמַ֫מְתִּי	קוֹמַ֫מְתִּי	בַּ֫נְתִּי
	2M	קַ֫מְתָּ	נְקוּמ֫וֹתָ	הֲקִימ֫וֹתָ	הוּקַ֫מְתָּ	קוֹמַ֫מְתָּ	קוֹמַ֫מְתָּ	בַּ֫נְתָּ
	2F	קַמְתְּ	נְקוּמוֹת	הֲקִימוֹת	הוּקַמְתְּ	קוֹמַמְתְּ	קוֹמַמְתְּ	בַּנְתְּ
	3M	קָם	נָקוֹם	הֵקִים	הוּקַם	קוֹמֵם	קוֹמַם	בָּן
	3F	קָ֫מָה	נָ֫קוֹמָה	הֵקִ֫ימָה	הוּקְמָה	קוֹמֲמָה	קוֹמֲמָה	בָּ֫נָה
PL.	1C	קַ֫מְנוּ	נְקוּמ֫וֹנוּ	הֲקִימ֫וֹנוּ	הוּקַ֫מְנוּ	קוֹמַ֫מְנוּ	קוֹמַ֫מְנוּ	בַּ֫נּוּ
	2M	קַמְתֶּם	נְקֹמוֹתֶם	הֲקִימוֹתֶם	הוּקַמְתֶּם	קוֹמַמְתֶּם	קוֹמַמְתֶּם	בַּנְתֶּם
	2F	קַמְתֶּן	נְקֹמוֹתֶן	הֲקִימוֹתֶן	הוּקַמְתֶּן	קוֹמַמְתֶּן	קוֹמַמְתֶּן	בַּנְתֶּן
	3C	קָ֫מוּ	נָ֫קוֹמוּ	הֵקִ֫ימוּ	הוּקְמוּ	קוֹמֲמוּ	קוֹמֲמוּ	בָּ֫נוּ

Imperfect		Qal	Niph'al	Hiph'îl	Hoph'al	*Pô'ēl*	*Pô'al*	Qal
SG.	1C	אָקוּם	אֵקוֹם	אָקִים	אוּקַם	אֲקוֹמֵם	אֲקוֹמַם	אָגִיל
	2M	תָּקוּם	תִּקּוֹם	תָּקִים	תּוּקַם	תְּקוֹמֵם	תְּקוֹמַם	תָּגִיל
	2F	תָּק֫וּמִי	תִּקּ֫וֹמִי	תָּקִ֫ימִי	תּוּקְמִי	תְּקוֹמֲמִי	תְּקוֹמֲמִי	תָּגִ֫ילִי
	3M	יָקוּם	יִקּוֹם	יָקִים	יוּקַם	יְקוֹמֵם	יְקוֹמַם	יָגִיל
	3F	תָּקוּם	תִּקּוֹם	תָּקִים	תּוּקַם	תְּקוֹמֵם	תְּקוֹמַם	תָּגִיל
PL.	1C	נָקוּם	נִקּוֹם	נָקִים	נוּקַם	נְקוֹמֵם	נְקוֹמַם	נָגִיל
	2M	תָּק֫וּמוּ	תִּקּ֫וֹמוּ	תָּקִ֫ימוּ	תּוּקְמוּ	תְּקוֹמֲמוּ	תְּקוֹמֲמוּ	תָּגִ֫ילוּ
	2F	תְּקוּמֶ֫ינָה		תָּקֵ֫מְנָה	תּוּקַ֫מְנָה	תְּקוֹמֵ֫מְנָה	תְּקוֹמַ֫מְנָה	תָּגֵ֫לְנָה
	3M	יָק֫וּמוּ	יִקּ֫וֹמוּ	יָקִ֫ימוּ	יוּקְמוּ	יְקוֹמֲמוּ	יְקוֹמֲמוּ	יָגִ֫ילוּ
	3F	תְּקוּמֶ֫ינָה		תְּקִימֶ֫ינָה תָּקֵ֫מְנָה	תּוּקַ֫מְנָה	תְּקוֹמֵ֫מְנָה	תְּקוֹמַ֫מְנָה	תָּגֵ֫לְנָה

	Qal	Niph'al	Hiph'îl	Hoph'al	*Pô'ēl*	*Pô'al*	Qal
Cohortative	אָק֫וּמָה	אֶקּ֫וֹמָה	אָקִ֫ימָה	אוּקְמָה	אֲקוֹמֲמָה	אֲקוֹמֲמָה	אָגִ֫ילָה
Jussive	יָקֹם	יִקּוֹם	יָקֵם	יוּקַם	יְקוֹמֵם	יְקוֹמַם	יָגֵל
With Vav-Consecutive	וַיָּ֫קָם	וַיִּקּוֹם	וַיָּ֫קֶם	וַיּוּקַם	יְקוֹמֵם	יְקוֹמַם	וַיָּ֫גֶל

Imperative		Qal	Niph‘al	Hiph‘îl	Hoph‘al	*Pô‘ēl*	*Pô‘al*	Qal
SG.	2M	קוּם	הִקּוֹם	הָקֵם		קוֹמֵם		בִּין
	2F	קוּמִי	הִקּוֹמִי	הָקִימִי		קוֹמֲמִי		בִּינִי
PL.	2M	קוּמוּ	הִקּוֹמוּ	הָקִימוּ		קוֹמֲמוּ		בִּינוּ
	2F	קֹמְנָה		הָקֵמְנָה		קוֹמֵמְנָה		

Participle		Qal	Niph‘al	Hiph‘îl	Hoph‘al	*Pô‘ēl*	*Pô‘al*	Qal
ACT	MS	קָם		מֵקִים		מְקוֹמֵם		בָּן
	MP	קָמִים		מְקִימִים				בָּנִים
	FS	קָמָה		מְקִימָה				בָּנָה
	FP	קָמוֹת		מְקִימוֹת				בָּנוֹת
PASS	MS	קוּם			מוּקָם		מְקוֹמָם	
	MP	קוּמִים			מוּקָמִים			
	FS	קוּמָה			מוּקָמָה			
	FP	קוּמוֹת			מוּקָמוֹת			
REFL	MS		נָקוֹם					
	MP		נְקוֹמִים					
	FS		נְקוֹמָה					
	FP		נְקוֹמוֹת					

Infinitive	Qal	Niph‘al	Hiph‘îl	Hoph‘al	*Pô‘ēl*	*Pô‘al*	Qal
ABSOLUTE	קוֹם	הִקּוֹם	הָקֵם				בּוֹן
CONSTRUCT	קוּם	הִקּוֹם	הָקִים	הוּקַם	קוֹמֵם		בִּין

R$_3$-HE (YOD/VAV) VERB

Perfect		Qal	Niph'al	Pi"ēl	Pu"al	Hithpa"ēl	Hiph'îl	Hoph'al
SG.	1C	גָּלִ֫יתִי	נִגְלֵ֫יתִי	גִּלִּ֫יתִי	גֻּלֵּ֫יתִי	הִתְגַּלֵּ֫יתִי	הִגְלֵ֫יתִי	הָגְלֵ֫יתִי
	2M	גָּלִ֫יתָ	נִגְלֵ֫יתָ	גִּלִּ֫יתָ	גֻּלֵּ֫יתָ	הִתְגַּלִּ֫יתָ	הִגְלִ֫יתָ	הָגְלִ֫יתָ
	2F	גָּלִית	נִגְלֵית	גִּלִּית	גֻּלֵּית	הִתְגַּלִּית	הִגְלִית	הָגְלֵית
	3M	גָּלָה	נִגְלָה	גִּלָּה	גֻּלָּה	הִתְגַּלָּה	הִגְלָה	הָגְלָה
	3F	גָּֽלְתָה	נִגְלְתָה	גִּלְּתָה	גֻּלְּתָה	הִתְגַּלְּתָה	הִגְלְתָה	הָגְלְתָה
PL.	1C	גָּלִ֫ינוּ	נִגְלִ֫ינוּ	גִּלִּ֫ינוּ	גֻּלֵּ֫ינוּ	הִתְגַּלִּ֫ינוּ	הִגְלִ֫ינוּ	הָגְלִ֫ינוּ
	2M	גְּלִיתֶם	נִגְלֵיתֶם	גִּלִּיתֶם	גֻּלֵּיתֶם	הִתְגַּלִּיתֶם	הִגְלֵיתֶם	הָגְלֵיתֶם
	2F	גְּלִיתֶן	נִגְלֵיתֶן	גִּלִּיתֶן	גֻּלֵּיתֶן	הִתְגַּלִּיתֶן	הִגְלֵיתֶן	הָגְלֵיתֶן
	3C	גָּלוּ	נִגְלוּ	גִּלּוּ	גֻּלּוּ	הִתְגַּלּוּ	הִגְלוּ	הָגְלוּ

Imperfect		Qal	Niph'al	Pi"ēl	Pu"al	Hithpa"ēl	Hiph'îl	Hoph'al
SG.	1C	אֶגְלֶה	אֶגָּלֶה	אֲגַלֶּה	אֲגֻלֶּה	אֶתְגַּלֶּה	אַגְלֶה	אָגְלֶה
	2M	תִּגְלֶה	תִּגָּלֶה	תְּגַלֶּה	תְּגֻלֶּה	תִּתְגַּלֶּה	תַּגְלֶה	תָּגְלֶה
	2F	תִּגְלִי	תִּגָּלִי	תְּגַלִּי	תְּגֻלִּי	תִּתְגַּלִּי	תַּגְלִי	תָּגְלִי
	3M	יִגְלֶה	יִגָּלֶה	יְגַלֶּה	יְגֻלֶּה	יִתְגַּלֶּה	יַגְלֶה	יָגְלֶה
	3F	תִּגְלֶה	תִּגָּלֶה	תְּגַלֶּה	תְּגֻלֶּה	תִּתְגַּלֶּה	תַּגְלֶה	תָּגְלֶה
PL.	1C	נִגְלֶה	נִגָּלֶה	נְגַלֶּה	נְגֻלֶּה	נִתְגַּלֶּה	נַגְלֶה	נָגְלֶה
	2M	תִּגְלוּ	תִּגָּלוּ	תְּגַלּוּ	תְּגֻלּוּ	תִּתְגַּלּוּ	תַּגְלוּ	תָּגְלוּ
	2F	תִּגְלֶ֫ינָה	תִּגָּלֶ֫ינָה	תְּגַלֶּ֫ינָה	תְּגֻלֶּ֫ינָה	תִּתְגַּלֶּ֫ינָה	תַּגְלֶ֫ינָה	תָּגְלֶ֫ינָה
	3M	יִגְלוּ	יִגָּלוּ	יְגַלּוּ	יְגֻלּוּ	יִתְגַּלּוּ	יַגְלוּ	יָגְלוּ
	3F	תִּגְלֶ֫ינָה	תִּגָּלֶ֫ינָה	תְּגַלֶּ֫ינָה	תְּגֻלֶּ֫ינָה	תִּתְגַּלֶּ֫ינָה	תַּגְלֶ֫ינָה	תָּגְלֶ֫ינָה

	Qal	Niph'al	Pi"ēl	Pu"al	Hithpa"ēl	Hiph'îl	Hoph'al
Cohortative							
Jussive	יִ֫גֶל/יִגְל יֶ֫גֶל/יִגֶל	יִגָּל	יְגַל	יְגֻל	יִתְגַּל	יֶ֫גֶל/יַגְל	
With VAV-Consecutive	וַיִּ֫גֶל	וַיִּגָּל	וַיְגַל	וַיְגֻל	וַיִּתְגַּל	וַיֶּ֫גֶל	

Imperative		Qal	Niph‘al	Pi“ēl	Pu“al	Hithpa“ēl	Hiph‘îl	Hoph‘al
SG.	2M	גְּלֵה	הִגָּלֵה	גַּל גַּלֵּה		הִתְגַּל הִתְגַּלֵּה	הַגְלֵה	
	2F	גְּלִי	הִגָּלִי	גַּלִּי		הִתְגַּלִּי	הַגְלִי	
PL.	2M	גְּלוּ	הִגָּלוּ	גַּלּוּ		הִתְגַּלּוּ	הַגְלוּ	
	2F	גְּלֶינָה	הִגָּלֶינָה	גַּלֶּינָה		הִתְגַּלֶּינָה	הַגְלֶינָה	

Participle		Qal	Niph‘al	Pi“ēl	Pu“al	Hithpa“ēl	Hiph‘îl	Hoph‘al
ACT	MS	גֹּלֶה		מְגַלֶּה			מַגְלֶה	
	MP	גֹּלִים		מְגַלִּים			מַגְלִים	
	FS	גֹּלָה גֹּלֵית		מְגַלָּה			מַגְלָה	
	FP	גֹּלוֹת		מְגַלּוֹת			מַגְלוֹת	
PASS	MS	גָּלוּי		מְגֻלֶּה				מָגְלֶה
	MP	גְּלוּיִם		מְגֻלִּים				מָגְלָה
	FS	גְּלוּיָה		מְגֻלָּה				מֻגְלִים
	FP	גְּלוּיוֹת		מְגֻלּוֹת				מָגְלוֹת
REFL	MS		נִגְלֶה			מִתְגַּלֶּה		
	MP		נִגְלִים			מִתְגַּלִּים		
	FS		נִגְלָה			מִתְגַּלָּה		
	FP		נִגְלוֹת			מִתְגַּלּוֹת		

Infinitive	Qal	Niph‘al	Pi“ēl	Pu“al	Hithpa“ēl	Hiph‘îl	Hoph‘al
ABSOLUTE	גָּלֹה	נִגְלֹה	גַּלֹּה גַּלֵּה		הִתְגַּלּוֹת	הַגְלֵה	הָגְלֵה
CONSTRUCT	גְּלוֹת	הִגָּלוֹת	גַּלּוֹת	גֻּלּוֹת	הִתְגַּלּוֹת	הַגְלוֹת	

היה Verb

Perfect		Qal	Niph'al	Pi"ēl	Pu"al	Hithpa"ēl	Hiph'îl	Hoph'al
SG.	1C	הָיִיתִי						
	2M	הָיִיתָ						
	2F							
	3M	הָיָה						
	3F	הָיְתָה						
PL.	1C	הָיִינוּ						
	2M	הֱיִיתֶם						
	2F							
	3C	הָיוּ						

Imperfect		Qal	Niph'al	Pi"ēl	Pu"al	Hithpa"ēl	Hiph'îl	Hoph'al
SG.	1C	אֶהְיֶה						
	2M	תִּהְיֶה						
	2F							
	3M	יִהְיֶה						
	3F	תִּהְיֶה						
PL.	1C	נִהְיֶה						
	2M	תִּהְיוּ						
	2F	תִּהְיֶינָה						
	3M	יִהְיוּ						
	3F	תִּהְיֶינָה						

	Qal	Niph'al	Pi"ēl	Pu"al	Hithpa"ēl	Hiph'îl	Hoph'al
Cohortative							
Jussive	יְהִי						
With Vav-Consecutive	וַיְהִי						

Imperative		Qal	Niph'al	Pi"ēl	Pu"al	Hithpa"ēl	Hiph'îl	Hoph'al
SG.	2M	הֱיֵה						
	2F	הֲיִי						
PL.	2M	הֱיוּ						
	2F	הֱיֶינָה						

Participle		Qal	Niph'al	Pi"ēl	Pu"al	Hithpa"ēl	Hiph'îl	Hoph'al
ACT	MS	הוֹיֶה						
	MP	הוֹיִים						
	FS	הוֹיָה						
	FP	הוֹיוֹת						
PASS	MS	הָיוּי						
	MP	הֱיוּיִם						
	FS	הֱיוּיָה						
	FP	הֱיוּיוֹת						
REFL	MS							
	MP							
	FS							
	FP							

Infinitive	Qal	Niph'al	Pi"ēl	Pu"al	Hithpa"ēl	Hiph'îl	Hoph'al
ABSOLUTE	הָיוֹ						
CONSTRUCT	הֱיוֹת						

Geminate Verbs

Perfect		Qal	Niph'al	Hiph'îl	Hoph'al	*Pô'lēl*	*Pô'lal*
SG.	1C	סַבּ֫וֹתִי	נְסַבּ֫וֹתִי	הֲסִבּ֫וֹתִי	הוּסַבּ֫וֹתִי	סוֹבַ֫בְתִּי	סוֹבַ֫בְתִּי
	2M	סַבּ֫וֹתָ	נְסַבּ֫וֹתָ	הֲסִבּ֫וֹתָ	הוּסַבּ֫וֹתָ	סוֹבַ֫בְתָּ	סוֹבַ֫בְתָּ
	2F	סַבּוֹת	נְסַבּוֹת	הֲסִבּוֹת	הוּסַבּוֹת	סוֹבַבְתְּ	סוֹבַבְתְּ
	3M	סַב / סָבַב	נָסַב	הֵסֵב/הֵסַב	הוּסַב	סוֹבֵב	סוֹבַב
	3F	סַ֫בָּה / סָֽבְבָה	נָ֫סַבָּה	הֵ֫סֵבָּה	הוּ֫סַבָּה	סוֹבְבָה	סוֹבְבָה
PL.	1C	סַבּ֫וֹנוּ	נְסַבּ֫וֹנוּ	הֲסִבּ֫וֹנוּ	הוּסַבּ֫וֹנוּ	סוֹבַ֫בְנוּ	סוֹבַ֫בְנוּ
	2M	סַבּוֹתֶם	נְסַבּוֹתֶם	הֲסִבּוֹתֶם	הוּסַבּוֹתֶם	סוֹבַבְתֶּם	סוֹבַבְתֶּם
	2F	סַבּוֹתֶן	נְסַבּוֹתֶן	הֲסִבּוֹתֶן	הוּסַבּוֹתֶן	סוֹבַבְתֶּן	סוֹבַבְתֶּן
	3C	סַ֫בּוּ / סָֽבְבוּ	נָ֫סַבּוּ	הֵ֫סֵבּוּ	הוּ֫סַבּוּ	סוֹבְבוּ	סוֹבְבוּ

Imperfect		Qal		Niph'al	Hiph'îl	Hoph'al	*Pô'lēl*	*Pô'lal*
SG.	1C	אָסֹב	אֶסֹּב	אֶסַּב	אָסֵב	אוּסַב	אֲסוֹבֵב	אֲסוֹבַב
	2M	תָּסֹב	תִּסֹּב	תִּסַּב	תָּסֵב	תּוּסַב	תְּסוֹבֵב	תְּסוֹבַב
	2F	תָּסֹ֫בִּי	תִּסְּבִי	תִּסַּ֫בִּי	תָּסֵ֫בִּי	תּוּסַ֫בִּי	תְּסוֹבְבִי	תְּסוֹבְבִי
	3M	יָסֹב	יִסֹּב	יִסַּב	יָסֵב/יַסֵּב	יוּסַב	יְסוֹבֵב	יְסוֹבַב
	3F	תָּסֹב	תִּסֹּב	תִּסַּב	תָּסֵב	תּוּסַב	תְּסוֹבֵב	תְּסוֹבַב
PL.	1C	נָסֹב	נִסֹּב	נִסַּב	נָסֵב	נוּסַב	נְסוֹבֵב	נְסוֹבַב
	2M	תָּסֹ֫בּוּ	תִּסְּבוּ	תִּסַּ֫בּוּ	תָּסֵ֫בּוּ	תּוּסַ֫בּוּ	תְּסוֹבְבוּ	תְּסוֹבְבוּ
	2F	תְּסֻבֶּ֫ינָה	תִּסֹּ֫בְנָה	תִּסַּבֶּ֫ינָה	תְּסִבֶּ֫ינָה	תּוּסַבֶּ֫ינָה	תְּסוֹבֵ֫בְנָה	תְּסוֹבַ֫בְנָה
	3M	יָסֹ֫בּוּ	יִסְּבוּ	יִסַּ֫בּוּ	יָסֵ֫בּוּ/יַסֵּ֫בּוּ	יוּסַ֫בּוּ	יְסוֹבְבוּ	יְסוֹבְבוּ
	3F	תְּסֻבֶּ֫ינָה	תִּסֹּ֫בְנָה	תִּסַּבֶּ֫ינָה	תְּסִבֶּ֫ינָה	תּוּסַבֶּ֫ינָה	תְּסוֹבֵ֫בְנָה	תְּסוֹבַ֫בְנָה

	Qal		Niph'al	Hiph'îl	Hoph'al	*Pô'lēl*	*Pô'lal*
Cohortative	אָסֹ֫בָּה	אֶסְּבָה					
Jussive	יָסֹב	יִסֹּב	יִסַּב	יָסֵב/יַסֵּב	יוּסַב/יֻסַּב	יְסוֹבֵב	יְסוֹבַב
With Vav-Consecutive	וַיָּ֫סָב	וַיִּסֹּב	וַיִּסַּב	וַיָּ֫סֶב			

Imperative		Qal	Niph'al	Hiph'îl	Hoph'al	*Pô'lēl*	*Pô'lal*
SG.	2M	סֹב	הִסַּב	הָסֵב		סוֹבֵב	
	2F	סֹ֫בִּי	הִסַּ֫בִּי	הָסֵ֫בִּי		סוֹבֲבִי	
PL.	2M	סֹ֫בּוּ	הִסַּ֫בּוּ	הָסֵ֫בּוּ		סוֹבֲבוּ	
	2F	סֻבֶּ֫ינָה	הִסַּבֶּ֫ינָה	הֲסִבֶּ֫ינָה		סוֹבֵ֫בְנָה	

Participle		Qal	Niph'al	Hiph'îl	Hoph'al	*Pô'lēl*	*Pô'lal*
ACT	MS	סֹבֵב		מֵסֵב		מְסוֹבֵב	
	MP	סֹבְבִים		מְסִבִּים			
	FS	סֹבְבָה		מְסִבָּה			
	FP	סֹבְבוֹת		מְסִבּוֹת			
PASS	MS	סָבוּב			מוּסָב		
	MP	סְבוּבִים			מוּסַבִּים		מְסוֹבָב
	FS	סְבוּבָה			מוּסַבָּה		
	FP	סְבוּבוֹת			מוּסַבּוֹת		
REFL	MS		נָסָב				
	MP		נְסַבִּים				
	FS		נְסַבָּה				
	FP		נְסַבּוֹת				

Infinitive	Qal	Niph'al	Hiph'îl	Hoph'al	*Pô'lēl*	*Pô'lal*
ABSOLUTE	סָבוֹב	הִסּוֹב	הָסֵב		סוֹבֵב	סוֹבַב
CONSTRUCT	סֹב	הִסֵּב	הָסֵב		סוֹבֵב	

INVITATION TO BIBLICAL HEBREW
HEBREW-ENGLISH VOCABULARY LIST

Numbers in parenthesis refer to chapter number in this grammar.

א

אָב	father (3)
אבד	Qal: perish, die, vanish Pi"ēl: make perish (destroy), make die (kill), make vanish (24)
אבה	to be willing, to consent (30)
אֲבִימֶ֫לֶךְ	Abimelek (14)
אֶ֫בֶן (*a*)	(f) stone (22)
אַבְנֵר	Abner (24)
אַבְרָהָם	Abraham (6)
אַבְשָׁלוֹם	Absalom (14)
אֱדוֹם	Edom (22)
אָדָם	man, Adam (4)
אֲדָמָה	land, ground (8)
אֲדֹנָי	Lord, lord, master (3)
אָהֵב, אָהַב	he loves, loved (21)
אֹ֫הֶל (*o*)	tent (19)
אַהֲרֹן	Aaron (6)
אוֹ	or (19)
אוֹיֵב	(participle) enemy (20)
אוֹר	light (9)
אָז	(adv.) then, at that time (10)
אֹ֫זֶן (*o*)	ear (24)
אָח	brother (13)
אַחְאָב	Ahab (15)
אָחוֹת	sister (13)
אחז	Qal: grasp, take hold of (frequently with ב or accusative) (30)
אַחֵר	(adj.) another, other (plural, אֲחֵרִים) (11)
אחר, אַחֲרֵי	(prep.) after, behind (6)
אַ֫יִל	ram (30)
אַיִן	there is no/not (literally: "non-existence of," from אַ֫יִן) (19)
אִישׁ	man (3)
אַךְ	only, surely, but (30)
אֹ֫כֶל (*o*), אָכְלָה	food (26)
אָכַל	(he) ate (5)
אַל	no, not (18)
אֶל־	(prep.) unto, toward, to (2)
אֵ֫לֶּה	these (c= common, masculine and feminine) (10)
אֱלֹהִים	God (3)
אֵלִיָּהוּ	Elijah (12)
אֱלִישָׁע	Elisha (32)
אֶ֫לֶף (*a*)	thousand, tribe(?), clan(?) (38)
אֵם	mother (13)
אִם	if (19)
אָמַר	(he) said (2)
אָמָה	(with 1cs suffix אֲמָהתִי) female slave, handmaid (38)
אמן	Niph'al: make firm, sure, establish Hiph'îl: trust, believe (sometimes with ב, believe in) (29)
אֱמֶת	truth (with 3ms suffix אֲמִתּוֹ, root אמן) (13)
אֲנַ֫חְנוּ	we (17)
אָנֹכִי/אֲנִי	I (17)
אֲנָשִׁים	men (3)
אסף	Qal: gather, collect Niph'al: passive of Qal (29)
אסר	Qal: bind, tie, imprison Niph'al: passive of Qal (29)
אַף	also, even (11)
אַף	nose, anger (31)
אפה	to bake (30)
אֲרוֹן	(with article הָאָרוֹן) ark, chest (22)

אֶ֫רֶז (*a*)	cedar (23)
אֲרָם	Aram (26)
אֶ֫רֶץ (*a*)	(with article הָאָ֫רֶץ) (f) earth, land (7)
ארר	Qal: curse (38)
אֵשׁ	(f) fire (18)
אִשֶּׁה	(construct singular אִשֵּׁה, construct plural אִשֵּׁי) offering by fire, fire offering (34)
אִשָּׁה	woman (4)
אַשּׁוּר	Assyria (18)
אֲשֶׁר	(relative pronoun) who, which, that, that which (3)
אַשְׁרֵי	happy, blessed (16)
אֵת	(prep.) with (2)
אֵת	direct object marker (7)
אַתְּ	you (f) (17)
אַתָּה	you (m) (17)
אַתֶּם	you (m) (17)
אַתֵּן	you (f) (17)

ב

בָּא	(he) came (4)
בָּבֶל	Babylon (24)
בֶּ֫גֶד (*i*)	garment (20)
בְּהֵמָה	large animal, cattle, crocodile(?) (19)
בּוֹר	pit (28)
בָּחַר בְּ	(he) chose (11)
בָּטַח	(he) trusts, trusted (12)
בֶּ֫טֶן (*i*)	womb (24)
בֵּין	(prep.) between (8)
בַּ֫יִת	house (5)
בֵּית־אֵל	Bethel (16)
בֵּית לֶ֫חֶם	Bethlehem (22)
בָּכָה	(he) wept (13)
בְּכוֹר	firstborn (36)
בלע	Qal: swallow, engulf Pi"ēl: swallow up, confound, destroy (32)
בֵּן	son (4)
בָּנָה	(he) built (8)
בַּ֫עַד (*a*)	(construct בְּעַד, separation) away from, behind, through, about, on behalf of (37)
בַּ֫עַל	owner, lord, Baal (21)
בער	Qal: burn, consume Pi"ēl: make burn (kindle), consume, destroy Pu"al: passive of Pi"ēl Hiph'îl: cause to burn (kindle), burn up, destroy (31)
בקע	Qal: split, break open or through Niph'al: passive of Qal Pi"ēl: split into pieces (32)
בֹּ֫קֶר (*a*)	morning (15)
בָּקָר	cattle (14)
בקשׁ	Pi"ēl: seek (23)
ברח	fled (19)
בְּרִית	covenant (13)
ברך	Qal: bless Pi"ēl: bless, pronounce a blessing on (29)
בְּרָכָה	blessing (20)
בָּשָׂר	flesh (7)
בַּת	daughter (13)
בְּתוֹךְ	(preposition) in the midst of (19)
בְּתוּלָה	virgin (36)
בַּת־שֶׁ֫בַע	Bathsheba (35)

ג

גאל	Qal: redeem, act as a kinsman redeemer Niph'al: reflexive and passive of Qal (31)
גְּבוּל	boundary, territory (26)
גִּבּוֹר	warrior, mighty man (28)
גָּדוֹל	(adj.) great (10)

גדל	(A/A) be (become) great, mature, strong (21) Qal: be great Pi"ēl: make great, magnify (23)
גּוֹי	people, nation (6)
גור	Qal: sojourn, journey, dwell for a time (37)
גִּלְבֹּעַ	Gilboa (36)
גלה	Qal: uncover (with אֹזֶן uncover the ear = reveal) Niph'al: reflexive and passive of the Qal: uncover oneself Pi"ēl: uncover, reveal Hiph'îl: cause to depart, take into exile (37)
גַּם	(adv. conj.) also, indeed, moreover (4)
גַּן	(with article הַגָּן) garden (7)
גֶּפֶן (*a*)	vine (27)

ד

דבק	Qal: cling, stick to, cleave Hiph'îl: cause to cling, stick to (36)
דִּבֶּר	(he) spoke (4)
דָּבָר	word, matter, thing (4)
דָּוִד	David (4)
דּוֹר	(pl. דּוֹרוֹת) generation (30)
דָּם	blood (18)
דָּמִים	bloodshed (plural of דָּם), murder (18)
דַּעַת (*a*)	knowledge (16)
דֶּרֶךְ (*a*)	way, road (15)
דרשׁ	Qal: seek (23)

ה

הָהֵמָּה, הָהֵם	those (m) (10)
הָהֵנָּה, הָהֵן	those (f) (10)
הַהוּא	that (m) (10)
הַהִיא	that (f) (10)
הוּא	(pronoun) he (2, 17)
הִיא	she (17)
הָיָה	(verb) (it, he) came to be, became, happened, has happened, was, were (2)
הֵיכָל	temple, palace (7)
הָלַךְ	(he) went, walked, has gone (2)
הלל	Qal: boast Pi"ēl: praise Hithpa"ēl: boast oneself, boast in (בְּ) (23)
הֵם/הֵמָּה	they (m) (12, 17)
הֵן/הֵנָּה	they (f) (17)
הִנֵּה	(particle) look, see, behold (5)
הפך	Qal: turn, turn over, overthrow Niph'al: reflexive of Qal (30)
הַר	(with article הָהָר) mountain (7)
הָרַג	(he) killed (13)

ו

...וְ	and, but, even, now (8)
וְהָיָה	And he (it) will be (20)
וְהָיוּ	And they will be (20)
וַיְהִי	And he (it) was (sg.) (20)
וַיִּהְיוּ	And they were (pl.) (20)

ז

זֹאת	this (f) (10)
זָבַח	(he) slaughtered, sacrificed (8)
זֶבַח (*i*)	sacrifice (8)
זֶה	this (m) (10)
זָהָב	gold (8)
זָכַר	(he) remembered (12)
זָכָר	male, man (34)
זעק	cry out (20)
זָקֵן	(adj.) old, elder (11)
זָקֵן	(A-e/A) be old (21)
זְרוֹעַ	arm (31)
זֶרַע (*a*)	seed, offspring (27)

זרע	Qal: sow, scatter seed Niph'al: be sown, be fruitful (32)

ח

חדל	Qal: cease, come to an end, desist, fail (35)
חוֹמָה	city wall (13)
חוּץ	(noun) the outside, street (30)
חָזָק	(adj.) strong, hard, mighty (31)
חזק	Qal: be strong, be firm, prevail Pi"ēl: put in a strong state, make strong Hiph'îl: cause to be strong, seize, take hold (with בּ) (29)
חִזְקִיָּהוּ	Hezekiah (18)
חָטָא	(he) sinned (missed the mark) (15)
חַטָּאת	(f) sin, sin-offering (16)
חָיָה	Qal: live, have life Pi"ēl: preserve alive, revive Hiph'îl: cause to be alive (preserve alive), revive (37)
חַיִּים	life (always in the plural) (15)
חַיִל	strength, mighty man, ability, army, wealth (29)
חָכָם	(adj.) wise (10)
חָכְמָה	wisdom (12)
חָלָל	slain, pierced, fatally wounded (36)
חֵמָה	heat, wrath, anger (31) חָרָה אַפִּי בּ – my nose became hot, i.e., I became angry with (12)
חֲמוֹר	(male) donkey (27)
חָמָס	violence, wrong (33)
חנן	Qal: favor, be gracious to Niph'al: be pitied Hithpa"ēl: seek favor (38)
חֶסֶד (*a*)	loyalty, lovingkindness, steadfast love (16)
חָפֵץ	Qal: delight in, take pleasure (with בּ) (29)
חָצֵר	settlement, enclosure (29)
חֹק	(pl. חֻקִּים) statute, law, rule (15)
חֶרֶב (*a*)	(f) sword (16)
חָרָה	be hot, angry (12)
חרם	Hiph'îl: devote to the ban, exterminate, destroy Hoph'al: passive of Hiph'îl (29)
חֶרְפָּה	reproach, disgrace (27)
חשׁב	Qal: think, account, plan, reckon, impute Niph'al: passive of Qal Pi"ēl: think upon, plan, derive, reckon (29)
חֹשֶׁךְ (*o*)	darkness (9)
חתת	Qal: be shattered, broken, be dismayed Hiph'îl: shatter, terrify (38)

ט

טָהוֹר	clean (adj.) (26)
טָהֵר	Qal: be clean (ceremonially or morally) Pi"ēl: put in a clean state, cleanse, purify Hithpa"ēl: reflexive of Pi"ēl (31)
טוֹב	(adj.) good (10)
טוּב	good thing(s), goodness (18)
טמא	Qal: be (or become) unclean, defiled Niph'al: defile oneself, be defiled Pi"ēl: put in an unclean state, defile, pronounce unclean

	Hithpa“ēl: put oneself in an unclean state, defile oneself (33)

י

יָד	(f) hand (3)
יָדַע	(he) knew, knows (4)
יָהּ	shortened form of יהוה (23)
יֵהוּא	Jehu (32)
יְהוּדָה	Judah (5)
יהוה	Lord, the Divine name; Yahweh (5)
יְהוֹנָתָן	Jonathan (18)
יְהוֹשֻׁעַ	Joshua (9)
יוֹאָב	Joab (14)
יוֹם	day (2)
יוֹסֵף	Joseph (8)
יַחְדָּו	all together, together (23)
יטב	Qal: be good, be pleasing Hiph‘îl: do good (to), deal well (with), do thoroughly (35)
יַ֫יִן (*e*)	wine (13)
יכח	Hiph‘îl: decide, judge, reprove, correct, convict (35)
יָכֹל (O/A)	Qal: be able, have power, prevail, endure (35)
יָלַד	bear a child (22)
יָם	sea (2)
יָמִין	the right, right hand, right side, south (32)
(ו)יסד	Qal: establish, found Niph‘al: passive, reflexive of the Qal Pi“ēl: establish, found Pu“al: passive of Pi“ēl (34)
יסף	Qal: add Niph‘al: be added, joined Hiph‘îl: add (יסף means “again” or “more” when followed by an infinitive or another verb – וַיֹּ֫סֶף ... וַיִּקַּח And he added and took = he took again) (35)
יעץ (י)	Qal: advise, counsel Niph‘al: consult together, exchange counsel (35)
יַעֲקֹב	Jacob (28)
יָצָא	(he) went out (5)
יצב	Hithpa“ēl (only): station oneself, take one’s stand (24)
יִצְחָק	Isaac (13)
יצר	Qal: form, fashion, plan, foreordain (participle: one who forms, a potter) Niph‘al: passive of Qal (35)
יָרֵא	(he) feared (14)
יִרְאָה	fear (20)
יָרַד	(he) went down (8)
יַרְדֵּן	Jordan (also written with the article הַיַּרְדֵּן) (8)
יְרוּשָׁלַ֫יִם	Jerusalem (5)
יִרְמְיָה, יִרְמְיָ֫הוּ	Jeremiah (22)
ירשׁ	Qal: take possession of, inherit, dispossess Hiph‘îl: cause to possess or inherit, cause to dispossess (35)
יִשְׂרָאֵל	Israel (3)
יֵשׁ	there is, there are (16)
יָשַׁב	(he) sat, dwelled (3)
יְשׁוּעָה	salvation (22)
יִשַׁי	Jesse (26)
יֵ֫שַׁע (*i*)	salvation, deliverance (34)
ישׁע	Niph‘al: be freed, saved Hiph‘îl: free, save, deliver, liberate (35)
יָשָׁר	(adj.) straight, right (10)
יֶ֫תֶר (*i*)	remainder, the rest (20)

כ

כַּאֲשֶׁר	(conjunction) as (5)

כָּבֵד	(adj.) heavy, severe (12)
כָּבֵד	(A-e/A) be heavy (21)
כָּבוֹד	(noun) glory, riches (12)
כבס	Pi"ēl: wash clothes (by treading); poetically – wash or cleanse a soul (31)
כֹּה	(adverb) thus, so (6)
כֹּהֵן	priest (5)
כִּי	(conj.) because, for, that, when, but, indeed (4)
כִּכָּר	(f) (round) valley, plain, loaf of bread (15)
כֹּל, כָּל־	all (with suffix כֻּלּוֹ) (5, 26)
כלה	Qal: be complete, come to an end, fail, finish, fulfill Pi"ēl: make an end of, finish, complete (37)
כְּלִי	vessel, weapon (21)
כֵּן	so, thus, rightly (12)
כְּנַעַן (*a*)	Canaan (12)
כִּסֵּא	chair, throne (19)
כסה	Pi"ēl: cover, clothe, conceal, overwhelm Hithpa"ēl: reflexive of the Pi"ēl, cover oneself (37)
כְּסִיל	fool (noun), insolent, stupid (adj.) (19)
כֶּסֶף (*a*)	silver (8)
כעס	Qal: be vexed, angry, irritated Pi"ēl: put in a vexed condition, anger Hiph'îl: vex, anger, provoke to anger (31)
כַּף	(f) palm (of hand), sole (of foot) (כַּפִּי with suffix) (28)
כפר	Pi"ēl: cover over; make propitiation (27)
כָּרַת	(he) cut (13)
כשל	Qal: stumble Hiph'îl: cause to stumble (24)
כָּתַב	(he) wrote (9)

ל

לֹא	no, not (2)
לֵאמֹר	saying (12)
לֵב, לֵבָב	heart (with suffix, לִבִּי my heart) (16)
לְבָנוֹן	Lebanon (הַלְּבָנוֹן with article) (23)
לְבַד	alone (with suffix, לְבַדִּי; with מִן: מִלְּבַדִּי besides, apart from) (30)
לוֹט	Lot (15)
לֵוִי	Levi (25)
לֶחֶם (*a*)	bread (7)
לחם	Niph'al: fight (25)
לַיְלָה	night (9)
לכד	capture (18)
לָכֵן	therefore (17)
למד	Qal: learn Pi"ēl: make learn (teach) (23)
לָמָה, לָמָּה	מה + ל prep. for what, why? (8)
לְמַעַן	so that, in order that, for the sake of (16)
לְעֵינֵי	to the eyes of, i.e., before (11)
לִפְנֵי־	to the face of, i.e., before (11)
לָקַח	(he) took, received (5)
לָשׁוֹן	tongue, language (22)

מ

מְאֹד	(adverb) very, exceedingly (9)
מאן	Pi"ēl: refuse, reject (36)
מאס	reject, despise (26)
מָגֵן	shield (21)
מִדְבָּר	wilderness (10)
מִדְיָן	Midian (28)
מִדְיָנִי	Midianite (28)
מֶה־, מָה־, מַה־	what, how? (7)
מוֹאָב	Moab (21)
מוֹעֵד	appointed time, place, meeting (26)

מָ֫וֶת	(construct מוֹת, see footnote 68) death (21)
מות	Qal: die Hiph'îl: cause to die, kill Hoph'al: passive of Hiph'îl (36)
מִזְבֵּחַ	place of sacrifice, altar (8)
מַחֲנֶה	camp, army (27)
מָחָר	tomorrow (18)
מַטֶּה	staff, tribe (27)
מטר	Hiph'îl: rain, cause rain to fall (35)
מָטָר	rain (35)
מִי	(אֶת־מִי) who? (whom?) (9)
מַ֫יִם	water (6)
מכר	sell (22)
מָלֵא	Qal: be full, fill Niph'al: passive of Qal Pi"ēl: put in a full state, fill, fulfill, wholly devote to (33)
מַלְאָךְ	messenger, angel (14)
מְלָאכָה	work (30)
מִלְחָמָה	war, battle (15)
מלט	Pi"ēl: deliver, save (23)
מֶ֫לֶךְ (*a*)	king (2)
מָלַךְ	(he) ruled, was king (8)
מַמְלָכָה	kingdom (construct מַמְלֶ֫כֶת [*a*]) (24)
מִן	(prep.) from, out of, because of, part of, than (in comparisons) the preposition can be compounded on another preposition – מֵעִם from with; מֵעַל from upon. This is common after verbs expressing motion. (2)
מִנְחָה	gift, offering (28)
מֵעִים	(the word only occurs in the plural) internal organs; inward parts (34)
מָצָא	(he) found, discovered, presented (19)
מִצְוָה	commandment (11)
מִצְרַ֫יִם	Egypt, Egyptian (4)
מָקוֹם	place (17)
מֶרְכָּבָה	chariot (27)
מֹשֶׁה	Moses (3)
משׁח	Qal: anoint (compare מָשִׁיחַ anointed one) (32)
מָשִׁיחַ	anointed one, Messiah (20)
מִשְׁכָּן	dwelling place, tabernacle (33)
מָשַׁל	(he) ruled (13)
משׁל ב	(he) ruled over (13)
מִשְׁפָּחָה	family, clan (20)
מִשְׁפָּט	judgment, justice, custom (11)

נ

נָא	now, please (19)
נְאֻם	utterance, declaration (25)
נבא	Hithpa"ēl and Niph'al: prophesy (23)
נָבִיא	prophet (6)
נֶ֫גֶב (*e*)	south, Negev region (37)
נֶ֫גֶד (*e*)	before, in front of, opposite to (with suffix נֶגְדִּי) (30)
נגד	Hiph'îl: declare, tell Hoph'al: passive of Hiph'îl (34)
נגע	Qal: touch (usually with ב), reach, strike Hiph'îl: cause to touch, reach, arrive, approach (34)
נָהָר	river (15)
נוס	Qal: flee Hiph'îl: cause to flee (36)
נַחֲלָה	inheritance (29)
נחם	Niph'al: be sorry, repent, suffer grief, be comforted Pi"ēl: comfort, console (25)
נָחָשׁ	snake (33)

נטשׁ	Qal: leave, forsake, permit Niph'al: passive of Qal (36)
נסע	Qal: (pull up, out) set out, journey, depart Hiph'îl: causative of Qal (34)
נְעוּרִים	youth (18)
נַ֫עַר (*a*)	lad, boy (16)
נָפַל	(he) fell (16)
נֶ֫פֶשׁ (*a*)	soul, life (22)
נֵ֫צַח (*i*)	eminence, glory, perpetuity (34)
נצח	Pi"ēl: act as a leader, overseer (34)
נצל	Niph'al: deliver oneself, be delivered Hiph'îl: take away, deliver (from) (34)
נָשָׂא	(he) lifted up (15)
נָשִׁים	women (4)
נָתַן	(he) gave (2)
נָתָן	Nathan (35)

ס

סָבִיב	all around, all about, surrounding (22)
סגר	Qal: shut Niph'al: be closed, shut Pi"ēl: deliver up (make closed up) Hiph'îl: deliver up, close up (24)
סוּס	horse (9)
סוּר	Qal: turn aside, depart Hiph'îl: cause to turn aside, depart, remove, take away (36)
סֵ֫פֶר (*i*)	scroll, book (15)
ספר	Qal: count Pi"ēl: recount, declare (in detail) (23)
סתר	Niph'al: hide oneself, be hid Hiph'îl: hide, conceal

ע

עֶ֫בֶד (*a*)	slave, servant (4)
עָבַד	(he) served (4)
עָבַר	(he) passed over, transgressed, has passed over (6)
עַד	(prep. and conj.) unto, to, as far as, when, until, עַד עוֹלָם forever (9)
עֵדָה	congregation (13)
עוֹד	(adverb) again, still, yet (9)
עוֹלָם	eternity (9)
עָוֹן	iniquity, guilt, punishment (27)
עֹז	(with suffix עֻזִּי) strength, might, power (21)
עָזַב	(he) abandoned, left, forsook (12)
עזר	Qal: help, aid Niph'al: passive of the Qal (29)
עַ֫יִן	(f) eye, well (11)
עִיר	(fem.) city (irregular plural עָרִים) (2)
עַל	(prep.) on, upon, over, against (2)
עָלָה	(he) went up (5)
עֹלָה	burnt offering (22)
עֵלִי	Eli (19)
עַם	(with article הָעָם) people (7)
עִם	(prep.) with (4)
עָמַד	(he) stood, has stood (6)
עמד	a longer form of עִם (38)
עַמּוֹן	Ammon (25)
עָפָר	dirt, ground (7)
עֵץ	tree (8)
עֵצָה	counsel, advice (35)
עֶ֫רֶב (*a*)	evening (15)
ערך	Qal: arrange in order (30)
עָשָׂה	(he) did, made (2)
עֵת	time, season (14)

עַתָּה	(adverb) now (6)

פ

פֶּה	mouth (24)
פַּ֫חַד (*a*)	trembling, terror (20)
פלא	Niph'al: be (or do) extraordinary (things), be (or do) wonderful (things) Hiph'îl: do wondrously, marvellously (33)
פלל	Hithpa"ēl: pray (23)
פְּלִשְׁתִּי	Philistine (30)
פְּלִשְׁתִּים	Philistines (10)
פֶּן	lest (25)
פנה	Qal: turn, face Hiph'îl: cause to face, turn (37)
פָּנִים	face (3)
פעל	Qal: do, make (31)
פקד	Qal: pay attention to, observe, visit, appoint Niph'al: passive of Qal Hiph'îl: set (over), cause (one) to be an overseer, entrust (24)
פַּר	bull (33)
פָּרָה	cow (33)
פְּרִי	fruit (7)
פַּרְעֹה	Pharaoh (7)
פרר	Hiph'îl: break, frustrate, make ineffective Hoph'al: passive of Hiph'îl (38)
פרשׂ	Qal: spread (out) Niph'al: be scattered, spread out (32)
פָּשַׁע	(he) revolted, transgressed (14)
פָּשַׁע בְּ	(he) revolted against (14)
פֶּ֫שַׁע (*i*)	rebellion, revolt, transgression (14)
פֶּ֫תַח (*i*)	opening, gate, entrance (30)
פתח	Qal: open Niph'al: be opened, loosened Pi"ēl: loosen, free, open (30)

צ

צֹאן	sheep (14)
צָבָא	army, host (12)
צַדִּיק	(adj.) righteous (11)
צֶ֫דֶק (*i*)	righteousness (15)
צְדָקָה	righteousness (11)
צִוָּה	(he) commanded (7)
צִיּוֹן	Zion (17)
צֵל	shade (17)
צלח	Qal: be successful Hiph'îl: succeed, prosper, cause to be successful (26)
צעק	Qal: cry, cry out, call Niph'al: passive of Qal; זעק is the same word (31)
צָפוֹן	north (33)
צָרָה	distress (21)

ק

קָבַץ	(he) assembled, gathered together (13)
קבר	bury (21)
קָדוֹשׁ	(adj.) holy (10)
קֶ֫דֶם	before, front, east (34)
קֹ֫דֶשׁ (*o*)	holiness, holy (17)
קדשׁ	Qal: be holy Pi"ēl: make holy Hithpa"ēl: make oneself holy (23)
קָהָל	assembly, congregation (32)
קוֹל	voice, sound (6)
קום	Qal: arise, stand up, stand Hiph'îl: cause to rise, arise, cause to stand, erect, raise up (36)
קָטָן, קָטֹן	(adj.) small, little, young (26)
קָרָא	(he) called, read (3)
קָרַב	(he) came near, approached (14)

קֶ֫רֶב (*i*)	(preposition) middle of; בְּקֶ֫רֶב in the middle of (27)
קרע	tear up, tear away (20)

ר

רָאָה	(he) saw, looked (3)
רֹאשׁ	head (6)
רַב	(adj.) much, many (16)
רֹב	multitude, abundance (33)
רבה	Qal: be or become many, numerous, great (37)
רִבְקָה	Rebecca (26)
רֶ֫גֶל (*a*)	(f) foot (28)
רָדַף	(he) pursued, persecuted (7)
רוּחַ	spirit, wind (20)
רֶ֫כֶב (*i*)	chariots (collective) (27)
רכב	Qal: mount, ride Hiph'îl: cause to mount, cause to ride (27)
רנן	Qal: give a ringing cry Pi"ēl: same as Qal Hiph'îl: same as Qal; cause a cry, give a ringing cry (38)
רֵעַ	friend (33)
רַע	(adj.) (f. רָעָה) evil (10)
רָעֵב	Qal: be hungry (compare the noun רָעָב hunger, famine) (32)
רָעָב	famine, hunger (13)
רעע	(stative) Qal: be evil, bad, be displeasing Hiph'îl: do evil, hurt, injure (38)
רפא	Qal: heal Niph'al: passive of Qal Pi"ēl: heal (33)
רָצוֹן	favor, will, pleasure, acceptance (31)
רַק	only, surely (38)
רָשָׁע	(adj.) evil, wicked (10)

שׂ

שׂבע	Qal: be satisfied, be in excess Hiph'îl: cause to be satisfied, satisfy (32)
שָׂדֶה	field (26)
שׂים	Qal: put, place, set, ordain (36)
שׂכל	Qal: be wise Hiph'îl: give attention to, ponder, have insight, give insight, act wisely, have success (24)
שְׂמֹאול (or שְׂמֹאל)	the left, left side, left hand, north (32)
שָׂמַח	(he) rejoices, rejoiced (13)
שִׂמְחָה	rejoicing, joy (22)
שָׂנֵא	(he) hates, hated (14)
שָׂפָה	lip, shore (22)
שַׂר	official, leader, prince (16)
שָׂרָה	(or שָׂרַי) Sarah (11)
שׂרף	Qal: burn (18) Niph'al: be burned (25)

שׁ

שָׁאוּל	Saul (7)
שָׁאַל	(he) asked (12)
שׁאר	Niph'al: be left over, remain Hiph'îl: cause (over) to be left over, spare (25)
שְׁאֵרִית	(abs. and const.) remainder, remnant (25)
שֵׁ֫בֶט (*i*)	rod, staff, tribe (28)
שׁבע	Niph'al: put oneself under oath, i.e., swear Hiph'îl: cause to swear, adjure (25)
שׁבר	Qal: break Pi"ēl: smash (23)
שַׁבָּת	Sabbath, rest (18)

שׁדד	Qal: destroy, slay, devastate Pi“ēl: destroy, assault Pu“al: be destroyed (38)
שׁוב	Qal: turn back, return, go back, come back (with another verb = again: return and do = do again) Hiph‘îl: cause to return, bring back (36)
שׁוֹפָר	horn, ram's horn (32)
שׁחת	Niph‘al: be marred, spoiled, corrupted Pi“ēl: spoil, ruin, destroy Hiph‘îl: spoil, ruin, destroy, corrupt, act corruptly (24)
שָׁכַב	(he) lay down, slept (14)
שָׁכַח	(he) forgot (11)
שׁכם	Hiph‘îl (only): rise early, make an early start (24)
שׁכן	dwell, settle (21)
שׁכן	Qal: dwell, settle (in a tent) Pi“ēl: make settle, establish (33)
שִׁלוֹ, שִׁלֹה	Shiloh (19)
שָׁלוֹם	peace, health (9)
שָׁלַח	(he) sent (5)
שׁלך	Hiph‘îl: throw, cast (down, away, off) (24)
שְׁלֹמֹה	Solomon (11)
שָׁם	(adv.) there (5)
שֵׁם	name (with suffix 3ms, שְׁמוֹ) (3, 12)
שׁמד	Niph‘al: be annihilated, exterminated Hiph‘îl: annihilate, exterminate (24)
שְׁמוּאֵל	Samuel (9)
שָׁמַיִם	heaven, heavens, sky (6)
שׁמם	Qal: be desolated, be appalled, awestruck Niph‘al: be desolated, be appalled Hiph‘îl: devastate, destroy (38)
שֶׁמֶן (*a*)	oil (28)
שָׁמַע	(he) heard, obeyed (3)
שָׁמַר	(he) kept, watched, guarded, has kept (6); Qal: keep Niph‘al: keep oneself, take heed, be careful (25)
שָׁנָה	year (15)
שַׁעַר (*a*)	gate (19)
שִׁפְחָה	female slave (38)
שָׁפַט	(he) judged (11)
שֹׁפֵט	(participle) a judge (20)
שֶׁקֶר (*i*)	falsehood, deception, lie (18)
שׁקר	Pi“ēl: act falsely, lie (compare שֶׁקֶר) (34)
שׁרת	Pi“ēl: minister, serve (often a participle: minister, officer) (31)
שָׁתָה	(he) drank (13)

ת

תְּהִלָּה	glory, praise (9)
תּוֹרָה	law, instruction (8)
תַּחַת	under, instead of (16)
תָּמִיד	continually, regularly (17)
תמם	(stative) Qal: be completed, finished, come to an end, cease Hiph‘îl: finish, complete, perfect (38)
תעה	Qal: wander about, go astray, err Hiph‘îl: cause to wander, mislead (37)
תקע	Qal: thrust, drive, clap, blow (horn) Niph‘al: passive of Qal (32)

INDEX

Numbers with decimals refer to section numbers in the grammar: 10.1-7 » chapter ten sections one through seven. Numbers in parenthesis with a dash refer to footnotes: (19-4) » chapter nineteen, footnote four.

NOTES

NOTES

NOTES

NOTES

Review of Particles

Article ה (7.6)

1. הַ□: before non-gutturals – הַדָּבָר
2. הָ: before א, ע, ר – הָרֹאשׁ
3. הַ: before ה, ח – הַהֵיכָל
4. הֶ: before חָ and unaccented הָ, עָ – הֶעָמָל
5. הָ: before הָ – הָהָר

Interrogative מה־ (7.6)

מַ□־: before non-gutturals – מַה־דָּבָר
מָה־: before א, ע, ר (or the article) – מָה־רֹאשׁ
מַה־: before ה (excluding the article), ח – מַה־הֵיכָל
מֶה־: before *Gָ (excluding ר) – מֶה־עָמָל

Inseparable Prepositions: כְּ, בְּ, לְ (8.4)

1. לְ: normal – לְדָבָר
2. לִ: 1) before vocal shewa – לִשְׁמוּאֵל
   2) before יְ – לִיהוּדָה
3. *Gלַ: corresponding short vowel before a composite shewa – לֶאֱדֹם
4. לָ/לְ□ֹ: pretonic open may receive qameṣ or shewa – לָלַיְלָה / לְלַיְלָה
5. לַ/לֵ: לַיהוה / לֵאלֹהִים
6. לַ□: the preposition supplants the ה of the article – לַדָּבָר

Conjunctive Vav: וְ (8.4)

וְ: normal – וְדָבָר
וִ: before יְ – וִיהוּדָה

*Gוַ: corresponding short vowel before a composite shewa – וֶאֱדֹם
וָ/וְ□ֹ: pretonic open may receive qameṣ or shewa – וָלַיְלָה / וְלַיְלָה
וַ/וֵ: וַיהוה / וֵאלֹהִים
וּ: 1) before vocal shewa – וּשְׁמוֹ
   2) before בומף (labial letters) – וּבֵן

Preposition מִן (9.4)

1. מִ□: normal – מִשָּׁאוּל
2. מִ: before יְ – מִיהוּדָה
3. מֵ: before Gutturals (including ר) – מֵהַמֶּלֶךְ

Interrogative ה (9.4)

1. הֲ: normal before a vowel – הֲשָׁלוֹם
2. הַ: 1) before vocal shewa – הַדְבַר
   2) before gutturals (excluding ר) – הַאֵלֵךְ
3. הֶ: before *Gָ (excluding ר) – הֶאָב

*G stands for guttural letters

Hebrew Boxes: Absolute and Construct (11.8)

	Abs. Sg.	Constr. Sg.	Abs. Pl.	Constr. Pl.
Masculine	None	□־	□ִים	□ֵי־
Feminine	□ָה	□ַת־	□וֹת	□וֹת־
Dual			□ַיִם	□ֵי־

Boxes for Pronominal Suffixes (12.2)		(12.4)	(15.3, 6)	(15.3, 6)	(15.3, 6)	(16.4, 5)
Singular		דָּבָר	מֶלֶךְ	סֵפֶר	קֹדֶשׁ	נַעַר
		דְּבַר־	מֶלֶךְ־	סֵפֶר־	קֹדֶשׁ־	נַעַר־
1cs	□ִי	דְּבָרִי	מַלְכִּי	סִפְרִי	קָדְשִׁי	נַעֲרִי
2ms	□ְךָ	דְּבָרְךָ	מַלְכְּךָ	סִפְרְךָ	קָדְשְׁךָ	נַעַרְךָ
2fs	□ֵךְ	דְּבָרֵךְ	מַלְכֵּךְ	סִפְרֵךְ	קָדְשֵׁךְ	נַעֲרֵךְ
3ms	□וֹ	דְּבָרוֹ	מַלְכּוֹ	סִפְרוֹ	קָדְשׁוֹ	נַעֲרוֹ
3fs	□ָהּ	דְּבָרָהּ	מַלְכָּהּ	סִפְרָהּ	קָדְשָׁהּ	נַעֲרָהּ
1cp	□ֵנוּ	דְּבָרֵנוּ	מַלְכֵּנוּ	סִפְרֵנוּ	קָדְשֵׁנוּ	נַעֲרֵנוּ
2mp	□ְכֶם	דְּבַרְכֶם	מַלְכְּכֶם	סִפְרְכֶם	קָדְשְׁכֶם	נַעַרְכֶם
2fp	□ְכֶן	דְּבַרְכֶן	מַלְכְּכֶן	סִפְרְכֶן	קָדְשְׁכֶן	נַעַרְכֶן
3mp	□ָם	דְּבָרָם	מַלְכָּם	סִפְרָם	קָדְשָׁם	נַעֲרָם
3fp	□ָן	דְּבָרָן	מַלְכָּן	סִפְרָן	קָדְשָׁן	נַעֲרָן
Plural		דְּבָרִים	מְלָכִים	סְפָרִים	קֳדָשִׁים	נְעָרִים
		דִּבְרֵי־	מַלְכֵי־	סִפְרֵי־	קָדְשֵׁי־	נַעֲרֵי־
1cs	□ַי	דְּבָרַי	מְלָכַי	סְפָרַי	קֳדָשַׁי	נְעָרַי
2ms	□ֶיךָ	דְּבָרֶיךָ	מְלָכֶיךָ	סְפָרֶיךָ	קֳדָשֶׁיךָ	נְעָרֶיךָ
2fs	□ַיִךְ	דְּבָרַיִךְ	מְלָכַיִךְ	סְפָרַיִךְ	קֳדָשַׁיִךְ	נְעָרַיִךְ
3ms	□ָיו	דְּבָרָיו	מְלָכָיו	סְפָרָיו	קֳדָשָׁיו	נְעָרָיו
3fs	□ֶיהָ	דְּבָרֶיהָ	מְלָכֶיהָ	סְפָרֶיהָ	קֳדָשֶׁיהָ	נְעָרֶיהָ
1cp	□ֵינוּ	דְּבָרֵינוּ	מְלָכֵינוּ	סְפָרֵינוּ	קֳדָשֵׁינוּ	נְעָרֵינוּ
2mp	□ֵיכֶם	דִּבְרֵיכֶם	מַלְכֵיכֶם	סִפְרֵיכֶם	קָדְשֵׁיכֶם	נַעֲרֵיכֶם
2fp	□ֵיכֶן	דִּבְרֵיכֶן	מַלְכֵיכֶן	סִפְרֵיכֶן	קָדְשֵׁיכֶן	נַעֲרֵיכֶן
3mp	□ֵיהֶם	דִּבְרֵיהֶם	מַלְכֵיהֶם	סִפְרֵיהֶם	קָדְשֵׁיהֶם	נַעֲרֵיהֶם
3fp	□ֵיהֶן	דִּבְרֵיהֶן	מַלְכֵיהֶן	סִפְרֵיהֶן	קָדְשֵׁיהֶן	נַעֲרֵיהֶן

Prepositions with Suffixes

(17.2) Independent Pronouns	(14.2) ל	(14.2) ב	(14.3) עם	(14.3) אתת	(14.3) את	(14.4) אל	(14.4) על	(14.4) לפני	(14.5) כ	(14.6) מן	(16.7) למען	(16.7) תחת	(16.7) אחר
אָנֹכִי/אֲנִי	לִי	בִּי	עִמִּי	אִתִּי	אֹתִי	אֵלַי	עָלַי	לְפָנַי	כָּמוֹנִי	מִמֶּנִּי	לְמַעֲנִי	תַּחְתַּי	אַחֲרַי
אַתָּה	לְךָ	בְּךָ	עִמְּךָ	אִתְּךָ	אֹתְךָ	אֵלֶיךָ	עָלֶיךָ	לְפָנֶיךָ	כָּמוֹךָ	מִמְּךָ	לְמַעַנְךָ	תַּחְתֶּיךָ	אַחֲרֶיךָ
אַתְּ	לָךְ	בָּךְ	עִמָּךְ	אִתָּךְ	אֹתָךְ	אֵלַיִךְ	עָלַיִךְ	לְפָנַיִךְ	כָּמוֹךְ	מִמֵּךְ	לְמַעֲנֵךְ	תַּחְתַּיִךְ	אַחֲרַיִךְ
הוּא	לוֹ	בּוֹ	עִמּוֹ	אִתּוֹ	אֹתוֹ	אֵלָיו	עָלָיו	לְפָנָיו	כָּמוֹהוּ	מִמֶּנּוּ	לְמַעֲנוֹ	תַּחְתָּיו	אַחֲרָיו
הִיא	לָהּ	בָּהּ	עִמָּהּ	אִתָּהּ	אֹתָהּ	אֵלֶיהָ	עָלֶיהָ	לְפָנֶיהָ	כָּמוֹהָ	מִמֶּנָּה	לְמַעֲנָהּ	תַּחְתֶּיהָ	אַחֲרֶיהָ
אֲנַחְנוּ	לָנוּ	בָּנוּ	עִמָּנוּ	אִתָּנוּ	אֹתָנוּ	אֵלֵינוּ	עָלֵינוּ	לְפָנֵינוּ	כָּמוֹנוּ	מִמֶּנּוּ	לְמַעֲנֵנוּ	תַּחְתֵּינוּ	אַחֲרֵינוּ
אַתֶּם	לָכֶם	בָּכֶם	עִמָּכֶם	אִתְּכֶם	אֶתְכֶם	אֲלֵיכֶם	עֲלֵיכֶם	לִפְנֵיכֶם	כָּכֶם	מִכֶּם	לְמַעַנְכֶם	תַּחְתֵּיכֶם	אַחֲרֵיכֶם
אַתֶּן	לָכֶן	בָּכֶן	עִמָּכֶן	אִתְּכֶן	אֶתְכֶן	אֲלֵיכֶן	עֲלֵיכֶן	לִפְנֵיכֶן	כָּכֶן	מִכֶּן	לְמַעַנְכֶן	תַּחְתֵּיכֶן	אַחֲרֵיכֶן
הֵם/הֵמָּה	לָהֶם	בָּם/בָּהֶם	עִמָּם/עִמָּהֶם	אִתְּהֶם	אֶתְהֶם/אֹתָם	אֲלֵיהֶם	עֲלֵיהֶם	לִפְנֵיהֶם	כְּמוֹהֶם	מֵהֶם	לְמַעֲנָם	(תַּחְתֵּיהֶם)תַּחְתָּם	אַחֲרֵיהֶם
הֵן/הֵנָּה	לָהֶן	בָּהֶן	עִמָּהֶן	אִתְּהֶן	אֶתְהֶן/אֹתָן	אֲלֵיהֶן	עֲלֵיהֶן	לִפְנֵיהֶן	כְּמוֹהֶן	מֵהֶן	לְמַעֲנָן	(תַּחְתֵּיהֶן)תַּחְתָּן	אַחֲרֵיהֶן

Paradigm of the Strong Verb

	Perfect (17.3)	Stative (21.3)	
1cs	קָטַלְתִּי	כָּבַדְתִּי	קָטֹנְתִּי
2ms	קָטַלְתָּ	כָּבַדְתָּ	קָטֹנְתָּ
2fs	קָטַלְתְּ	כָּבַדְתְּ	קָטֹנְתְּ
3ms	קָטַל	כָּבֵד	קָטֹן
3fs	קָטְלָה	כָּבְדָה	קָטְנָה
1cp	קָטַלְנוּ	כָּבַדְנוּ	קָטֹנּוּ
2mp	קְטַלְתֶּם	כְּבַדְתֶּם	קְטָנְתֶּם
2fp	קְטַלְתֶּן	כְּבַדְתֶּן	קְטָנְתֶּן
3cp	קָטְלוּ	כָּבְדוּ	קָטְנוּ

Participle (19.2-3)		Abs.	Const.	Abs.	Const.	Abs.	Const.
	ms	קֹטֵל	קֹטֵל	כָּבֵד	כְּבֵד	קָטֹן	קְטֹן
A	fs	קֹטְלָה	קֹטֶלֶת	כְּבֵדָה	כִּבְדַת	קְטַנָּה	קְטַנַּת
C	(t)	קֹטֶלֶת	קֹטֶלֶת				
T	mp	קֹטְלִים	קֹטְלֵי	כְּבֵדִים	כִּבְדֵי	קְטַנִּים	קְטַנֵּי
	fp	קֹטְלוֹת	קֹטְלוֹת	כְּבֵדוֹת	כִּבְדוֹת	קְטַנּוֹת	קְטַנּוֹת
P	ms	קָטוּל	קְטוּל				
A	fs	קְטוּלָה	קְטוּלַת				
S	mp	קְטוּלִים	קְטוּלֵי				
S	fp	קְטוּלוֹת	קְטוּלוֹת				

	Imperfect (18.2)	Stative (21.4)	
1cs	אֶקְטֹל	אֶכְבַּד	אֶקְטַן
2ms	תִּקְטֹל	תִּכְבַּד	תִּקְטַן
2fs	תִּקְטְלִי	תִּכְבְּדִי	תִּקְטְנִי
3ms	יִקְטֹל	יִכְבַּד	יִקְטַן
3fs	תִּקְטֹל	תִּכְבַּד	תִּקְטַן
1cp	נִקְטֹל	נִכְבַּד	נִקְטַן
2mp	תִּקְטְלוּ	תִּכְבְּדוּ	תִּקְטְנוּ
2fp	תִּקְטֹלְנָה	תִּכְבַּדְנָה	תִּקְטַנָּה
3mp	יִקְטְלוּ(ן)	יִכְבְּדוּ	יִקְטְנוּ
3fp	תִּקְטֹלְנָה	תִּכְבַּדְנָה	תִּקְטַנָּה

Imperative (18.4)		(21.5)	
Cohortative	אֶקְטְלָה	אֶכְבְּדָה	אֶקְטְנָה
2ms	קְטֹל	כְּבַד	קְטַן
2fs	קִטְלִי	כִּבְדִי	קִטְנִי
Jussive	יִקְטֹל	יִכְבַּד	יִקְטַן
Emphatic	קָטְלָה		
2mp	קִטְלוּ	כִּבְדוּ	קִטְנוּ
2fp	קְטֹלְנָה	כְּבַדְנָה	קְטַנָּה

Infinitive (19.4)		(21.7)	
Abs.	קָטוֹל	כָּבוֹד	קָטוֹן
Const.	קְטֹל	כְּבַד	קְטַן

Synopsis of the Strong Verbs: Derived Stems

(22.6)	Pi(a)"ēl	Pu"al	Hithpa"ēl
	A-ē[3ms]/E	A/A	A-ē[3ms]/Ē-a[2, 3fp]
Perfect	□▣□	□▣□	הִתְ□▣□
Imperfect	יְ□▣□	יְ□▣□	יִתְ□▣□
Imperative	□▣□		הִתְ□▣□
Infinitive	□▣□		הִתְ□▣□
Participle	מְ□▣□	מְ□▣□	מִתְ□▣□

	Hi(a)ph'îl	Hoph'al	Niph'al
	A-î[3's]/Î-ē[2, 3fp]	A/A	A/Ē-a[2, 3fp]
Perfect	הִ□□□	הָ□□□	נִ□□□
Imperfect	יַ□□□	יָ□□□	יִ▣□□
Imperative	הַ□□□		הִ▣□□
Infinitive	הַ□□□		הִ▣□□/נִ□□□
Participle	מַ□□□	מָ□□□	נִ□□□

Infinitive Absolute

1. Orange: Pi"ēl, Pu"al, Niph'al
2. Green: Pi"ēl, Hiph'îl(□ַ), Hoph'al, Hithpa"ēl

Infinitive Construct

Green: Pi"ēl, Hiph'îl(□ִי), Hithpa"ēl, Niph'al

Participle

1. Green (pretonic reduction): Pi"ēl, Hiph'îl(□ִי), Hithpa"ēl
2. Red (irreducible qameṣ): Pu"al, Hoph'al, Niph'al

Proto (Pre-Biblical) Hebrew Rules (6.2)

1. Qameṣ in Biblical Hebrew was a pataḥ in Proto-Hebrew – דָּבָר « *דַּבַר.
2. Vocal shewa (□ְ, □ֱ, □ֲ, □ֳ) in Biblical Hebrew was a short vowel (frequently pataḥ) in Proto-Hebrew – דְּבַר « *דַּבַר.
3. Historic long vowels are the same in Proto-Hebrew and Biblical Hebrew – סוּסִים is both Proto-Hebrew and Biblical Hebrew.
4. The short vowels, pataḥ, ḥireq, qibbuṣ, and qameṣ-ḥatuf in Biblical Hebrew, are the same in Proto-Hebrew – גַּם is both Proto-Hebrew and Biblical Hebrew.

Five Rules of Biblical Hebrew (6.3)

דְּ בָ רִים מְ לֶךְ דְּ בָר
1 2 3 4 5

1. In a closed accented syllable, Hebrew *prefers* a long vowel.
2. In an opened pretonic syllable, Hebrew *requires* a long vowel.
3. In a closed unaccented syllable, Hebrew *requires* a short vowel.
4. In an opened accented syllable, Hebrew *prefers* a short vowel.
5. In an originally opened pro-pretonic syllable, Hebrew reduces the original short vowel to a vocal shewa. (The vocal shewa, unable to constitute an independent syllable, attaches to the pretonic syllable – דְּבָ)

Hebrew Pronominal Suffixes

	Perf: Direct	Perf: Connecting Vowel	Impf/Impv: Direct	Impf/Impv: Connecting Vowel	Impf/Impv: Energic Nun
1cs	□ַנִי	□ָנִי	□נִי	□ֵנִי	□ֶנִּי
2ms	□ְךָ	□ְךָ	□ְךָ	□ְךָ	□ֶךָּ
2fs	□ֵךְ	□ֵךְ 3fs □ַתֵךְ	□ֵךְ	□ֵךְ	
3ms	□הוּ	□וֹ	□הוּ	□ֵהוּ	□ֶנּוּ
3fs	□ָהּ	□ָהּ	□ָהּ	□ֶהָ □ָהּ	□ֶנָּה
1cp	□נוּ	□ָנוּ	□נוּ	□ֵנוּ	□ֶנּוּ
2mp			□ְכֶם	□ְכֶם	
2fp			□ְכֶן	□ְכֶן	
3mp	□ם	□ָם 3fs □ָתָם	□ם	□ֵם	
3fp	□ן	□ָן 3fs □ַתָן	□ן	□ֵן	

	Qal	Niph'al	Pi"ēl	Pu"al	Hithpa"ēl	Hiph'îl	Hoph'al
R¹-Guttural	Impf: GP – non-1cs, non-R¹-א GP – 1cs, R¹-א, stative אP – R¹-א vocalic ending	Perf: נG/נG Impf, Impv, IC: הG/יG IA, IC: הG/נG Ptc: נG/נG	Strong	Strong	Strong	Perf: הG/הG Impf, Impv, Inf; Ptc: GP/GP	GP/GP
R¹-Alef	(Reg / Vav-Cons) Non-pausal: □(□) / □(□) Pausal: □ / □						
R²-Guttural	Strong	Strong א ה ח ע ר	R *I* *I* *I* R	R R *I* R R	R *I* *I* *I* R	Strong	Strong
R³-Guttural	Perf: Strong Impf, Impv: Pataḥ	A/Ē-a » A/A	A-ē/Ē » A/A	A/A » A/A	A-ē/Ē-a » A/A	A-î/Î-ē » A-î/Î-a	A/A » A/A
	Non-finite: Forms retain the thematic vowel and receive a furtive pataḥ (*if necessary*)						
R³-Alef	Perf: A/ » Ā/ (A-ē » Ē[stative])	Perf: A/ » Ē-ā/	Perf: A-ē/ » Ē/	Perf: A/ » Ē-ā/	Perf: A-e/ » Ē/	Perf: A-î/ » Ē-î/	Perf: A/ » Ē-ā/
	Impf, Impv: pataḥ » qameṣ ימצא[3ms] תמצאנה[2fp/3fp] מצא[2ms] מצאנה[2fp]	All other thematic vowels are like strong verbs except, 1) When R³-Alef ends a word, Alef quiesces, and the short thematic vowel (pataḥ) lengthens; 2) All 2fp/3fp Impf/Impv quiesce Alef and take segol for the thematic vowel – תמצאנה[Niphal imperfect] Ptc: All t-form participles quiesce R³-Alef and lengthen preceding segol to sere – מצאת[Qal]					
R¹-Nun	Perf, IA, Ptc: Strong Impf: Assimilation Impv: Orange – Strong Red/Green – Nun AWOL IC: Orange – Strong Red/Green – Nun AWOL + ת (גשת/תת[segolate pattern])	Perf, Ptc: Assimilation Impf, Impv, Inf: Strong	Strong	Strong	Strong	Assimilation	Assimilation
R¹-Vav/Yod	Impf: R¹-Vav drops (thematic vowel – ē) R¹-Yod – Ḥireq-Yod (thematic vowel – a) IC: Yod/Vav – AWOL + ת (שבת[Segolate pattern]) IA, Ptc: Strong *Irregular*: יוכל/יכל	Perf, Ptc: aw » ô נושב » נושב[Perf 3ms]; נושב » נושב[Ptc ms] Impf, Impv, Inf: Strong with Vav retained יושב[Impf 3ms]	Strong Original Vav » Yod	Strong Original Vav » Yod	Strong *Sometimes* Vav/Yod	aw » ô הושיב » הושיב ay » ê היטיב » היטיב	uw » û יושב » יושב

	Qal	Niph'al	Pi"ēl	Pu"al	Hithpa"ēl	Hiph'îl	Hoph'al
R²-Vav/Yod	Pref. vowels: A or I[Stative] Thematic Vowels: A-ā/Î [R²-Yod]; A-ā/Û[R²-Vav] Stative: A-e/Û; Ô/Ô מֵת; בּוֹשׁ Perf: קָם[3ms]; קָמָה[3fs]; קַמְתִּי[1cs]; קַמְתֶּם[2mp] Impf: יָקוּם[3ms]; יָשִׂים[3ms] Juss: יָקֹם; יָשֵׂם V-C: וַיָּקָם; וַיָּשֶׂם Impv: קוּם[2ms]; שִׂים[2ms] IA: קוֹם; שׂוֹם IC: קוּם; שִׂים Ptc: קָם[ms]; קָמָה[fs]	Preformative Vowels: A[Perf. Ptc] or I Thematic Vowel: Ô Perf: נָקוֹם[3ms] נְקוּמֹתִי[1cs] Dissimulation of thematic vowel ô » û Impf: יִקּוֹם[3ms] Impv: הִקּוֹם[2ms] Inf: הִקּוֹם Ptc: נָקוֹם[ms]; נְקוֹמָה[fs]				Preformative Vowels: I[Perf. Ptc] or A Thematic Vowel: Î (Ē) Perf: הֵקִים[3ms]; הֵקִימָה[3fs]; הֲקִמֹתִי/(הֵ)הֲקִימֹתִי[1cs] Impf: יָקִים Juss: יָקֵם V-C: וַיָּקֶם Impv: הָקֵם[2ms] IA: הָקֵם IC: הָקִים Ptc: מֵקִים[ms]; מְקִימָה[fs]	R²-Vav » R²-Yod Perf: הוּקַם[3ms] Impf: יוּקַם[3ms] Ptc: מוּקָם[ms]; מוּקָמָה[fs]
R³-Vav/Yod	Perf "3's": 3ms ◻ָה – בָּנָה; 3fs ◻ְתָה – בָּנְתָה; 3cp ◻וּ – בָּנוּ Others: Ḥireq-Yod – Pi"ēl, Hithpa"ēl, Hiph'îl – בָּנִיתִי[Qal 1cs]; Ṣere-Yod – Niph'al, Pu"al, Hoph'al – נִגְלֵיתִי[Niphal 1cs]						
	Impf: 1) Non-ending ◻ֶה – יִבְנֶה[Qal 3ms]; 2) Vocalic-ending directly to R² – יִבְנוּ[Qal 3mp]; תִּבְנִי[Qal 2fs]; 3) Syllabic-ending 2/3fp ◻ֶינָה – תִּבְנֶינָה[Qal 2/3fp] Jussive/V-C: Drop ◻ֶה and may have segolatization – Qal: יִגֶל/יִגְל/יִגֶל/יִגֶּל (סֵפֶר [i]); Hiph'îl: יֶגֶל/יַגֶל (מֶלֶךְ [a])						
	Impv: 1) 2ms ◻ֵה – גְּלֵה; 2) Vocalic-endings directly to R² – בְּנִי, בְּנוּ; 3) Syllabic-ending 2fp ◻ֶינָה – גְּלֶינָה						
	IA: 1) ◻ֹה: Qal, Niph'al, Pi"ēl, Pu"al – Qal בָּנֹה; 2) ◻ֵה: Hiph'îl, Hoph'al, Hithpa"ēl – הַגְלֵה[Hiph'îl] IC: ◻וֹת: Qal בְּנוֹת						
	PA: ms ◻ֶה – בֹּנֶה; fs ◻ָה – בֹּנָה, בֹּנִית; mp ◻ִים – בֹּנִים; fp ◻וֹת – בֹּנוֹת PP: בָּנוּי[ms]; בְּנוּיָה[fs]; בְּנוּיִם[mp]; בְּנוּיוֹת[fp]						
R²-R² Geminate	Preformative Vowels: A/I Thematic Vowel: A/Ō[standard]; A/A[stative] Perf:[strong/collapsed/stative] 3ms קַל/סַב/סָבַב 3fs קָלָּה/סַבָּה/סָבְבָה 1cs קַלּוֹתִי/סַבּוֹתִי/◻◻◻◻ Impf: 1) Normal Gemination: יָסֹב[3ms]; יָסֹבּוּ[3mp] 2) Transposed Gemination: יִסֹּב[3ms] Impv: סֹב[ms]; סֹבּוּ[mp]; סֹבִּי[fs]; סֻבֶּינָה[fp] IA: סָבוֹב[Strong] IC: סֹב or סְבֹב[strong] Ptc: Strong סֹבֵב	Preformative Vowels: A[Perf. Ptc]; I[Impf. Impv. Inf] Thematic Vowel: A/A Niph'al » Naph'al Perf: נָסַב[3ms]; נְסַבּוֹתִי[1cs] Impf: יִסַּב[3ms]; תִּסַּבִּי[2fs]; תִּסַּבֶּינָה[2fp] Impv: הִסַּב[2ms]; הִסַּבִּי[2fs] IA: הִסּוֹב IC: הִסֵּב Ptc: נָסָב[ms]; נְסַבָּה[fs]				Preformative Vowels: I[Perf. Ptc]; A[Impf. Impv. Inf] Thematic Vowel: Ē/Ē Perf: הֵסֵב/הֵסַב[3ms]; הֲסִבּוֹתִי[1cs] Three Imperfect Forms: 1) Normal Gemination: יָסֵב[3ms]; יָסֵבּוּ[3mp] 2) Transposed Gemination: יַסֵּב [3ms] 3) Double Gemination: יַסֵּבּוּ[3mp] Impv: הָסֵב[2ms]; הָסֵבִּי[2fs] IA: הָסֵב IC: הָסֵב Ptc: מֵסֵב[ms]; מְסִבָּה[fs]	Preformative Vowel: Û Thematic Vowel: A/A R¹-Vav in the first syllable Perf: הוּסַב[3ms]; הוּסַבּוֹת[1cs] Impf: יוּסַב[3ms] Ptc: מוּסָב[ms]; מוּסַבָּה[fs]

Synopsis of the Strong Verbs: Derived Stems

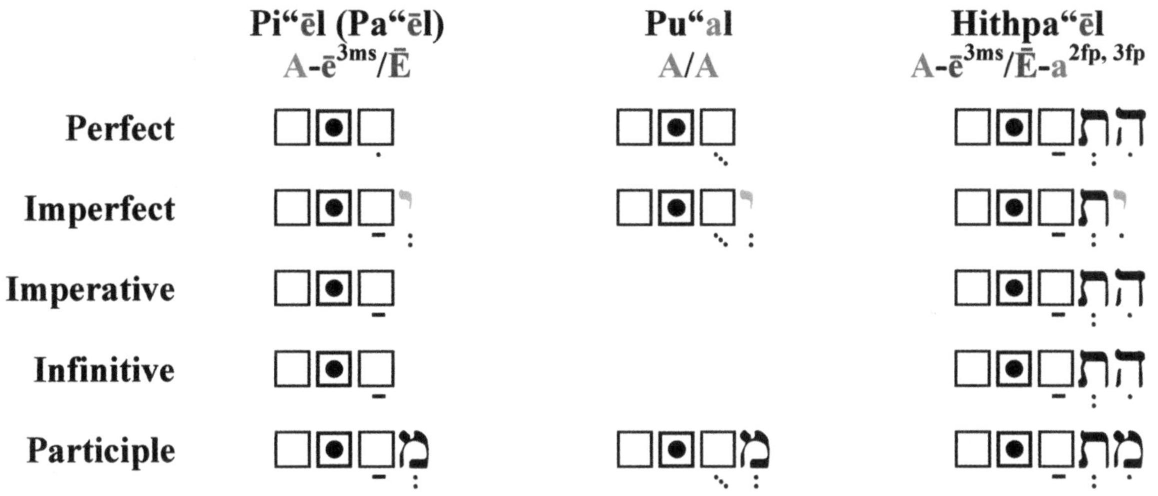

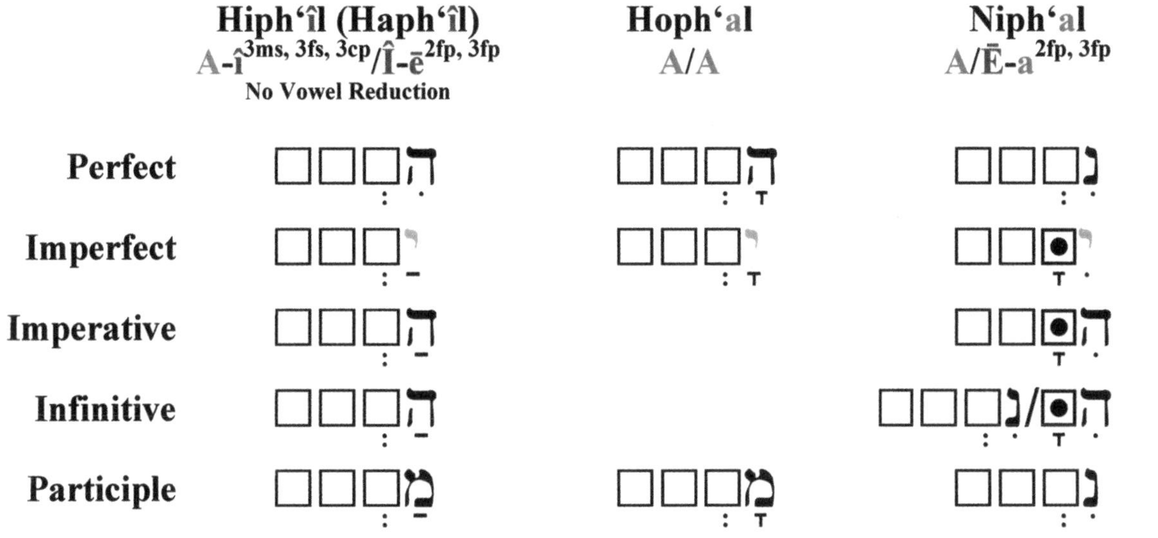

	Pi"ēl (Pa"ēl) A-ē^3ms^/Ē	Pu"al A/A	Hithpa"ēl A-ē^3ms^/Ē-a^2fp, 3fp^
Perfect	□ִ◉□	□ֻ◉□	הִתְ□ַ◉□
Imperfect	יְ□ַ◉□	יְ□ֻ◉□	יִתְ□ַ◉□
Imperative	□ַ◉□		הִתְ□ַ◉□
Infinitive	□ַ◉□		הִתְ□ַ◉□
Participle	מְ□ַ◉□	מְ□ֻ◉□	מִתְ□ַ◉□

	Hiph'îl (Haph'îl) A-î^3ms, 3fs, 3cp^/Î-ē^2fp, 3fp^ No Vowel Reduction	Hoph'al A/A	Niph'al A/Ē-a^2fp, 3fp^
Perfect	הִ□ְ□□	הָ□ְ□□	נִ□ְ□□
Imperfect	יַ□ְ□□	יָ□ְ□□	יִ◉ָ□□
Imperative	הַ□ְ□□		הִ◉ָ□□
Infinitive	הַ□ְ□□		הִ◉ָ□□/נִ□ְ□□
Participle	מַ□ְ□□	מָ□ְ□□	נִ□ְ□□

In the Imperfect, the Yod (י) stands for all Imperfect preformatives (אֵיתָן)

Infinitives:

1. **Absolute**
   Orange: **Niph'al, Pi"ēl (!)**
   Green: **Pi"el, Hiph'îl (□ֵ), Hithpa"ēl**

2. **Construct**
   Green: **Pi"el, Hiph'îl (□ִי), Hithpa"ēl, Niph'al (!)**

Participles:

1. **Green (pretonic reduction):** **Pi"ēl, Hithpa"ēl, Hiph'îl (□ִי)**
2. **Red (irreducible Qameṣ):** **Pu"al, Hoph'al, Niph'al**

Standard vs. Stative Verbs

		Standard			Stative			
		כתב	נתן	שלח	מלא	כבד	גדל	קטן
Perfect		A/Ō	A/Ē	A/A	Ē/A	A-ē/A	A/A	Ō/A
sg.	1c	כָּתַבְתִּי	נָתַתִּי	שָׁלַחְתִּי	מָלֵאתִי	כָּבַדְתִּי	גָּדַלְתִּי	קָטֹנְתִּי
	2m	כָּתַבְתָּ	נָתַתָּ(ה)	שָׁלַחְתָּ	מָלֵאתָ	כָּבַדְתָּ	גָּדַלְתָּ	קָטֹנְתָּ
	2f	כָּתַבְתְּ	נָתַתְּ	שָׁלַחְתְּ	מָלֵאת	כָּבַדְתְּ	גָּדַלְתְּ	קָטֹנְתְּ
	3m	כָּתַב	נָתַן	שָׁלַח	מָלֵא	כָּבֵד	גָּדַל	קָטֹן
	3f	כָּתְבָה	נָתְנָה	שָׁלְחָה	מָלְאָה	כָּבְדָה	גָּדְלָה	קָטְנָה
pl.	1c	כָּתַבְנוּ	נָתַנּוּ	שָׁלַחְנוּ	מָלֵאנוּ	כָּבַדְנוּ	גָּדַלְנוּ	קָטֹנּוּ
	2m	כְּתַבְתֶּם	נְתַתֶּם	שְׁלַחְתֶּם	מְלֵאתֶם	כְּבַדְתֶּם	גְּדַלְתֶּם	קְטָנְתֶּם
	2f	כְּתַבְתֶּן	נְתַתֶּן	שְׁלַחְתֶּן	מְלֵאתֶן	כְּבַדְתֶּן	גְּדַלְתֶּן	קְטָנְתֶּן
	3c	כָּתְבוּ	נָתְנוּ	שָׁלְחוּ	מָלְאוּ	כָּבְדוּ	גָּדְלוּ	קָטְנוּ

Imperfect		A/Ō	A/Ē	A/A	Ē/A	A-ē/A	A/A	Ō/A
sg.	1c	אֶכְתֹּב	אֶתֵּן	אֶשְׁלַח	אֶמְלָא	אֶכְבַּד	אֶגְדַּל	אֶקְטַן
	2m	תִּכְתֹּב	תִּתֵּן	תִּשְׁלַח	תִּמְלָא	תִּכְבַּד	תִּגְדַּל	תִּקְטַן
	2f	תִּכְתְּבִי	תִּתְּנִי	תִּשְׁלְחִי	תִּמְלְאִי	תִּכְבְּדִי	תִּגְדְּלִי	תִּקְטְנִי
	3m	יִכְתֹּב	יִתֵּן	יִשְׁלַח	יִמְלָא	יִכְבַּד	יִגְדַּל	יִקְטַן
	3f	תִּכְתֹּב	תִּתֵּן	תִּשְׁלַח	תִּמְלָא	תִּכְבַּד	תִּגְדַּל	תִּקְטַן
pl.	1c	נִכְתֹּב	נִתֵּן	נִשְׁלַח	נִמְלָא	נִכְבַּד	נִגְדַּל	נִקְטַן
	2m	תִּכְתְּבוּ	תִּתְּנוּ	תִּשְׁלְחוּ	תִּמְלְאוּ	תִּכְבְּדוּ	תִּגְדְּלוּ	תִּקְטְנוּ
	2f	תִּכְתֹּבְנָה	תִּתֵּנָּה	תִּשְׁלַחְנָה	תִּמְלָאנָה	תִּכְבַּדְנָה	תִּגְדַּלְנָה	תִּקְטַנָּה
	3m	יִכְתְּבוּ	יִתְּנוּ	יִשְׁלְחוּ	יִמְלְאוּ	יִכְבְּדוּ	יִגְדְּלוּ	יִקְטְנוּ
	3f	תִּכְתֹּבְנָה	תִּתֵּנָּה	תִּשְׁלַחְנָה	תִּמְלָאנָה	תִּכְבַּדְנָה	תִּגְדַּלְנָה	תִּקְטַנָּה

Imperative		A/Ō	A/Ē	A/A	Ē/A	A-ē/A	A/A	Ō/A
sg.	2m	כְּתֹב	תֵּן	שְׁלַח				
	2f	כִּתְבִי	תְּנִי	שִׁלְחִי				
pl.	2m	כִּתְבוּ	תְּנוּ	שִׁלְחוּ				
	2f	כְּתֹבְנָה	תֵּנָּה	שְׁלַחְנָה				

R_1-GUTTURAL (PE GUTTURAL) VERBS

<table>
<tr><th></th><th>Qal</th><th>Niph‘al</th><th>Pi“ēl</th><th>Pu“al</th><th>Hithpa“ēl</th><th>Hiph‘îl</th><th>Hoph‘al</th></tr>
<tr><td>Perfect</td><td>Strong 29.3
(or Gֲ in 2mp, 2fp)</td><td>Gֱ נֶ (Gְ נֶ)
29.6.1</td><td colspan="3" rowspan="7">Strong
29.3</td><td>Gֱ הֶ (Gְ הֶ)
29.6.1</td><td rowspan="7">Gֳ Pָ
(Gְ Pָ)
29.6.1</td></tr>
<tr><td>Imperfect</td><td>1cs Gֱ אֱ
Stative Gֱ Pֶ
R_1-א אֱ Pֶ
R_1-ה, ח, ע Non-1cs and non-stative forms Gֲ Pַ
(exception: vocalic, non-pausal or with suffixes Gְ Pַ)</td><td rowspan="3">Dagesh rejection:

Ḥireq becomes Ṣere

29.4</td><td rowspan="6">Gֲ Pַ
(Gְ Pַ)
29.6.1</td></tr>
<tr><td>Imperative</td><td>Vocal shewa position: Gֲ »
R_1-ה, ח, ע; אֱ » R_1-א
2fs, 2mp are strong 29.5</td></tr>
<tr><td>Infinitive Construct</td><td>Gֱ for R_1-א
Gֲ for R_1-ה, ח, ע 29.5</td></tr>
<tr><td>Infinitive Absolute</td><td rowspan="2">Strong
29.3</td><td>□הֵ or □נֵ</td></tr>
<tr><td>Participle Active</td><td rowspan="2">Gֱ נֶ (Gְ נֶ)
29.6.1</td></tr>
<tr><td>Participle Passive</td><td>Gֲ 29.5</td></tr>
</table>

Qal Imperfect (29.6.2)

	Standard (/Ō)							Stative (/A) 29.6.2 or Standard with Pataḥ thematic vowels	
	R₁-א 29.6.2	R₁-ה 29.6.2		R₁-ח 29.6.2		R₁-ע 29.6.2			
		Composite Shewa	Silent Shewa	Composite Shewa	Silent Shewa	Composite Shewa	Silent Shewa	Composite Shewa	Silent Shewa
1cs 29.6.2	אֶאֱסֹר	אֶהֱרֹג	אֶהְדֹּף	אֶחֱלֹף	אֶחְתֹּם	אֶעֱזֹב	אֶעְשֹׁר	אֶאֱמַץ	אֶחְסַר
2ms	תֶּאֱסֹר	תַּהֲרֹג	תַּהְדֹּף	תַּחֲלֹף	תַּחְתֹּם	תַּעֲזֹב	תַּעְשֹׁר	תֶּאֱמַץ	תֶּחְסַר
3ms	יֶאֱסֹר	יַהֲרֹג	יַהְדֹּף	יַחֲלֹף	יַחְתֹּם	יַעֲזֹב	יַעְשֹׁר	יֶאֱמַץ	יֶחְסַר
2fs Non-pausal 29.6.2	תַּאַסְרִי	תַּהַרְגִי	תַּהְדְּפִי	תַּחַלְפִי	תַּחְתְּמִי	תַּעַזְבִי	תַּעְשְׂרִי	תֶּאֶמְצִי	תֶּחְסְרִי
2fs Pausal 6.5.3	תֶּאֱסֹ֫רִי	תַּהֲרֹ֫גִי	תַּהְדֹּ֫פִי	תַּחֲלֹ֫פִי	תַּחְתֹּ֫מִי	תַּעֲזֹ֫בִי	תַּעְשֹׁ֫רִי	תֶּאֱמָ֫צִי	תֶּחְסָ֫רִי
2/3fp Pausal and Non-pausal	תֶּאֱסֹ֫רְנָה	תַּהֲרֹ֫גְנָה	תַּהְדֹּ֫פְנָה	תַּחֲלֹ֫פְנָה	תַּחְתֹּ֫מְנָה	תַּעֲזֹ֫בְנָה	תַּעְשֹׁ֫רְנָה	תֶּאֱמַ֫צְנָה	תֶּחְסַ֫רְנָה

Chart courtesy of Isaac Jerusalmi

Note: Usually, suffixed forms are like vocalic, non-pausal forms – יַאַסְרֻ֫נוּ.

Dissimilation of Thematic Vowels (30.4)
(אחז), אבד, אכל, אמר

	Regular (without Vav-consecutive ◻וַ)	Vav-Consecutive ◻וַ
Non-pausal	יֹאמַר יֹאכַל יֹאבַד (יֹאחֵז) 30.4.1	וַיֹּאמֶר וַיֹּאחֶז וַיֹּאכַל (וָאֹמַר 1cs only) 30.4.3
Pausal	יֹאמֵ֑ר יֹאכֵ֑ל יֹאבֵ֑ד 30.4.2	וַיֹּאמַ֑ר וַיֹּאכַ֑ל 30.4.4

□ַ (□ֵ) 30.4.1	□ֶ/□ַ 30.4.3
□ֵ 30.4.2	□ַ 30.4.4

Notes:

1. Bracketed words are exceptions.
2. אבד never occurs with Vav-consecutive (◻וַ).
3. יֹאחֵז/אחז (30.4.1) is like the regular, pausal form (30.4.2; 30.4.3) – וַיֹּאחֶז.
4. אבה, אפה – Third weak verbs (chapter 37) do not dissimilate thematic vowels.
5. Imperfect 2, 3fp forms always take Pataḥ.

R_2-GUTTURAL (AYIN GUTTURAL) VERBS

	Qal	Niph'al		Pi"ēl	Pu"al	Hithpa"ēl	Hiph'îl	Hoph'al
Perfect			א	R	R	R		
Imperfect			ה	I	R	I		
Imperative	Strong		ח	I	I	I	Strong	
Infinitive			ע	I	R	I		
Participle			ר	R	R	R		

Chart courtesy of Isaac Jerusalmi

R: **Rejects Dagesh Forte with compensatory lengthening**

I : Implies Dagesh Forte

R_3-GUTTURAL (LAMED GUTTURAL) VERBS

FINITE FORMS (E » A: ṢERE » PATAḤ, 32.4.1)

The Hebrew world goes Red

	Qal	Niph'al	Pi"ēl	Pu"al	Hithpa"ēl	Hiph'îl	Hoph'al	
Perfect **Imperfect** **Imperative**	Pataḥ 32.5.1 (Imperfect and Imperative only)	A/Ē-a » A/A	A-ē/Ē » A/A	A/A remains A/A	A-ē/Ē-a » A/A	A-î/Î-ē » A-î/Î-a (In jussive, Vav-consecutive and imperative 2ms forms ē » a)	A/A remains A/A	In pausal forms, the usual thematic vowel is retained and the R_3-Guttural receives a Furtive Pataḥ

NON-FINITE FORMS (32.4.2)

Infinitive Absolute **Infinitive Construct** **Participle**	Usual thematic vowels are retained, and the R_3-Guttural receives a Furtive Pataḥ (an occasional exception of Ṣere » Pataḥ)	Pausal and Non-Pausal forms

R_3-Guttural (Lamed Guttural) Verbs (32.4)

	Non-Pausal	Pausal
Finite Forms (Perfect, Imperfect, Imperative)	Ṣere becomes Pataḥ Ḥireq-Yod takes Furtive Pataḥ 32.4.1	Ṣere thematic vowel restored, and Furtive Pataḥ added when necessary 32.4.1
Non-Finite Forms (Infinitives and Participles)	Pausal and Non-Pausal: Thematic vowels retained, and Furtive Pataḥ added when necessary 32.4.2	

Chart courtesy of Isaac Jerusalmi

R_3-ALEF (LAMED ALEF) VERBS

The Hebrew world goes Green

	Qal (Standard)	Qal (Stative)	Niph'al	Pi"ēl	Pu"al	Hithpa"ēl	Hiph'îl	Hoph'al	
Perfect 33.4.2	A » Ā	A-ē » Ē	A » Ē-ā	A-ē » Ē	A » Ē-ā	A-ē » Ē	A-î » Ē-î	A » Ē-ā	"Greening Effect"
Imperfect	/Ā 33.5.2		All other thematic vowels are like strong verbs except, (1) When R_3-Alef ends the word, the Alef quiesces, and the short thematic vowel (Pataḥ) lengthens (33.4.1) (2) All 2, 3fp imperfect-imperative forms quiesce the Alef and take Segol for the thematic vowel (33.5.3).						
Imperative									
Infinitive Absolute									
Infinitive Construct									
Participle	All T-form participles quiesce the R_3-Alef and lengthen preceding Segol to Ṣere: מֹצֵאת 33.5.4.								

Notes: R_3-Alef in the silent shewa position (also at the end of the word) quiesces, and the preceding vowel, if short, lengthens.

R_1-NUN (PE NUN) VERBS

<table>
<tr><th></th><th colspan="3">Qal</th><th>Niph‘al</th><th>Pi“ēl</th><th>Pu“al</th><th>Hithpa“ēl</th><th>Hiph‘îl</th><th>Hoph‘al</th></tr>
<tr><td>Perfect</td><td colspan="3">Strong
34.3.1</td><td>Assimilation
34.4.1</td><td colspan="3" rowspan="6">Strong
34.3.1</td><td colspan="2" rowspan="6">Assimilation
34.4.1</td></tr>
<tr><td>Imperfect</td><td colspan="3">Assimilation
34.4.1</td><td rowspan="4"></td></tr>
<tr><td>Imperative</td><td>(Orange)
Strong
34.3.2</td><td>(Red)
Nun goes
AWOL
34.4.2</td><td>(Green)
Nun goes
AWOL
34.4.2</td></tr>
<tr><td>Infinitive Absolute</td><td colspan="3">Strong
34.3.1</td></tr>
<tr><td>Infinitive Construct</td><td>(Orange)
Strong
34.3.2</td><td>(Red)
Nun goes
AWOL Plus
Tav (Segolate)
34.4.2</td><td>(Green)
Nun goes
AWOL Plus
Tav (Segolate)
34.4.2</td></tr>
<tr><td>Participle</td><td colspan="3">Strong
34.3.1</td><td>Assimilation
34.4.1</td></tr>
</table>

R_1-YOD (ORIGINAL PE VAV) VERBS (35.1-5)

	Qal	Niph‘al » Naph‘al	Pi“ēl	Pu“al	Hithpa“ēl	Hiph‘îl » Haph‘îl	Hoph‘al
Perfect	Strong: Yod replaces Vav 35.3.2	aw » ô *נַוְשַׁב » נוֹשַׁב 35.4.1.3	Strong (In Pi“ēl, Pu“al, the original Vav becomes Yod; Hithpa“ēl sometimes retain Vav; sometimes it becomes Yod) 35.3.2			aw » ô *הַוְשִׁיב » הוֹשִׁיב *יַוְשִׁיב » יוֹשִׁיב etc. 35.4.1	uw » û *יֻוְשַׁב » יוּשַׁב etc. 35.4.1
Imperfect	Impf./Impv. have thematic vowels /Ē-a. Impf. drops Vav and lengthens preceding Ḥireq to Ṣere 35.4.2	Strong with Vav retained by Dagesh Forte יִוָּשֵׁב 35.3.1					
Imperative	Drops Vav (like R_1-Nun green/red) 35.4.2						
Infinitive Construct	Drops Vav, adds ת and forms Segolate patterns (like R_1-Nun green/red) 35.4.2						
Infinitive Absolute	Strong: Yod replaces Vav 35.3.2						
Participle		aw » ô *נַוְשָׁב » נוֹשָׁב 35.4.1					*מֻוְשָׁב » מוּשָׁב

הלך is a R_1-Yod (Vav) verb in the Qal imperfect, imperative, infinitive construct, and the Hiph‘îl. Elsewhere, it is regular – הֹלֵךְ Qal participle masculine singular absolute, יִתְהַלֵּךְ Hithpa“ēl imperfect 3ms (35.5.3).

	R₁-Yod (original Yod) (35.6-10)		Mixed Forms: ירא 35.12.1		Mixed Forms: ירשׁ 35.12.2		Irregular Form: יכל (Ō/A) 35.14
	Qal	**Haph'îl (« Hiph'îl)**	**Qal R₁-Yod (Yod)**	**Derived Conjugations R₁-Yod (Vav)**	**Qal R₁-Yod (Yod)**	**Derived Conjugations R₁-Yod (Vav)**	**Qal**
Perfect	Strong 35.8.		יָרֵא		יָרַשׁ	Niph'al perf. 3ms נוֹרַשׁ	יָכֹל 3ms
Imperfect	Yod in silent shewa position quiesces: short Ḥireq lengthens to Ḥireq-Yod 35.9.2		יִירָא		יִירַשׁ	Hiph'îl impf. 3ms יוֹרִישׁ	יוּכַל Imperfect 3ms
Imperative	All impf./impv. has Pataḥ for thematic vowels 35.10	ay » ê Perf. 3ms הֵיטִיב » הַיְטִיב* 35.9.1	יְרָא	Niph'al perf. 3ms נוֹרָא Niph'al impf. 3ms יִוָּרֵא	R₁-Yod (Vav) רֵשׁ		
Infinitive Absolute			Strong		Strong		
Infinitive Construct	Strong 35.8		יִרְאָה/יְרֹא*		R₁-Yod (Vav) רֶשֶׁת		
Participle			Strong		Strong		

*irregular

R_2-Vav/Yod (Ayin Vav/Yod) Verbs

		Qal 36.4.4				(Niph'al ») Naph'al 36.4.3	Hiph'îl 36.4.2		Hoph'al 36.4.1
Preformative Vowels		A		A or I		A (Perfect, Participle) or I	I (Perfect, Participle) or A		
		Standard		Stative					
Thematic vowels		A-ā/Û	A-ā/Î	A-ē/Û	Ô/Ô	Ô	Î (Ē)		
		(R_2-Vav)	(R_2-Yod)				Ḥireq-Yod	Pataḥ	R_2-Vav
Perfect	3ms	קָם	שָׂם	מֵת	בּוֹשׁ	נָקוֹם	הֵקִים		verbs
	3fs	קָ֫מָה	שָׂ֫מָה	מֵ֫תָה	בֹּ֫שָׁה		הֵקִ֫ימָה		become
	3cp	קָ֫מוּ	שָׂ֫מוּ	מֵ֫תוּ	בֹּ֫שׁוּ		הֵקִ֫ימוּ		R_1-Vav
	1cs	קַ֫מְתִּי	שַׂ֫מְתִּי	מַ֫תִּי	בֹּ֫שְׁתִּי	נְקוּמֹ֫תִי	(הֱ)הֲקִימֹ֫תִי	הֵקַ֫מְתִּי	verbs
Imperfect	3ms	יָקוּם	יָשִׂים	יָמוּת	יֵבוֹשׁ	יִקּוֹם	יָקִים		הוּקַם
Jussive	3ms	יָקֹם	יָשֵׂם	יָמֹת	יֵבוֹשׁ		יָקֵם		Perfect 3ms
Vav-Consecutive	3ms	וַיָּ֫קָם	וַיָּ֫שֶׂם	וַיָּ֫מָת	וַיֵּבוֹשׁ		וַיָּ֫קֶם		
Imperative	2ms	קוּם	שִׂים	מוּת	בּוֹשׁ	הִקּוֹם	הָקֵם		
Infinitive	Absolute	קוֹם	שׂוֹם	מוֹת	בּוֹשׁ	הִקּוֹם	הָקֵם		
	Construct	קוּם	שִׂים	מוּת	בּוֹשׁ	הִקּוֹם	הָקִים		
Participle	ms	קָם	שָׂם	מֵת	בּוֹשׁ	נָקוֹם	מֵקִים		
	fs	קָמָה	שָׂמָה	מֵתָה	בּוֹשָׁה	נְקוֹמָה	מְקִימָה		

R_2-Vav/Yod (Ayin Vav/Yod) Verbs

בּוֹא

		Qal (Ā/Ō) 36.6.1			Hiph'îl (Green) 36.6.2		
Perfect	3ms	בָּא	1cs	בָּ֫אתִי	3ms	הֵבִיא	1cs: הֵבֵ֫אתִי/(הֱ)הֲבִיאֹ֫תִי
	3fs	בָּ֫אָה	2mp	בָּאתֶם	3fs	הֵבִ֫יאָה	
	3cp	בָּ֫אוּ			3cp	הֵבִ֫יאוּ	
Imperfect	3ms	יָבוֹא				יָבִיא	
Jussive	3ms	יָבוֹא				יָבֵא	
Vav-Consecutive	3ms	וַיָּבוֹא				וַיָּבֵא	
Imperative	2ms	בּוֹא				הָבֵא	
Infinitive	Absolute	בּוֹא				הָבֵא	
	Construct	בּוֹא				הָבִיא	
Participle	ms	בָּא				מֵבִיא	
	fs	בָּאָה				מְבִיאָה	

R$_3$-Vav/Yod (Lamed Vav/Yod) Verbs

Perfect 37.4.1	3's 3ms □ָה בָּנָה 3fs □ְתָה בָּנְתָה 3cp □וּ בָּנוּ Other forms preserve Yod: Ḥireq-Yod: Qal, Pi"ēl, Hithpa"ēl, Hiph'îl Ṣere-Yod: Niph'al, Pu"al, Hoph'al Qal 1cs בָּנִ֫יתִי Niph'al 1cs נִגְלֵ֫יתִי
Imperfect 37.4.2	(1) Without ending □ֶה : Qal 3ms יִבְנֶה (2) Vocalic endings directly connect to R$_2$: Qal 3mp יִבְנוּ 2fs תִּבְנִי (3) Syllabic ending 2, 3fp □ֶ֫ינָה : Qal 3fp תִּבְנֶ֫ינָה Jussive, Vav-consecutive forms drop the ending □ֶה and may have Segolatization Qal יִגֶל, יִגְל, יִ֫גֶל, יֶגֶל (סֵ֫פֶר [*i*]) Hiph'îl יַגְל, יֶ֫גֶל (מֶ֫לֶךְ [*a*])
Imperative 37.4.3	(1) 2ms □ֵה גְּלֵה (2) Vocalic endings 2fs, 2mp connect directly to R$_2$ בְּנִי, בְּנוּ (3) Syllabic ending 2fp □ֶ֫ינָה גְּלֶ֫ינָה
Infinitive Absolute 37.4.4	(1) □ֹה in Qal, Niph'al, Pi"el, Pu"al: Qal בָּנֹה (2) □ֵה in Hiph'îl, Hoph'al, Hithpa"ēl: Hiph'îl הַגְלֵה
Infinitive Construct 37.4.4	□וֹת Qal בְּנוֹת
Participle 37.4.5	Qal Active ms □ֶה בֹּנֶה fs □ָה בֹּנָה T-Form בֹּנִית mp □ִים בֹּנִים fp □וֹת בֹּנוֹת Qal Passive ms בָּנוּי fs בְּנוּיָה The Yod is consonantal like a strong verb mp בְּנוּיִם fp בְּנוּיוֹת

$R_2R_3=R_2R_2$ Geminate (Ayin-Ayin: Double Ayin) Verbs

	Qal 38.5.4	Niph‘al 38.5.3	Hiph‘îl 38.5.2	Hoph‘al 38.5.1
Preformative vowels / **Thematic vowels**	A (Standard) I (Transposed): A/Ō; I (Stative): A/A	A – Perfect, Participle; I – Imperfect, Imperative, Infinitive; A/A	I - Perfect, Participle; A - Imperfect, Imperative, Infinitive; Ē/Ē	Û; A/A
Perfect	Third persons Strong / Collapsed / Stative 3ms סָבַב / סַב / קַל 3fs סָבְבָה / סַבָּה / קַלָּה 3cp סָבְבוּ / סַבּוּ / קַלּוּ 1cs — / סַבּוֹתִי / קַלּוֹתִי	Niph‘al » Naph‘al A/A		R_1-Vav in the first syllable הוּסַב
Imperfect	Two imperfect forms (theoretically) 1. Normal Gemination (Stative) יָסֹב יָסֹבּוּ (יֵקַלּוּ) 2. Transposed Gemination יִסֹּב		Three imperfect forms (theoretically) 1. Normal Gemination יָסֵב יָסֵבּוּ 2. Transposed Gemination יַסֵּב 3. Doubled Gemination יַסֵּבּוּ	
Imperative	ms סֹב mp סֹבּוּ fs סֹבִּי fp סֻבֶּינָה			
Infinitive Absolute	(strong) סָבוֹב	הִסּוֹב		
Infinitive Construct	סֹב (or strong סְבֹב)	הִסֵּב		
Participle	(strong) סֹבֵב	נָסָב נְסַבָּה	ms מֵסֵב (R_1-Yod analogy) fs מְסִבָּה	

General Notes:

1. Transposed gemination is possible in all stems (38.6.1).
2. There are numerous analogies to R_2-Vav/Yod verbs (38.6.2).
3. The Pi“ēl, Pu“al, and Hithpa“ēl are rare and like strong verbs (footnote 38-1 and 36-1).